BRAINWASH

ALSO BY DOMINIC STREATFEILD

Cocaine

BRAINWASH

The Secret History of Mind Control

DOMINIC STREATFEILD

THOMAS DUNNE BOOKS

St. Martin's Press ⚏ New York

THOMAS DUNNE BOOKS
An imprint of St. Martin's Press.

BRAINWASH. Copyright © 2007 by Dominic Streatfeild.
All rights reserved. Printed in the United States of America.
No part of this book may be used or reproduced in any manner
whatsoever without written permission except in the case of brief
quotations embodied in critical articles or reviews.
For information, address St. Martin's Press, 175 Fifth Avenue,
New York, N.Y. 10010.

www.thomasdunnebooks.com
www.stmartins.com

ISBN-13: 978-0-312-32572-5
ISBN-10: 0-312-32572-X

First published in Great Britain by Hodder & Stoughton,
a Division of Hodder Headline

First U.S. Edition: March 2007

10 9 8 7 6 5 4 3 2 1

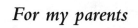

For my parents

Contents

BRAINWASH

1

Brain Warfare

IRAQIS DRUGGED, BRAINWASHED AND SENT TO DIE FOR
BIN LADEN *FROM JAMES HIDER IN KARBALA*
Terrorists linked with al-Qaeda are increasingly recruiting young Iraqis to
carry out suicide bombings, brainwashing them with Osama bin Laden's
sermons and drugging them before sending them off to wreak mayhem,
Iraqi police believe.

—*The Times*, 22 March, 2004

'I couldn't believe it. My son had gone from a docile mouse to a suicidal
killer? No. Not without being brainwashed. Someone got to him. I am sorry
to say it, but he was brainwashed.'

—Robin Reid, father of shoebomber, Richard

Dr András Zakar was returning from morning mass at Vizivaros Con-
vent on Sunday, 19 November 1948 when an unmarked car pulled up
alongside him. Silently, three men in dark suits leaped out, grabbed the
doctor by the arms and bundled him on to the back seat. They climbed
in after him, slammed the doors and, with a screech of tyres, accelerated
away.

To passers-by there was nothing especially remarkable about this incident. Hungarians had been told that the state was under threat and that
conspirators were everywhere: the secret police were snatching dissidents
more or less continuously. What made this case unusual was the victim. Dr
Zakar was personal secretary to Jósef Mindszenty, head of the Catholic
Church in Hungary and the most senior cardinal in Eastern Europe.

Mindszenty, a potential successor to Pope Pius XII, was a powerful man; the 'disappearance' of his secretary was ominous.

Five weeks later the secret police returned Dr Zakar to the cardinal's official residence in Esztergom. But the Zakar they delivered on Christmas Eve 1948 wasn't the same Zakar who had left the month before. Something had happened to him. His eyes looked strange. He was confused and disoriented, as if in a twilight state of consciousness. The normally taciturn thirty-five-year-old doctor of theology behaved like a child, babbling and giggling constantly. At one point he ran down the corridors, shrieking. Officers accompanying Zakar treated him like a madman, repeatedly reminding him that they fed him meat twice a week. In return, he simpered as if they were his closest friends. 'He seemed,' recalled Gyula Mátkai, the cardinal's chief secretary, 'to be having a very good time with them.'

Ordered to search the building for incriminating evidence, Zakar took off at a gallop, leading the officers to a room in the basement where he pointed to a spot on the ground. Digging a few inches beneath the soil, the policemen discovered a metal box full of Mindszenty's confidential correspondence. They then congratulated the smirking Zakar and shepherded him back to the secret police headquarters at 60 Andrassy Street in Budapest for more 'treatment'.

At 6.45 p.m. on Boxing Day, Mindszenty and his elderly mother were making their way downstairs after evening mass when there was a furious banging at the door. The cardinal ordered it to be opened, to find himself facing a group of armed men. Lieutenant-Colonel Gyula Décsi stepped forward. 'We have come to arrest you,' he told Mindszenty. The cardinal asked to see the warrant but Décsi shook his head. 'We don't need one.'

Mindszenty knelt, kissed his mother's hand and said a prayer, then picked up his coat and hat and handed himself in to the custody of the arresting officers. The last sounds he heard as he was led away into the night were the voices of his colleagues who, realising that his arrest spelt the end of Catholicism in Hungary under Soviet occupation, had spontaneously started singing the national anthem.

Mindszenty's staff were dumbfounded by his arrest but initially it was the behaviour of his secretary that most baffled everyone. How could the loyal Dr Zakar have betrayed the cardinal? Why had he behaved so bizarrely? Clearly, they thought, something strange had happened to him.

By the time he arrived in court five weeks later, something strange had happened to Cardinal Mindszenty, too. In the dock he swayed backwards and forwards, unsteady on his feet. His eyes were half closed and he was uncoordinated, like a sleepwalker. He spoke in a monotone, as if repeating facts by rote. At times he paused for up to ten seconds between words. Apparently unable to follow the course of his own trial, this highly educated, intelligent man stood, eyes glazed, totally bewildered.

Worse than his appearance, however, was what he said. As Mindszenty stared into the middle distance, he confessed that he had orchestrated the theft of Hungary's crown jewels—including the country's most sacred relic, the Crown of St Stephen—with the explicit purpose of crowning Otto von Habsburg emperor of Eastern Europe. He admitted that he had schemed to remove the Communist government; that he had planned a Third World War and that, once this war was won by the Americans, he himself would assume political power in Hungary.

The confessions were patent nonsense. Since the end of the war, Mindszenty had indeed opposed the Communist takeover of Hungary but he was no revolutionary, and he certainly wasn't a traitor. At one point in court he agreed that he had met Otto von Habsburg in Chicago on 21 June 1947; in fact, Habsburg had not been in Chicago and the cardinal had not been in the United States on that date. Moreover, Western observers soon discovered that Mindszenty had specifically warned Church officials of his impending arrest by the Communists. Afraid that he might buckle under torture, he had written letters just weeks before he was picked up to the five most senior Catholic officials in Hungary with instructions that they were to be opened only in the event of his arrest. The letters stated categorically that he had not taken part in any conspiracy and that he would never resign his episcopal see.

Asked in court about them, Mindszenty appeared to have changed his mind. 'I did not see then many things which I see today,' he slurred. 'The statement I made is not valid.' He also offered to resign.

To those who knew him, Mindszenty had undergone a radical transformation. A source close to Pope Pius XII commented that the Mindszenty on trial was 'not the man that we knew'. British Foreign Office analysis concluded that he was 'a tired or resigned man wholly unlike what we know of the Cardinal's real personality'. Even his mother agreed, telling the press that when she was allowed to see him in jail 'he was a completely changed man, without will and without consciousness'. At one point when she visited him, he had failed to recognise her altogether.

The cardinal's handwriting seemed to have changed, too. Comparisons of his signature before and after the arrest revealed considerable differences. According to an Italian graphologist, Mindszenty was 'no longer capable of writing his customary signature'. Sure enough, in the month of the trial, two Hungarian handwriting experts, Laszlo Sulner and Hanna Fischhof, defected to Austria and confessed to working on the case. Initially, they said, they had been called in to forge the cardinal's confessions but it soon became clear that this would not be necessary: he was signing them of his own accord. According to the two experts, documents emerging at the start of Mindszenty's interrogation contained denials, but within a fortnight they were full of confessions. 'The mind which impelled the pen in the first instance,' reported Sulner, 'was not the mind which impelled the pen in the second instance.' Something strange, indeed, had happened to the cardinal.

In the West, the appearance of a powerful, resolute man publicly confessing to crimes he couldn't possibly have committed immediately rang a bell. The same thing had happened in Moscow a decade earlier. At the time, Stalin had arrested a number of his inner circle and placed them on trial for horrendous—but wholly implausible—crimes.

The Moscow Show Trials (1936–38) presented the macabre spectacle of the Soviet state prosecutor, Andrei Vyshinsky, howling repeatedly that the accused were 'mad dogs', 'dogs gone mad' and 'dirty dogs' that should be 'taken out and shot', while the supposed conspirators fell over each other to agree with him. Many stated from the outset that their crimes were so heinous that they had no right even to offer a defence. Sergei Mrachovsky—a man with impeccable revolutionary credentials— confessed to a bizarre plot to murder Stalin. Lev Kamenev stated that he was a 'bloodthirsty enemy' of the Soviet Union who, in an act of 'contemptible treachery', had tried to assassinate Kirov. Richard Pickel admitted to assisting with the planning for this assassination, referring to himself as 'the dregs of the land'. And yet there was not a shred of evidence that any of these confessions was true. The defendants then turned on themselves and each other. Edouard Holtzman declared that he and his friends were 'not only murderers but fascist murderers'. To Yuri Piatakov, meanwhile, the crimes of his fellow defendants were so grave that he asked permission to shoot them himself. One was his ex-wife.

In this Kafkaesque nightmare, defendants not only demanded to be found guilty, but also requested the most severe punishment. Arkady Rosengoltz stated that 'I don't want to live after this disgrace', A.A. Shestov that 'The proletarian court must not, and cannot, spare my life.' Shestov's only remaining goal, he said, was to 'stand with calmness on the place of my execution and with my blood to wash away the stain of a traitor to my country'. He wasn't the only one who wanted to die. 'I am a traitor to my party,' concluded Mrachovsky, 'who should be shot.' He was. They all were—after first thanking the prosecutor, Vyshinsky, for honouring them with the ultimate sentence.

The spectacle of hardened revolutionaries lining up to sign their own death warrants created worldwide consternation. Was it really possible that these men were guilty? In response to public concern the United States established the Dewey Commission to find out. It eventually decided that the Soviet confessions were so inherently improbable that they couldn't possibly be true. 'We therefore find,' concluded the report, 'the Moscow Trials to be frame-ups.'

But if they were 'frame-ups', how was it done? What would it take to make grown men publicly vilify themselves and their lives' work like this? There were no outward signs that any of the defendants had been tortured. And even if they had, why didn't any of them burst out with the truth in court? They must have known that they were going to be shot anyway. It was speculated that the Soviets had used drugs or hypnosis on the victims. But no one knew. 'No mystery in history,' reported the *Daily Mail*, 'matches what is going on in Moscow.'

A decade after the mysterious Show Trials, history seemed to be repeating itself in the Mindszenty case. The cardinal, reported the *Evening Standard*, was a 'bewildered man, ready like all other Soviet victims to confess to whatever was laid to his charge'. The *Daily Telegraph* agreed that he was 'not in full possession of his faculties'. Some commentators even speculated that the man in the dock was not Mindszenty but an impostor. It was a supremely unlikely theory but, faced with such an improbable spectacle, what theory wasn't?

As had been the case during the Show Trials, the press was keen to attribute the strange confessions to the use of drugs. In a piece entitled

'Mindszenty: drug? Third degree? Hypnosis?' the *Daily Mail* reported that the cardinal had been dosed with 'confession drugs such as Benzedrine, amphetamine, scopolamine and actedron'. A RAND Institute study of the confession phenomenon concurred, concluding that the Soviets were using drugs and hypnosis, among other techniques, to prepare victims for trial. Church authorities felt the same: a spokesman for Pius XII commented that if Mindszenty had indeed confessed, he had been forced to do so by drugs. Whatever the technique used to make him talk, however, someone was going to pay for it. On 31 December 1948, the pope excommunicated everyone involved in the cardinal's arrest and interrogation.

The British Foreign Office debated the issue for some time. Admittedly, the cardinal was 'not normal' at his trial, and there was some evidence that Soviet interrogators used drugs to 'undermine the nerves and will-power'. But generally the mood was sceptical. Accounts of widespread drug use were, says one dispatch from Vienna, 'journalistic embroidery'. According to a top-secret document dated 10 February 1949, Mindszenty had probably been persuaded to confess by less subtle means: Dr Zakar had been beaten 'half dead' and paraded in front of his boss, who had immediately buckled.

But the diplomats weren't entirely convinced by their own theory: if Zakar had been savagely beaten, why did he show no sign of it at the trial? 'All told,' concludes the Foreign Office file, 'the Cardinal's confession remains as much of a mystery as ever.'

American authorities agreed. The trial was an enigma. The only thing that was clear was that *something* had happened to Mindszenty and, whatever it was, it was deeply sinister. 'Somehow,' wrote US Army intelligence adviser Paul Linebarger, 'they took his soul apart.'

Three years after Mindszenty was sentenced to life imprisonment for his 'crimes', another bombshell hit. In Korea.

On the night of 13 January 1952, pilots Kenneth L. Enoch and John S. Quinn of the 3rd US Air Force Bomb Group were shot down over North Korea. Four months later, on 16 May, the two men made an extraordinary confession to a group of Chinese interrogators. They had, they said, been deploying biological weapons, including anthrax, typhus, cholera and plague, over Korea. The weapon-delivery systems, said Quinn, were 'still in the experimental stage' but effective. 'I was forced,' he stated, 'to be the tool of these [American] warmongers and made to . . . do this awful crime against the people of Korea and the Chinese volunteers.' The men's confessions were taped and broadcast on Peking Radio the next day. Moscow Radio soon took up the cause, and the East began accusing the West of war crimes.

Nine months later, in February 1953, Colonel Frank H. Schwable, Chief of Staff of the US First Marine Wing, confirmed Enoch and Quinn's allegations. Schwable, who had been shot down on 8 July the previous year, gave explicit details of the operation. According to his statement, the US biological-weapons programme was numbered VMF-513 and codenamed SUBPROP. The US Joint Chiefs of Staff had green-lighted the project in October 1951.

First operational tests had been run, said Schwable, in November that year using B-29s from Okinawa, Japan, but pretty soon bacteria-delivery devices were being fitted to other aircraft including Tiger Cats, Skyraiders, Corsairs and Panthers. The testing was so secret that even the pilots concerned were not allowed to know what they were carrying. Naturally, other allies in the United Nations were not informed, either.

Schwable explained that canisters containing the germs were dropped at various altitudes across diverse terrain and over different-sized cities to enable the US military to determine how the bacteria spread, and thus to calculate the most effective ways of deploying them in the future. The weapons were specifically designed to harm civilians.

Operational uses of germ weapons were numerous. Schwable even gave squadron numbers and the names and ranks of senior officers involved. Everything the two junior pilots had alleged was true: the United States had been—and was still—dropping germ weapons all over North Korea. It was, he agreed, 'shameful'.

With the names, the technical details and the dates, there was enough information here to convince anyone of the veracity of the biological-warfare claims. As if that wasn't enough, Schwable's statement was shortly followed by confirmations from another thirty-five US pilots, all confessing to their involvement in the operation.

But there was a problem: all the confessions were false. There were no bacteriological weapons in use over Korea.

With the Mindszenty trial, the Moscow Show Trials and the statements of the American prisoners-of-war in Korea, there now appeared to be compelling evidence that the Soviets had a technique capable of inducing confessions and of making hostile prisoners pliable. It seemed to go a lot further, too: throughout the Korean War, more and more soldiers and air-men made public broadcasts rejecting capitalism and embracing Commu-nism. A typical broadcast from one indoctrinated British soldier states that 'the Chinese are a very friendly, peace-loving nation and they bear no ill-will towards us . . . This war is an unjust war . . . all the things we fought for in World War II have been betrayed.' Another British private reported the unlikely assertion that during the battle in which he was captured, the Chinese had been so concerned for their enemy's welfare that they had been shooting over their heads, so as not to harm them. Ultimately, when the war came to a close in 1953, twenty-one Americans, three Belgians and one British soldier refused to come home to the West, preferring to stay in Communist China.

Unsurprisingly, Western intelligence services were extremely con-cerned. What were the Soviets up to? Why didn't *we* know anything about it? Military and intelligence hawks sprang into action: what was going on behind the Iron Curtain?

In 1953 the United Kingdom's Joint Intelligence Committee established the Evasion, Escape and Prisoner-of-War Intelligence Sub-committee to determine what had happened to the Korean prisoners-of-war. Chaired by the Air Ministry, its members were recruited from each of the armed ser-vices, together with a representative from the Secret Intelligence Service (MI6). Foreign Office requests went out early in the year to all departments requesting assistance in collating 'information on enemy interrogation methods'.

Clearly, background experience was needed, so the sub-committee searched around for suitably knowledgeable experts to advise on indoctri-nation and interrogation techniques, selecting a number of wartime mem-bers of MI19, the military-intelligence department in charge of prisoner interrogation, including the organisation's famed interrogator, Major Cyril Hay. To this expertise was added the experience of the department in charge of PoW escape, evasion and conduct after capture during the Second World War, MI9. As it happened, MI9 was already up and run-ning, having been reactivated in the early 1950s to brief troops in Korea on how to behave should they fall into enemy hands. It was taken under the wing of the Air Ministry and rechristened A19.

In November 1952, a young occupational psychologist called Cyril Cunningham received a call, inviting him to an interview, from the senior officers of the clandestine A19. At the time Cunningham, who had never heard of the organisation and had no idea what he was actually being interviewed for, was working in a boring desk job at the Air Ministry's Science 4 Department, evaluating selection procedures for national servicemen. In a spare moment, he had written a report describing the German use of hidden microphones in the interrogation of downed RAF pilots during the Second World War that had apparently impressed someone influential.

In the interview Cunningham was asked how he had managed to come by the supposedly highly classified material in his report. He replied that he had found some of it at the back of an old filing cabinet in an air station in Cornwall, and had dug up the rest in the Holborn Public Library. 'I think,' chortled the lead A19 interviewer, Wing Commander Jim Marshall, 'that you had better come and work for me.' A month after his interview, Cunningham was given his brief: to find out what was going on in Korea. Sworn to secrecy, he was unable to tell even his Air Ministry colleagues what he was up to as he began to piece the story together.

Initially, Cunningham was taken under the wing of the former MI9 and MI19 men and taught all the methods used by British Intelligence in the Second World War to interrogate and break foreign agents. His next step was to find former Korean PoWs and interview them about life in the camps. Assuming the rank and uniform of a lieutenant in the Army Dental Corps to avoid press attention, he travelled around the country with a reel-to-reel tape-recorder, gathering recollections from those who had been released. Shocked to discover that, on completion of his courses, he was the only War Office employee qualified to interrogate foreign agents, he became the British government's Communist indoctrination expert and soon found himself inundated with requests for information from the Cabinet Office, the Foreign Office, the Security Service (MI5) and MI6, all of whom wanted to know what was going on.

Naturally, MI5 was interested in men who had collaborated with their Korean and Chinese captors. Once these men returned from the war, there was a serious question concerning their allegiance. And with good cause: one soldier admitted to Cunningham that his Communist interrogator had given him two hundred dollars in cash, told him to buy a typewriter and sit tight in the UK for five years, whereupon he would be contacted by a representative from the Chinese Embassy who would give him further instructions concerning his future as a Communist mole. MI5 was alerted and the Chinese recruiter, when he turned up in London as an embassy 'chauffeur', was picked up and deported, along with two Romanians. The issue of Korean and Chinese-indoctrinated 'sleeper' agents in the UK became a pressing one. 'We knew damn well that they were [trying to recruit agents],' Cunningham says today. 'This happened. And if they'd done it once, they could do it again.'*

In the meantime in the United States, the CIA—then just two years old—began to research interrogation and indoctrination techniques, too. For the Agency, the starting point was also the Moscow Show Trials. It was clear that in Moscow and Hungary, the minds of the confessors had undergone a forcible reorientation but it was also clear that this had happened without torture. Mindszenty, figured the Agency, had confessed 'under the influence of some unknown force'.

Early CIA officers were not naïve. Many had served in the Agency's precursor, the Office of Strategic Services (OSS), during the Second World War and had first-hand experience of interrogation. But they'd never seen anything like this before. German brutality may have gained tactical information, but it never made *converts*: generally, the harder you beat people, the more they hated you. They didn't suddenly turn round and want to be your friend. 'There is adequate historical evidence,' wrote one expert in June 1949, 'to establish that basic changes in the functional organisation of the mind cannot be brought about by psychological duress

* Did they do it again? One of the first British prisoners taken in Korea was George Blake, MI6's head of station in Seoul. Repatriated after the war, Blake continued to work for SIS, but fed details of all his operations directly to the KGB, compromising, according to one former intelligence officer, 'every East German agent of MI6 . . . He betrayed every single person we had.' In 1961 Blake was sentenced to forty-two years in prison, one for each agent whose death he had allegedly caused. Since his case became public, there has been endless speculation that he was 'turned' to Communism during his experiences as a PoW in Korea. Blake has always denied this: 'I joined the Communist side not because I was well or badly treated' he wrote in his autobiography. 'That had nothing to do with it. I joined because of its ideals.'

or physical torture alone.' On this basis, the Agency men concluded that they were witnessing the birth of a new, and terrifying, phenomenon.

In an attempt to work out what was going on, the US military and intelligence communities assembled a bank of experts to assess the psychological states of returning American prisoners-of-war. At the head of these experts were psychiatrist Lawrence Hinkle and neurologist Harold Wolff of Cornell University. Hinkle and Wolff's CIA report largely disregarded accounts of drugs and hypnosis, focusing instead on the physical and psychological treatment meted out to prisoners.

In the Soviet Union, they wrote, interrogation initially involved a great deal of solitary confinement designed to persuade the prisoner that he was alone, unloved and abandoned. Nothing softened up a prisoner, the KGB figured, like leaving him alone with his own fear. During an initial four- to six-week period in solitary, the individual was also subjected to mind-numbing routines designed to induce stress. He was made to stand for prolonged periods, sleep in specific positions, and was verbally and physically abused if he wavered from the routine. He was not allowed any contact with the outside world and was kept in a cell with no natural light so that he lost all track of time. Mealtimes and other routines were varied to confuse him further. Prisoners were underfed and kept cold to weaken them physically and emotionally; sleep patterns were disrupted (frequently prisoners were not permitted to sleep at all, or made to sleep facing a bright light) to further the sense of discomfort and unreality.

After a prolonged softening-up period, the prisoner would be a nervous wreck, terrified, isolated and confused. He would sit in his cell weeping, muttering prayers to himself. He would begin to hallucinate. Only when this stage had been reached would the interrogation begin.

Once again, it was designed specifically to disorient the subject. At the start of the process, no accusations were made. Instead, the victim was asked to name his crimes. Repeatedly he was ordered to write an account of them only for it to be ridiculed and torn up in front of him each time. Refusal to comply or inconsistencies between stories led to abuse, until the subject was unsure what, exactly, he was supposed to be confessing to, and what, exactly, he had already confessed to. In the meantime, he was alternately humiliated and exhausted, made to stand until he collapsed, and frequently denied use of toilet facilities until he soiled himself in front of his interrogators.

Forthright behaviour was sometimes rewarded with a cigarette, a cup of coffee, or a toilet break. At other times the interrogators reacted unpredictably, either chastising or rewarding the victim for no reason at all. To make their point, instead of rewarding positive statements, an interrogator might draw a pistol and tell him he was about to be shot. Again, the unpredictable nature of the responses furthered the sense of confusion. Ultimately the situation would become so intolerable that the subject was willing to say anything to bring the process to an end—even if it meant death.

Realising that the interrogation would not end until he submitted absolutely, the victim would fabricate confessions, then try pitifully to justify them to his interrogators. In this way he would, effectively, persuade himself of his own guilt. So demoralised that he was no longer able to distinguish between true and false, 'the victim', wrote Hinkle and Wolff, 'does not consciously change his value system; rather the change occurs despite his efforts. He is no more responsible for the change than is an individual who "snaps" and becomes psychotic.'

Hinkle and Wolff noted a difference between Soviet and Chinese interrogation techniques. The Soviets were usually content with a full confession to whatever imaginary crimes they had cooked up; the Chinese, meanwhile, were more interested in 're-educating' the subject so that he might usefully be re-inserted into society. Prisoners were sorted into groups, then pressurised until they conformed. For twelve hours a day they might be interrogated, then returned to their shared cell, where their entire group would work on them for the next twelve hours. The combination of interrogators' pressure and extreme peer pressure soon proved unbearable—and the subjects' will broke.

Hinkle and Wolff's (and, in the UK, Cunningham's) conclusions, that Communist confessions and conversions were the result of brutal psychological manipulation rather than magical pharmacological compounds, seemed to gel with scientific developments at the time, particularly in the emerging field of psychology. Since the early 1920s, psychologists had been making huge breakthroughs, prising open the human mind and revealing the various factors that conditioned it. If these factors were disrupted, they argued, almost anything was possible.

In the United States, one psychologist who seemed to have proved this was John B. Watson. Known as the father of behaviourism—the science of predicting and controlling human behaviour—in 1920 Watson decided to prove the impact of conditioning on the human personality by running a bizarre (and cruel) experiment on an eleven-month-old baby boy called Little Albert.

In the experiment, Albert was given a tame white rat to play with, and the two immediately became firm friends. Watson then decided to see if he could modify Albert's perception of the rat artificially, transforming it from a friend into a threat. From that point on, every time the white rat was introduced to Albert's playpen, Watson banged a large piece of metal with a hammer just behind the child's head, producing a deafeningly loud noise. Albert, terrified, quickly associated the noise with the rat. Soon the sight of the rat alone was enough to make him cry. Ultimately other small animals, or anything with fur, reduced him to tears. Santa's beard, or men with white hair, provoked a tantrum.

Watson thought he had stumbled on a way to mould the human personality. For him, the right kind of conditioning made it possible to programme children from birth. 'Give me a baby,' he famously boasted, 'and I'll make it climb and use its hands in constructing buildings of stone or wood . . . I'll make it a thief or a gunman or a dope fiend . . . Make him a deaf mute, and I will still build you a Helen Keller . . . Men are built, not born.'

In the course of his work, Watson used technical terms that might well have influenced George Orwell when he invented 'Newspeak' twenty-eight years later in the novel *1984*, such as 'building-in', 'implanting' and 'unlearning'. It all sounded terribly scary. If, speculated the CIA, it was possible to construct character like this, then why was it not possible to *deconstruct* character in the same way?

One image of what might be possible emerged with the defection of Hungarian dissident Lajos Ruff in 1956. Ruff, who had been arrested in Budapest in 1953 for distributing political leaflets, had been interrogated in the same secret police centre as Cardinal Mindszenty (he claimed to have met Mindszenty a number of times in prison). As such he appeared to be uniquely qualified to comment on what was going on inside the Hungarian state interrogation centres.

In front of a US Senate Committee—and later in his book, *The Brainwashing Machine*—Ruff detailed the horrific treatment he had received at the hands of the secret police. After the usual attempts at heavy-handed interrogation (as an opener, he was asked to confess; when he refused, his interrogator smashed him in the face with a cast-iron ashtray, knocking out two teeth), Ruff was led to the room where, he was told, Mindszenty had been 'broken'. A doctor took him aside and warned him that in the 'Magic Room' he would either confess or end up schizophrenic.

The room itself, and everything in it, was irregularly shaped to eliminate right angles and create visual disorientation. The door was oval. Inside, lights rotated constantly and moving images were projected on to the walls. Furniture was translucent and the bed sloped at an angle to make sleep impossible. Strange sounds were played through hidden speakers, so that Ruff might go to sleep listening to music but wake to the screams of women being tortured. Mealtimes were varied: he was sometimes served meals twice, five minutes apart, to confuse him. Repeatedly drugged, he would go to sleep naked but wake up dressed, or vice versa. At one point he was roused by a doctor who asked him why he had tried to commit suicide. Sure enough, when he felt his neck it was sore and bruised, as if he had tried to hang himself.

The Magic Room, wrote Ruff, was 'the most frightening workshop of Soviet mental destruction, a psychological atomic reactor which is the symbolic apex of Communist organisation—like the diamond on top of the driller.' He was only released after going on hunger strike and smashing everything that could possibly be broken.

Ruff's account smacks of journalistic enhancement but there was more than enough to convince many of the veracity of claims that psychological experiments such as John B. Watson's had reaped results in the Eastern bloc. Meanwhile, the CIA's own interest in behaviourism soon led to further speculation. Watson's work owed a huge debt to the physiologist Ivan Pavlov, who, twenty years earlier, had rung bells and flashed lights at dogs to make them salivate. Pavlov, who had coined the term 'conditioned reflex' to describe the phenomenon, and who had taken his experiments further than anyone else on the planet, was Russian. If classical conditioning was applicable to humans like this, the secret to its applications was probably residing in the Soviet Union.

The idea that the Soviets were using Pavlovian conditioning to indoctrinate political prisoners originated with an American journalist called Edward Hunter. In the late 1940s Hunter, intrigued by reports of Communist dissidents being 're-educated' against their will in China, began investigating the phenomenon. Having spent time in Hong Kong interviewing former Communist prisoners, he came up with a term for the process that was to galvanise intelligence and press speculation.

The Chinese, Hunter decided, had set about trying to reform errant Communists by mistreating them, then using measured rewards and punishments to persuade them of the beauties of socialism. In Chinese the term for this process was '*xi-nao*': 'mind cleanse'. On 24 September 1950, in the *Miami Daily News*, he published a landmark article on the process, bastardising 'mind cleanse' to produce a word that he thought would prove more evocative with Western readers: 'brainwash'.

Following the success of his article on 'brainwashing' in China, Hunter directed his attention to the Show Trials, Cardinal Mindszenty and the strange confessions of the PoWs in Korea. Wasn't it possible that the Eastern bloc victims had been 'brainwashed'? He concluded that it was. In two books that followed, he examined the process in detail. 'The intent,' he wrote, 'is to change a mind radically so that its owner becomes a living puppet—a human robot—without the atrocity being visible from the outside.' Brainwashing transformed victims into helpless automata, their confessions pouring out 'as if pressed on a disc'.

According to Hunter, the Bolsheviks had been quick to realise the implications of Pavlov's work. Soon after the Russian Revolution, in fact, Pavlov had been wooed by the Communist Party and hailed publicly as the Soviet Union's greatest living scientist. He shortly began to receive generous research grants, and an impressive new laboratory was built for him in Koltushy. Unlike other Russian academics, he was given unlimited opportunities to travel around the world to further his research. 'There can be no doubt,' wrote Hunter, 'that [Pavlov] was the most protected and privileged character in the Soviet Union outside the Kremlin.'

There was a method behind this special treatment. On a visit to London in 1928, when he was made an honorary fellow of the Royal College of Physicians, Pavlov apparently told a former colleague, Michael Korostevetz, that shortly after the Revolution he had been surprised to receive a personal invitation from Lenin to visit the Kremlin.

When the two men met and Lenin enquired about his research, Pavlov gave him a potted history of his work with dogs. 'Yes, that's all very fascinating,' interrupted the impatient Lenin—but he was interested in human beings, not dogs. What had Pavlov learnt about *people* during the course of his experiments? According to Hunter, Lenin then gave Pavlov a special task.

Pavlov's assignment was to write a summary of his life's work—but he was to apply this knowledge to human beings, not animals. For the time it took him to write this report he was to remain in Moscow, a 'guest' at the Kremlin.

Lenin, it seems, had realised that it was impossible to create the New Soviet Man by persuasion alone. If the Revolution was to succeed, a means of converting the Russian population *en masse* to socialism was needed. Pavlov's new conditioning techniques would be applied first to the Russians, then the Chinese, the Central European republics and, finally, to the rest of the world.

Three months after their meeting, Pavlov handed Lenin a 400-page manuscript. Lenin took it, read it and returned a day later, beaming. He shook Pavlov's hand firmly and told him he had guaranteed the future of the Revolution. 'Pavlov's manuscript,' reported Hunter, 'which became the working basis for the whole Communist expansion control system, has never left the Kremlin.'

Since then, Pavlov's techniques had been applied all over the world including, most recently, to American troops in Korea. US Marine Colonel Frank Schwable was proof of that. When he returned to the United States at the end of the war, Schwable told a Military Court of Inquiry that he had known at the outset of his interrogation that the First Marine Air Wing was not deploying biological weapons over Korea. 'I knew we hadn't,' he said, 'but the rest of it was real to me—the conferences, the planes and how they would go about their missions . . . The words were mine but the thoughts were theirs.' The technique really seemed to work.

There is every indication that Hunter's story and the theory that Pavlovian conditioning was being deliberately applied to humans in the Soviet bloc were taken seriously. An article in the March 1953 edition of the *American Journal of Psychiatry* demonstrates that there really was a spike in Russian interest in Pavlov's work in the late 1940s and 1950s. The CIA picked up on this immediately. 'Much of Soviet psychology is concerned,' wrote one expert in 1958, 'with adaptation of the conditioned reflex concepts of Pavlov.' The Agency was also aware that the techniques were being applied to humans. In 1955 an informant who had recently visited the Brain Institute in Moscow told a case officer:

> The Soviet government requires that all physiological laboratories produce work in conditioned reflex responses. . . . [Informant] observed two cases in which reflexes had been conditioned. In one of these cases—that of a young boy—a salivary fistula had been produced. The boy was conditioned so that when he thought or said the number '4' he salivated. When they demonstrated him for [informant], they asked him to divide 8 by 2 and before he could actually verbalise the number '4' he salivated.

The true nature of Pavlov's brainwashing techniques came to light only with the publication of William Sargant's *Battle for the Mind* in 1956. Sargant, a noted psychiatrist at St Thomas's Hospital in London—and who will crop up a number of times in this book—postulated a theory about how the techniques could cause man to reverse his most personal beliefs.

According to Sargant, Pavlov's most important discovery came about not as a result of his meticulous experiments but by accident. In 1924 there was a terrible flood in Leningrad. The waters had risen so fast that Pavlov's dogs, trapped in the laboratory, were in danger of drowning and were forced to swim around their cages, desperately holding their noses above the water. Luckily, a research assistant arrived just in time to free them.

Once the water had subsided and Pavlov's team got back to work, however, it became clear that something strange had happened: all the dogs' conditioned reflexes—salivating and so forth—had gone. For the dogs, the near-drowning experience had been so terrifying that their learnt behaviour had been erased. Pavlov's dogs had been brainwashed by their own fear.

Months later, when the dogs had been retrained, Pavlov decided to try an experiment. He positioned a hosepipe beneath the door of his laboratory and turned on the tap to see what happened. As the water ran into the animal compound, the dogs immediately panicked as they had during the great flood. Sure enough, when tested after the experiment, they had forgotten all their conditioning cues again. This phenomenon made Pavlov rethink his theories, with profound implications.

Pavlov already knew that there were two levels of conditioning in dogs. If you repeatedly rang a bell before feeding them, they would eventually salivate in response to the sound of the bell. This he called the 'Equivalent Phase'. If you trained the dogs to salivate upon hearing the bell and then rang the bell without feeding them, however, the dogs eventually became confused and acted unpredictably, either salivating or not salivating, reacting strongly to a weak impulse or weakly to a strong one. This he termed the 'Paradoxical Phase'.

To these two levels he now added a third, which he termed the 'Ultra Paradoxical Phase'. In this case, he said, extreme fear or trauma transformed positive conditioning into negative conditioning. As had happened during the flood, the dogs became so traumatised that they did the exact opposite of what they had been trained to do. An aggressive dog might become docile; a friendly dog might bite a laboratory attendant. In the Ultra Paradoxical Phase, character traits were reversed.

From Pavlov's work, Sargant concluded that if an experience was violent or traumatic enough, it was possible to reverse behavioural traits outright. Under severe trauma the mind reached a point at which it simply could not function properly any longer and its wires crossed, reversing the polarity. The result was radical personality change.

Sargant, who had treated shell-shocked patients throughout the Second World War, said he had seen similar cases numerous times: brave soldiers became cowardly, demure ones intent on rushing into impossibly dangerous situations. In the Blitz, such patients tended to present as underweight, with a distant look in their eyes and a strange 'bomb-happy' smile on their faces. Their physical appearance, in fact, was similar to that of the confessors at the Moscow Show Trials. Given enough pressure and fear, he said, everyone would break down eventually.

Most importantly, such traumatised patients had a further trait: they were immensely, abnormally, suggestible.

Sargant speculated that shell-shock and violent interrogation were not the only causes of such changes. Religion could perform the same function. Almost invariably, in ceremonies where acolytes went into trances or spoke in tongues, there was a great deal of drumming, dancing, shouting and excitement. In some cases, feelings of intense guilt were deliberately induced, or fear—such as in the Christian snake-handling cults of the southern United States. The function of these stimuli was to push the human psyche into an unnaturally high level of excitement resulting, ultimately, in psychic release and irrational behaviour: ecstatic experience and religious conversion.

In the atmosphere of the early 1950s, when the Mindszenty trial and the Korean confessions were on people's minds, it wasn't hard to see the similarity between Sargant's shell-shocked patients, new religious converts and the Eastern bloc confessors. All had been pushed beyond their natural limits; all had undergone apparently inexplicable transformations and ended up reversing their beliefs. For Sargant, the possibility that the Soviet Union had picked up on these conversion phenomena, isolated the causes and was now actively applying them aggressively as weapons was comparable only to the threat of 'total physical destruction through atomic warfare'.*

Sargant wasn't the only one to see the danger. Aldous Huxley, who was himself to play a role in the brainwashing mêlée following the Korean War, parroted Sargant's 'very remarkable' theory to anyone who would listen. 'Pavlov's findings,' he wrote, in 1958, 'have important practical applications. If the central nervous system of dogs can be broken down, so can the central nervous system of political prisoners. It is simply a matter of applying the right amount of stress for the right amount of time.' The whole thing was, he thought, terribly depressing. 'The prophecies I made [in *Brave New World*] are coming true much sooner than I thought they would.'

But Pavlovian theory was not the only explanation for what had happened in Korea and the Soviet Union. A couple of other ideas had been waiting in the wings.

---

* As often seems to have been the case with Sargant, his revolutionary theory (and, in this case, his analogy) owes more than a little to the work of other researchers. In March 1953 the *American Journal of Psychiatry* specifically noted that the Soviets were interested in Pavlov's 'experimental neurosis'—the induction of psychological breakdown through deliberate application of intolerable stress. A year later, Joost Meerloo, former chief of psychiatry for the Dutch military and an expert witness at the Schwable tribunal, coined a term for it: 'menticide'. To Meerloo, the implications of the deliberate induction of Pavlov's 'experimental neurosis' were terrifying: 'Maybe the perverted conditioning of mankind is even worse than an atomic explosion. The human mind may be incarcerated for years to come.'

★ ★ ★

In July 1951, the CIA apprehended two Russian agents in Germany, both of whom, when searched, were found to be carrying 4 1/2-inch-long clear plastic cylinders. Inside the cylinders, collapsible tubes contained a viscous grey-white liquid, fitted with hypodermic needles. Under interrogation the agents admitted that the liquid was a powerful drug capable of turning a human being into a zombie. Resistance was impossible. Given the drug unwittingly, they said, a man would do exactly as he was told, regardless of the consequences. Moreover, throughout the period of the drug's action, the victim would be fully capable of walking, and would show no outward signs of narcosis. The CIA immediately dispatched the tubes to various laboratories for analysis. No one in the United States was able to identify the contents.

Although CIA doctors Hinkle and Wolff had concluded that there were no psychologically 'magic' brainwashing drugs, suspicion lingered that they might be wrong. Like the popular press, the Agency speculated for some time that drugs or hypnosis held the answer to what had happened in Korea and Hungary. 'There is a strong indication', reported a 1949 assessment, that Eastern bloc countries were 'further advanced than we might care to believe' in the extraction of information through the use of amphetamines, such as Benzedrine, and barbiturates, such as sodium pentothal. Moreover, 'new' drugs, such as SHE—scopolamine ephotamine hukatal (which caused 'slow mental excitement')—were known to be in use behind the Iron Curtain. In fact, work on truth and brainwashing drugs, along with hypnosis, was suspected of having been undertaken by the Hungarians and the Nazis during the Second World War.

According to CIA information, the Soviets had also been investigating the techniques. In 1954 a Russian defector, Nikolai Khokhlov, told the Agency that research had been under way in the USSR for some time. He was in a position to know: he was in charge of 'executive actions' (i.e. assassinations) for the KGB's thirteenth directorate at the time. According to his debrief, the KGB maintained two special laboratories in which they were cooking up all sorts of drugs and poisons for use on Western agents.

Khokhlov's information seemed to gel with other, older reports. In the 1930s, said another source, Lavrenti Beria—head of the OGPU, forerunner to the KGB—had built a top-secret laboratory in Moscow, in which doctors and other scientists had developed new poisons to eliminate enemies of the state. This 'super secret' Soviet laboratory, known as Kamera ('The Chamber') was apparently situated somewhere in Spets Byuro #1, but its location and function were so secret that even senior KGB officers were not allowed to know what or where it was. Inside the Chamber, work was conducted on 'powders, beverages, liquors and various types of injections' as a means of forcing confession.

Hypnotism was another field that seemed to offer answers. Mindszenty's performance, noted a 1949 CIA assessment, demonstrated regression to an infantile state of abject dependency 'characteristic of hypnosis'. Three years later, a follow-up report indicated that there was 'ample evidence' of the use of both drugs and hypnosis.

Throughout the 1950s, there were recurring reports that the Soviets were using drugs to extract information from victims. 'They realised that something nasty had been done [to Mindszenty],' recalls Cyril Cunningham. 'He was injected with a substance but nobody ever found out what that substance was.' A CIA informant likewise concluded of the Mindszenty case that

> The Cardinal was drugged. His confession was induced by the alternate use of aktedron and scopolamine, the former speeding up the physiological reactions and the latter slowing them down. It was estimated that if this procedure was carried on for four days, all of the Cardinal's inhibitions would be completely annihilated.

Further reports indicated that the Chinese were in possession of truth-drug technology, too. One of Edward Hunter's interviewees, American lawyer Robert T. Bryan, who had served sixteen and a half months in a Shanghai jail for political crimes, recalled being held down on a table, his trousers removed and a hypodermic needle jabbed into the base of his spine. One of his interrogators referred to the injection as containing 'true words serum'. Another, Lieutenant John A. Ori, reported finding a strange white powder in his food in one of the Korean prison camps. At first he thought the powder was salt but it turned out to be sweet. Ori soon found himself 'talking and talking. I was hardly able to control what I was saying. I talked a blue streak.'

'Strong evidence' existed, reported a 1949 CIA analysis, that some of this information was sound. The idea of using drugs for interrogation was not new to the Agency and, if that was the case, it certainly wasn't new to the Russians or the Chinese. Throughout the 1950s a host of reports warned of the dangers of drugging by the Soviets. Former inmates of Soviet prisons said that coffee was often given during interrogations with cigarettes 'of a peculiar odour', which increased the stimulating effects of the caffeine. Meanwhile, in May 1953, a debriefed Korean PoW reported that he had been drugged on the train returning him from Manchuria— apparently in an attempt to knock him out while he passed through a militarily sensitive area. The request went out for more information: had anyone else been drugged by the Chinese? It seemed that they had:

> The individuals who had come out of North Korea across the Soviet Union to freedom recently had apparently had a 'blank' period or period of disorientation while passing through a special zone in Manchuria. [Deleted] pointed out that this had occurred in all individuals in the party after they had had their first meal and their first coffee on the way to freedom.

The idea that something secret was going on in Manchuria and that the soldiers were put to sleep as they passed through the 'special zone' seemed farfetched, but what other explanation could there be? 'Drugging,' concluded the CIA document, 'was indicated.'*

Further reports went into detail concerning the origins of the Soviets' mysterious drugs. One CIA informant, recently back from Moscow, reported the existence of special sub-tropical propagation houses at the Nikita Botanical Gardens, where strange medicinal plants were being cultivated for their speech-producing effects. There, top Soviet botanists were apparently cross-breeding hallucinogenic and poisonous plant species to create hybrids, producing new drugs with effects on the human body and mind as yet unknown. Drugs from the centre could be administered surreptitiously to American agents, causing any number of effects from unconsciousness to death. In between the two a number of compounds

---

* It was almost certainly the rumour cited in this document, with various pieces of information gleaned from experiments detailed in chapter 5, that inspired the most famous 'brainwashing' story of all: Richard Condon's *The Manchurian Candidate*. We'll come to it later in the story.

induced 'loquaciousness, or lowered resistance to persistent questioning'. Another plantation was known to be in existence in Dakchisarai in the Crimea. All evidence pointed to the fact that the Soviet Union had made provision for the 'large-scale production' of truth drugs. Such drugs, noted a CIA document, 'might win or lose battles' in war.

The combination of such intelligence, together with the Moscow Show Trials, the Korean confessions and the work of Edward Hunter and William Sargant, proved explosive. Soon everyone in the US intelligence community was speculating wildly about what the Soviets and the Chinese were up to. Whatever it was, it was deeply sinister. The 'perverse science' of mind control, a bastard son of psychiatry and military research, was too terrible even to contemplate. In 1953 a meeting of the CIA's Psychological Strategy Board warned that Soviet drugging was so likely that US politicians should be monitored closely for 'signs of a changed personality'. Any suspect officials should be restrained, isolated and monitored for at least twenty-four hours. If it had come to this, reasoned Agency experts, it was time that the world was warned.

In April that year director of the CIA Allen Dulles gave a lecture at Princeton University detailing Soviet developments in the field of mind control. The Soviets, said Dulles,

> take selected human beings whom they wish to destroy and turn them into humble confessors of crimes they never committed, or make them the mouthpiece for Soviet propaganda. New techniques wash the brain clean of the thoughts and mental processes of the past and, possibly, through the use of some 'lie serum', create new brain processes and new thoughts which the victim, parrot-like, repeats.

Such an 'abhorrent' experiment in brain perversion, warned Dulles, had never before been undertaken. Its target was the minds of free men, both collectively and individually. Echoing Edward Hunter, he said that brainwashing effectively enabled the Soviets to tamper with the mind until it became 'a phonograph playing a disk put on its spindle by an outside genius over which it has no control'. With this technology in hand, the Cold War was moving into a new era of psychological warfare, which Dulles characterised as the battle for men's minds. 'We might call it in its new form,' he concluded, 'brain warfare.'

Six months later, in a meeting of the United Nations Political and Security Council, US representative Dr Charles W. Mayo launched a tirade against the Communist deployment of 'brainwashing and menticide' techniques. Detailing the use of Pavlovian conditioning and drugs in interrogation, he explained that brainwashing was in a different league from ancient torture apparatuses, such as racks and thumbscrews. Instead of simply inducing physical pain, it made victims willing accomplices to the destruction of their own identity.

With such reports from the military, the intelligence and civilian authorities, the press—perhaps justifiably—panicked. While no one knew exactly what it entailed, brainwashing appeared to be a terrible alchemy of the techniques featured in Huxley's *Brave New World*, Arthur Koestler's *Darkness at Noon* and Orwell's *1984*. ('No one whom we bring to this place ever stands out against us,' Winston Smith's interrogator told him in *1984*. 'We shall squeeze you empty, and then we shall fill you with ourselves.') It was a sneak attack on the human will: a dirty, underhand, horrific technique that violated all known moral standards. 'Nothing less,' reported the *Journal of Social Issues*, 'than a combination of the theories of Dr I.P. Pavlov and the wiles of Dr Fu Manchu could produce such results.' It was a rape of the soul.

The public was further alarmed in 1955 by the worldwide distribution of *Brainwashing: a Synthesis of the Communist Textbook on Psycho-politics*. The booklet, which purported to be a translation of a secret speech given by KGB chief Lavrenti Beria in Moscow, detailed Soviet plans for the deployment of the new weapon. It advocated the use of severe interrogation techniques including drugs, torture and 'pain-drug hypnosis', which were capable of inducing anything from confessions to sexual perversions in the subject. With the right psychological techniques, said Beria, families could be broken up, interrogation victims driven insane and the careers of politicians wrecked. Enemies' loyalties could be subverted and their minds destroyed until they were crushed like insects. 'There will never be an atomic war,' he predicted, 'for Russia will have subjected all of her enemies.'

The document was sent to the National Security Council (NSC) and the FBI for evaluation. Neither agency was able to prove that it was a hoax, one NSC official commenting: 'If the booklet is a fake, the author or authors know so much about brainwashing techniques that I would consider them experts, superior to any that I have met to date.'

The greatest brainwashing evangelist, however, was the man who had invented the term, Edward Hunter. Hunter saw it as the mission of all free men to combat this sinister new Communist weapon in which 'shadow takes form and form becomes shadow'. In 1958 he was called to testify before the US Committee on Un-American Activities (CUAA):

HUNTER: The objective of Communist warfare is to capture intact the minds of the people and their possessions, so they can be put to use. This is the modern conception of slavery that puts all the others in the kindergarten age.

Q: Is the United States part of this battlefield?

HUNTER: The United States is the main battlefield in this Red war.

To the American public, the threat of brainwashing was not simply the risk of servicemen getting into trouble in wars or trials overseas. What the Communists were doing threatened world freedom. If they could capture servicemen in Korea or cardinals in Hungary and subvert them, it wouldn't be long before free thought everywhere was jeopardised. And if that happened, it wouldn't be much longer before all Americans became potential enemies. Brainwashing shortly became a battle: freedom versus slavery, liberty versus oppression. 'This is psychological warfare on a scale incalculably more immense than any militarist of the past has ever envisaged,' Hunter told the committee. 'If we and the other free nations permit this to go on, and if the same thing is being done in the other countries of the Soviet bloc, the price our children will have to pay makes the heart sick.'

Psychiatrist Joost Meerloo agreed. 'It is acknowledged that modern warfare has brought the challenge to the doorstep of every citizen, and that the final front of the cold war line is in every citizen's mind.'

Faced with such a threat, there was little doubt that someone needed to do some research into this phenomenon. In August 1954 the US Secretary of Defense set up a special committee to see how Allied prisoners could be taught to resist Communist indoctrination and brainwashing techniques in the future. The committee concluded that the United States and Britain were 'obliged' to invest time and money in the study of what the Soviets were up to so that the threat could be neutralised.

The CIA was way ahead of them.

In fact, the Agency had been interested in drugs and interrogation techniques since its inception in 1947. Two years later, immediately after the Mindszenty trial, the CIA's head of Scientific Intelligence made a fact-finding trip to Europe to learn more about Soviet developments in the field, interviewing numerous refugees from the Eastern bloc—sometimes with drugs—to discover what they had been through in Soviet prisons. On his return to the US that summer, it was decided to set up a 'special-interrogations' team to handle all future incidents, and to look out for possible techniques in use in Eastern Europe.

Since other CIA branches were wondering about the use of hypnosis and drug-based interrogation, it was proposed that a single research unit be established to serve them all, under the umbrella of the Office of Security. In charge was placed former US Army colonel Sheffield Edwards. He classified the project top secret and codenamed it BLUEBIRD.

On 20 April 1950, CIA director Richard Hillenkoetter authorised project BLUEBIRD. CIA documents from the time are often patchy and undated, and no specific goal is stated, but a later summary reports that the programme's goals, broadly, were

(a) Discovering means of conditioning personnel to prevent unauthorized extraction of information of them by known means.
(b) The possibility of obtaining control of an individual by the application of special interrogation techniques.
(c) Memory enhancement, and
(d) Establishing defensive means for preventing hostile control of Agency Personnel.

'CIA,' noted a follow-up document in 1950, 'will consider . . . special or unorthodox methods such as brain damage, sensory stimulation, hypnosis, so-called "black psychiatry", Pavlovian conditioning, "Brainwashing" or any other methods having pertinence for such procedures as interrogation, subversion or seduction.'

Understandably, the realisation that such interrogation techniques might be possible, that hypnosis and drugs might be used to control human beings, exerted a powerful fascination on the Agency. But it was on a slippery slope. What appears to have started as a defensive programme—researching interrogation techniques as a means of preparing US servicemen for capture—

soon became an *offensive* one. Investigations into mind-control techniques would continue under the Agency's aegis for the next twenty-three years. In August 1951, BLUEBIRD would be renamed ARTICHOKE and, in April 1953, assume its most notorious codename, MKULTRA.

The seeds of the transformation were present from the start. Point (b) above—'the possibility of obtaining control of an individual'—gives a fair indication that it had occurred to someone very early on that these techniques might be usefully applied on foreign agents. Diabolical they might be but, if current intelligence on the Soviets was wrong and they weren't using the techniques, it was only a matter of time before they were. And in the meantime, well, why shouldn't *we*? A Security Study under ex-President Herbert Hoover stated the problem succinctly:

> We are facing an implacable enemy whose avowed objective is world domination by whatever means and at whatever cost. There are no rules in such a game. Hitherto acceptable longstanding concepts of 'fair play' must be reconsidered. We must . . . learn to subvert, sabotage, and destroy our enemies by more clever, more sophisticated and more effective methods than those used against us.

Following the scare created by the confessions of the late 1940s and early 1950s, the CIA became involved in an extraordinary clandestine search for brainwashing techniques, in the course of which it spiralled into a morass of ethical issues. It crossed and recrossed boundaries of morally acceptable behaviour with impunity, broke laws in the name of justice, and subverted human rights in the name of freedom. The starting point for all this was the quest for the philosopher's stone of interrogation: a truth drug. Did such a drug exist? Was it possible to force someone to tell the truth? As it happens, it was a quest that had already been going on for some time.

2

Truth Drugs

EX–CIA CHIEF REVITALISES TRUTH SERUM DEBATE
WASHINGTON—Former CIA and FBI director William Webster said
Thursday that the United States should consider administering 'truth drugs'
to uncooperative al-Qaeda and Taliban captives at Guantanamo Bay, Cuba,
and elsewhere to try to obtain more details about terrorist operations.

Speaking to a small group of reporters here, Webster said the use of
drugs such as Sodium Pentothal or other 'invasive' tactics short of torture
might make US agents more effective in penetrating al-Qaeda's worldwide
network. 'We ought to look at what options are out there,' said Webster.

USA Today, 26 April 2002

The moment Susan Wall opened her eyes, she was confused. Why was
her father sitting beside the bed? He was supposed to be at home in England. More to the point, why was she unable to feel the left-hand side of
her body? Oh! she thought. It's Dad! Then she lapsed back into unconsciousness.

When Sue woke up again, two Spanish policemen were in the room.
They asked her if she could remember the accident. She had no idea what
they were talking about. The men produced some tattered clothes and a
pair of gold shoes that seemed familiar. Perhaps they were her shoes, she
thought. But, then again, perhaps they were Claire's. She couldn't remember.

Then a thought struck her. Claire! Where was Claire?

The last image Sue had of Claire was at a party the pair had thrown
in their flat in Notting Hill in June. Sue had made the invitations—

collages—and photocopied them at work. Since they were leaving for a holiday in Mallorca the next day, they had called it their 'coming-out party'.

The evening had been a huge success. It was the summer of 1965, and the Beatles were top of the charts. Sue, Claire and their friends had danced until the walls of the flat ran with condensation. Then Sue had opened the skylight window so that everyone could climb out on to the roof. Claire, laughing, had danced across the neighbours' rooftops. It was a magical night.

Unfortunately, it was also the last thing Sue could remember. And it was six weeks ago.

Sue told her father that she wanted to write to Claire. After all, Claire was her best friend: she'd want to know that Sue was all right. Her father said that was a good idea, and offered to post the letter. When Claire didn't reply, Sue wrote again. Still no reply. It was all a bit strange—but, then, everything was a bit strange. The hospital, the nurses, the police. Everyone told her not to worry: these things took time. She'd be home soon.

When Sue arrived back in England a fortnight later, she complained to her mother that Claire hadn't written to her once while she was in hospital. Wasn't that unlike her? 'I think we ought to have a chat,' said Sue's mum. 'Let's have a cup of tea.' Then, sitting in the lounge, she told her that Claire was dead. She had been killed in the accident in Mallorca.

On receipt of the news that Claire was dead, Sue's condition deteriorated. She failed to recover the use of the left-hand side of her body. She also failed to recover her memory. The only thing she could recall about the holiday was that she and Claire had had an argument. Convinced that she was to blame for her friend's death, she became depressed. Doctors told her that there was no serious damage, that she would get better. But as time went by, she didn't. Her amnesia bothered her: she could remember her name, where she lived and where she had gone to school but that was about it. Everything was disconnected, mystifying. It was as if she was watching her own life on television, lost in a vacuum.

In late 1965, Sue was admitted to the Belmont Hospital and treated for depression. When the drugs didn't work, it was clear that something new was called for. And that was when she met William Sargant.

Sue knew that Sargant was a big man in psychiatry. He had written a book on brainwashing that had made him famous. The reaction of the staff and patients in the ward reinforced the impression that he was a terribly important man. When he walked in, everyone seemed to inhale: 'The great William Sargant!' It wasn't only his reputation. Sargant was a large man physically who had, in his day, played rugby for Cambridge. He had a powerful, authoritative personality and a habit of barking at people. There was something about his demeanour that compelled respect. He didn't ask: he told. 'It was really a kind of a parting of the waves when he walked in,' recalls Sue. 'Awe-inspiring. An awe-inspiring human being.' She felt honoured when he took an interest in her case.

Sargant told Sue that her paralysis and amnesia were not due to any physical injuries but were the result of the psychological trauma she had suffered. Basically, he said, her mind had found the whole incident so terrifying that it had shut down, leaving her in limbo. The only way to recover her memory, and her health, was to retrieve the experience so that she could come to terms with it and finally let it go. He could help her to do this. There was a drug, he said, that would bring back the past.

A week later, Sue was taken to a treatment room and instructed to lie down on the bed. A junior doctor and a couple of nurses stood by, waiting for Sargant to arrive. When he swept in a few minutes later, there were few preliminaries and no chat. He wasn't that kind of man. Sargant gave Sue an injection and everyone in the room waited silently. Then, as the drug began to take effect, he began to talk to her quietly, asking questions—and leading her back into the past.

Moments later, Sue began to talk. There were geraniums, she remembered. Red ones. And a party. And a sports car.

Sargant instructed Sue to tell the story in the present tense. The important thing, he told her, was not to remember the incident, but to *relive* it. She was in Mallorca, he said. She was on holiday. What could she see?

Before Sue knew it, it was the last night of her holiday again. She and Claire had had an argument, but because they were flying home tomorrow they decided to go out to a bar with a couple of local boys anyway. They drank rum and Coke, forgot their differences and began having a good time. When the bar closed at three or four a.m., the boys offered them a lift back to their house. On the way they stopped off at one of the boys' homes. His father's open-topped red sports car stood in the drive. 'Hey,' said Sue. 'Let's go in this car!' The four climbed in, boys at the front, girls in the back.

By now the drug had taken full effect and Sue felt an urgent, gushing need to talk. The memories began returning fast, graphically, like a feature film. As the accident drew closer, however, she became agitated and began to fidget and squirm on the bed. Convinced that her hospital gown was riding up her thighs, she became embarrassed and tried frantically to pull it down. 'Be still! Stop moving!' Sargant ordered, making her feel like a little girl. He began to push her harder and harder, back to the night in Mallorca. Then, in a glut, the memory returned.

As one of the Spanish boys started the sports car's engine, Claire sat down on the back seat. Sue wasn't having any of it. 'No!' she said. 'Up here!' Hauling herself on to the boot of the car she placed her feet on the seat and sat up above the driver. She then told Claire to join her so that the two could feel the wind in their hair. Claire laughed and climbed up. The car pulled out of the driveway.

The next recollection was of the flowers.

Sue was lying on the ground, her head next to a pot of geraniums. The road was wet and slippery. Someone had hosed it down. As the car had hit the water it had aquaplaned. Sitting on the boot, instead of in the seats, the two girls had been flung out. Claire had been trapped between the car and a tree. Sue, thrown in the other direction, was lying in the road, next to the flowers.

After a period of unconsciousness, Sue remembered waking up inside the house with the geraniums. Claire had gone ahead in a taxi, she was told. The ambulance was on its way. Then more unconsciousness. Then her father, sitting beside her bed in the hospital.

The technique William Sargant used to help Sue recover her memory was not new. In fact, it dated back to the late nineteenth century, when Sigmund Freud had discovered that physical ailments could have psychological causes. According to Freud, the recollection of unhappy events in the past caused emotional pain. Since the mind didn't enjoy pain, it tended to bury traumatic memories in the unconscious by 'forgetting' them. Unfortunately, however, such memories often refused to stay buried. Sometimes the stress created by the process of repression caused them to resurface in the form of apparently unrelated physical symptoms. Only once the repressed memories were brought out into the open and dealt with, said Freud, would the physical symptoms be relieved. There were various ways of going about this. Intensive psychotherapy was one, hypnosis another. Freud's colleague, Breuer, termed the coaxing-out of such emotions 'abreaction', and Freud called the resulting sudden relief of psychic pressure 'catharsis'.

Abreaction had come into its own in Britain during the First World War when it was used to draw hidden traumas out of shell-shocked soldiers. After the war, however, the technique was largely forgotten until a decade later it received an unexpected boost. In 1931 at the London Hospital, a physician named J. Stephen Horsley noticed that when women in labour were anaesthetised with the barbiturate Nembutal, they appeared to lose their inhibitions, often confiding intimate personal details to their doctor. When the drug wore off, they had no recollection of what they had said. Horsley knew that it usually took months of psychoanalysis to get patients into a state as relaxed as this. Yet here was a drug that removed inhibitions in a matter of seconds. Perhaps Nembutal might have important uses in psychiatry. He began to experiment with other barbiturates, such as sodium amytal and sodium pentothal, to see if they might be used to remove personal inhibitions, too.

Horsley's technique (later aped by intelligence agencies all over the world) was to give an intravenous injection of the barbiturate at a very slow rate. The goal was to reduce the patient to a state half-way between sleep and wakefulness in which he would be uninhibited enough to let the barriers down and start revealing personal secrets, but still capable of talking coherently. The trick was to leave the needle in the vein: if the patient stopped talking or became uneasy, a little more barbiturate would put him under again; if he became unconscious, he could be roused, and the process restarted.

As they received the barbiturates, Horsley's patients invariably became relaxed and amiable—and willing to share all kinds of personal details. Long-forgotten childhood memories emerged all over the place. Barbiturate treatment, Horsley concluded, offered a new means of establishing contact with the unconscious mind. He christened the technique 'narcoanalysis'.

To measure the narcotic's effectiveness in eliciting information, Horsley tried an experiment with twenty of his staff nurses. The plan was to give them 2 ccs of sodium pentothal and see if they revealed personal information. Prior to the experiment, the nurses had laughed: there was no way they were going to reveal any secrets, even under the influence of a drug. But, following the injections, that was precisely what they did. Eighteen out of the twenty found themselves unable to refuse to answer his questions.

Had Horsley discovered a truth drug? He certainly considered the possibility. A technique similar to narcoanalysis, he speculated, might have been behind the recent confessions in the Moscow Show Trials. By 1936, the popular press was debating the possible applications of the technique in medicine, psychotherapy and forensic investigations.

Horsley's technique was not widely used. In fact, it seems largely to have vanished until the start of the Second World War, when an ambitious young psychiatrist—William Sargant—stumbled upon it by accident.

In June 1940, working at the Belmont Hospital, Sargant was presented with a swathe of shell-shock victims recently evacuated from Dunkirk. All of the men needed urgent medical attention but one in particular was in an especially pitiful state: mute, shaking, terrified and clearly in great distress. No one knew what had happened to him but he was so traumatised that he had been unable to urinate for three days. As a result his bladder was terribly swollen, 'like a pumpkin', causing him extreme discomfort. Sargant had no idea how to treat him but, seeing that he was under a great deal of stress, gave him a shot of the barbiturate sodium amytal.

The result was immediate. The man began to talk about what had happened to him and, spontaneously, emptied his bladder all over the couch. By the time the drug wore off, he was talking coherently and had stopped shaking.

A few days later Sargant was confronted by another amnesic patient, trembling with fear and unable to use his right hand. Once again, he administered an injection of sodium amytal, upon receipt of which the man stopped trembling and recalled, in vivid detail, how he had emerged from a battle to find his brother lying beside a road, mortally wounded in the stomach. At his brother's request, the man had dragged him into a field and put him out of his misery with a rifle shot. 'It was the hand that pulled the trigger,' noted Sargant, 'that had suddenly become paralysed.'

As more and more traumatised evacuees were paraded before him, Sargant began giving sodium amytal more frequently. When they were sedated he would persuade them that they were back on the battlefield, that the tanks were coming down the road towards them, and that they were about to die. They would go red in the face, start to hyperventilate, and the hidden memories would pour out. But the soldiers weren't simply remembering the incidents. They were *reliving* them. Soon Sargant found himself with a series of soldiers running around his office, screaming and acting out their nightmares. Sometimes the abreactions were so violent that it was necessary to hold them down. 'I remember,' he joked later, 'the third or fourth patient almost chasing me around the room.'

It wasn't long before other drugs proved themselves, too. Many of the barbiturates seemed to work. Ether, suggested to Sargant by an American colleague, caused even more violent abreactions. And it wasn't only depressants that had this effect: the amphetamines worked, too. It seemed that when they were given to shell-shocked patients intravenously, they led to such a rush of energy that the individual felt an unstoppable need to talk. The result was a sudden outpouring of memories and emotions, which could be channelled usefully by a therapist. With drugs, Sargant had rediscovered the technique of cathartic abreaction pioneered by Freud and Breuer in the 1890s.

Then something unexpected happened. On 12 July 1940—six days after Sargant's discovery had appeared in the *Lancet*—he received a letter from a Brigadier J. Rees, medical director of the Tavistock Clinic and later chairman of the Army Psychiatry Advisory Committee. The letter, congratulating him on 'the beginning of what I hope will be a lot of first-class work', appears to have been the starting point for a relationship between William Sargant and Whitehall that was to last for the best part of thirty years. It led him into the heart of the British Security Service, MI5.

Sargant's personal documents are incomplete but it appears that he was on the verge of producing another paper on the use of sodium amytal when he received an 'urgent' call from Brigadier Rees, who told him of 'the undesirability of this work getting into enemy hands' and instructed him not to publish. A letter from Sargant to the War Office dated 1 February (no year is given) makes it clear that his work had been classified. 'This morning,' wrote Sargant, 'I have been on the phone to Colonel Hargreaves [Brigadier Rees's partner] and apparently they have now definitely made up their minds that they do not want it published.'

It is entirely understandable that, during the war, academic papers detailing new treatments for battle stress would be suppressed, since this sort of information might conceivably assist the enemy. It is equally possible, however, that there was another reason why Sargant's work was classified: that his paper accidentally shed light on far more highly classified work— research by the British military and intelligence communities into the feasibility of a truth drug.

There was certainly reason to believe that the Germans were hunting for just such a drug themselves. According to intelligence historian M.R.D. Foot, there was no shortage of 'bar-room' talk among the British intelligence community that the Germans were using drugs to break informants. A Special Operations Executive (SOE) training manual dated September 1943, meanwhile, gives specific advice on what to do if interrogated under ether.

Concrete proof of German interest in truth drugs came on 24 July 1942, when a coded Enigma cable was decrypted at the Government Code and Cypher School at Bletchley Park in Buckinghamshire. The signal, from the SS Führer in Dnjepropetrowsk, Ukraine, was a request for mind-altering drugs from the SS medical headquarters in Berlin.

MOST SECRET

Experiments to date of injecting parachutists with scopolamine were successful. Therefore experiments with Mescaline are to be undertaken, since these injections produce an enhanced effect through intoxication.

The experiments, the cable reported, involved injecting airborne troops with 0/4 to 0/6 grams of scopolamine (an alkaloid derivative of belladonna, commonly used as an analgesic at the time)* every half-hour. Filing data at the Public Records Office suggest that these tests were being conducted

---

* Scopolamine had been mooted as a truth drug since Texan obstetrician Robert E. House had discovered its abreactive properties in Dallas in 1916. Like Horsley, House made his discovery after administering the drug to a woman in labour. Leaving the mother unconscious on the bed, he had asked her husband for a set of scales with which to weigh the baby. The man didn't know where they were—but his wife did: 'They're in the kitchen, on a nail behind the picture,' piped a clear voice from the bedroom. It was following this incident that the popular press first homed in on the idea of a truth drug, the *Los Angeles Record* of 1922 coining the term 'truth serum'.

on Allied prisoners but due to the number of recipients—between fifty and a hundred—it seems more likely that the guinea pigs were, in fact, German troops. Fifty grams of mescaline hydrochloride was requested. 'The effect,' noted the writer, 'lasts up to 5 hours.'

Details of the mescaline and scopolamine tests have long since been destroyed but, sixty years on, there is no doubt that the Nazis were indeed searching for a truth drug. In addition to the Ukrainian experiments, research was also under way in Poland and Germany. This time, however, the guinea pigs were not parachutists but civilian prisoners.

The man behind the German truth-drug tests was Standartenführer Wolfram Sievers, a member of Heinrich Himmler's personal staff, and secretary-general of the Ancestral Heritage Research and Teaching Society, or 'Ahnenerbe'. Founded in 1935, Ahnenerbe was a supposedly academic organisation dedicated to researching, and proving, the supremacy of the Aryan race. Originally a faintly ludicrous outfit, Ahnenerbe sponsored hare-brained projects analysing Teutonic rituals, excavating Viking warships and studying native folk music in the Tyrol.

As the war moved on, however, the organisation became increasingly involved in military research and in 1942, when Himmler established the Institute of Scientific Research for Military Purposes, the two groups merged. Ahnenerbe now became the source of funds and supplies for a series of barbaric 'medical' tests on civilians incarcerated in concentration camps across Eastern Europe. Sievers, a former book dealer, received directly from Himmler lists of research projects to be undertaken, then authorised the equipment, the facilities and the guinea pigs.

Medical tests run at the camps are well documented. Prisoners were forced to drink untreated seawater, placed in pressurised cabins, shot with live rounds to see how their blood coagulated, and frozen to death in tanks of iced water to determine how long downed pilots could expect to survive if they ditched over the sea. Originally these experiments took place at Dachau but they were soon moved to Auschwitz for more privacy ('The camp is so extensive,' commented one doctor, 'that less attention will be attracted to the work. The subjects howl frightfully when they freeze').

The Ahnenerbe-sponsored medical experiments have rightly received a lot of attention. One aspect of the organisation's work that has never been explored, however, is its search for a truth drug.

According to one source, truth-drug experiments at Auschwitz resulted from the Gestapo's inability to break Allied troops with physical pain. Members of the Polish resistance proved especially intractable. Torture didn't seem to be working, 'so the next question,' recalled one former researcher, 'was why don't we do it like the Russians, who have been able to get confessions of guilt at their Show Trials?' Since it was common knowledge that the Russians were using drugs, this seemed a good place to start.

The tests were run in Block 10, a unit that one commentator describes as 'quintessential Auschwitz'. There, medical doctors tested vaccines by infecting inmates with contagious diseases, perfected methods of sterilising men and women with drugs and X-rays and carried out blood transfusions from one victim to another, deliberately mismatching the blood types to see what happened.

Even for Auschwitz, Block 10 had a terrible reputation: it was rumoured that women sent to the block for experimentation were 'impregnated with monsters'. The shutters were permanently drawn and research was punctuated by the regular sound of gunshots, as firing squads laboured round the clock in the courtyard of Block 11 next door.

Truth-drug tests, referred to by one witness as 'brainwashing with chemicals', were run under the supervision of Dr Bruno Weber, the officer in charge of the Hygienic Institute. For some time, Weber had been collaborating with SS doctors, including the organisation's chief pharmacist, Viktor Capesius, and a Professor Mrugowsky, chief physician of the Waffen SS's Central Hygienic Institute in Berlin. Mrugowsky was behind the logistics of the camp tests and, presumably, the man to whom the request for mescaline for the Ukrainian experiments would have come. Another collaborator was SS Obersturmführer Dr Werner Rohde.

Capesius and Weber experimented for some time with barbiturates and morphine derivatives, feeding various cocktails of drugs to inmates and monitoring the results. One witness to these tests, Dr J. Wolman, later recounted watching prisoners being fed unidentified drugs before they were interrogated. Another, Professor J. Olbrycht, recalled Capesius forcing inmates to drink a substance 'that looked and smelled very much like coffee'. The result was a strong manic excitement.

The next day, Capesius tried the experiment again. This time, the dose was higher: two of the four recipients of the drug collapsed and had to be carried out of the room. Within twelve hours both were dead. A doctor at the camp later told a researcher ambivalently: 'Within the context of Auschwitz, what difference did two people make—people who were in the hands of the Gestapo and so already dead anyhow?' Werner Rohde was even less bothered, bursting into 'ironic laughter'. The way he saw it, they were lucky to have received the drugs at all. 'At least they died a pleasant death,' he told another doctor.

Meanwhile, another truth-drug programme was up and running in Block 5 at Dachau. Interviews with former prison medic Walter Neff by American investigators in 1945 revealed some of the details. The experiments, said Neff, were run under a Dr Kurt Ploetner, lecturer in medicine at the University of Leipzig. Their goal was 'to eliminate the will of the person examined'.

Recommendations for tests apparently came to Ploetner directly from the SS; Wolfram Sievers' duty diary indicates that a number of meetings took place between the Ahnenerbe chief and Dr Ploetner. Presumably Sievers supplied the drugs. A number of compounds were tested but the one that Neff recalled most vividly was mescaline, a 'Mexican drug that has been reputed to dissolve repressions and to encourage talkativeness', which was given to prisoners on about thirty separate occasions. The experiments' protocols were simple: unwitting inmates were fed the drug, then interrogated to see what information they revealed.

> The best results were achieved giving the [prisoners] Messkalin mixed with coffee. The [prisoners] had to remain quiet afterwards. In single cases the [prisoners] got furious, in other cases very gay or melancholy showing the same symptoms as in a state of intoxication . . . The examining person succeeded in every case in drawing even the most intimate secrets from the [prisoners] when the questions were cleverly put.

Although some secrets were revealed—all inmates were quite open to the interrogators about their feelings of hatred for them—Ploetner concluded that mescaline was too unreliable to be a truth drug. Sometimes it worked, sometimes it didn't. In addition, it had strange side-effects: it induced vivid hallucinations and, when the dose was increased, the result was vomiting, headaches and nausea.

★ ★ ★

It is not clear whether the British or the Americans had hard evidence of any of these projects during the war, but they certainly had their suspicions. And, with those suspicions, it would have been foolish not to look into the issue, especially as neither country was inexperienced in the field of chemical experimentation.

In 1942, SOE's Physiology Section at Porton Down had begun work on Project SACCHARINE, the procurement of drugs for the intelligence community. The idea was to provide agents with a choice of small-scale chemical agents that might, at a push, save their lives. Chemicals for the tests were provided by Imperial College, London, and Cambridge University.

SACCHARINE was eventually to lead to such handy devices as tear-gas grenades, contact poisons and smoke generators. 'Special requirements' were 'A Tablets', to counter travel sickness, 'B Tablets', Benzedrine, for extra energy in an emergency, 'Mecodrin', another amphetamine, for energy, 'E Capsules', containing a fast-acting anaesthetic, 'K Tablets', morphine-based chemicals designed to be slipped into foreign agents' drinks to knock them out, and 'L Tablets', suicide pills.

There is no doubt that research was conducted into truth drugs in the United Kingdom, and it seems reasonable to assume that background information, if not more explicit advice, on narcoanalysis and abreactive techniques would have come from William Sargant, who was at the forefront of the doctors utilising the technique at the time. It seems, however, that the drugs were discarded fairly quickly. 'The use of the so-called "truth drugs"', reports a British Government principal medical officer in 1950, 'was discontinued in the army after a very short period in the recent war.' The results of such use were apparently found to be 'unreliable'.

Further evidence of British intelligence services' disregard for truth drugs comes from MI5. In a document declassified in September 2005, an MI5 officer was encouraged by an American agent to use the 'truth drug', benzedrine sulphate, to obtain information from captured Germans. The officer concerned—who admitted to testing the drug on himself—was not impressed: 'I tried a compound of the drug,' he wrote, 'but the effects were deleterious temporarily to the body rather than to the mind.' Another document, declassified in January 1999, contains a suggestion from the War Office that MI5 use the barbiturate, Evapam Sodium, to 'pick the brains' of Rudolf Hess. Again the response was not favourable. Hess, states the MI5 reply, was 'a poor type, completely devoid of intellectual (or even intelligent) interests'.

As with everything relating to the work of the Security and Secret Intelligence Services, information is scarce, but a CIA document dated 22 June 1948 refers to 'the United States-Britain combined operation' to utilise truth drugs, indicating that the British intelligence community occasionally made use of them. Sodium amytal, says the document, 'was considered only in top echelon cases. This use was strictly unauthorised and no account of it was made in writing.'

Details of the operational use of truth drugs by the British have never emerged. It is clear, however, that haphazard research into barbiturates and amphetamines continued into the Cold War. One psychiatrist who worked for MI6 after the war agrees that work was indeed conducted into their efficacy—but says that experiments were never very well organised or thought-out. 'Experimentation took place in a vague sort of way,' he says. 'I mean, at the Royal Waterloo Hospital, part of Thomas's, we used to experiment in whether or not we could get confessions from people who . . . were suspected of this or that. But it wasn't done in any sort of scientific way . . . we experimented on a wide range of people and problems.'

There is no indication that MI5 or MI6 specifically sponsored or encouraged these experiments. It seems reasonable, however, to assume that since one of the main perpetrators was working for them, they were kept aware of the results. Certainly, the psychiatrist concerned backs up the notion that British Intelligence was less than impressed with their outcome. 'You know,' he says, 'you might as well stick a pin in somebody's testicles and expect an answer as give someone a truth drug and expect an answer. I can tell you from experience that that's what we found and that was generally accepted.'

Another former intelligence officer recalls his unit coming to the same conclusion. 'The time that I was active,' he says 'I think if someone had suggested it, it would have been regarded as "what a curious thing to be doing. Let's experiment with some funny people down at Porton!" But it was never even considered [in the field]. "Let's do it the old fashioned way, darling!" '

While the British seem to have been sceptical, though, the Americans were enthused. On 31 October 1942, the US National Research Council, alerted by American military intelligence to the possibility that both Russians and Germans were using truth drugs, activated a committee to investigate the feasibility of their use in the interrogation of prisoners-of-war. The Office of Strategic Services (OSS) was placed in charge of the committee.

Before the OSS could start their search, it needed an academic capable of the task. As it happened, the organisation already had one. Stanley P. Lovell, a short, bespectacled research chemist from Boston, had received a summons from the OSS's legendary boss, Colonel William ('Wild Bill') Donovan in the summer of 1942, and had been told, in no uncertain terms, what was required. 'I need,' said Donovan, 'every subtle device and every underhand trick to use against the Germans and the Japanese . . . You'll have to invent them all, Lovell, because you're going to be my man. Come with me!'

After airing initial qualms that the underhand application of science in the taking of human life was 'not cricket', Lovell eventually got into the swing of things, realising that the project might be quite fun. 'What I have to do,' he told Donovan, 'is stimulate "Peck's Bad Boy" beneath the surface of every American scientist and say to him "Throw all your normal law-abiding concepts out the window. Here's a chance to raise merry hell. Come, help me raise it." ' Donovan slapped him on the back. 'Stanley,' he responded, 'go to it!'

Lovell attacked the task with gusto, and built anything that could conceivably be used to kill, maim, harass or simply embarrass the enemy. His creations included bat bombs, cat bombs, stink bombs, silenced flashless pistols for assassinations, apparatus for derailing trains, exploding camel faeces, exploding candles, exploding cookie dough and any number of other household objects designed to detonate in the Germans' faces. On a number of occasions Lovell concocted chemicals specifically for Hitler's ingestion including, famously, a cocktail of female hormones designed to make his moustache fall out and to cause him to grow breasts.

Every time the Americans had someone they thought could get close to Hitler, in fact, Lovell was asked to provide a new poison for 'der Führer's carrots'. A number of lethal poisons were dispatched; none was ever applied. At one point Lovell designed a minute assassination device for Japanese Army officers consisting of a gelatine ball the size of a pin-head containing the deadly botulinus toxin. It was sent by sea to Asia for distribution to prostitutes, who were supposed to slip it into their clients' drinks. The device was never used: officers on the ship concerned decided to test the device to make sure it worked, and fed one of the gelatine balls to a donkey. When nothing happened, they fed the animal another. After a few minutes, they assumed that the poison was inert and threw the rest away. Lovell was livid: donkeys are the only mammals on earth immune to botulinus toxin.

With a background like this, it was no great surprise that, in the autumn of 1942 when the OSS asked Lovell to look into the possibility of a truth drug, he was enthusiastic. 'The mission,' he related, 'was most urgent . . . everyone wanted it, and quite properly so.' The mysterious, elusive drug was transparently codenamed 'TD', and the hunt began.

Winifred Overholser, director of St Elizabeth's Hospital in Washington DC, headed the 'Truth Drug Committee', which also included, for reasons that will become clear, the head of the Federal Bureau of Narcotics, Harry Anslinger, and one of his most trusted agents, George Hunter White.

While there was no shortage of drugs for testing, the committee originally narrowed down the choice to six. At the top was mescaline, the drug the Nazis were using at Dachau. On Saturday and Sunday, 30 and 31 January 1943, two members of the team checked into St Elizabeth's where they were fed 'experimental quantities' of the drug and interrogated. The results were not good. 'The experiment was negative,' reports the summary paper, 'in producing a proper relaxation of the men.' No new information was divulged. Worse, both men shortly complained that they were feeling ill and the experiment had to be stopped. Similar results were soon gained from the testing of scopolamine, which led to hallucinations, headaches, blurred vision and a 'fantastically, almost painfully, dry "desert" mouth' that proved a barrier to all conversation, let alone truth-telling.

Concluding that mescaline and scopolamine were not the most suitable drugs for their purposes, the committee men went back to the drawing-board. In their place they procured three different types of marijuana that they thought might be suitable: cannabinol from Indian charis, tetrahydrocannabinol (THC) acetate and synthetic cannabinol. Of these three, THC acetate—tasteless, colourless and odourless—was deemed the most promising. Preparations were made for oral ingestion.

In the meantime, requests went out for guinea pigs on whom to test the drug. According to John Marks's *The Search for the Manchurian Candidate*, the first volunteers were taken, for security reasons, from the staff of the Manhattan Project—the clandestine plan to build an atom bomb at Los Alamos in New Mexico. 'Our secret was so great,' one team member told Marks, 'I guess we were safer than anyone else.' The men were given 'secrets' and told not to divulge them under any circumstances. Then they were fed a concentrated dose of THC acetate.

The first marijuana experiments, in May 1943, went as badly as the mescaline tests had before them. The first four recipients threw up. Concluding that the dose must have been too high, the researchers tried again with another eight volunteers. Once again, however, the marijuana preparation was too strong. The recipients were sick, and one was hospitalised. Six weeks later, the man had still not resumed active duty.

Reasoning that the subjects became unwell because the human body could not take such high doses of the drug orally, the researchers now set about finding a better way of getting it into the body. They soon settled on the idea of inhaling it. Experiments were run with a form of cannabis that vaporised when poured over hot smokeless charcoal, and with another form that was put into an aerosol and sprayed into the room containing the subjects. In both cases, the results were unsatisfactory: the drug irritated the throat and eyes. The best way of getting cannabis into the system, everyone soon realised, was by smoking it. This ensured that it got into the system fast enough to be useful but that the dose could be easily controlled. It was to this technique that they now turned.

The first recipient of the OSS's new truth drug (the first recipient of most OSS drugs, in fact) was one of its own men: Federal Bureau of Narcotics agent George Hunter White.

Even before the truth-drug tests, White was recognised as something of a character. 'There was never any officer in uniform,' wrote Stanley Lovell, fondly, 'like Major White. He was roly-poly, his shirt progressing in wide loops from neck to trousers, with tension on the buttons that seemed more than bearable. Behind his innocent, round face with the disarming smile was the most deadly and dedicated public servant I've ever met.'

'Deadly' was about right. Since his recruitment into the Federal Bureau of Narcotics in 1934, White appeared to have spent eight years being threatened, stabbed, beaten and shot at. It was rumoured that in the line of duty he had shot and killed a 'Jap spy', blasted his way out of a bar in Marseille in a gunfight, and infiltrated, then broken up the notorious Chinese 'Hip Sing Tong' opium ring in Seattle. In 1949 he busted Billie Holliday for opium possession. Five feet seven inches tall and weighing 200 pounds, the shaven-headed White had been recruited by the OSS at the start of the war and immediately become an aide to William Donovan, travelling widely, interrogating prisoners-of-war and attending the British spy school 'Camp X', in Canada, where he had struck up a friendship with Ian Fleming, creator of James Bond.

White's diary records the first test of the new technique. 'May 24, 1943: Conduct experiment on T-drugs. Volunteer as subject'. After inserting a gram of marijuana acetate into a cigarette, he sat down and smoked it. The result was immediate: 'Knock myself out.'

Having titrated the dose and concluded that marijuana held promise as a truth drug, White now set about doctoring cigarettes so that they could be given to unwitting test subjects without alerting suspicion. The trick to the operation, he noted, was to use a hypodermic syringe with a blunted needle:

> The needle should be thrust into the cigarette along its axis for about one inch. Slowly withdrawing the needle, the plunger should be slowly depressed so that the drug is deposited evenly along this portion of the cigarette. Care must be taken to avoid the drug seeping through and staining the paper.

Cigarettes prepared in this way were allowed to dry out and placed back in the packet, which was resealed, giving the impression that they could not possibly have been tampered with. When they burned, there was no smell to indicate that they contained anything other than tobacco.

Three days after he had rendered himself unconscious with the drug, White set out to test it in the field. The unwitting recipient was a 'notorious' New York gangster in his mid-forties called August del Gracio. Under the pretence of discussing the Mafia's future role in the liberation of Italy, White invited him to his flat for a drink. Del Gracio arrived at two p.m., stating that he had to run: he had a friend, he said, waiting for him in the car outside. At two ten he accepted a cigarette. When, after twenty minutes, nothing had happened, White offered him another. This time the result was evident: shortly after smoking it, the gangster became 'obviously high and extremely garrulous'. He then began to talk.

In the two-hour monologue that ensued, he gave White an in-depth account of his various criminal activities. He appeared to know that he was being indiscreet but was unable to stop himself, so he entreated White (who was, after all, a federal agent) not to tell anyone else. 'Whatever you do,' he told him at one point, 'don't ever use any of the information I'm telling you.'

Best of all, del Gracio had no idea that he had been drugged, and appeared to have lost all track of time. He had completely forgotten, for example, that his friend was still waiting for him in the car outside. In fact, there was every indication that he planned to talk all afternoon. Eventually, at four thirty, White insisted that he had to leave: he was expecting another visitor. Clearly, he figured, the first test had been a success.

Two days later, White invited del Gracio for a game of chess. This time, however, he pushed things too far. After two cigarettes, the gangster closed his eyes, leaned back in his chair and complained that the room was spinning. His hands and feet felt like they had pins and needles sticking into them. White gave him a glass of brandy and suggested that he take a quick nap. But the drug still seemed to be working. Just before he went to lie down, del Gracio offered to have a mutual acquaintance murdered, if the OSS officer 'thought that would be helpful'. 'Care must be taken,' reported White later, 'not to administer unnecessary amounts of the drug because . . . it will probably cause him to lose consciousness . . . and no further questioning will be possible.'

Despite this small glitch, White was convinced he was on to something. 'There is no question,' he concluded, 'but that the administration of the drug was responsible for loosening the subject's tongue . . . the cigarette experiments indicated that we had a mechanism which offered promise in the relaxing of prisoners.'

After a further test, in which White dosed thirty suspected Communists with his special cigarettes in an attempt to make them confess (all of the men revealed personal information apart from one, who didn't smoke; five admitted to harbouring Communist sympathies), the technique was deemed effective. Effects of the cigarettes, noted OSS documents, appeared within a quarter of an hour and lasted somewhere between thirty and ninety minutes. Care should be taken, though, to make sure that the recipient had drunk alcohol prior to smoking them; this way, feelings of dizziness could be blamed on the drink.

When placed in food ('potatoes, butter . . . mayonnaise, sausage or chocolate creams') the effect was slower but longer-lasting. Smoked or eaten, the result was the same: a state of chatty carelessness that often resulted in the disclosure of personal information. As marijuana users sixty years later may recognise, the OSS also discovered that the drug led to an accentuation of the sense of humour 'to the point where any statement or situation can become extremely funny to the subject'. It also tended to make the ensuing conversation rather one-sided. Someone given the drug to smoke 'becomes excessively interested in a topic of conversation to the point where he will insist on giving his opinion on subjects under discussion . . . the subject will probably want to do all of the talking himself.' In such a condition, they were ripe for spilling the beans.

Further tests were carried out by OSS officers on themselves and each other. One truth-drug man, who worked with White at the time, told John Marks that the cigarettes gave him a pleasant feeling of floating, as if he was walking a couple of feet above the ground. 'The fellows in my office', he joked, 'wouldn't take a cigarette from me for the rest of the war.'

After White had delivered his reports, OSS officials decided it was time to find out if the technique worked for real. Their first victim was a German U-boat captain in a detention camp in Virginia. The results, as recorded by Stanley Lovell—who monitored the interrogation via a microphone link—were unintentionally hilarious. For security reasons, Lovell later wrote that the drug was administered to the German in a glass of beer. CIA documents reveal the truth: that it was actually given to him in a series of cigarettes. Either way, there was a disastrous mix-up.

The captain was invited to the camp officer's mess for a beer, where his young OSS interrogator sat him down and offered him a smoke from a packet of doctored cigarettes—being careful to make sure his own cigarettes came from a separate packet—and attempted to start a conversation. Over the course of the next few hours, the pair sank a few beers and smoked while, next door, Lovell listened in. The interrogator had been instructed to extract information from the German about the maximum depth of his country's submarines but the subject was clearly wary, stating that he knew nothing. At each denial, the American became more and more distraught, until eventually he erupted. 'I'm going to tell you something, Heinie,' he declared. 'My boss, Major Quinn, is making passes at my wife. I'm going to shoot him, sure as hell, if he doesn't stop it!'

Next door, the prison-camp commandant realised what had happened and burst out laughing. The interrogator had got the drugged cigarettes mixed up with the innocuous ones. 'Our boy has got your truth drug!' he told Lovell. 'This ought to be real good!'

The situation was eventually resolved but the results were unimpressive. Although the submariner was given a total of three THC acetate cigarettes—more than were used to knock out the New York gangster completely—he maintained his reserve. Eventually he volunteered some information about the state of morale in the German Navy but no facts about the submarines. There are no further records indicating that 'TD' was used again during the war.

Which is not to say, however, that American truth-drug research stopped. Far from it. After the war was over, in 1946, George White was back in business. Records indicate that he was busily checking the effects of a mysterious drug codenamed SUGAR, which could be placed in either food or alcohol or inserted in crystalline form in a cigarette. That same year, a memorandum for the record suggested that it might be worth assembling a special kit for interrogators containing all the necessary equipment for the deployment of marijuana, including the syringe with the filed-down needle for inserting it into cigarettes. That way, agents could pass through international border checkpoints explaining that they were diabetic, arousing no suspicion. Intelligence staff should be informed, said another memo, that 'the use of the truth serum is successful in between 50% and 75% of all cases'.

But while small-scale truth-drug projects were on the back-burner in the United States, it was Cardinal Mindszenty's strange confessions that resuscitated the issue. A year after his trial, in April 1950, the CIA greenlighted BLUEBIRD, the clandestine project to investigate 'brainwashing' and other thought-control techniques. At the top of BLUEBIRD's things-to-do list was the search for a truth drug. By now, however, the CIA wasn't the only interested party.

In the period between the winding up of the OSS and the establishment of the CIA, other American agencies had become interested in the idea of a truth drug. On 23 July 1951, noting the widespread interest and hoping to control research by other (no doubt less qualified) organisations, the CIA held a meeting with representatives of the US Army, Navy, Air Force and the FBI. Rather sensibly, the FBI backed out early on, but the three military organisations agreed to collaborate with the Agency in a new search for a truth drug. Since the US Navy already had an operation codenamed BLUEBIRD it was requested that the project be redesignated ARTICHOKE. On 20 August that year, it was officially renamed.

A summary of the project dating from its inception describes ARTICHOKE as having four main goals:

(a) Extraction of information from unwilling subjects.
(b) Preventing extraction of information from our agents.
(c) Control of activity of individuals whether they wish it or not.
(d) Preventing control by others of our agents.

Areas of suggested research included hypnosis, drugs and other techniques, including 'gases, sound, light, electricity, heat, cold, etc . . . fatigue [and] lobotomy'. A later memo adds 'electricity', 'supersonic vibrations' and 'sleep-inducing machines'. The search was not to be half-hearted: 'No area of human knowledge,' instructs a memo of 1953, 'is to be left unexplored in connection with the ARTICHOKE program.'

Soon after ARTICHOKE received the go-ahead, the CIA assembled two or three 'crack' interrogation teams, each comprising three men, and instructed them to be ready to travel 'at a moment's notice' to any part of the world to interrogate potential informants. One of the teams' goals was the extraction of useful information. The other was far more dubious. According to a 1951 CIA document, the teams were to 'conduct at the overseas bases operational experiments utilising aliens as subjects'. The Agency, it seems, was less interested in gathering intelligence than it was in exploring the possibilities of drugs, hypnosis and interrogation. Possible targets were 'potential agents, defectors, refugees, POWs and others'.

From the outset, ARTICHOKE's interrogation teams were beset with problems. For a start, there was the question of finding people with the right sort of qualifications to run such experiments. What sort of qualifications were needed, anyway? As Alan Scheflin demonstrates in his book

The Mind Manipulators, the first teams were gloriously under-qualified to conduct research into the complex issues of confession and interrogation: of the original three-man team, none spoke any languages other than English, had a college degree or any useful medical qualification. To combat their ignorance of the subject in hand, the team members took twice-weekly evening classes in hypnosis (for details of their discoveries in this field see Chapter 5). In the meantime, they spent their days concocting impressive reports to persuade their superiors that they were making great progress.

ARTICHOKE operatives seemed to consider work done during the war on truth drugs as rather old hat. Science had moved on since then. Or, if it hadn't, the CIA had. Work was conducted into the use of individual drugs such as sodium amytal, scopolamine and marijuana but the teams' specialisation was the use of cocktails of drugs.

A notable favourite—and staple of espionage thrillers ever since—was the old barbiturate technique developed by Horsley and Sargant (Horsley's book, *Narcoanalysis* was on the reading list for CIA men in 1948), but with a twist. Instead of simply shooting subjects full of barbiturates such as sodium amytal or pentothal, the drugs were combined with amphetamines, such as Benzedrine or methedrine. This trick apparently enhanced the truth-inducing nature of both drugs: barbiturates loosened the tendency for self-censorship but tended to put people to sleep; amphetamines induced a fast, unstoppable urge to talk, and counteracted the effects of the sedatives. In this way, thought the CIA, stomping simultaneously on the accelerator and the brake, it was possible to put anyone into a 'twilight state' far advanced of what either drug was capable of on its own. An Agency document reports the technique in some detail:

> The subject is given an injection of 2½% sodium pentothal until he is asleep. At this point he is given an intravenous injection of five to twenty milligrams desoxyn, depending on the response. The hoped for response is easy verbalization. The sodium pentothal needle should be kept in the vein for control in case the subject becomes too excited from the desoxyn. If excitement does not appear within a few minutes, both needles may be withdrawn and the result expected to continue for about 45 minutes. If it is desired to continue the examination further, both injections may be repeated.

The CIA's technique of mixing uppers and downers was nothing new. It had been pioneered in Britain in an attempt to stop patients on sodium amytal falling asleep in the middle of therapy. William Sargant, among others, had used it. Neither was it secret, having been widely reported in the medical press. No matter. To the ARTICHOKE men, the barbiturate-amphetamine combination appeared to offer what the drugs on their own could not: a reliable way of forcing people to tell the truth. And if it didn't work straight away, it was always possible to add another drug, or two, and see what happened. In conjunction with the drugs, they planned to use their newly acquired hypnosis skills. The drug cocktails, combined with hypnosis, appear to have been an attempt to induce violent cathartic reactions: alternately putting subjects to sleep, then waking them up until they were sufficiently confused to be coerced into reliving an experience from their past.

Early CIA records are scattered with reports referring to ARTI-CHOKE missions. In July and October 1950 the interrogation teams—then working under the BLUEBIRD umbrella—travelled to the Far East to interrogate Korean PoWs with sodium amytal, Benzedrine and other drugs, including coramine and the stimulant picrotoxin. A total of twenty-nine individuals were interrogated, apparently successfully. One subject was regressed so effectively that he believed he was back at a party, even becoming drunk on the imaginary alcohol the Americans were giving him. A female subject had a lengthy chat with an interrogator, quite sure that he was her boyfriend.

During the course of a later ARTICHOKE mission in June 1952, interrogators used Desoxyn in conjunction with sodium pentothal to make the subject talk. Once persuaded that he was at home, it wasn't hard to convince him that one of the Agency men was an old friend whom he had last seen fifteen years ago. The interrogator asked him what had happened since then, and the secrets, apparently, fell out. Over the course of the next few years, ARTICHOKE teams went into action in a number of countries. Reports of their missions are cursory, usually consisting of cables from one embassy to another asking how the team should proceed, but one operation has been well documented. The mission, codenamed CASTIGATE, took place in August 1952. Organised by the US Navy under its own truth-drug project, CHATTER, it was a fiasco.

For some time, the Navy had been paying Professor G. Richard

Wendt, an academic at the University of Rochester, in New York, to study narcotic aids to interrogation. Finally, at the start of 1952, after two years' experimentation on university undergraduates—at a total cost of some £300,000—he told his sponsors that he had completed the search, and discovered an effective truth drug.

Through the CIA, the US Navy managed to procure a number of suspected double agents for interrogation in Frankfurt and rigged up a suitable location for the process: an isolated farmhouse, fully kitted out with two-way mirrors and electronic eavesdropping devices. When Wendt arrived, however, with his attractive female secretary, he refused to reveal to the excited Agency men what drugs he was planning to use, referring to them only as 'L', 'C' and 'Q'.

In the end, the three drugs turned out to be a barbiturate, an amphetamine and an extract of marijuana: exactly what the CIA was already using, and what the OSS had experimented with a decade earlier. Agency men were appalled, especially when Wendt insisted on measuring out the drugs with the blade of a penknife. They were equally unimpressed when he kept asking them what they thought he should do next. 'At no point,' notes a summary, 'did [Wendt] appear to be self-assured or in command of the situation.'

The tests went ahead anyway: it was too late to stop them. Over a series of days, five potential double agents were paraded before the professor, who gave them various doses of his three drugs dissolved in coffee or beer. Although he had assured the Agency men that the drugs were tasteless, some of the subjects complained that the drinks had an unpleasant, bitter flavour.

Before the trip Wendt had told the CIA that the drugs would make interrogation subjects 'friendly . . . and disposed to talking'. The opposite was true. Some became extremely aggressive. Clearly out of his depth, intimidated by the CIA men and terrified by the experience, Wendt told his colleagues that the subjects had reacted differently from the college seniors he had been experimenting on at home. He did, however, offer an explanation: this particular mixture of drugs, he said, was only effective on people who were naturally truthful. If the subject was a liar by nature, the drugs would 'cause him to lie more and with more conviction'. One can only imagine the reaction of the CIA men upon being told that Wendt's new truth drug would only work on people who were already telling the truth.

The situation went rapidly from bad to worse. Following the failure of his tests, Wendt proceeded to get drunk, play the piano and flirt with his secretary—until his wife showed up and found the pair together, whereupon he threatened to kill himself. CIA reports on the operation state that Wendt was 'bewildered, confused and uncertain', then ask some pertinent questions, including the most pertinent of all: 'How can we smother this trip?' Morse Allen, in charge of the ARTICHOKE programme at the time, was livid: he asked whether it might be worth suing Wendt for fraud—after all, the man had squandered 'hundreds of thousands of dollars'—but was clearly concerned that a prosecution might have side effects for the Agency, should Wendt end up 'in trouble, such as divorce . . . or suicide'.

Attempting to make the best of a bad job, the ARTICHOKE team accompanying Wendt decided not to let his guinea pigs go to waste and tried a few techniques of their own. Generally, these involved shooting the agents full of barbiturates and amphetamines until they were thoroughly confused, at which point they hypnotised them and tried to persuade them they were their friends, or, in one case, an agent's wife, back in the Soviet Union.

Bearing in mind that none of the hypnotists spoke a word of Russian so everything had to be relayed to the subjects through a translator (and that in the last case the translator—supposed to be the agent's wife—was a man), the technique proved remarkably successful. According to ARTICHOKE reports, valuable information was extracted. However, as the interrogation teams were clearly trying to justify their existence, the term 'success' might have been used subjectively.

Although the Agency's verdict on the operation was 'generally unsatisfactory', everyone tried hard to look on the bright side. 'Can it be said in any way except negative,' asked Morse Allen, 'that the test was successful?' It couldn't. In the end, the Agency drew a line under the operation. Wendt was fired, and funding for the US Navy's CHATTER project was abruptly terminated.

Not that the CIA's truth-drug programme suffered. The ARTICHOKE teams now went on a charm offensive, persuading their superiors that the techniques were reaping substantial rewards. The tactic seems to have worked. 'We're now convinced', states a memo of November 1952, 'that we can maintain a subject in a controlled state for a much longer period of time than we heretofore had believed possible.' By the use of its new techniques, they said, the Agency was capable of producing relevant information in a 'very high percentage of cases'. Authorities believed that ARTICHOKE had done so well that nothing is impossible'. A later assessment, just before the Wendt fiasco, reported that the ARTICHOKE techniques were 'Unquestionably worthwhile . . . There will be many a failure but . . . every success with this method will be pure gravy'.

Unfortunately for the ARTICHOKE teams, the 'gravy' proved mysteriously elusive. In its place arose a series of questions that no one seemed able to answer. One advantage of drug-based interrogation—and the reason why so much effort was put into finding suitable ways to deliver the drugs in food—was that the subject could undergo the process without knowing he had been drugged. Sodium amytal, for example, was concluded to be delivered most inconspicuously in chocolate syrup. But this led to problems: how much chocolate syrup would the subject eat? Sodium amytal needed repeated topping-up if it was to remain effective. What if he didn't eat enough? 'It was tricky,' reports a CIA man, 'to persuade someone that they really needed to eat more syrup this often.'

Other delivery systems led to complications: how many doctored cigarettes would a target smoke? How deeply would he inhale? If the dose was too weak, the operation would be a waste of time; too strong, and the victim would simply keel over. The techniques clearly needed practice. But this proved hard to arrange.

One of ARTICHOKE's key problems was how to locate suitable subjects for the testing of their burgeoning list of interrogation drugs. Wendt had screwed up royally in Frankfurt but he had had a point: the people he had been asked to drug *weren't* like his college students. Nor were they like Agency volunteers, or shell-shocked soldiers. They were professional, experienced and hostile. How could the ARTICHOKE teams test techniques for men like this? Clearly, they needed real foreign agents to practice on.

But when the ARTICHOKE men requested that CIA foreign stations come up with suitable candidates, the result was a thundering silence. No one wanted to risk their own valuable informants—especially not for a team of no-hopers whose techniques were widely seen as harebrained. The ARTICHOKE teams found themselves stuck.

When they managed to get themselves into the field, they faced an even more difficult problem. The only way the interrogation teams had of measuring their own success was in the application of the very techniques that were under evaluation. Drugs might confuse people and make them talkative but did this mean that they were telling the truth? How much of it? All? Or just some? How hard should they be pushed? On various occasions the Agency drugged subjects until they collapsed and had to be hospitalised. Did this make the process any more authentic? Should they lower the dose, or raise it? How could they tell?

Trying to work out whether subjects under narcoanalysis were actually telling the truth had concerned the inventors of the abreactive techniques that had kick-started the search for a truth drug in the first place. Both William Sargant and Stephen Horsley had noted early on that while sodium amytal and pentothal appeared to drive hidden memories out into the open, very often they drove out fantasies too. In fact, even for a psychiatrist who knew his patient well, it was difficult to tell the difference between the two.★

The whole point of using barbiturates on traumatised patients was to break down their ability to censor themselves, to make them talk openly about what they were thinking, and what had happened to them. But once they were in the 'twilight state' between waking and sleeping, they were unable to censor their fantasies. Once they started talking, the flotsam and jetsam of all kinds of psychological trauma simply poured out. Even they didn't know what was true.

Most psychiatrists acknowledged that revelations induced by drugs were tainted. Edwin Weinstein, a US Army doctor, recalled the case of a shell-shocked member of the 601st Clearing Company who had apparently gone blind due to the trauma he had experienced. Questioned under barbiturates, the man re-enacted a fearsome battle followed by a frenzied search for his brother who, he was convinced, had been killed. The man

---

★ In the late nineteenth century Freud had stumbled on this problem, too, when many of his patients, under hypnosis, recalled they had been the victims of sexual molestation. Initially he concluded that he was on the trail of an epidemic of paedophilia. Eventually he realised that the stories they were telling him were fantasies. His error resurfaced again in the late 1970s and 1980s, when 'repressed memories' of sexual abuse were recovered from women and children in the United States. True to form, many of these memories proved to be fantasies. See Chapter 9.

recalled stumbling across the battlefield, turning over corpses to find him. Once this memory had been recovered, he regained his sight. Dr Weinstein learned later that the man's brother had not taken part in the battle: at the time he had been at home on leave in the United States.

Similar cases emerged in civilian hospitals: the 1948 *Experimental Journal of Clinical and Experimental Psychopathology* details a number of cases in which narcoanalysis led to fantasies that were, initially, accepted as fact. One man said he had taken part in an armed robbery when he was nowhere near the scene; a woman claimed to have a non-existent child. Even when the drugs were withdrawn and the subjects woke up, they were confused and not sure of the truth.

Ultimately the fact that the 'memories' of subjects on barbiturates were highly suspect ruled out the technique when it came to criminal prosecution cases in Europe and the United States. In 1945 the French Medico-Legal Society determined that confessions extracted under sodium pentothal were too unreliable to be used as evidence in court. Its conclusion was accepted by legal systems around the world.

Rightly so. Jean Rolin, author of the only contemporary study of truth drugs in the 1950s, concluded that it was just as possible for innocent people to admit that they had committed crimes as it was for hardened criminals to deny crimes they had clearly committed. 'Any confession made is not necessarily true,' he wrote, 'and if no confession is made this does not necessarily prove that the patient has not committed the crime.' The *American Journal of Psychiatry* agreed. So did the *Lancet*.

Moreover, it was quite possible for narcoanalysis subjects to remain silent. A 1957 study by Henry Beecher (whom we'll meet again in Chapter 3) revealed that when subjects were given secrets and told not to reveal them, then dosed with a number of the CIA's 'truth drugs', including atropine, pentothal, amphetamines, alcohol, scopolamine, morphine, caffeine and mescaline—singly and in combination—they refused to talk at all.

The conclusion of all these authorities was that abreactive 'recollections' were bound to contain contradictions, meaningless imagery and fantasies. Revelations emerging from narcoanalysis might be true, false, or somewhere in between. Two of the main proponents of abreactive therapies during the Second World War, Roy Grinker and John Spiegel, agreed that while drug therapy offered a short-cut to normal therapeutic goals—dredging out lots of interesting psychiatric material—it involved serious risks. 'In some respects,' they noted, 'the demands on [the psychiatrist's] skill will be *increased* by the baffling mixture of truth and fantasy in drug-induced output.'

For William Sargant, the fact that the memories he was eliciting were often false was not a problem. The point was the emotional outburst that accompanied them, not the veracity of the stories. In fact, he later argued that sometimes it helped, when leading someone to abreact, to feed the patient emotional and violent information that specifically *wasn't* true: anything to make the process more dramatic. To Sargant, what was happening wasn't so much remembering the incident but *forgetting* it: allowing it to slip into the past, so that the subject could move on with his life. The thing was to make the patient better. Who cared what had really happened?

The CIA didn't see it like that. They didn't care about the abreaction: they were looking for a drug that delivered the *truth*. A chemical that might deliver truth, fantasy, lies or—worse—a combination of the three wasn't helpful at all. In fact, when it came to abreactive drugs, the Agency found itself in a maze where all the walls seemed to be moving. Instead of interrogators who could give a quick shot of a drug cocktail, now they needed analysts or psychiatrists capable of deciphering fantasy from reality on behalf of the interrogation subject. This required huge amounts of preparation and background information. It was a task the 'crack' interrogation teams were hopelessly unqualified to perform.

Intelligence operations rely on the evaluation of information: is your informant telling you the truth? Can what you've been told be trusted and, if so, how far? Traditionally, officers made such decisions with a combination of experience, research and intuition. In the hunt for truth drugs, the Agency was attempting to eliminate the uncertainty in this equation. But, as intelligence historian Thomas Powers writes, agent-running is an art, not a science. This was a fact that the ARTICHOKE teams seemed unwilling to accept.

None of the Agency's truth drugs seem to have proved substantially more efficient than the oldest 'truth drug' of all: alcohol. In fact, this was a conclusion the OSS had reached in 1946, following a test comparing the speech-inducing effects of scopolamine, caffeine, Benzedrine, alcohol and marijuana. After 132 experiments on forty-four subjects, marijuana turned out to be the most effective drug, but it was closely followed by a combination of alcohol and caffeine: beer and coffee.

Alcohol and caffeine, of course, had the advantage that most people drank, while some didn't smoke. Moreover, since marijuana was illegal, the beer/coffee combination was recommended 'for ordinary use in interrogation'. Tests a year earlier had revealed that when marijuana was rated for its efficiency on a scale of 1–10, it scored 1–2. In other words, using truth drugs was about as helpful as not using them. 'Indications are,' reported another summary, 'that uninhibited truthfulness cannot be obtained by this method.'

When it came to barbiturates, the Agency seems to have realised that they weren't reliable enough for practical use. 'Even under conditions most favourable for the interrogator,' reported an officer in 1961, 'output will be contaminated by fantasy, distortion, and untruths.'

That year one study concluded that the entire search had largely been a waste of time. 'There is no "truth serum",' wrote Dr Louis A. Gottschalk, 'which can force every informant to report all the information he has.' Another report by George Bimmerle agreed: 'No such magic brew as the popular notion of the truth serum exists.'

Instead of giving up the search, however, ARTICHOKE moved onwards and upwards to more elaborate techniques in an increasingly sinister search for effective control mechanisms, and the 'magic bullet' that would enable the Agency to make people behave as it wanted them to.

3

Eating the Flesh of God

Allan felt cold and wrapped himself in a blanket. A few minutes later he leaned over to me and whispered, 'Gordon, I am seeing things!' I told him not to worry. I was, too. The visions had started.

'The Discovery of Mushrooms that
Cause Strange Visions', *Life,* 10 June 1957

'Turn on, tune in, drop out!'

Timothy Leary

María Sabina knew that the strangers were coming well before they arrived: she had watched them approach in her dreams. Initially baffled, she sought out Guadalupe García, wife of the village mayor. 'I see strange people', she told her. 'I don't know what's happening.' At night as she slept she saw the men traversing the hills to the south of Huautla de Jiminez. In her visions, their outlines were shadowy and indistinct but it was clear that they had white faces and even whiter hair.

A lesser Wise One might have mistaken the figures for ghosts. María Sabina, however, knew better: they weren't ghosts. They were foreigners.

When the men arrived in the village on 29 June 1955 María Sabina realised she had been correct in her prediction. They were, indeed, foreigners. One was middle-aged, a dignified gentleman with greying hair; the other, younger, a photographer. They had clearly come a great distance: behind them trailed a train of mules loaded with hessian sacks. The men spoke good Spanish but barely a word of Mazatec, which made it easy for the village children to poke fun at them without their knowing it.

As soon as the men had arranged accommodation, the older one requested an audience with the mayor, Cayetano García. The pair pulled up chairs in the municipal building and sat on opposite sides of a wooden table. Introductions made, the white man asked if he could speak to the mayor in confidence. García encouraged him to go on. The man leaned forward and whispered into his ear, at which point the Mexican was visibly surprised. Thinking for a moment, he asked the American if he understood what he was asking for. The white man indicated that he did. 'Well,' said García, 'If you're really sure . . .' The men shook hands, and parted.

A couple of hours later, García tracked down María Sabina. 'Some blond men arrived at the municipal building,' he told her. "They've come from a faraway place in search of a Wise One.'

María Sabina nodded. Huautla de Jiminez was in the middle of nowhere; no gringos had ever come looking for a Wise One before. But that wasn't all they wanted. 'The thing is,' said García, 'That one of them, looking very serious, put his head up close to my ear and said, "I am looking for the Little Ones that Spring Forth." I couldn't believe what I was hearing.' He shook his head. 'For a moment I doubted it,' he said, 'but the blond man appeared to know a lot about the matter.'

The blond man might have known a lot about the matter, but he certainly didn't know as much as María Sabina. No one did. Since she had been a teenager nearly fifty years earlier she had been the village Wise One, and throughout that period the Little Ones that Spring Forth had been the lead weapon in her sacred medical armoury. When something was wrong in the village she would consult them, and the solution would become clear.

When María Sabina ate the Little Ones that Spring Forth she was drawn into the realm of the Principal Ones, who told her how to solve problems and cure ailments. Sometimes the Little Ones would lift her high into the mountains, where she would walk with God. Occasionally they showed her the Baby Jesus but she was only ever allowed to look, not touch. 'I enter another world,' she explained later, 'different from the one we know in the daylight.' Did she want to share this other world with the two gringos?

When García asked María Sabina if she would see the two foreigners, she wasn't sure what to say. 'The man seems sincere and good,' he reassured her. 'I promised to bring them to your house.'

'If you want to,' she replied. 'I can't say no. You are an official and we are friends.'

Later that afternoon, when García relayed the news to the two men that María Sabina would see them, they were jubilant. Gordon Wasson and his photographer, Allan Richardson, were nearing the end of a six-year quest.

Wasson's journey had started in January 1949 when his wife, Valentina, had fired off a letter to the British war poet and playwright Robert Graves. Graves's response, and the events that took place after it, were unexpectedly to play a bizarre role in popular culture over the next half-century. Unknown to either Graves or Wasson, they were also to influence intelligence operations on both sides of the Atlantic.

At the time, Wasson and his wife, amateur mycologists (she was a paediatrician, he was vice president of J.P. Morgan), were writing a textbook on mushrooms. They had recently read Graves's stage play *I, Claudius,* in which the eponymous hero was poisoned by his wife, Agrippina. According to Graves's account, the poison concerned, which proved fatal, had been derived from a mushroom. Did the poet happen to know, asked Valentina, in her letter, which mushroom Agrippina had used?

As it happened, Robert Graves did know. Mushrooms had fascinated him since, one autumn as a young child, he had licked the cap of a poisonous fly agaric toadstool, burning his mouth and causing his tongue to swell. The mushroom responsible for Claudius's death, he told the Wassons, was almost certainly *Amanita phalloides.*

In September 1952, knowing that the Wassons were intrigued by fungi with strange pharmacological properties, Graves sent them an account of some mushrooms that had apparently been eaten during Mexican religious ceremonies in ancient times. Last reported in the annals of the conquistadors, the mushrooms had eluded botanists and explorers for nearly five hundred years and, as a result, were generally considered to be mythical. Evidence was emerging in academic circles, however, that they might be real. There was even a chance that the religious ceremonies were still practised. But the mushrooms were a mystery. The only thing that was known about them, wrote Graves, was the name they had been given by sixteenth-century Spanish chroniclers: *teonanácatl,* 'the flesh of God'.

Gordon and Valentina Wasson decided to investigate. They knew that if the mushrooms existed they were likely to be found in the mountainous region around Oaxaca, 150 miles south-east of Mexico City. Together, during the summers of 1953 and 1954 they set about exploring the region, reconvening with Graves at his home in Mallorca to relate their adventures and ask for advice. It was only now, in 1955, that their quest was about to reach its conclusion.

Back in Huautla de Jiminez, Cayctano García and his two brothers led Wasson into a wide ravine where they found a pile of old sugarcane mulch, in the middle of which sprouted a large colony of mushrooms. García pointed at them with a grubby finger. 'Nti-sheeto,' he said. The Little Ones that Spring Forth. Wasson had found the Flesh of God.

Richardson photographed the scene for posterity while Wasson picked a handful of the fungi, placing them carefully in a specially made cardboard box.

At eight o'clock that night, the men converged at García's house, where they found María Sabina waiting for them. When Wasson showed her his mushrooms, the Wise One picked them up one by one, caressing them and speaking to them softly in Mazatec.

The ceremony began immediately. María Sabina sat cross-legged on a mat in front of a makeshift altar decorated with a bunch of flowers and a picture of Jesus. Hot chocolate was served. She removed the mushrooms from the box, brushed them clean of soil and passed them through copal incense smoke, chanting quietly. Then she handed them out in pairs to each supplicant.

Aware that he was about to become the first white man ever to participate in a ritual so secret that most experts denied its existence, Wasson was 'on tiptoe of expectancy'. Richardson was less excited: before he had left for Mexico he had promised his wife he wouldn't do anything stupid—like taking part in a ceremony that involved eating poisonous mushrooms 150 miles from the nearest hospital. 'My God!' he muttered, as he was handed the first pair. 'What will Mary say?' Richardson took the fungi, put them into his mouth and began to chew.

The mushrooms had a bitter, acrid taste, with a rancid odour that remained in the nasal passages, like a gassy soft drink. Everyone present ate them silently with the exception of García's father, Emilio, who smacked his lips and jerked his head violently. After consuming six pairs each, Wasson and Richardson were instructed to sit silently in the corner. María

Sabina and her daughter ate their mushrooms—twenty-six each—crossing themselves before they swallowed the last pair. Then they waited.

At midnight, María Sabina snuffed out the only candle, plunging the room into darkness. The only sound now was her quiet, rhythmic chanting, accompanied by the chirping of crickets outside.

About half an hour later, both men began to feel violently ill. Over the next few hours Richardson had to leave the room three times to vomit, Wasson twice. The darkness was punctuated by the sound of the other men leaving to be sick, too. Every now and then María Sabina reached across, searching through the darkness for Wasson's hand and grasping it. At about twelve thirty, Richardson started to shiver violently. He was given a blanket and wrapped himself in it. A few minutes later, he leaned over to Wasson. 'Gordon,' he whispered, 'I'm seeing things.'

Wasson turned to him in the darkness. 'Don't worry,' he reassured his friend. 'So am I.' The visions had started.

Before taking the mushrooms, Wasson and Richardson had agreed that, in the name of scientific investigation, they would try to fight the symptoms to work out how powerful the drug might be. But once it started to take effect, they discovered that this was impossible.

Regardless of whether they opened or closed their eyes, the images emerged from the centre of their fields of vision. Sometimes they came at them fast, sometimes slowly; the pair had no control. Starting with intense, brightly coloured geometric motifs, the images soon evolved into vivid three-dimensional hallucinations: in Wasson's case, ornate palaces with cloisters and beautiful gardens, the walls inlaid with onyx and precious stones. At one point he glanced at the bouquet of flowers on the altar, only to find himself face to face with a mythological beast drawing a regal chariot.

But the images were only the beginning. Soon Richardson and Wasson weren't just seeing things: they were *feeling* them too. As though their senses had skipped a groove, the pair began to hear colours and see voices. María Sabina's chanting took physical form and flew round the room, as if it was something that Wasson and Richardson could catch in their hands. The images were so sharp that it was as though everything the two men had ever seen before was blurred or imperfect. Repeatedly the men reached physically into their hallucinations to grasp what they were seeing, only to find the images dissolving into the darkness and regenerating as they withdrew their hands.

To Wasson, it suddenly became clear that the walls of the house had been blown apart, or dissolved, the spirits of the men inside ejected, catapulted at great velocity over the jungles of southern Mexico and into the mountains that rose, tier above tier, into heaven.

A normally eloquent man, he found himself unable to describe the experience adequately when he got home. 'When a state of mind is utterly distinct,' he later wrote, 'then our words fail. How can you tell a woman who has been born blind what it is like to see?' The experience, he said, was 'soul-shattering'.

Of course, Wasson and Richardson's experience was not unique. White men had experienced chemically induced hallucinations before. In fact, twelve years earlier, in Switzerland, Albert Hofmann had discovered the pharmacological properties of a chemical derivative of the ergot fungus by accidentally ingesting some, and had experienced a most peculiar bicycle ride home through the countryside outside Basel. 'I was seized,' wrote Hofmann, in his laboratory notes afterwards, 'with the terrible fear of going insane. I was taken to another world, another place, another time. My body seemed to be without sensation, lifeless, strange. Was I dying?' He had named the chemical lysergic acid diethylamide-25: LSD.

News of his discovery had been strangely muted. At the time Hofmann, employed by Sandoz Pharmaceuticals in Basel, was hunting for a circulatory stimulant that might prove useful in childbirth. After his startling first trip, he had realised that LSD did not fit the bill and had put the drug away. It was only in 1948 that he had returned to it for a second look.

It soon became clear to the Swiss chemist that his new drug was extraordinarily powerful. In fact, the only known chemical with similar properties, mescaline, was somewhere between five thousand and ten thousand times *less* potent. Any drug active in such small quantities had to be worth investigation, so at Sandoz work began to determine what LSD was, and what it did.

To the handful of scientists in the world working with LSD in the late 1940s and early 1950s, the chief interest was in the nature of the hallucinations it induced. To many, it seemed that LSD brought about a state of temporary insanity, triggering delusions similar to those suffered by chronic schizophrenics. If this was true, it offered a unique opportunity for researchers to break into the world of mental illness. It seemed possible, for example, that schizophrenics might have a genetic imbalance that caused their bodies to produce minute quantities of LSD, bringing about the hallucinations and symptoms that had, for generations, confined them to institutions. If this was the case, and chemists were able to synthesise an antidote to the drug, schizophrenia itself could be consigned to history. It was a tall order, but it was the strongest lead on the illness that had emerged in the history of psychiatry.

But psychiatrists were not the only professionals interested in the temporary insanity caused by LSD. Other, more shadowy researchers were watching, too.

With the BLUEBIRD and ARTICHOKE programmes, the CIA had pioneered the deliberate induction of unstable mental states as a means of interrogation. When news broke in the United States of a magical drug that appeared to make people go crazy it was only natural that the Agency would become interested. When they were compared to LSD, mescaline, sodium amytal, sodium pentothal and the other drugs explored so far were small beer.

The driving force behind most of the CIA's experiments in mind control from the early 1950s was the head of its Technical Services Staff (TSS). Sidney Gottlieb, a thirty-three-year-old chemistry Ph.D., was a brilliant man whose personal life contained the sort of quirks that would have made him an implausible character in a spy novel. He lived on a farm some way outside Washington, DC, where he raised his own livestock, making cheese and only drinking goats' milk; he had been born with a club foot and suffered from a pronounced stutter. An obsessive folk-dancer, he apparently spent a good proportion of his CIA-funded missions abroad hunting out new routines. These foibles—together with his Germanic surname—have ensured that he has since become the hub of all CIA-based brainwashing conspiracy theories.

Not, it must be said, without good cause. Gottlieb's career highlights include the production of deadly pathogens for various Agency assassinations around the world, including one for an attempt in 1960 on the life of Congolese leader, Patrice Lumumba. (Gottlieb selected a suitably lethal African bacterium, which he personally carried to the Congo for deployment. In the end, the assassination was cancelled.) He was also responsible for the mailing of an incapacitant-impregnated handkerchief to a suspected

Russian spy in the Iraqi Army, the deliberate shredding of the CIA's entire back catalogue of brainwashing experiments in 1973 when it appeared that news of them was about to come out, and a laughable performance before Frank Church's Senate Intelligence Committee in 1975 in which he claimed to have forgotten virtually everything he had spent the last twenty-five years researching. It should come as no surprise, then, that it was Sidney Gottlieb who turned the CIA's attention to LSD.

News of the drug seems to have arrived in the Agency in November 1951, when an outside consultant informed an officer that the work he was doing with LSD was 'of great importance to national security'. Attempts were immediately made to procure some, and a memo shortly arrived with a small vial of the drug, purchased with untraceable funds through 'cutouts' in Switzerland on behalf of ARTICHOKE. In tones of wonder, the writer reminded the recipient that the attached drug was tasteless and odourless and 'capable of being easily concealed in any drink, hot or cold'. A 'heavy dose', he noted, would comfortably balance on the head of a pin.

For the CIA, the first objective was to test it. To do this, the Agency created a series of 'charitable' front organisations to farm out pharmacological research to civilian colleges, hospitals and universities. The Society for the Investigation of Human Ecology, The Geschickter Fund for Medical Research and the Josiah Macy, Jr, Foundation offered grants, support and encouragement to researchers in a number of fields deemed useful by the CIA. In return for the cash, the institutions were expected to feed their results back to the Agency.

Operating under the aegis of the CIA's new (and most notorious) brainwashing umbrella project, MKULTRA*—signed into existence by CIA director, Allen Dulles, in April 1953—the front organisations offered

---

* In its search for items that might eventually deliver 'behaviour control [and] behaviour anomaly production' MKULTRA sponsored 149 'subprojects', investigating hallucinogenic drugs, sensory deprivation (see Chapter 4) hypnotic agent programming (see Chapter 5) and subliminal perception (see Chapter 6). Other topics receiving research grants included handwriting analysis, manual magic tricks (for use in slipping drugs into foreign agents' drinks), lip-reading, the chemical induction of stress, the stimulation of monkey brains with radio waves, brain concussion (experiments were conducted on cadavers in a specially prepared blast range, see Chapter 7) and many other techniques of so-called 'black psychiatry'.

the Agency both credibility and security as it searched for new mind-control techniques. CIA official David Rhodes, who ran one of the societies, explained, 'If we picked up a *Newsweek* one morning and discovered so-and-so was doing something exciting in such-and-such field, I would get on the phone . . . and say, "I'm a rep of the Human Ecology Fund, and I'm excited about what you're doing. Can I come by and have lunch with you?"—which at the time was a lot easier than saying, "I'm from the CIA . . . " '

While some researchers were fully aware of the true source of their grants, the majority of the recipients of the CIA's money did not know that the Agency was paying their bills, or the wider goals of their own research. 'In a great many instances,' notes an early memo, 'the work must be conducted by individuals who are not and should not be aware of Agency interest.' By sending grants to unwitting recipients, the Agency was protecting itself as well as its researchers: why tell them they were working for the CIA if they didn't need to know?

By the end of the brainwashing programmes, the CIA would have done deals with eighty separate institutions including forty-four colleges or universities, fifteen research facilities or private companies, twelve hospitals or clinics and three penal institutions. The most notorious in the field of LSD research was the Addiction Research Center in Lexington, Kentucky. Lexington, a huge drug rehabilitation centre, was characterised by Bureau of Narcotics chief Harry Anslinger as a 'place of salvage' where inmates were forced to confront, and beat, their addiction before they were released back into the community. Under the centre's CIA-funded doctor Harris Isbell, however, it became something rather different.

The deal was pretty simple. The CIA needed a place to test dangerous and possibly addictive drugs; Isbell had a large number of drug users in no position to complain. From the early 1950s onwards the Agency shipped LSD, with any number of other potentially dangerous narcotics, to Kentucky to be tested on human guinea pigs. To encourage inmates to 'volunteer' for the drug tests, Isbell offered them shots of their own particular drug of choice. In this way, addicts incarcerated for using drugs were paid to use drugs—with more drugs.

Declassified MKULTRA documents contain reams of material from Isbell detailing the various concoctions he fed Lexington inmates. Whatever the drug was, he seems to have been willing to try it on his patients. A famous memo to the CIA in February 1963 reports his uncertainty concerning the effects of a new compound: 'I will write you a letter,' he reports, 'when I have had the chance to get the stuff into a man or two . . .'

LSD was a clear favourite. Isbell offered to feed the drug to inmates in varying doses and, in some cases, in conjunction with other drugs that he thought might work as an antidote. A report of 14 July 1954 details the results of one of his more notorious experiments: to see how much LSD a human being could physically take:

> Our experiments on tolerance to LSD-25 have been proceeding well, although I continue to be somewhat surprised by the results, which to me are the most amazing demonstration of drug tolerance I have ever seen. I have 7 patients who have now been taking the drug for more than 42 days . . . all 7 are quite tolerant to both the physiological and mental effects of the drug.
>
> We have attempted to break through this tolerance by administering double, triple and quadruple doses . . .

In the end, the seven men took LSD for seventy-seven days, a feat that must surely have qualified as the most macabre and bizarre experiment ever to have been conducted with the drug at the time. This dubious honour was only trumped in 1962 when, in an attempt to duplicate the annual 'rut madness' that made male elephants go crazy during the mating season, CIA-sponsored researcher Dr Louis Jolyon West used a dart gun to inject 300,000 micrograms of the drug into a 7000-kilogram bull elephant called Tusko at the Oklahoma City Zoo. According to West's account of the incident, five minutes after the shot, Tusko 'trumpeted, collapsed, fell heavily onto his right side, defecated and went into *status epilepticus*'. West swiftly administered first aid in the form of a 2800-milligram injection of thorazine, followed by another of the barbiturate pentobarbital sodium but it was to no avail. Tusko died an hour and a half later.

Elephant trials aside, the main result of the CIA's widespread bankrolling of drug research in the 1950s was that LSD and other possibly useful drugs were soon being tested all over the United States. The Agency now found itself plugged directly into some of the world's leading pharmacologists, all of whom sent the results of their research directly to its various offices in downtown Washington, DC. When the CIA moved to its current head-quarters in Langley, Virginia, in 1949, the building became the epicentre of an unprecedented research effort to unlock the secrets of the hallucino-gens.

With proper academic work on LSD under way, and some degree of confidence that the drug was not likely to prove fatal, the MKULTRA men now set about trying it out on themselves. Sometimes this self-testing was due to a shortage of volunteers at the hospitals where the drug was being evaluated; more often than not, however, it seems simply to have been the result of curiosity. The results were predictable: the Agency men, knocked sideways by the drug, concluded that it definitely deserved a place in their arsenal.

The next step was to test the drug on people unawares. According to John Marks, certain staff members agreed in their offices that anyone might slip a dose into anyone else's drink at any time. This didn't work out as well as they might have hoped. While some officers realised their drinks had been spiked and managed to pull themselves together, others freaked out. On one occasion a CIA man panicked and ran, tripping, out of his offices into the Washington, DC, traffic. MKULTRA staff launched a frantic search for him, scouring the city until he was eventually found, cowering beneath a fountain on the other side of the Potomac river. Since the unfortunate LSD recipient was quite sure that every passing car was a terrible monster with fantastic, glaring eyes, out to get him, his colleagues had serious trouble in convincing him to come out. 'It was awfully hard,' recalled one MKULTRA veteran, 'to persuade him that his friends were really his friends at that point . . . He'd become a full-blown paranoid.'

Occasional accidents don't seem to have hampered the Agency's enthu-siasm for the drug. Elsewhere, experiments were going well. In July 1954 an officer was given a series of 'secrets', told not to reveal them and dosed with LSD. In no time at all 'he gave all the details'. The Agency concluded that the drug had real potential in the field of 'eliciting true and accurate statements from subjects under its influence during interrogation'. Such was the CIA's zeal for experimentation that a security memo in December 1954 specifically warned that 'Testing in the Christmas punch bowls usu-ally present at the Christmas office parties' was not to be encouraged. Christmas pranks aside, unwitting dosing with LSD continued inside (and outside) the Agency for some time to come, with disastrous effects.

In the meantime, the Americans made a concerted effort to interest the British in LSD.

The British intelligence community was first alerted to LSD's potential by Harvard's professor of anaesthesiology, Henry Beecher, in early 1952. Beecher, who had advised the US Army on medical matters since the end of the Second World War, appears to have been the man who first alerted the OSS to the Nazi truth-drug experiments at Dachau—details of the mescaline tests are to be found among his personal papers at Harvard.

In the spring of 1952 Beecher took a working tour of Europe, pausing in Berlin, where he acted as a consultant to the US armed forces 'on matters of national security'. His next stop was Basel, Switzerland, home of Sandoz Pharmaceuticals and LSD. After that he went to England and was named an honorary member of the Royal Society of Medicine for 'services to science'. Also, in London, he touched base with representatives of the British Joint Intelligence Bureau (JIB)—and passed on the news about LSD.

Not sure what to make of the drug, British Intelligence turned to someone they regarded as an expert: Professor Joel Elkes, head of the Department of Experimental Psychiatry at Birmingham University. Elkes, a refugee from Lithuania, had established the department in 1951 and was researching the actions of various drugs on the brain. He went on to perform the first blind test of the antipsychotic, chlorpromazine—(Largactil) in 1954, writing himself into the history books. Today he is regarded as one of the founding fathers of of psychopharmacology.

During the war, Elkes and his colleagues at Birmingham had been researching human nerve conduction, which led them into the field of cholinesterases—enzymes that cause muscles to relax after contracting. Soon his work held more than academic interest: with the discovery of the new generation of Nazi nerve agents, work on the cholinesterases attracted attention from the highest levels, and Elkes received a call from Whitehall.

Elkes, now 92 years old and living in Florida, recalls the importance of his research. 'Our military intelligence had given us insights into the secret German chemical warfare work,' he says. 'We were asked to work with the anti-cholinesterases—DFP, TEPP and the like.' The British Chemical Defence Experimental Establishment (CDEE) at Porton Down in Wiltshire shipped various chemicals to Elkes, who tracked the way they worked inside the brain and sent regular progress reports. The work, he says, was 'humdrum' but the CDEE paid him 'quite a small grant' through the Ministry of Supply.

In the winter of 1952, Elkes was in bed with influenza, catching up on some medical literature, when he came across one of the first published papers on LSD. What he read shocked him: 'When I read the dose level, I jumped out of my skin!' According to the report, LSD was more active, and in smaller doses, than strychnine or cyanide. He immediately concluded that there had to be a printing error: no drug known to man had effects so serious in such minute doses. He rang the article's reviewer and told him that there had been a mistake, only to be informed in no uncertain terms that LSD really *was* that powerful. 'I said, "You mean to say that there's a drug available which influences mental function so profoundly which is only in a millionth of a gram?" And he said, "Yes." And that's what interested me.' Upon receipt of the information, Elkes called Sandoz Pharmaceuticals and ordered a shipment of the drug for investigation.

When the LSD arrived in Birmingham, Elkes and his team were eager to see what it could do. The first test, with himself as the guinea pig, took place that Christmas Eve. He swallowed half a microgram per kilogram of his bodyweight and waited to see what, if anything, would happen. It wasn't long before he noticed the results. 'You enter a different world,' he says today. 'It's as simple as that—as if you go through a looking glass. The vision is impaired, there's a trembling of vision . . . and colours were greatly enhanced . . . the world looked very strange and different . . . It's quite understandable how these drugs led to the origins of religious practice.'

Fifteen members of Elkes's department took the drug under different circumstances; it was shortly discovered that LSD's effect was greatly enhanced if it was taken under flickering lights. Elkes concluded that the effects were not unlike those induced by 'massive sensory deprivation', an observation that was to have interesting repercussions (see Chapter 4).

Not long after these experiments, Elkes's sponsors at Porton Down were contacted by the Secret Intelligence Service, MI6, and tasked to conduct their own experiments on LSD and, specifically, its potential use as an aid to interrogation. Don Webb, a nineteen-year-old corporal in the

Royal Air Force, was one of the guinea pigs. In the spring of 1953 he bumped into a colleague who had recently taken part in some experiments at Porton Down: he had been put to bed and the military had tried to give him a cold. At the end of the week, he was sent home with an extra week's pay. The whole thing, he said, was a skive. He encouraged Webb to volunteer.

Webb applied and was given a rail warrant from Southampton to Salisbury, where he was grouped with eleven other volunteers. It was a Sunday so the atmosphere was relaxed, 'like a holiday camp. It was quite jolly.' Once they arrived at Porton Down, the group was split up. Ten men were told they were to test various types of military clothing. Webb and one other man, Logan Marr, were siphoned off for special treatment.

The next day, while the other ten men were put through their paces in the clothing, Marr and Webb were taken to see a polite civilian psychologist, who tested their spatial skills, verbal and numerical reasoning ability. Then they answered a series of personal questions, designed to uncover their goals and ambitions. The final question, he remembers, was 'Have you ever had any doubt about your capacity for normal love?' He burst out laughing.

Webb and Marr were then instructed to strip naked: they were to be photographed. The photographer—a woman, strangely—told them to stand on a small rotating disc so that they could be photographed from all angles. When the men made it to the NAAFI that evening, 'the inevitable had happened': the photographs had been shown to the female bar girls and waitresses. Over supper, they were passed round for everyone to look at. The whole thing was a bit of a joke. 'There were great shouts of glee! It was really good-natured.'

The next morning, Tuesday, the two men were taken into another laboratory kitted out with Bunsen burners and test benches. Two men in civilian clothes and white coats were waiting for them with two glasses of water, which the pair were instructed to drink. 'They told us there was something in [the water],' recalls Webb. 'They told us, "We're going to see how you react to this stuff."' Dutifully, Marr and Webb picked up the glasses and downed the contents.

Shortly after they had drunk the water, the men in white coats began to fire questions at them: 'How are you feeling now?' 'How do you feel, and what do you feel?' Webb said that he didn't feel anything. Then, suddenly, he burst out laughing. So did Marr. Unable to stop, or to work out what was funny, they were led to another room and questioned but nothing emerged except more laughter. Eventually they were told to return to their barracks.

Back in barracks that evening the two men noticed that their eyes were bloodshot, which they found hysterically funny. When the other ten men, who had been running on treadmills all day, asked what was going on, Webb and Marr didn't know. They just laughed. Eventually their colleagues became angry with them and left for the NAAFI, which the two men found even more hilarious.

Since Webb and Marr don't appear to have hallucinated on that Tuesday, it appears that they received a low dose of LSD, to see what it would do. The next day, Webb was taken away alone and given another glass of water to drink. The results were startling: 'Really weird things started happening in the walls and the floor', he says. 'Everything looked as if it was covered with about six inches of clear fluid . . . Then people's faces started to peel open. That was weird! The faces, the flesh would peel open, and there was a skull looking at you, and you knew perfectly well that the guy was talking to you because you could hear him but you couldn't get to grips with it. It was horrible.'

The doctors supervising the test asked Webb to read a paragraph from a book, but as he looked at the words on the page, they turned into fish scales and eyes. Webb tried desperately to pull himself together but was unable to regain his composure. 'I was absolutely at my wit's end. I just couldn't work it out.'

As Webb tried to stop himself panicking, the doctor accompanying him, clearly fascinated by what was happening, tried to reassure him by telling him that everything was all right and repeatedly thanking him for taking part in the experiment. Every time Webb calmed down, the doctor gave him psychological tests: Rorschach inkblots, pictures to interpret. 'Can you understand this?' he was asked. 'What happened here?' Webb was placed in front of a Heath-Robinson contraption to measure the speed of his reactions.

For the next three days, he was left alone to recover, and spent the time sunbathing on one of Porton Down's lawns. When the time came to leave he was told not to discuss with anyone what had happened to him, and was handed a brown envelope. Back in Southampton he opened it to discover not a week's extra wages, as he had been promised, but two.*

MI6's LSD experiments ran throughout 1953 and 1954. The format appears to have been similar to Webb's experience, as do the results. In June 1953 another guinea pig, twenty-three-year-old Royal Naval rating Derek Channon, was given a lump of sugar impregnated with the drug and told to sit in front of a wall on to which coloured lights were projected. Convinced that he was about to be eaten by a tiger that had just leaped out of the wall, Channon became terrified, and Porton doctors had trouble in persuading him to allow them to take frequent blood samples.

The results of the tests were unsatisfactory. Bill Ladell, who worked on the trials, reported to Porton's Applied Biology Committee in 1965 that the experiments were 'tentative and inadequately controlled'. Perhaps because of their slipshod nature, a second wave of experiments was begun almost at the moment the first was complete. This time instructions came not from MI6 but from the Joint Intelligence Committee (JIC).

In a meeting of the medical section of the Joint Intelligence Bureau's Consultant Panel on Psychiatry on 7 July 1955, it was decided that LSD merited further attention. Four months later, on 23 November, the panel reconvened. Dr Harry Cullumbine, who had supervised the MI6 tests at Porton Down, attended with Birmingham University's Professor Joel Elkes. The minutes of the meeting make clear that, like the CIA, the panel was now interested in the *unwitting* dosing of interrogation subjects with LSD. There is some evidence that such tests had already taken place. Dr Cullumbine told the panel that

> Subjects to whom the drug had been administered without their knowledge were affected to the extent that their reactions were beyond their control when subjected to interrogation by a skilled interrogator experienced in the application of the drug.

* Webb's experience came back to haunt him. Two weeks after the Porton experiment, he attended an ice-hockey match with his girlfriend. Glancing down at his feet, he saw an immense gaping mouth open up on the floor, as if it was about to swallow him. A number of weeks later, unable to sleep and plagued with flashbacks, he visited the base doctor and explained that the problem appeared to have started after his strange experience at Porton. 'It's nothing to do with me, son,' the doctor told him. 'I've been warned off it.' He was given a bottle of sleeping tablets and sent away.

Likewise, Elkes commented on the administration of LSD in doses of '50–100 micrograms' to subjects 'quite unaware that they had been given anything'. Asked about this comment in 2004, Elkes was emphatic: 'Oh; no! No! Absolutely not! All the subjects were aware of it! They were all volunteers! Absolutely not!' If Elkes's subjects were volunteers, though, the question arises as to whom Harry Cullumbine was referring when he talked of LSD tests 'without their knowledge'. The meeting concluded that 'further investigation into the possible applications of LSD-25 and its analogues was required' and that 'Research is desirable into the use of LSD-25 as a possible effective agent for use in interrogation.'

These 'further investigations' went way beyond MI6's original LSD tests. Details of the experiments, still classified half a century later, emerged only at the inquest into the death of Ronald Madison, an aircraftsman killed by accident following exposure to the nerve agent sarin during an experiment at Porton Down, in 2005. In a written statement delivered to the court, former Royal Artillery captain Ronald Wilkerson recalled taking part in an experiment to test a 'truth drug'. Wilkerson, responsible for the army staff at Porton, was asked to volunteer for the test some time between May 1953 and August 1955 by one of the establishment's scientific officers, a 'Dr Silver' (actually Alfred Leigh-Silver).

The next day Wilkerson, Dr Silver (who participated in the experiment), and another man were led into a laboratory and shown three glasses of water. Silver explained that one of the glasses contained a truth drug but that no one knew which one. He did not explain to the other men what the drug was, or what it would do to them, but instructed them to choose a glass and drink. Wilkerson was apprehensive about the experiment but, assuming that nothing bad would happen, drank the water. Silver and the other man followed suit.

Half an hour later Wilkerson was led into a room that contained two men in civilian clothes, who informed him that he was about to be interrogated. For an hour or so, he was questioned in an 'aggressive' manner, and encouraged to reveal details about his duties at Porton. 'In my opinion,' said Wilkerson, in his statement to the court, 'the form of questioning was in fact an intense interrogation.' When he refused to buckle under the pressure, the interrogators told him he had done well, and that the questioning was over. Then they threw him a curve ball. 'By the way,' one asked, 'what exactly is it that you do here?'

Wilkerson realised that this was a ploy and refused to answer. The interrogators eventually gave up. They did tell him, however, that they were from 'military intelligence'.

Afterwards, even though it must have been clear that Wilkerson had not drunk the LSD-saturated water, he was taken to the station hospital for a check-up. There, he bumped into Dr Silver, who also seemed to be behaving normally. The third guinea pig, however, was missing.★

The tests appear to have been expanded in the summer of 1956. In March that year, at the request of the Joint Intelligence Committee, the Defence Research Policy Committee (DRP) was invited to consider whether work should be undertaken into the use of abreactive drugs 'for military purposes'. DRP staff concluded that 'The Committee [JIC] should authorise a limited effort on this subject at CDEE Porton, at the discretion of Chief Scientist, Ministry of Supply, C(M) and the Chief Superintendent, CDEE.'†

One man who seems to have been involved in the tests was Cyril Cunningham, the Air Ministry's brainwashing and interrogation expert, now, of course, working for the clandestine AI9 to determine what the Soviets were up to in Korea. Certainly Cunningham was kept aware of recent American developments in LSD research. At the time, he says, the Americans were keen that the British conduct further research into LSD and other so-called truth drugs. 'They were very excited about it,' he recalls. 'I had alarms continually about drugs pouring out of America . . . I was fed with huge lists of drugs—and I'm not going to tell you what we did with them!'

★ Another guinea pig in this test series appears to have been Geoffrey Baker, later Field Marshall Sir Geoffrey Baker, who, in a confidential memo on counter-insurgency and security operations in 1964, commented that 'Some years ago, I took part in experiments with a "truth drug"; I wonder what the present form is here.' A handwritten response reads: 'Position v doubtful—not a worthwhile project. MI5 are in possession of the facts.'

† At the request of Alan Care, the solicitor representing the Porton Down guinea pigs, details of some of these tests have been declassified under the disclosure law. The documents remain the property of the court, however, and despite a written request, the Ministry of Defence has not seen fit to allow me access to them. Other records relating to the deliberations of the Consultant Panel on Psychiatry have, apparently, been destroyed.

When I asked Cunningham what he meant by this statement, he was reluctant to explain: 'I'm in a very difficult position,' he said, 'and I'm frightened of getting my arse fried [under the Official Secrets Act].' He revealed, however, that he had visited Porton Down on a number of occasions, that he had been offered the opportunity to take LSD (he turned it down) and that he knew Basil Clarke—who, MI6 has admitted, was responsible for dosing Derek Channon with it in 1953.

When we met, I put it to Cunningham that after MI6's initial LSD tests were complete, further experiments were conducted at Porton Down, this time with officers as guinea pigs and active interrogations following the drug's administration. Cunningham, now in his late seventies, relented somewhat. 'I'm frightened of getting my arse fried,' he repeated, '[but] there's a lot more to come out.'

Part of the urgency for the British drug tests had resulted from a scare story perpetrated by the CIA. In 1951, and again in 1953, the Agency received word that the Soviet Union had managed to procure its own supplies of LSD. Naturally it was assumed that the Russians would be interested in such a drug but it was too soon for them to be in on the story: the CIA and MI6 had been trying to keep LSD quiet. Although the drug was made only at one location—Sandoz Pharmaceuticals in Switzerland—it was reported to the Agency that the Communists had enough for fifty million doses. Clearly, something had to be done.

Cyril Cunningham recalls the British reaction to the Soviet LSD scare: 'I think nobody paid any attention [to LSD] until they found that the Swiss were making a synthetic derivative of it, then flogging it to the Russians . . . ninety per cent of this stuff was being exported to Russia, which set alarm bells ringing all over the place . . . Our secret services went to find out what was going on.'

Details of MI6's attempts to stem the flow of LSD to the Soviet Union (if they made any) are unlikely ever to be declassified. But the CIA's operations are well documented. On 4 September 1953, a CIA representative visited Sandoz to see if the rumours were true and reported back to the Agency that the company had stockpiled ten kilograms of the drug—enough to send every citizen in the greater New York area on a three and a half day-long psychedelic trip. 'This,' commented the agent, 'is a fantastically large amount.' In order to stop Sandoz selling the LSD to the Soviets,

Allen Dulles, director of the CIA, decided on 22 October that the Agency should purchase all of it. The price suggested was $240,000. On 2 December, two CIA officers were dispatched to Switzerland to buy up all the LSD in the world.

When they got to Basel, they discovered that someone unfamiliar with metric measurements had mistaken a milligram for a kilogram. Sandoz had never produced anything like ten kilograms of LSD; in fact, they had made less than forty grams. Of those forty grams, ten were still in stock, and another ten were in the United States.

To prevent such a misunderstanding occurring again, the CIA men negotiated a deal with Sandoz. The company agreed not to sell LSD to the Soviet Union. Perhaps strangely, it also agreed that in order to remove the financial incentive that might encourage other pharmaceutical companies to synthesise the drug, all LSD from that point on would be distributed free of charge. Sandoz's managers were not put out by this undertaking: the drug was making them no money and, one of the American officers reported, the company was 'sorry that they had discovered this material since it had been a source of many headaches and bother'. Clutching their bag of cash, the CIA men beat a hasty retreat.

Back in the United States, the Agency now set about trying to cut Sandoz out of the LSD business. In response to repeated reports that the Soviet Union was cultivating huge amounts of ergot in Bulgaria, Czechoslovakia, East Germany, Poland and the USSR—to be used, no doubt, in the synthesis of LSD for their own brainwashing projects—the CIA decided that it needed a lot more of the drug. Representatives were dispatched to the pharmaceutical house Eli Lilly in Indianapolis to discuss the possibility of synthesising LSD in the US. In October 1954, the company finally discovered a technique using 'readily available raw materials'. The result, stated a report, was that 'in a matter of months LSD could be available in tonnage quantities'.

LSD was not the only hallucinogen that the Agency was watching. As early as 1952 it had been scouring botanical journals for naturally occurring drugs that might be of use. Initial interest seems to have emerged from an ARTICHOKE conference in October 1952 when an academic researcher informed Morse Allen that a Mexican plant, *piule,* was used by indigenous Indians as a 'sort of truth serum'. Allen decided that the mysterious plant 'clearly warranted extensive research' and another project was born.

'Research has shown,' Allen concluded a month later, 'that these plants have strong narcotoxic properties which are of vast interest to ARTI-CHOKE.' As a result, an officer was sent immediately to Mexico to col-lect *piule* seeds, along with any other indigenous narcotic plants that might be of use to the ARTICHOKE programme. The agent concerned, who knew Mexico well and spoke fluent Spanish, was to travel under cover with no identification or apparatus that might reveal the true nature of his mission. If he was asked about his trip, he would explain that he was re-searching native plants with anaesthetic properties for medical use.

Over two months in early 1953, the officer collected ten kilograms of *piule* seeds, which were hastily dispatched for analysis. In the meantime, the CIA began collating lists of other flora and fauna thought to produce inter-esting narcotics. By 1956 the Agency boasted that it had dispatched botanists to twelve different countries in the hunt for 'hidden treasures on potential plant resources', including Puerto Rico, Tobago, Jamaica, Haiti and Cuba. Useful plant and animal resources included erythrina flowers, 'Guatemalan rhubarb', *Rivea corymbosa* (morning glory) seeds, *piscipla* bark, New Mexican 'sleepy grass', bufetonine, derived from the backs of poison-ous toads, harmine from Peruvian *ayahuasca* and ibogaine from *iboga*. Such was the volume of new organic material coming in that in August 1954 the Agency complained that it was 'swamped by deliveries' and requested a break so that the scientists could analyse what they already had.

Over the next ten years the CIA compiled an extraordinarily compre-hensive pharmacopoeia of potentially useful animal and plant poisons. In July 1962 requests for exotic materials reached a delightfully eccentric peak when the Agency decided that it was important to investigate a poi-son derived from the gall bladder of the Tanganyikan crocodile. For some time the CIA debated how best to procure such a thing: 'We have ap-proached the problem of picking up a Tanganyikan crocodile's gall blad-der from two points of view. The first is to have one of our [deleted] buddies in Tanganyika find, capture and eviscerate a native crocodile . . . the second alternative would be to acquire a crocodile on the spot in Tan-ganyika . . . and ship the live animal to the United States.'

Eventually the second plan was deemed best since 'Dr [deleted] feels that the only way of getting the gall bladder to the United States intact is in the live crocodile.' The Agency speculated that about two hundred dollars would cover the cost of a 'medium-sized' croc. History does not relate what became of this particular project—or the unfortunate crocodile.

Of all the plants and animals of interest to the CIA, the ones deemed most immediately relevant were mushrooms. Morse Allen told an ARTI-CHOKE conference on 18 June 1953 that there were 'very strong indications' that some mushrooms had powerful effects on the human mind, which made them ideal candidates for a truth drug. For some reason, the mushrooms that looked most promising were Mexican. A week later, after a search of the available literature, he confirmed that Mexican witch-doctors used mushrooms in special ceremonies to locate stolen items or to predict the future. It now became 'essential', noted Allen, that the Agency launch a project to explore the subject.

At this point it was more or less clear that the CIA's interest in exotic flora was about to collide with those of Robert Graves, Gordon Wasson and the Wise One of Huautla de Jiminez, María Sabina.

After they had experienced the mushroom ceremony on 25 June 1955, Wasson and his photographer Allen Richardson had vowed never to eat the Little Ones that Spring Forth again. Three days later, however, Wasson succumbed to temptation. Once again, the results were mind-blowing. The visions, he later reported, were 'so sharp that they seemed more real to me than anything I had ever seen with my own eyes. I felt that I was now seeing plain, whereas normal vision gives us an imperfect view; I was seeing the archetypes, the Platonic ideals, that underlie the imperfect images of everyday life.'

No sooner had Wasson got home to New York than he was telling everyone about the Flesh of God. One of the first to receive the news of the discovery was the man who had put him on the trail of the mushrooms in the first place: Robert Graves. 'My man is very elated,' wrote Graves, to a friend in 1956, 'since he actually found the mushroom oracle I sent him after in Mexico, and ate the sacred mushrooms . . . and there's the next wonder drug to watch out for.'

Wasson also alerted a friend of Graves', William Sargant. In a bizarre turn, the war poet and the psychiatrist had struck up a friendship and agreed to collaborate on a book about brainwashing. Two years later *Battle for the Mind* was a bestseller and had cemented Sargant's fame. Sargant provided the opinions, Graves the structure and layout to 'make the saliva flow', as he put it.

When Wasson reported news of his discovery to Sargant, he compared the drug in the mushrooms to LSD. Sargant agreed that the chemicals were likely to prove similar, and maintained an interest in Wasson's work for some time, occasionally firing off letters enquiring after his latest discoveries. Despite his generally open attitude, however, the psychiatrist was guarded about British research into hallucinogenic drugs. 'Quite a lot of interesting work,' he reported cryptically, 'is going on over here with regard to lysergic acid.' Part of the reason for his reticence may have been Sargant's relationship with MI5 (see Chapter 7).★

With Gordon Wasson crowing to everyone he could find about his mushroom discovery, it wasn't long before the CIA, now themselves in search of the Flesh of God, heard about his activities in Mexico. In December 1955, five months after Wasson's trip, a CIA cable from Mexico City warned the ARTICHOKE team that 'an amateur mycologist' had made three expeditions to the country, during the course of which he had located and eaten the mushrooms concerned. 'I understand,' said the source, 'this man plans to make another trip to Mexico in the summer of 1956 for the purpose of learning more about these Mexican mushrooms.'

To Morse Allen, there were no two ways about it. If Wasson was returning to Mexico to collect more mushrooms next summer, he wasn't going alone. This time, the CIA would be there, too. The mission to infiltrate his team now became MKULTRA's Sub-project 58. The agent chosen to handle the operation was a twenty-nine-year-old research chemist at the University of Delaware. In 1953 Dr James Moore had been recruited by the CIA to analyse chemicals picked up from botanical materials around the world. When news came in that Wasson was on his way back to Mexico, Moore was instructed to seek him out and make contact.

★ Graves was also behind a strange introduction to the British Ministry of Defence: he personally recommended that Sargant meet with a colleague of Cyril Cunningham, the MoD psychologist Dr Mary Allen, on 17 June 1964. 'Dear Robert' wrote Sargant, 'Of course I will see Mary Allen . . .'. He fired off a letter to her the same day agreeing to meet to discuss 'anything I know about the subject you mention'. (This meeting may be connected to an interest in the use of abreactive drugs for interrogation by the British military). Two days later, Sir Geoffrey Baker initiated the debate formally within the MoD. Despite Sargant's repeated insistence that he was not subject to the Official Secrets Act, his personal papers reveal no details about his discussions at the MoD.

Finding Wasson didn't prove too difficult: after all, the man was vice-president of J.P. Morgan. Moore rang him 'out of the blue' and asked if he was interested in securing funding for the trip from the 'charitable' organisation he represented, the Geschickter Fund for Medical Research. Wasson was, and two thousand dollars changed hands. The only condition for the funding was that Moore be allowed to tag along. CIA documents make clear that the other members of Wasson's contingent had no idea that their new friend was a CIA mole: Wasson 'is uncleared and unwitting of US government's interest in his project'.

It might have been a classic infiltration operation. But it wasn't. When the team arrived in Mexico in June 1956 Moore hated the place. A rather conventional man, he wasn't up for the adventurous nature of the trip. On day one the single passenger plane carrying him to Huautla de Jiminez nearly crashed on takeoff, scaring the pants off him. Once in town, he was appalled to discover that he was expected to sleep on the floor of a thatched hut. He immediately contracted food poisoning and lost more than a stone. While Wasson and his pals relished the back-to-basics adventure, Moore was a creature-comforts man: 'I had a terribly bad cold,' he later recalled, 'we damn near starved to death and I itched all over.'

Inevitably, the CIA stooge became known as the group complainer, and was left out of everything. Even when the time came for the ceremony things didn't go right for him: María Sabina gave him too low a dose. 'I did feel the hallucinogenic effect,' he said, 'although "disorientated" would be a better word to describe my reaction.' The whole thing was a bit of an anticlimax, but he procured a large bag of mushrooms for his CIA bosses.

Back in the United States Moore faced further disappointment. The CIA wanted him to extract and isolate the active constituent of the Flesh of God for use in interrogations. Unfortunately, isolating the chemical proved trickier than he had anticipated. In his laboratory, he fed the mushrooms to cats, dogs and monkeys but it was hard to conclude anything more than that they appeared 'relatively non-toxic'.

Worse, while Moore was struggling with his top-secret chemistry project at the University of Delaware, one of Wasson's mycological friends in Paris succeeded in propagating the mushrooms, then harvested and dried 100 grams of them. He popped them into an envelope and posted them to Albert Hofmann at Sandoz Pharmaceuticals.

Hofmann fed samples to mice and dogs in the laboratory but, unable to tell whether or not they were tripping, eventually resorted to the time-honoured method: he ate them himself.

Even for the man who had discovered LSD, the results were impressive. Half an hour after he had swallowed thirty-two mushrooms, Hofmann's world transformed itself. Everything became Mexican. When he closed his eyes all he could see were Mazatec patterns and motifs. At one point a colleague checked his blood pressure and was instantly transformed into an Aztec priest. Eventually the rush of images became too much for him: 'I feared I would be torn into this whirlpool of form and colour,' he wrote, 'and would dissolve.'

For Hofmann this was clearly a drug that merited further attention and he set about chemical analysis right away, eventually publishing his results in 1958. The mushrooms contained two new drugs, which he named psilocin and psilocybin. Sandoz, still in control of the CIA's number-one brainwashing drug, LSD, now set up a production line and started marketing the secret ingredient of their number-two drug, psilocybin, under the brand name 'Indocybin'.

James Moore must have been terribly upset to be trumped but there was little he could do except order a consignment from Sandoz. The CIA wasn't too pleased, either. Still, the Agency consoled itself, it might still be possible to keep the true *source* of the drug secret. But that was where things went really wrong.

In June 1957 Wasson published a seventeen-page story, lavishly illustrated with Richardson's photographs, in *Life* magazine. It detailed how, on the night of 29 June 1955, he had taken a form of Holy Communion in Mexico in which the participants had swallowed not bread but divine mushrooms. 'The mushrooms were of a species with hallucinogenic powers,' he wrote. 'That is, they cause the eater to see visions.'

Now the cat really was out of the bag. It was about to cause all kinds of problems.

In the meantime the CIA had run into a problem with its LSD testing, too. By 1952 the Agency had enough hospitals and universities testing hallucinogenic drugs to produce a hundred Ph.D. papers. It was interesting stuff but rather dry: dosing hospital patients or volunteers with LSD didn't teach the Agency much about the deployment of the drug *in the field*. What Sidney Gottlieb needed were real tests on real people who didn't know they were being drugged.

Naturally the CIA didn't want to slip its drugs to just anyone: the operation was supposed to be secret. What would happen if the Soviets heard about it? Testing the drugs abroad was becoming increasingly risky. An Agency memo of 1963 warned that drugs had been tested on foreigners so indiscriminately that it was 'making an inordinate number of nationals witting of our role in this very sensitive activity'. For reasons of national security, concluded Gottlieb, the drugs had to be tested in the US on American citizens.

What Gottlieb needed was a group of guinea pigs who were unable, or at least unlikely, to spill the beans or—if that couldn't be arranged—wouldn't be believed if they did. In his eyes, the people who best fitted this category were criminals. After all, they would never go to the police and complain that they had been illicitly drugged.

Of course, when it came to the practicalities of testing drugs on underworld characters, there was only one man who mattered. 'Man in Bureau of Narcotics' notes an early CIA memo, 'has good access to criminal types in NY.' Then the memo names an old friend: 'George White'. In June 1952 Gottlieb contacted the former OSS officer and asked for his assistance.

In the eyes of many CIA men, rerecruiting White was a mistake: there was some reluctance within the Agency to allow into its ranks a man whom other officers seem to have regarded as an ill-educated Neanderthal. White himself was well aware of opposition within the Agency. The way he saw it, he was being blackballed by the CIA's 'crew-cut, pipe-smoking punks'. 'It was only when my sponsors discovered the root of the problem,' he wrote later to a friend, '[that] they were able to bypass the blockade. After all, fellas, I didn't go to Princeton . . .'

The CIA 'punks' were right to be wary of White. Not only were his methods cavalier, he seems to have had an alarming capacity for indiscretion. On 9 June 1952, the day Gottlieb contacted him, White broke all security regulations by noting in his diary, 'Gottlieb proposed I be a CIA consultant. I agree.'

Labouring under MKULTRA sub-projects 3, 14, 16, 42 and 149, White's task was to conduct 'experiments involving the covert administration of physiologically active materials to unwitting subjects'. In other words, to repeat the tests he had run on the New York gangster August del Gracio in 1943 but with different drugs. Under the pseudonym Morgan Hall, he set about procuring a series of safe-houses across the United States, luring unwitting punters into them, then administering various combinations of the CIA's drugs to see how they reacted. Targets came from the 'borderline underworld', recalled one CIA officer who was involved in the tests. 'Prostitutes, drug addicts and other small-timers who would be powerless to seek any kind of revenge in case they found out'.

The first safe-house, at 81 Bedford Street, Greenwich Village, New York, was rented in June 1953. It consisted of two adjoining apartments: one for the people to be monitored, another for the agents doing the monitoring. White instructed his builders to carve out a 'window' in the bedroom, which he fitted with a two-way mirror so that the MKULTRA men could watch the goings-on from next door. He spent thousands of dollars furnishing the place in a suitably gaudy manner and installed state-of-the-art surveillance apparatus to film, tape-record and photograph what happened. When the apartment was finished, he set about bringing in criminal contacts and spiking their drinks.

In 1955 White was transferred by the Bureau of Narcotics to San Francisco, where he established another CIA safe-house at 225 Chestnut Street, overlooking the Golden Gate Bridge. Once again, he hired builders to install two-way mirrors and instructed an electronics company to rig the place for sound and vision. By the time the flat was finished, one visiting agent noted, 'it was so wired that if you spilled a glass of water you'd probably electrocute yourself'.

White recruited a bevy of prostitutes and encouraged them to bring their clients back to his flat. Once inside it was business as usual for the women except that at some point they would offer each punter a drink spiked with whatever drug the CIA wanted tested. They were paid for their time, either in fifty-dollar instalments (the highest single payment was three hundred dollars) or in get-out-of-jail-free chits, redeemable the next time they were arrested. Account slips in his CIA files list White's payments to prostitutes as 'cash—undercover agent for ops (cf authorization)'. Gottlieb's records of the tests are likewise euphemistical. He described the prostitutes as 'certain individuals' indulging in 'highly unorthodox activities'.

Naturally, the process had to be monitored by someone. White would pour himself a drink, sit down on the opposite side of the bedroom's two-way mirror and watch.

In 1955, when it became clear that the observation sessions often lasted a long time, White decided that he had better equip himself for unavoidable calls of nature: an invoice in his files dated 3 August indicates the purchase (appropriately from 'Criminal Investigation, Intelligence and Law Enforcement Equipment') of a portable toilet (twenty-five dollars) and fifteen disposable bags (fifteen cents each) for use in case of emergency in the monitoring room.

The toilet has become a key element of the White legend. According to one source who visited him at the time, White spent his working evenings sitting on it and drinking martinis while he enjoyed the action.

White's safe-houses served a number of purposes. It was common knowledge that the KGB used prostitutes to lure unwitting Westerners into compromising situations, secretly photographing them and using the pictures to blackmail them. On other occasions Westerners were drugged unconscious and laid in bed beside naked 'partners'.

Such underhand methods were not beyond the scruples of the CIA, but if they were to use them, they needed to conduct some research into the techniques of launching a successful 'honey trap'. White's safe-houses offered the perfect testing ground for such operations, as well as Agency surveillance equipment.

The CIA was also interested in the extraction of information through sex. For some time, according to one officer, it was assumed that women should sexually provoke the target, then reward loose talk with favours. After monitoring events in White's safe-houses, CIA psychologists discovered that men were much more likely to talk *after* sex, when they were relaxed. The moment the prostitute started a conversation, the man didn't know what to say, and felt vulnerable: 'What the hell's he going to talk about?' the agent explained to researcher, John Marks. 'Not the sex, so he starts talking about his business. It's at this time she can lead him gently. But you have to train prostitutes to do that . . .'

The main goal of White's operation ('Midnight Climax' . . .) was to discover the properties of the drug currently in vogue. But White, an overweight anti-narcotics agent perched on a portable toilet behind a two-way mirror, was not really qualified to judge. All he could report was what the subjects did physically. Naturally, after a dose of LSD, they acted strangely—but that must have been predictable. Nevertheless more drugs were sent to California for testing. BLUEBIRD boss Sheffield Edwards had earlier ruled that hallucinogenic drugs were 'extremely dangerous' and 'not to be used under any circumstances on Agency personnel'. So, 'If we were scared enough of a drug not to try it on ourselves,' an agent told John Marks, 'we sent it to San Francisco.'

By the end of 1957, the CIA could boast of having discovered six new chemical products available for operational use. Three, P1, C1 and C9 were LSD variants designed to make people freak out and embarrass themselves in public (a note in the files records that the three chemicals had already been used in six different foreign operations on thirty-three subjects); there was also K2, a knockout drug, K3, which enhanced the effects of alcohol, and A2, a stimulant like Benzedrine 'but without its undesirable side-effects'.

Following these successes, further safe-houses were established in Marin County, California, and New York. Various chemicals were tested in the Marin County house including stink bombs, itching powders and high-tech methods of injecting drugs into drinks. In 1959 a bizarre experiment tested a method of incapacitating an entire room of people by spraying an aerosol mist of LSD over their heads. David Rhodes, one of the MKULTRA officials behind the plan, later admitted to a Senate committee that the experiment had been a fiasco. He and a colleague, John Gittinger, invited a group of strangers to the safe-house for a party, then prepared to spray the drug. Unfortunately it was a hot day, and revellers kept opening the windows and doors, creating a draught. In frustration, Gittinger took the aerosol can into the bathroom and emptied it into the air round his own head. Nothing happened. The experiment and the party came to an abrupt halt.

Useful though the safe-house experiments might have been, the CIA was well aware that they crossed moral and ethical lines. A 1957 memo on 'Influencing Human Behaviour' admits that 'some of the activities are considered to be professionally unethical and in some instances border on the illegal'. Even Agency men involved in the operations realised that they were overstepping the mark. 'I think every last one of us felt sorry to attempt this kind of thing' one participant recalled. 'We knew that we were crossing the line. Every decent kid knows he shouldn't steal but he does it sometimes. We knew damn well we didn't want anyone else to know what we were doing.'

The ethics of the tests only really became an issue, though, when the CIA's inspector-general, John Earman, stumbled upon the safe-house operations during an audit of the MKULTRA programme six years later in 1963. In his twenty-four-page report, he stated that various aspects of its testing regime were 'professionally unethical' and raised 'questions of legality'. Of all the projects, he noted, the 'most sensitive' were clearly the safe-house activities, where experimentation 'places the rights and interests of US citizens in jeopardy'.

Earman was less worried by the ethics of the testing than he was by the risks it entailed. What would happen, he asked, if George White talked about the experiments, or if someone else went to the press? He noted that some subjects had become violently ill after receiving doses of CIA narcotics, and that at least one had needed hospitalisation. 'A test subject,' he wrote, 'may on some occasion in the future correctly attribute the cause of his reaction and secure independent professional medical assistance in identifying the nature of the substance involved, and by whom.' In other words, the CIA might get caught.

Earman was sympathetic to the Agency's plight. When the aims of the drug tests were explained to him he agreed that they were necessary but deemed that, in future, such tests should be conducted away from United States soil 'on foreign nationals'. He recommended that the dosing of US citizens with drugs be terminated.

It wasn't. Unwitting testing of LSD and other drugs in CIA safe-houses continued until 1965 in San Francisco and 1966 in New York.

How many people were drugged in the decade during which the houses were run? Presumably for fear of legal suits the CIA has never admitted to dosing a single civilian with LSD, and now that all of the major participants are long gone, the true extent of its drug testing will never be known.

Fear of lawsuits does not seem to have bothered George White, who clearly thought the operation was a huge joke. 'I toiled wholeheartedly in the vineyards because it was fun, fun, fun!' he wrote to Sidney Gottlieb, some time later. 'Where else,' he asked, 'could a red-blooded American boy lie, cheat, rape and pillage with the sanction and blessing of the All Highest?'

Perhaps testing LSD on ignorant civilians was preferable to the alternative, which was using the drug in real interrogation situations. CIA records are sparse on this topic. One documented case, however, took place in Europe in the spring of 1961. The operation was run under the US Army Intelligence Center and codenamed THIRD CHANCE. Eleven men were interrogated, ten of whom were foreigners; one was an American.

The subject was a black soldier named James R. Thornwell, suspected of stealing classified documents. Before the experiment took place, Thornwell was interrogated periodically for six weeks. His captors kept him awake and, alternately, hot or cold; they denied him food and drink, verbally 'degraded' him and made him stand in stress positions. They then told him that they wanted to inject him with sodium pentothal because they had not tried it 'on Negroes before'. Without warning of what the drug would do, they gave him a shot of 'EA1729', the Army's then codename for LSD. The idea seems to have been not that the drug would induce any special mental state but that it would scare him out of his wits. In this respect, the test was a great success. Thornwell freaked out—especially when his interrogators told him that the drug was making him insane, and offered 'to extend this state indefinitely'. Although he appeared willing to confess to almost anything to end the interrogation, no new information was forthcoming and he was eventually released.

Not that that was the end for the unfortunate GI. According to his medical reports, Thornwell was fine a month before he was interrogated under LSD. Two months later, he was diagnosed by an army doctor as 'schizoid personality, chronic, severe' and discharged from the army for 'unsuitability'. Court-martial procedures were halted when his attorney requested that Thornwell's interrogators be present to explain what they had done to him. For some reason, no one thought this was a good idea. Instead, he was discharged; there was still no evidence that he had stolen the documents.

The army seems to have been some way behind the CIA in its discovery that LSD was not an effective truth drug. Initially, the key attraction of the substance had been that it brought out truthful statements. It was also rumoured to lead to amnesia for the time spent hallucinating—a bonus, since it ensured that interrogation subjects would be unsure what, exactly, they had admitted to. In fact, interrogators were as likely to get a stream of gibberish from their victims as anything meaningful. LSD was unpredictable: sometimes people enjoyed it, sometimes they panicked. However they reacted, they invariably remembered the experience vividly.

In the UK the response was much the same. 'The trouble with that damn stuff,' recalls Cyril Cunningham, 'is that some people have psychotic episodes. And if the individual does have a psychotic episode, God help him and all around him!'

In the mid-1950s, the CIA did a swift about-turn and decided that, rather than a truth drug, LSD might be an *anti*-truth drug: people on it were incoherent and completely out of control. Mightn't it be a good idea to give agents a small supply of the drug in case they were captured? Soviet interrogators wouldn't know what to make of *that*! Hopefully after their victim had rambled long enough, they would call off the interrogation.

By the early 1960s, though, something bigger was afoot than whether or not LSD was a truth drug. The public was discovering the wonders of the CIA's brainwashing drugs, and attitudes towards hallucinogens in the United States were shifting.

The shift had resulted partly from the fateful chain of events set in motion in September 1952 when Robert Graves had alerted Gordon Wasson to the existence of *teonanácatl*, the Flesh of God. This stage had culminated in 1957 with the publication of 'The Discovery of Mushrooms that Cause Strange Visions' in *Life* magazine. That year, Graves visited Wasson in New York, and the two men spent an evening listening to a recording of María Sabina's mushroom ceremony. This, wrote Graves, was 'the most exciting event' of his stay in the United States.

On 31 January 1960 the pair listened to the recording again, this time after they had eaten some mushrooms. Graves found the experience revelatory. A week later he wrote to Wasson that 'this was not merely a red letter day but a day marked with all the colours of the rainbow'. The mushrooms, he said, had broken down the barriers in his consciousness with the result that 'I am now able to see pictures in my mind far more clearly than I did before.' He concluded that the sacred mushrooms should be distributed across Europe and America. 'Why reserve these drugs for the mentally sick?' he wrote. 'They should be given to the mentally whole. Especially to poets and artists.'

Four months later he indulged again, this time taking synthetic psilocybin tablets made by Albert Hofmann at Sandoz Pharmaceuticals. On 8 July 1960 he reported to his friend William Sargant that the synthetic product did not compare favourably to the real thing. 'Don't be deceived,' he told the psychiatrist. 'It has left out the magical principle and sends you to Coney Island not to Eden (like the other).'

While Robert Graves was dabbling with the drug, Gordon Wasson was immersing himself in it. Two months after he had fed Graves psilocybin, Wasson took Albert Hofmann and his wife to Mexico to meet María Sabina and participate in a mushroom ceremony. Hofmann offered Maria Sabína a sample of his psilocybin, which she judged to be nearly as good as the mushrooms.

Unknown to Wasson and his friends, while they were exploring the possibilities of psilocybin, the CIA was running its own experiments with the drug at the Addiction Research Center in Lexington, Kentucky, under Dr Harris Isbell. In November 1958 Isbell received his first batch of 500 milligrams of psilocybin. He immediately set up a special ward for twenty-eight 'Negro males' and fed them the drug dissolved in raspberry syrup. Shortly after they had swallowed it, all of the men reported feeling unwell, and half an hour later they were convinced that 'something evil was going to happen'. Some complained that they felt that they were going insane, or dying, or both. Then they hallucinated, seeing colours and kaleidoscopic patterns, which soon took on wondrous forms. 'Some patients,' reported Isbell, 'felt they had become very large, or had shrunk to the size of children. Their hands or feet did not appear to be their own, and sometimes took on the appearance of animal paws.' Others reported elaborate fantasies, such as flying to the moon.

But the CIA's plans to keep psilocybin and LSD secret were going awry. With Isbell testing the drugs on addicts and Wasson telling his friends about it, it wasn't long before other figures became interested in the new wonder drugs. And they were going to kick open the doors.

In the summer of 1959 a young Harvard psychology professor read Wasson's article in *Life* and decided to investigate. The next year he took a trip to Mexico, hiring a villa with a swimming-pool outside Cuernavaca. That August he received a visitor, a Mexican professor of anthropology called Gerhardt Braun, who had also read the article. As they sat beside the pool, Braun told the American that there really was something in this mushroom business. He had recently visited a small village called Toluca where he had tracked down a lady called Old Juana who had sold him a bag of 'magic mushrooms'. Would he like to try some? The young professor agreed and on 9 August, ate seven mushrooms. The taste, he complained, was bitter—but the effect was explosive. 'Wow!' he wrote to his friend Arthur Koestler. 'I have learned more in six hours than in the last sixteen years!'

For any other Harvard professor, this experience might have been an interesting after-dinner story. Not this one. He was Timothy Leary.

'It was the classic visionary voyage,' reported Leary later, 'and I came back a changed man. You are never the same after you've had that one flash glimpse down the cellular time tunnel. You are never the same after you've had the veil drawn.'

Back in the United States Leary ordered a hundred psilocybin tablets from Sandoz. The day they arrived, he threw a party for a handful of friends and cracked open the bottle. The next morning, all hundred tablets were gone and he placed another order. When the shipment arrived, he established the Harvard Psilocybin Project and fed the drug to thirty-four prison inmates in Concord, Massachusetts, in an attempt to rehabilitate them. 'Let's see if we can turn the criminals into Buddhas!' he told his post-graduate students.

Leary handed out the drug to friends and colleagues, who passed it on to others. He gave it to writers Jack Kerouac and Robert Lowell, then to the Beat poets, Allen Ginsberg and Peter Orlovsky. (Half an hour after Ginsberg had taken it, he erupted naked into the room: 'I'm the messiah! I've come down to preach love to the world!' he announced, before deciding to phone President Kennedy and the Soviet premier, Khrushchev, 'to settle this thing about the Bomb once and for all'.) Ginsberg introduced it to the pianist Thelonious Monk and the trumpeter Dizzy Gillespie. Gillespie was so enthused by the experience that he took enough tablets home with him for his entire band to try. Word was spreading.

Leary and Wasson's distribution of psilocybin supported the buzz of interest in mystical experience that Aldous Huxley had ignited a few years earlier. In the spring of 1953 he had been offered mescaline by a British doctor, Humphrey Osmond. Led around town by Osmond, he had been most impressed by the folds in his own trousers when he sat down, staring at them and repeating, 'This is how one ought to see; this is how things really are.'

Now mescaline was deemed a consciousness expander rather than a brainwashing drug. In 1954 Huxley published an account of his experience with the drug, *The Doors of Perception*—he purloined a line from William Blake for the title—which soon became a landmark text for the emerging counter-culture.

Having read accounts of psilocybin in *Life*, Huxley and Osmond visited Wasson to ask him about it. Soon Huxley had made a new 'dear friend' in Timothy Leary, and the pair took the drug together.

News of Wasson's wonder drug was spreading in England, too. In 1961 Robert Graves lectured to members of Oxford's Humanist Society about his experiences with the mushrooms. After eating them, he said, he had travelled to Paradise via the deepest blue-green grottoes of the sea, passing along a blazing trail of bejewelled paths. A published version of the lecture, 'The Universal Paradise', gives an indication of the enthusiasm he brought to his subject. 'In this mountain-top Eden,' he wrote, 'the musical notes of the curandera's song could be watched as they slowly fell and turned into leaves, flowers or twisted golden chains . . . A sense of utter peace and profound wisdom held me.' The experience, he said, was 'wholly good, an illumination of the mind'. The lecture, notes Graves's biographer Miranda Seymour, was for many of his young audience 'their first authoritative account of "tripping".'

The British military was not ignoring the new drug either: Porton Down documents from December 1959 show that research was under way on a number of plant-based drugs under investigation by the CIA, including reserpine, yohimbine and harmine. They also refer to the discovery of a useful chemical from *Psilocybe mexicana*, the mushroom Wasson had discovered four years earlier. The drug, of course, was psilocybin.

Civilian researchers were picking up on the possibilities of hallucinogenic drugs, too. In 1951 Ronald Sandison, a psychiatrist, visited Albert Hofmann at Sandoz and came home with a free box of 100-microgram ampoules of LSD. After testing the drug for abreactive qualities at Powick Hospital in Worcestershire and recording promising results, Sandison published a paper on LSD's use in the treatment of mental illness. Then things went crazy. 'Within five minutes of publishing that first paper', Sandison recalls, 'I had somebody from the *News Chronicle* on my doorstep, who wanted to know what all this was about . . . It created a sensation. I never expected anything like it.' Sandison became the key figure in British hallucinogenic research. On Hofmann's recommendation, he began to run trials with psilocybin, distributing it to his patients.

Sandison's research was conducted on a small scale until a friend stepped in. That friend was Professor Joel Elkes, head of the Department of Experimental Psychiatry at the University of Birmingham, at the time advising Porton Down (and thus MI6) on the interrogation possibilities of LSD. Elkes encouraged Sandison's work and eventually ensured that he received a fifty-thousand-pound grant from the regional hospital board to build a special LSD wing at Powick. The therapy spread across the UK.

Elkes then chose Sandison to represent the British medical community at World Health Organisation (WHO) conferences on LSD, where he rubbed shoulders with Aldous Huxley and Dr Harold Abramson, one of the leading lights of American LSD research. Unknown to Elkes, Sandison or Huxley, Abramson was working for the CIA, and many of the meetings they attended were sponsored by the CIA front organisation the Josiah Macy, Jr, Foundation. In this way, the results of Elkes's and Sandison's work were channelled directly into the CIA's MKULTRA project.

The role of Elkes and Sandison in the LSD story has another important angle. In 1951 Sandison made the acquaintance of an eccentric American millionaire named Alfred M. Hubbard. Hubbard, a former OSS officer, was fascinated when he heard about LSD and tried some immediately, apparently witnessing his own conception. 'It was the deepest thing I've ever seen,' he later recalled. 'I saw myself as a tiny mite in a big swamp with a spark of intelligence. I saw my mother and father having intercourse. It was all clear.' Suitably impressed, Hubbard contacted Sandoz and ordered forty-three cases of the drug—'Cost me a couple of hundred thousand dollars,' he said later— which he shipped to America. There, he tracked down Aldous Huxley and Humphrey Osmond and gave it to them in 1955. Persuaded of the value of the experience, Osmond coined the term 'psychedelic' to describe it.

Since Hubbard had lots of money as well as lots of LSD—six thousand vials in his initial shipment—Huxley and the former spy formed an alliance. The goal seems to have been to alert the American intelligentsia to the beauties of hallucinogenic drugs as fast as possible. Hubbard, who refused to charge for his various drugs, flew all over the country collecting and distributing interesting pharmaceuticals to an ever-increasing circle of fans.

One of the people he introduced to LSD was LA society psychiatrist Oscar Janiger, who later recalled that he waited for Hubbard's arrival 'like the little old lady in the prairie waiting for a copy of the Sears-Roebuck catalogue'. He and his friends began to take LSD and psilocybin socially, and fed it to their patients. Janiger gave LSD to writers, actors and musicians including Anaïs Nin, André Previn, Jack Nicholson, James Coburn and Cary Grant—who gave an outspoken interview in 1959 extolling its virtues. Now that A-list celebrities were experimenting with the drug, its spread was inevitable.

In the meantime, of course, the CIA was still sending the drug into its universities and hospitals for testing, where their subjects suddenly became less random. Friends of friends who had heard about, or tried LSD, showed up and offered to have a go. In 1959 Harold Abramson gave LSD to the anthropologist Gregory Bateson, who encouraged Allan Ginsberg to take part in an LSD experiment at the Mental Research Unit in Palo Alto, California. Ginsberg became paranoid, convinced that he was about to be 'absorbed into the electrical grid of the entire nation' but passed on the word of the drug afterwards.

The next year Ken Kesey, a postgraduate creative-writing student at Stanford University, was paid seventy-five dollars to take part in a series of CIA-sponsored experiments at Menlo Park Veterans' Hospital. Galvanised by the effects of LSD, he dropped out, took a job as a psychiatric nurse and began to research a novel 'both on the ward, and on drugs'. The novel turned out to be *One Flew Over the Cuckoo's Nest*. Following its success, Kesey lost no time in gathering together a group of like-minded individuals, putting them into a Dayglo painted 'magic bus' and driving all over the United States organising 'acid test' parties at which thousands of participants were given LSD.

With Kesey on the west coast of the United States and Leary on the east, use of the magic drug was spiralling out of control. Leary, by now well on the way to assuming the mantle of the 'high priest of LSD', coined the aphorism 'Turn on, tune in, drop out!' which reverberated across the country for the next decade, earning himself the impressive sobriquet (from Richard Nixon, no less) of 'the most dangerous man in America'.

The result was that, completely by accident, LSD and psilocybin were catapulted into the public consciousness. This took the CIA by surprise. It had never occurred to Agency men that people might take brainwashing drugs for *fun*. In 1963 the Agency recognised that things were going awry: 'There is information that some non-Agency groups particularly on the West Coast, have taken to using these drugs in a type of religious experimentation . . .

Any information concerning the use of this type of drug for experimental or personal reasons should be reported immediately . . .'

The memorandum warned that Timothy Leary's LSD research group had established 'chapters' in Mexico City, Cambridge, Massachusetts, Los Angeles and New York. The drugs they were using, including mescaline, psilocybin, LSD and 'some mind-affecting mushrooms' were 'extremely dangerous'. They were also exactly the same drugs with which the Agency had been ham-fistedly experimenting—and trying to keep secret—for a decade.

The CIA might have been shocked by the movement it had inadvertently started but nowhere were the effects of the discovery of hallucinogenic drugs more poignant than in a small village 150 miles to the south-east of Mexico City.

María Sabina, the Wise One of Huautla de Jiminez, should have realised something was wrong from the beginning. Normally when she ate the Little Ones That Spring Forth she was taken into the hills around Oaxaca, but in 1955 when she gave them to Wasson and Richardson for the first time this changed. 'I had different visions than usual,' she later recounted. 'I saw places I had never imagined existed. I reached the place the foreigners come from. I saw cities. Big cities. Many houses, big ones.'

At first María Sabina was quite pleased to be the focus of attention for Wasson, Leary, Hofmann and their friends. She especially enjoyed being given copies of the articles they wrote about her: unable to read the text, she liked to look at the pictures. She and Wasson became great friends and at one point he presented her with a copy of an LP he had produced of her chanting, and a gramophone to play it on. Most exciting for her, once it became known what she had done for the reputation of Oaxaca, the governor of the province came to visit, and presented her with a pair of mattresses, enabling her to sleep on a bed for the first time in her life.

Wasson had gone to great lengths to protect María Sabina's identity, changing her name, location, and even the language she spoke when he wrote about her in *Life* magazine. But it wasn't long before clues to her real identity came out—and Western pilgrims found her. As more and more people turned up expecting to be introduced to the Little Ones that Spring Forth, she became dissatisfied: 'Before Wasson,' she recalled, 'the mushrooms were always taken for the sick to get well. After the first visits, foreign people came to ask me to do vigils for them. I asked them if they were sick, but they said no—that they had only come to "know God".'

The mushrooms were also supposed to be a secret. 'It's true,' she later told a researcher, 'that before Wasson nobody spoke so openly about the *children*. When we Mazatecs speak of the vigils we do it in a low voice.' The Americans didn't speak in low voices. The youngsters, long-haired and wearing bright clothing, didn't understand that this was an ancient ritual and deserved respect. 'It was difficult for me to explain to them that the vigils weren't done from the simple desire to find God, but were done with the sole purpose of curing the sicknesses that our people suffer from.'

As time went by the visitors became progressively younger and more unkempt. If María Sabina refused to perform the ritual for them, they bought the mushrooms from someone else in the village and got high. They were also badly behaved. Without proper supervision, they ate too many mushrooms and became ill, or caused trouble. One foreigner got stoned and 'roared like a lion'. Another ran around the village at dead of night with a live turkey in his mouth. 'These young people,' she said, 'blond and dark-skinned, didn't respect our customs. Never, as far as I remember, were the Saint Children eaten with such a lack of respect.'

Others offered to pay her for the ritual, but had no money. A young foreigner in sandals offered her a dog in lieu of cash. 'What's it going to eat?' she asked him. 'Shit?'

The influx of young people in search of drugs soon brought the Mexican federal authorities to Huautla de Jiminez. Eventually the inevitable happened: María Sabina was arrested and taken into custody. Although she was released shortly afterwards, the experience was not a happy one: when she got home she discovered that the officials had ransacked her home and stolen everything of value, including the gramophone that Gordon Wasson had given her. In 1967 a permanent contingent of Mexican soldiers had to be stationed in the village to expel kick-seeking travellers who were turning the place into a commune.

Worse than the police presence, though, was the way María Sabina was treated by her own community. With the invasion of young people, she soon assumed the status not of a Wise One or priestess but of a whore, selling secrets, mysteries and magic for cash. One night some locals burned down her home, destroying all her possessions. She and her family were forced to move into the forest and root for food like animals.

The single most tragic aspect of the affair, however, was the loss of the Little Ones that Spring Forth. 'Before Wasson,' she later said, 'I felt that the Saint Children elevated me. I don't feel like that any more . . . From the moment the foreigners arrived, the Saint Children lost their purity. They lost their force. The foreigners spoiled them. From now on they won't be any good. There's no remedy for it.'

In old age, María Sabina told a French magazine that when Cayetano García had come to her that day in June 1955 and asked if she would meet Gordon Wasson and Alan Richardson, 'I should have said no.'

The tragedy was not lost on Wasson himself. 'These words,' he wrote in 1976, 'make me wince. I, Gordon Wasson, am held responsible for the end of a religious practice in Mesoamerica that goes back far, for a millennia. I fear that she spoke the truth . . . A practice carried on in secret for centuries has now been aerated and aeration spells the end.'

María Sabina, the Wise One of Huautla de Jiminez, died in 1985 at the grand old age of ninety-one. In the bus and railway stations of Oaxaca it is still possible to buy posters and postcards of her. It is also possible to buy and eat the mushrooms that made her famous

It is no longer possible, however, to witness or to participate in the ceremony of the Little Ones that Spring Forth.

4

In the Black Room

The soldiers arrived on Beragh's Main Street at 4.30 a.m. on Monday, 9 August 1971. They parked their Saracen armoured personnel carrier outside number seventy-six. Cautiously, a small search party climbed out of the vehicle, approached the house and hammered on the front door.

Inside, Paddy Joe McClean had just got off to sleep. McClean, a thirty-eight-year-old remedial teacher and father of eight, had recently returned from a holiday in St John's, Northern Ireland. He and his wife, Annie, who was eight months pregnant, had driven the family there in a battered minibus and rented a house on the beach. 'It was', he recalls, 'the greatest

98

time ever.' Their stay had been cut short, however, when news arrived that Annie's mother was seriously ill. The night before the troops arrived he was sitting with her in hospital until two a.m., when he returned home and collapsed into bed, exhausted.

Woken by the knocking, McClean shouted from a window that he would be right out, then headed downstairs to see what all the fuss was about. Opening the door in his pyjamas, he found himself facing a group of armed Paras. They had bad news. 'They said, "You're coming with us,"' recalled McClean, in his kitchen in November 2004. 'Words to that effect. "You're arrested. We're taking you." I would have said, "I have to get my clothes."'

The Paras followed McClean upstairs. On the landing the heavily pregnant Annie asked what was going on and was informed by an officer that her husband was being arrested. As he got dressed, she remonstrated with the soldiers, and the baby in the cot in their bedroom began to cry. Then they pulled McClean out of the room. Annie grabbed Paddy Joe and tried to drag him back upstairs but the soldiers refused to let go. She started to scream, demanding to know where they were taking him. Her cries woke the other children, who howled, too. As the noise reached a crescendo Paddy Joe McClean was herded out of the building into the back of the waiting Saracen, and spirited away into the night.

Sixty-five miles away, at 88 Iris Drive, Belfast—a quarter of a mile from the Falls Road—a similar scenario was unfolding. This time the target was nineteen-year-old mechanic Joe Clarke. Clarke was involved in Formula 2 racing, working on two Lotus cars in the local garage. One had recently been written off by John Watson; Clarke was fixing it. One day he hoped to become a driver. That hot summer of 1971 he had been abroad racing, then come back to Ireland for a week off in Donegal with his fiancée. The pair had stayed at a small guesthouse before returning to work in Belfast.

That night there had been a riot on the Falls Road. Clarke had gone out to watch and, as he puts it, 'nosy about'. He had visited his fiancée and returned to his parents' house at midnight. Like Paddy Joe McClean, he was fast asleep when the troops arrived at four thirty. Woken by the noise of their arrival, he got dressed and headed downstairs to discover that his father had answered the door. Four Paras entered the house and set about searching it. To make sure that they didn't plant anything, Clarke followed them around.

The search complete, soldiers and the Clarke family met in the hallway, where one asked for Joe by name. 'That's me,' he admitted.

'Well,' said the officer in charge, 'we're arresting you under the Special Powers Act.'

When Clarke was informed that if he tried to escape he would be shot, his father interrupted. 'Don't be harming him.' Clarke turned to his father and told him not to worry before being led out of the house to an army truck, where his shoes were removed and his wrists tied with plastic cuffs. Four more Paras put him into the back, alongside another man who had been arrested. A soldier then produced a long metal bolt and smacked it theatrically into his open hand. 'Don't make me use this,' he said.

Initially Clarke was not scared. But as the truck left the Catholic district he became apprehensive. Along the streets, families were emerging from their homes to see what was going on. Girdwood was in a mainly Protestant area, not far from the Crumlin Road, and it didn't take the residents long to work out what was happening. 'That was when they started banging,' he says. 'Women were banging their bin lids. They'd heard all this coming from the Catholic area, and thought, This is it, you know? When they saw all the lorries going in there, they realised what was going on.'

The sight of the crowds on the street, cheering on the British troops, convinced Clarke that his predicament was more serious than he had thought: 'Oh, shit! I'm in trouble here!'

McClean and Clarke had been picked up as part of Demetrius, the British Army's operation to arrest IRA suspects for internment, which had been sold to the Government by Northern Ireland's prime minister, Brian Faulkner, on 5 August 1971. A fortnight earlier, on 23 July, 1800 troops had raided houses across the Province, confiscating documents and address books. Intelligence from these sources had been collated and, with the Royal Ulster Constabulary (RUC), the army had produced a list of 500 Catholic suspects. Faulkner wanted to arrest 450; the army suggested that 150 was a more reasonable number. In the end, on the morning of 9 August, 342 were taken. There was now the matter of what to do with them.

In the back of the Saracen, Paddy Joe McClean was driven in silence to a collection point in Omagh. There, he was transferred to another army truck where he met other detainees and the scale of the arrest operation became clear. As trucks from all over Fermanagh and Tyrone converged and began to fill, people he knew were shoved into his truck and told to sit alongside him. 'The funny thing was,' he says, 'I recognised pupils of my own, that I had taught, and they were saying "Master this", and "Master that"!'

As the truck moved off, the detainees discussed where they were being taken. McClean's former pupils, who knew that he had been interned before, asked him what was going on. He told them there was no prison in the direction they were headed and that it was possible they were going to be interned on the British mainland. He was wrong.

In fact, the army's plan was to accommodate the initial wave of detainees in three regional holding centres: Magilligan Weekend Training Centre in County Londonderry, Ballykinler Weekend Training Centre in County Down, and Girdwood Barracks in Belfast. There, internees would be screened before they were either released or transferred to prison.

McClean's truck arrived at Magilligan at ten fifteen but he was not unloaded until one o'clock. Sixty-eight men were then herded into the training centre, and the waiting began. They were fed adequately and given camp beds for the night. Not that they got much sleep: that night, say the internees, soldiers in charge of the operation made a deliberate effort to keep them awake, running batons along the outside of the corrugated-iron Nissen huts, throwing stones at them and shouting.

The next day, McClean was called for sorting. To his surprise, the RUC man in charge was an old acquaintance, who appeared as shocked to see him as he was to be there. 'He looked aghast at me . . . He said, "Why are you here?" and I said, "Well, you tell me—that's what I want to find out." He says, "I don't know. But," he said, "Here's what I'll do." '

McClean's friend gave him a coloured card and told him to report to a particular hut, but on his way there he was stopped by a soldier who checked his name on a clipboard. 'No,' said the soldier, shaking his head. 'That's wrong. You're not going there. You're going to another one.'

It was a fateful decision. Internees in the hut to which McClean had originally been allocated were released later that day; those in the hut to which he was redirected were not. Inside he met three men, one of whom, Patrick Shivers, he recognised. The other two, Micky Montgomery and Micky Donnelly, were strangers.

The four men were not interrogated that day. Left to themselves when everyone else was being called in, they became edgy and at one point one panicked; McClean told him to cool it. They were fed porridge, sausages and beans and, later, a fish roll. That night, once again, the soldiers kept them awake before charging into the hut at four a.m. 'Right, you bastards!' announced a Scottish soldier. 'I'm up! Get up there!' Baffled by the early start, they were led to the canteen and fed beans, sausages and bread. It was the last proper meal they were to eat for nearly a week.

After breakfast the four men were handcuffed together and lined up in a corridor. One asked if they were going to be transferred to Rathlin Island. They weren't. 'Where you're going,' an RUC man told him, 'is far worse than Rathlin.' Then, without any warning, Special Branch men appeared, placed heavy denim hoods over the suspects' heads and herded them out of the building into a waiting helicopter. Paddy Joe McClean's real ordeal was about to begin.

Fifty miles away at Girdwood Barracks, Joe Clarke was undergoing a similar procedure. He was kept in a large gymnasium with 184 other suspects—all sitting in silence on the floor. Gradually, men were siphoned out for interrogation. Although they were supposed to keep quiet, the men whispered to one another. Sometimes they were caught and made to do press-ups as a punishment. Sometimes the soldiers seemed to pick on them for no reason. One soldier approached Clarke. 'You've got a smirk on your face,' he said. 'Take it off, or I'll take it off for you.' The IRA suspect tried a joke: ' "It's just the way my face is!" It was more banter than anything else, you know,' he recalls, 'but at the time you were really frightened. A nineteen-year-old lad who hadn't seen a terrible lot of the world.'

After two days of this treatment—again, the internees were denied sleep—everyone had been screened out, with the exception of Clarke and one other suspect, Francis McGuigan. The pair was sitting together in the empty gymnasium at two a.m. on Wednesday when they were surprised by the arrival of Belfast's most notorious Special Branch officer, Harry Taylor. He wandered over to say hello. 'Well, boys!' he announced. 'There's no more room left for you two. You two are going home.' Clarke's heart leaped. Then Taylor burst out laughing. 'No,' he said. 'I've got something else in store for you.'

Three hours later, at five a.m., Clarke and McGuigan were ordered to parade in one of the corridors at Girdwood, where they were joined by Kevin Hannaway and Jim Auld, who lived a few streets away. Hannaway had clearly been beaten and was bleeding from a cut above the eye;

McGuigan was visibly shaking. A soldier told the four prisoners that they were being moved, and that for this they were to be hooded.

McGuigan, who suffered from claustrophobia, shouted that he could not be hooded. Ignoring his cries, the soldiers hooded them all, hand-cuffed them together and shoved them into a lorry. They were driven to a field where they were manhandled into a waiting RAF Wessex helicop-ter, which revved up and lifted off.

In the air above Magilligan, Paddy Joe McClean tried to determine where he was being flown. Convinced that he was on his way to Scotland, he thought at one point he could smell the sea air. But hooded, in a swerving and banking helicopter, he soon lost all sense of direction. No one would tell him anything.

While McClean was left in silence, the soldiers accompanying Clarke took grim pleasure in detailing their plans for him. 'You've seen the photo-graphs of Vietnam, prisoners getting thrown out of helicopters?' one asked. Inside his hood, Clarke nodded. 'That's what's going to happen to you.'

Clarke did not believe for a minute that British soldiers would actually throw a prisoner out of an airborne helicopter. But, sure enough, after a flight of about an hour, that was exactly what they did. He was told, 'You can go now, boy . . . You're getting thrown out!' and was pitched out of the door—to discover that they had been hovering just a few feet above the ground. 'I hadn't time to think,' he recalls. 'Milliseconds before you hit the ground, and when you hit the ground, you think, fuck! Thank God for that!'

The stories of McClean and Clarke now merge. With ten other men snatched from all over Northern Ireland, they were delivered to the same site for interrogation. It is possible that the interrogation centre was lo-cated at Palace Barracks, Holywood, but nearly thirty-five years later this is still apparently a state secret. Likewise the identities of both British and RUC interrogators have never been officially revealed; none was willing to help, on or off the record, with the research for this book. Accounts of what happened next are thus taken from the testimonies of the interroga-tion subjects, the official enquiries that ensued and records from the 1974 European Commission of Human Rights at Strasbourg, where what the British Government euphemistically termed 'interrogation in depth' was eventually deemed not to be torture but rather 'inhuman and degrading treatment . . . in breach of Article 3 of the Convention'.

The twelve suspects were roughed up and hauled into the interrogation centre where they were forced to strip naked—apart from the hoods. Numbers were painted on to the backs of their hands (Paddy Joe McClean was 1, Joe Clarke 4) and they were photographed. They were taken for a medical examination, then issued with dark blue boiler suits and told to put them on. Although they were not informed of it at the time, they would not be allowed to change this clothing until the interrogation process was over. They were not allowed to remove it, even to use a bathroom. 'Major operation, minor operation, same thing,' says McClean, 'You had to go in the suit.'

With the prisoners medically examined, logged, photographed and dressed, the interrogation procedure could begin. Each suspect was now forced to stand, hands above his head, a metre from a wall, then to lean against it, spreading his hands and feet as far apart as possible. He was not allowed to move again. 'The order,' recalls McClean, 'would be "Stand against that wall! Throw up your hands, fingertips as far apart as you can place them. Feet as far apart as you can place them." And if you didn't do that, you got a kick in the inside of the leg to move your leg out. And the order was "That's where you are. Stay there. Don't move."'

'Every time you moved a limb', Clarke remembers, 'They would beat it until you put it back up again. When you put it back up again, if you put it down, they would give you a couple of slaps with a baton, to force you to put it back up against the wall.'

Thirty years later, McClean shakes his head. 'Try it yourself some time against a wall. As far back as you can that you're just depending on your fingertips against the wall, and you're at full stretch. And your feet as far apart as you can stand. And just stand there. Stand there. And stand there. That's how it was done.'

But that wasn't entirely how it was done. There was also white noise: a loud rushing, hissing sound that enveloped the interrogation centre and everyone in it.

'I can only describe it,' recalls McClean, 'as the noise of a jet engine. If I had been under a jet engine, that sort of a high-pitched scream all the time.'

Clarke agrees: 'It was very loud. Like steam, escaping out of a pipe. That sort of a noise . . . it was continuous all the time, and it never altered. Tone or anything.'

At this point, since they were all hooded, none of the twelve suspects was aware of the others in the room. They did not know where they were, or why. They had no idea how long the ordeal would last, or whether they would survive it. Hungry, tired, stressed, terrified, effectively blinded by the hoods and deafened by the white noise, each now felt utterly alone.

Although the twelve men did not realise it, they weren't entirely alone. In fact, efforts were already being made to locate them. On Wednesday, 11 August two days after the internment raids, a Catholic priest and teacher, Father Denis Faul, was visited by one of his parishioners, who told him that he had been arrested and beaten at Ballykinler. Faul called a colleague in Belfast, Father Brian Brady, and discovered that reports of beatings were common among those who had been released. The two priests set up an office at the bottom of the Falls Road and recorded statements from men coming out of the internment camps, gradually assembling a dossier to reveal exactly what had happened to each of the 342 men arrested that week. Word soon circulated that Faul and Brady's office was a good information point and Catholics began to arrive in large numbers.

It wasn't long before worrying news emerged. Of the 342 arrested, the priests were only able to account for 330. Twelve men had vanished. One happened to be an acquaintance of Father Faul: Paddy Joe McClean.

McClean's whereabouts were of particular concern because his wife, Annie, was almost due to deliver their child. Also, in a tragic coincidence, her mother had died on the day that he had been arrested. Unable to attend the funeral, she sat at home waiting for the phone to ring, just in case anyone called with news. She telephoned friends and lawyers, but no one had any idea where her husband might be.

Armed with the names of the twelve missing men, the priests set about trying to find them. Faul repeatedly rang the Northern Ireland Office only to find that the staff there seemed not to know what was happening. Each time he called, the answer was the same: 'We'll try and find out something for you.' 'I must say,' he told me, 'they were polite enough.'

Other callers were not treated so considerately. Trying to locate her husband, who was one of the twelve missing men, Patrick Shivers's wife was bounced from one prison to another until eventually she was given a telephone number, only to discover that it was Ian Paisley's 'Dial a Prayer' line. A (possibly apocryphal) story indicates that even Father Faul received short shrift: when he was hunting for another 'interrogation-in-depth' victim in October 1971, a soldier answered the phone at Holywood

Barracks, then announced to a colleague 'This is that fucker Faul again. He wants to know who we've got here.'

'Tell him to fuck off' was the reply.

What neither Father Faul nor the interrogation victims—or even the soldiers—knew was that the events taking place had resulted from a top-secret meeting in Canada almost twenty years earlier.

The meeting was held for the benefit of Sir Henry Tizard, head of the British Defence Research and Policy Committee, a 'brilliant and mercurial scientist', who had been active in the Air Ministry during the Second World War, and was known affectionately in RAF circles as 'Tizard the Wizard'. Tizard had fallen from favour in 1940: he had believed that in Germany the use of radar was less advanced that it was in Britain, and had failed to predict that the Germans might guide bombers to their targets in London by transmitting radar beams from the Continent. He resigned when bombs began to hit their targets with alarming accuracy. However, after Dunkirk he had made a comeback when he arranged for Britain to share her secret scientific military developments with the United States in the build-up to its involvement in the war. Tizard was a somewhat outspoken man, who made himself available to the British Joint Intelligence Bureau and always kept a close eye on innovations in the intelligence field.

In May 1951 he received an invitation to visit Canada from the chairman of the Canadian Defence Research Board, Dr Ormond W. Solandt. Ostensibly the reason for the visit was to discuss military technology, including new radio advances, nerve-gas production, hydrofoil transport and 'flame warfare'. But there was another item on the agenda—which resonated with what was then going on in Korea.

'You may recall,' wrote Solandt on 2 May, 'that you once suggested calling a meeting in Canada to discuss the possibilities of research on the uses and misuses of drugs, hypnosis, etc., in war. It occurred to us that we might usefully have such a meeting in Montréal while you were there.'

Tizard, a keen fly-fisherman who appreciated the excellent salmon prospects in Canada, lost no time in replying that he should 'be glad to attend the suggested meeting on the possibilities of research on the uses and misuses of drugs'. After all, he noted, 'We had a recent meeting of experts here so I shall be able to come over with their opinion.'

The meeting took place at the Ritz Carlton Hotel in Montréal on 1

June 1951. Eight experts, including Tizard, were present, two of whom were representatives of the CIA. From the summary Solandt sent later to Tizard, together with the Canadian and CIA minutes of the event, it is possible to reconstruct what took place.

The meeting, which Solandt classed as 'entirely informal and unofficial', started in Tizard's absence and concerned 'research into the general phenomena indicated by such terms as "confession", [and] "menticide".' The group discussed brainwashing and the Moscow Show Trials, concluding that it might be a good idea to interview refugees who had undergone interrogation in the Soviet bloc to discover what the Russians had subjected them to. It was suggested that since Cardinal Mindszenty's sister lived in Halifax, Nova Scotia, she might be a useful starting point.

At this point Sir Henry Tizard and Ormond Solandt appeared. Tizard, according to the CIA minutes, was not impressed: '[Tizard] stated at the outset that there was nothing new in the whole business from what was practised during the Inquisition days and there was little hope of achieving any profound results through research.'

Tizard might not have been keen to discuss the Show Trials but everyone else was. The Americans were interested because, according to later documents, they wanted to be kept 'informed as to the activities of the British and the Canadians' in the field. The CIA had decided before the meeting that, while they would disclose nothing about their own brainwashing programme (then codenamed BLUEBIRD), especially not that they were actively testing truth drugs on supposed double agents around the world, they would play along with their allies to find out what they had.

The Canadians, meanwhile, were fascinated by the subject, largely thanks to the presence of their lead scientific brain, the brilliant Dr Donald W. Hebb, head of Psychology at McGill University in Montréal. Hebb tried to prolong the debate, suggesting that it might be worth discussing the idea of 'sensory isolation'. According to the Canadian minutes, 'He suggested a situation whereby an individual might be placed in a situation . . . in which, by means of cutting off of all sensory stimulation . . . and by the use of "white noise", the individual could be led into a situation whereby ideas, etc., might be implanted.'

Hebb's notion of implanting ideas under 'sensory isolation' clearly related to brainwashing but initially had nothing to do with intelligence work. For years he had been working on a theory to explain the development of the brain. At McGill he had kept Scottish terrier puppies in isolation for varying periods of time. When released into the real world the puppies were terrified, displaying retarded behaviour, sticking their noses into flames or lit cigars to smell them and burning themselves. Hebb thought that sensory isolation might provide answers concerning the structure and development of the mammalian brain. His theory intrigued Tizard.

'[Tizard] was obviously impressed with the idea,' according to the CIA minutes, 'and agreed to its importance from a research standpoint. The others present had been convinced prior to the meeting and had little difficulty in reaching a common understanding that this is a vital field in the defence of the Western Powers.' He even became 'quite enthusiastic' about Hebb's sensory-isolation experiments and 'agreed to put some of his scientists . . . in touch with the [Canadians] and it is believed that co-ordinated . . . programs will result'.

Follow-up documents from the CIA reveal that:

> The American programs through Dr Webster of [CIA] will be co-ordinated with British and Canadian programs . . . it was agreed that we would continue the conversations along the same lines initiated by [deleted]: namely that research in each of the three countries is needed and that an exchange of information and continuing liaison in connection with such research is needed.

The question of what was happening to political prisoners in the Soviet bloc, and whether confession and 'brainwashing' could be brought about by sensory isolation was not only interesting to Tizard from an intelligence standpoint. For some years, there had been stories of humans losing their faculties through isolation: solo sailors often reported hallucinations, as did mariners stranded on life-rafts, solitary mystics, explorers and people trapped in dark caves. It was said that Eskimos never went hunting or fishing alone: lacking human contact and with no prominent visual cues on the ice pack, they became disoriented and tended to paddle their canoes out to sea, never to be heard of again.

There was a pressing reason why this was of interest in the 1950s. With the advent of the jet engine and aircraft that could fly at high altitudes for long periods, the problem of isolation had raised its head once more. In the early 1950s there was concern in military circles over pilots who, for no apparent reason, suddenly lost control of their aircraft at high altitude and jeopardised the lives of their crews. At the RAF Institute of Aviation Medicine, A.M. Hastin Bennett made a study of the phenomenon: a number of RAF pilots had become disoriented at altitudes above twenty thousand feet and altered the course and aspect of their aircraft without re-alising it. The reason? Isolation.

'When the aircraft is flying straight and level the aviator has very little to do,' wrote Hastin Bennett. 'The pilot is strapped into his seat and can-not move about; often he cannot see the wings behind him or the nose of the plane sloping away in front. The background noise of the engines and of the oxygen system is monotonous and unvarying. Outside there is an unchanging vista.' The result was disorientation and, occasionally, com-plete loss of control.

Such incidents were termed the 'Break-off Phenomenon' and it was possible that Hebb's experiments on sensory isolation might shed some light on it. This explained part of the Canadian, British and American in-terest in his proposal. It certainly provided a convenient excuse.

Hebb's experiments on sensory isolation were codenamed 'X-38' and funded for two years in September 1951 by the Canadian Defence Research Board to the tune of $21,250. All concerned were instructed not to reveal the true nature of the work—brainwashing—and, if anything became pub-lic, to explain that this was really a study of the effects of monotony on hu-man performance that would eventually save the lives of pilots, long-distance drivers and anyone who worked long hours with heavy machinery.

Ron Melzack, at the time a postgraduate student of Hebb, recalls, how-ever, that the secrecy was cursory: 'Hebb said, "This is being supported by the Defence Research Board, and they are looking into this problem [brainwashing], and they're doing it with American counterparts, and it's supposed to be secret, so don't go around telling your mother or father or your best friends. Just keep it to yourselves." . . . It wasn't entirely secret. It was semi-secret. All the graduate students knew exactly what was going on and why.'

Hebb began Project X-38 by constructing a series of air-conditioned isolation cells measuring $4 \times 6 \times 8$ feet on the top floor of McGill's psychol-ogy block. Each cell was soundproofed. Postgraduate students were paid twenty dollars a day to lie in them wearing opaque goggles, gloves, card-board tubes over their hands to prevent tactile sensation, and headphones broadcasting white noise. They were instructed to stay in the room for as long as they could. As Hebb wrote, after the project was partially declassified:

> The subject is paid to do nothing 24 hours a day. He lies on a comfortable bed in a small closed cubicle, is fed on request, goes to the toilet on request. Otherwise he does nothing. He wears frosted glass goggles that admit light but do not allow pattern vision. His ears are covered by a sponge-rubber pillow in which is embedded a small speaker . . . His hands are covered with gloves, and cardboard cuffs extend from the upper forearm beyond his fingertips, permitting free joint movement but little tactile perception.

These experiments were not as sinister as they may sound. Hebb's subjects were volunteers; they had been fully briefed about the experience they would undergo, and were well paid. The cubicles were fitted with intercom, so that they could communicate with the experimenters, and with observation windows, so that they could be monitored. They could demand to stop the experiment whenever they wanted. At the time it was joked that the worst thing about staying in the isolation rooms was not the weird psychological effects they might produce, but that the subjects would have to eat food cooked by one of Hebb's co-authors, Woodburn Heron. Hebb saw the funny side himself: 'This experiment is too cruel to do with animals,' he joked, 'but not with college students.'

Although the experiments were treated lightheartedly, when the data came in, Hebb was shocked. He had had no idea how hard the subjects would find the isolation experience. On the first day, six of his initial group of volunteers refused to enter the chambers. Eleven out of twenty-two managed the twenty-four-hour minimum inside. Few lasted more than two days, and the toughest of all stuck it out for just 139 hours. Many of those who took part said they found the experience unsettling and sometimes extremely unpleasant. At least one reported that sensory deprivation was 'a form of torture'. After one subject nearly crashed his car on the way home it was determined that sensory isolation led to a loss of ability to measure distance and to put visual objects into perspective. Some subjects became so disoriented that when they were taken out of the chamber for a lavatory break they got lost in the bathroom and had to call a researcher to help them find their way out.

Then there was the matter of the 'brainwashing'. To make things more interesting, Hebb included a choice of deliberately repetitive and dull listening material in the isolation rooms. There was a repeated chorus of 'Home On The Range', a long list of audio stock-market reports, or a religious message for six-year-olds. Subjects could choose whether they wanted to listen to the tapes or not. Most chose to listen: anything, however monotonous, was preferable to the white noise.

Hebb then tried a new tack: if subjects would choose to listen to meaningless and repetitive tapes rather than silence, would they choose to accept propaganda? He replaced 'Home On The Range' with a series of lectures aimed at persuading the listener of the reality of various paranormal phenomena. When asked before they entered the chambers, the volunteers denied believing in the supernatural. By the time they came out, however, their views had changed. Some subjects later admitted to visiting the local library after the experiment to read up further on extrasensory perception; a handful reported a newly discovered fear of ghosts. When Hebb had faced the Defence Research Board in June 1951, he had said that the goal of his experiments was to determine whether isolation and white noise might facilitate the 'implanting' of new beliefs. The answer, it seemed, was yes.

But a more worrying phenomenon emerged. After just a few hours in the rooms, some of the subjects saw things that weren't there. The hallucinations started anywhere between twenty minutes and seventy hours into the experiments. Usually they began with simple visual anomalies: coloured dots before the eyes and geometric patterns. These soon evolved into transient images, often sliding over one another in different directions. Finally the hallucinations became concrete, integrated scenes that subjects likened to 'dreaming when awake'.

Some were clearly amusing. One subject saw a roll-top bathtub gliding through a field with an elderly man inside it, wearing an old tin battle helmet. Another reported a row of squirrels marching in single file across a snowy field, wearing snowshoes and with rucksacks on their backs. Another enjoyed a vivid scene of naked women diving and swimming in a woodland pool. While the hallucinations were initially seen as a comic distraction, the novelty soon wore off. Some subjects reported feelings of paranoia, such as the man who became convinced that Hebb and his colleagues were projecting images on to his frosted goggles from the outside.

Paranoid hallucinations were reported, too: 'One man,' wrote Hebb, 'saw a pair of spectacles, which were then joined by a dozen more, without wearers, fixed intently on him; faces sometimes appeared behind the glasses, but with no eyes visible. The glasses sometimes moved in unison, as if in procession.'

Subjects worried about what they saw, became unable to sleep, and questioned their sanity. Some reported long, vivid dreams, which apparently continued even though they were awake; others were incapable of distinguishing between sleep and waking. One panicked when he became convinced that someone else was in the box with him. The two 'hims' began to overlap and he was unable to determine which was himself.

Hebb, clearly surprised, confessed that a person not used to being alone might well 'crack up' in the room, and admitted that his results were 'very unsettling':

> It is one thing to hear that the Chinese are brainwashing their prisoners on the other side of the world; it is another to find in your own laboratory, that merely taking away the usual sights, sounds and bodily contacts from a healthy university student for a few days can shake him, right down to the base: can disturb his personal identity.

Paranoia, confusion, fear, hallucinations: there was more interesting material here than Hebb could have imagined when he made his proposal to the Defence Board in 1951. Twenty years later, his discoveries would have important practical implications in Northern Ireland.

Hooded and spreadeagled against a wall in a secret location somewhere in the Province, Paddy Joe McClean was not enjoying his interrogation experience. After nine hours of this treatment, however, it stopped. He was shoved into a helicopter and flown to Crumlin Road prison, where he was presented with a detention order. Having been hooded, he was unable to read it. An RUC officer read it out aloud to him. 'I signed it and I thought, That's it all over now. I'm going to go home,' recalls McClean. 'But then we were put on the helicopter again and taken right back . . . imagine how disappointed, crestfallen, lost hope, when you find yourself right back in that noise again.'

Joe Clarke was equally distressed to find himself back in what the soldiers were now calling the 'Music Room'. After three nights without sleep, both men were so exhausted that they were physically collapsing from the wall. Another internee, Micky Donnelly, later recalled that he was collapsing from the wall every twenty to thirty minutes. But as soon as they hit the floor, soldiers would force them to stand up again. If they refused to stand, there was special treatment. Paddy Joe McClean was grabbed by four men who took a leg and an arm each, flung him up and down in the air, spun him round, then dropped him on to the floor. Joe Clarke lost his temper, ran around the interrogation room until he bumped into a guard, and attacked him. The two scrapped until a number of soldiers intervened and picked him up bodily. He was beaten, his wrists and ankles were handcuffed and he was 'rolled up and down a flight of stairs'. 'Also,' says Clarke, 'they would put your legs up your back and drop you on to the floor—put your ankles up your back, two of them were holding you, and you're a couple of feet off the ground, or three feet off the ground, and they'd drop you. On to your knees.'

At various intervals the soldiers would grab a suspect and haul him into another room where he would be sat down and his hood removed. A volley of questions was fired at him. Clarke recalls being interrogated by an officer with an English accent: ' "Were you in the IRA? Who do you know in the IRA?" This sort of stuff. "There's been explosions around your district—were you involved in them?" They mentioned different things that went on at the time. They were being forceful but they weren't shouting at you . . . "Well, you'd better start talking, or you'll go back out." "Look, I don't know anything." So they'd throw you back out again.'

Sometimes the interrogators deliberately misled the subjects. Micky Montgomery asked where he was being held and was told he was in the Channel Islands. Others were told lies to scare them. Francis McGuigan was asked for his home address. When he gave it, he was told that a bomb had exploded there that morning and more than seventy civilians had been killed. Perhaps his family were among the dead.

Generally, questions were asked about IRA arms dumps, the names of terrorists and subversive activities. However, Paddy Joe McClean says he was not questioned about the IRA. 'It was general conversation. In fact at one stage they asked me about Republican versus Democratic programmes in America. It had got nothing at all to do with what was here in Northern Ireland.'

When subjects refused to answer the questions, or when the answers were not the ones the interrogators wanted, the response was the same: 'Take him back to the Music Room.'

In the 'Music Room', Paddy Joe McClean now made a discovery: at regular periods the white noise featured a break before repeating itself. He concluded that it was coming from a tape and that it must be part of a tactic to break him down, to make him talk. 'I know what you're trying to do,' he told the soldiers. 'This is torture. This is systematic.' The soldier behind him shouted, 'This boy's trying to break the system!' and he was roughed up. The incident persuaded him of one thing: if this was indeed a torture session, he wasn't going to co-operate. He sat down and refused to get up. The soldiers picked him up and propped him against the wall, wedging his arms behind a radiator. He fell down again. He was handcuffed and hung by the wrists from a nail in the wall.

With the hoods, the noise, the loss of sense of time and the exhaustion, it wasn't long before Joe Clarke noticed strange things happening. Things that Donald Hebb could have predicted. 'I thought I was doing bodyguard for James Callaghan,' says Clarke, 'and somebody had tried to shoot him. I actually started shouting a name out. They said, "Tell us about him! Tell us about him!" and I realised I was hallucinating.'

In another hallucination, Clarke dreamed that he and his fiancée's brother had bought a scrapyard together; during one interview he was convinced that the interrogator was his brother. Paddy Joe McClean also became confused. At one point he was sure the white noise contained hidden messages and tunes: he heard a funeral march and the sounds of a firing squad preparing to shoot him. He then witnessed his own funeral in graphic detail: 'I can still see [it],' he says. 'I can still see the hearse in front of my own door, and I can see the children, as they were then, following the funeral.'

To a scientist like Hebb, these phenomena would have been understandable. The difference was that while he was interested in sensory deprivation as a means of solving academic questions relating to the mechanics of the brain, others were more interested in the technique's practical applications. At the head of these were the American military and the CIA.

To the CIA, sensory deprivation offered a solution to the question of how the Soviets handled interrogations. CIA-funded scientist Lawrence

E. Hinkle later reported, in a paper sponsored by the CIA front organisation the Society for the Investigation of Human Ecology, that in their interrogations the Soviets were inducing what he termed the 'Brain Syndrome'. This was brought about by withholding substances that the human mind needed to work in a balanced way. Excessive sweating, deprivation of water, rapid breathing, prolonged standing and decreased oxygen intake all interfered with the brain's healthy operation, causing anomalies. 'Brain function,' he wrote, 'is readily impaired by disturbances in homeostasis.'

In such circumstances, a subject experienced pain, fatigue, thirst, hunger and drowsiness. As the experience went on, he lost the ability to carry out complex tasks. He was irritable, depressed, jumpy and tense. Eventually he became unsure about things he had formerly known, even doubting his own identity. One way of inducing such a state was to deprive the brain of information: 'Deprived of information, the brain does not function "normally" . . . the brain has special vulnerabilities of its own; it cannot function "normally" unless it receives a certain amount of information upon which it can operate, and it cannot carry out a single pattern of activities unremittingly and indefinitely'. 'There can be no doubt,' concluded Hinkle, 'that isolation, fatigue and sleep deprivation produce disturbances of brain function . . . it is probably correct to say that if any of these are carried on long enough they will disorganise the brain function of anyone.'

Donald Hebb abandoned his experiments at McGill after three and a half years. Ironically, Project X-38 was shut down partly because the scientists monitoring the experiments found waiting outside a silent booth too monotonous. But when word of his findings crept out, other scientists became intrigued. In 1955 Jack Vernon obtained a grant from the Surgeon General of the US Army to build an isolation chamber in the basement of the Eno Hall at Princeton University. He recruited a series of postgraduate students and, like Hebb, offered them twenty dollars for every day they remained in it. Although he did not record the same high percentage of hallucinations, his subjects generally found the experiment disturbing. Half complained of concentration difficulties. 'It was as though,' he wrote, 'they had lost disciplinary control over the thinking process.' Twenty per cent used the panic button and demanded to be let out.

A colleague repeated the experiments and managed, by playing propaganda tapes to his subjects, to change their attitudes about a random foreign country. Compared to a control group, subjects emerging from isolation were eight times more positive towards Turkey—about which they had formerly displayed ambivalence—after listening to the tapes. Vernon theorised that it might be possible to convert a Christian to Islam using sensory deprivation by giving him a choice of tapes to listen to: a dull thirty-second fact reel about Christianity or a series of interesting ones about Islam. To escape the monotony the subject would undoubtedly choose to listen to the Islamic tapes over the Christian one. At the same time, because of the deprivation process, he would become more susceptible to the propaganda. 'We may conclude,' Vernon wrote, 'that the effects of Sensory Deprivation are similar to those of brainwashing. This is to say, confinement rendered people more susceptible to propaganda and led to greater attitude change . . . Although America has never used such a technique and presumably never will, there can be no doubt that we could build a very effective brainwashing technique.'

Admittedly, not everyone hated the experience. Some loved it. Equally, many participants, after demanding to be let out of the chamber, offered to go back in—once they had been reassured that they were safe. A couple of key factors emerged that offered observers the opportunity to predict how long subjects might withstand the procedure. If the subject was not informed that he was being monitored by experts, paranoia would set in faster; if he was not sure about the safety of the experiment, he would back out sooner. (One summer Vernon hired non-Princeton students, who did not know him. Ninety per cent backed out before the time limit was up.) Most importantly, if no upper time limit was set it became far harder to endure.

Hebb's and Vernon's work sparked interest all over America, and soon sensory-deprivation experiments were taking place in universities across the US. Much of this work was underwritten by either the military or the CIA. Questions that interested them were: 'How can we use this?' and 'How can we make it more intense?'

One answer came from John Lilly, a professor at the National Institutes of Health (NIH) in Bethesda, Maryland. In 1954 Lilly took sensory deprivation a step further by attempting to remove outside distractions *completely*. After a series of discussions with Hebb at McGill, he designed a tank filled with water at exactly body temperature in which the subject was submerged, wearing a full face mask and breathing apparatus. Now there was no sound other than the subject's own breathing, and no sensation at all. The tank was used for very short periods of isolation; Lilly recalled one long session of two and a half hours, at the end of which he began to hallucinate. He was shortly contacted by the CIA, who wanted to know about the operational applications of the tank. He refused to help and, hounded by intelligence organisations, eventually bowed out of sensory-deprivation research altogether.

In the office next door to Lilly's, however, one of his colleagues had no such qualms. A former postgraduate student of Hebb and a lieutenant in the US Navy, Dr Maitland Baldwin was recruited by CIA officer Morse Allen in 1955. Baldwin went on to perform all sorts of bizarre experiments for the Agency—irradiating monkeys' brains, inplanting electrodes in humans, and attempting complete head transplants from one animal to another. In 1955 he asked Hebb to look over the protocols for a new isolation experiment he had devised. The plan was to build a padded box $8 \times 3 \times 3$ feet. Sound would be piped into it and liquid food supplied by tube.

Baldwin figured that once the subject had lost all sense of time, the experience would rapidly became intolerable. A subject put into a deprivation environment, with no idea how long he was going to stay there—and no panic button—would break down faster and more completely than hitherto believed possible. He would put people into the box and not tell them how long they would have to remain there.

To prove his theory, he put a US army volunteer into his black box for forty hours. After 'an hour of crying loudly', he noted, 'and sobbing in a most heartrending fashion', the soldier eventually kicked his way out. Baldwin concluded that enforced sensory deprivation would lead to 'complete psychic breakdown', and possibly permanent brain damage. But how long would it take? And what would be the end result?

In 1955 he offered to answer these questions with an extraordinarily macabre experiment.

[Baldwin] frankly admits that unless he can carry out 'terminal experiments' he cannot find out the real answers to total isolation . . . The [CIA case officer] asked [Baldwin] that if subjects could be obtained and an absolutely safe area located would he be willing to leave his present work for 30 or so days and participate in such experiments? [Baldwin] stated that not only would he enthusiastically participate but stated that he would donate his services (if some official cover could be arranged).

Baldwin added a proviso: '[Baldwin] stated that he would not want any other agency to know about this experiment unless it proved to be successful'.

Maitland Baldwin's plan to conduct a 'terminal' sensory deprivation experiment was deemed 'immoral and inhuman' by the CIA, and vetoed. As far as can be established, it never took place.

Work on sensory deprivation was not confined to the United States and Canada, of course. Details of classified work conducted in the UK are hard to find but research certainly took place. One doctor who is open about his involvement with sensory deprivation in the UK is Stanley Smith, who worked at the Moor Hospital in Lancaster in the 1950s. Smith was interested in the treatment of patients who were losing their hearing and specifically in why they sometimes experienced attacks of paranoia. Having heard of Hebb's results at McGill, he wondered if his patients' deafness worked as a form of sensory isolation, disorienting them. In 1958 he obtained permission to use three rooms on the top floor of an isolated ward building, and instructed the hospital engineer to build a deprivation chamber. Inside one room another was constructed, suspended from the ceiling by nylon cords to minimise vibration and sound penetration. The chamber was, to all intents and purposes, completely silent. It was fitted with a Dunlopillo mattress and an observation window made of one-way glass. Inside, subjects wore translucent goggles to restrict their vision, and their arms and hands were fitted with fur gauntlets. Cotton gloves and thick woollen socks were worn. Volunteers, who were offered one full day off for every day they remained in the chamber, were selected from the hospital's nursing staff. Some loved the experience, in particular one nurse who remained inside for four or five days, and came out beaming that it was the best holiday she had ever had. Others, however, did not fare so well.

Smith himself spent thirty-eight hours in the chamber, and hated it. 'I found it extremely unpleasant indeed. Very unpleasant,' he says. 'In fact, had I been asked [to go back in again] I would vehemently have said, "Not on your life would I ever do that, or I would be in a bad state." I persuaded myself that I was doing no good in there, to myself or to any truth or information that we might be looking at. I tried to get out. I was not a great person to have in that place at all.'

There were other problems. Many of Smith's subjects had nightmares, often of their own death. All reported problems with concentration. There were mental disturbances and obsessive thoughts. In twelve of the initial twenty subjects these thoughts led rapidly to fear, then panic. One nurse commented later, 'I thought I was going mad.' Another burst into tears and had a hysterical depressive attack. Reasons for quitting the experiment were 'unbearable anxiety, tension, or panic attacks'. Often subjects emerged sweating profusely, trembling, with dry mouth and tachycardia. Interestingly, the only group of volunteers who really thrived were four chronic schizophrenic patients, all of whom seemed content to spend unlimited periods of time in the room. 'They loved it!' recalls Smith.

Smith published the results of his experiment in the *Lancet* in 1959. Shortly afterwards, he received a phone call. 'I had the usual problem with—who was it now?—I think somebody from the War Office.' He sighs. 'They wanted to know whether this had any military use . . . They didn't ask for any help. They just said, "Have you been doing anything else?" That was what they were after. What was the object of it all? They were rather taken aback when I told them about hearing and that sort of sensory loss.'

Although evidence is scarce, it is clear that the British military conducted classified work into sensory deprivation. In a paper before the Royal Institution in 1960 entitled 'The Scientific Lessons of Interrogation' Alexander Kennedy, professor of Psychological Medicine at Edinburgh University, reported on a startling array of interrogation techniques apparently learned during the Second World War. Kennedy, a former lieutenant-colonel in British Intelligence, had been stationed at MI5's Combined Detailed Interrogation Centre (CSDIC) in Cairo during the war, so presumably knew what he was talking about. He cited the results of Hebb's work and discussed one period of 'waiting for the construction of a sensory deprivation chamber' with a colleague, Dr H. Bethune. Inside this chamber, he said, subjects were blind and deaf, with no sense of touch. After eighteen hours, this led to 'a severe state of confusion'. One of Kennedy's subjects appears to have been a young RAF doctor, Peter Roper, who recalls being locked inside a stainless-steel cylinder and told to remain in it until the situation became intolerable (we'll meet Dr Roper again in Chapter 7).

'I certainly knew' says an MI6 psychiatrist who conducted experiments into the efficacy of truth drugs 'that there was a lot [of sensory-deprivation work] going on . . . I think there was something going on at George's [in south London] and one certainly heard about it. There were labs here and there. I wasn't involved myself because I didn't know much about it.'

A further paper in 1960–61 reveals that the British military was interested—if not actively involved—in more radical sensory-deprivation techniques. A.M. Hastin Bennett, of the RAF Institute of Aviation Medicine, reporting on the 'Break-off Phenomenon', wrote:

> It is not the intention of this chapter to present detailed accounts of experimental work carried out by the author, but it is of interest to note that several subjects immersed under 3 ft of water, with the visual field in darkness, have reported feelings of unreality or detachment within the first hour of the experiment. Illusions of turning and of other sorts of motion have been prominent also within the first hour.

The Parker Committee's report into the interrogation of the twelve IRA suspects reveals further proof of British military research into sensory deprivation. In March 1972 Lord Gardiner, author of the Minority Report, admitted that 'some experiments [in sensory deprivation] have been done in England with troops and civilian volunteers'. Other than this, however, the scientific record appears blank. But different sources reveal how sensory deprivation penetrated the British military and intelligence communities. The starting point was the strange confessions that emerged during the Korean War.

At the end of the conflict it was recognised that members of Britain's special forces and other 'prone to capture' agents were likely to reveal sensitive information to the enemy if they were taken prisoner. Since it was suspected that the Russians, Chinese and North Koreans were using extreme interrogation, and possibly even 'brainwashing', techniques, it was decided that steps should be taken to inoculate these troops. The JIC's Evasion, Escape and Prisoner of War Intelligence Sub-committee was put in charge of the assignment, and Cyril Cunningham of AI9, the War Office's psychologist and resident 'brainwashing' expert, interviewed former Korean prisoners-of-war to discover what kind of treatment they had received. He prepared a series of briefs, which were dispatched to the Joint Services Interrogation Wing (JSIW) at Maresfield in Sussex and others. Home of the Intelligence Corps, Maresfield now assumed a crucial role in the training of British special forces—which were on the move.

With the reactivation of the Special Air Service (SAS) for the Malayan Emergency (1948–60), the Regiment assumed an increasingly important role. Officially reformed in 1958–9, the SAS began to grow. 'The SAS at the time was a one-war unit that had been reinstigated for the Malayan Emergency,' recalls one former veteran, 'and that's what we were training for. But as soon as that was over and the carryings-on in the Middle East began, they saw the potential, and then we got a hell of a lot of training in all sorts of things, including the Cold War thing, the counter-interrogation . . . we came back [to the UK] in about February, March '59, and then the training went berserk.'

As special-forces training courses multiplied, potential recruits were siphoned off and given a course in what to expect if the worst came to the worst. John Hughes-Wilson, a former colonel in the Intelligence Corps, explains, 'Resistance to Interrogation was [for] certain types of submariners, very few, a rather larger clutch of aircrew, particularly special forces aircrew, and of course the special forces themselves. By special forces I include MI5 and MI6 officers . . . You have to give these people the chance to withstand the pressures they might get from people who don't believe in the Geneva Convention—or haven't even heard of the bloody Geneva Convention.'

SAS troops were sent on escape and evasion exercises around Europe. If they were caught, they were subjected to the techniques the Intelligence Corps thought were being used by the Soviets. These included wall-standing, physical exhaustion, deception, a certain level of brutality, sleep and sensory deprivation. Understandably, Resistance to Interrogation ('R to I') training was not a popular billet.

The SAS veteran shakes his head. 'That's the thing that always got to me. Sensory deprivation. We used to get it in 1960, '61. It was a lightless room, somewhere where you got no sense of daylight or dark, mostly pitch dark. Occasionally [it was] broken by loud, very loud music and flashing lights. And the thing that amazed me is that it caught on. They have these bloody discos nowadays! It's exactly the bloody same! It was a great incentive not to get caught.'

So unpopular was the course that members of the Regiment went to extreme lengths to avoid it. Before operational exercises, officers would ask who had yet to go through the training. Names were noted and those who had not experienced it were first to be caught. It transpired that when they transmitted their location back to headquarters during the exercises, the SAS passed the information to the 'enemy', who picked them up for interrogation.

It wasn't long before SAS rank and file began to play the game. 'They never caught me!' laughs another veteran. 'I wouldn't send my location, you see. Which caused a bit of bother all round because eventually, the whole bloody Regiment was sending bloody rubbish all the time, and not getting caught. It took years for them to live that down . . . For years after those sessions, the SAS was never quite where they said they were. It got so your own people couldn't find you. It was a bit of a menace.'

Meanwhile, at the JSIW, more information was compiled about Soviet 'brainwashing' techniques. Colonel Roy Giles of the Gloucestershire Regiment was sent there for an interrogation course in 1963. Nothing was taught about sensory deprivation. In 1966, however, he attended a JSIW counter-interrogation course in Aden. This time he was shown a film of what he assumed to be SAS Resistance to Interrogation training. In it, soldiers were hooded, lined up and 'bashed about'.★

Giles was also lectured on sensory deprivation, specifically the technique invented by John Lilly at NIH in 1954, and mentioned by the RAF's A.M. Hastin Bennett eight years earlier. 'The technique that all of us in Aden listened to agape,' he says, 'was a method that had been developed allegedly very recently, which was to suspend the prisoner in a tank of liquid gelatine, which was at 94.8 degrees Fahrenheit. Naked. With your arms and legs tied and your head encased in a sort of diver's helmet, through which

★ The film was probably *I Can't Answer That Question*, made in 1966 at MI6's 'Fort' near Southsea. In the film, subjects are hooded, physically exhausted, roughed up, lied to, kept cold and verbally abused. White noise is used. Over footage of a series of blindfolded men chained to walls, a cod-Russian voiceover explains, 'Depriving a man of all contact with reality puts him into a most receptive state of mind. Only those who can anchor their reason firmly in the world they can remember will be able to resist.'

you were breathing. You were hung into this tank, so all you could hear was the sound of your own breath. In theory you would go bonkers.'

Giles and his colleagues were shown a film of the technique in action, with a man being lowered into the tank. But the procedure, while horrific, was not without its flaws. There was, he was instructed, a handy means of beating underwater sensory deprivation: 'They said, "Don't worry! Don't worry!" This is what the guys who practise this haven't thought about. They may have deprived you of all sort of external capability, but the male person has one very sensitive organ—between his legs—over which, under these circumstances, it has been proved, you still have control.' Giles laughs. 'The answer is, you can do all sorts of *amazing* things in a tank of gelatine at 94.8 degrees!'

As well as researching different ways of producing sensory deprivation, Britain's special forces—and those of her NATO allies—were looking at the nature of the noise to be used during the interrogation process. An Intelligence Corps veteran recalls visiting the US Air Force Survival School at Fairchild, Spokane, where the Americans were experimenting with different types of white noise: 'We were being shown how the Americans did it,' he says, 'and they had a couple of women going through interrogation and they told us, "Oh, by the way, we've got babies crying," and the idea was to appeal to their maternal instinct. There was a couple of us Brits there, and we looked at each other and were like "Oh, don't be so bloody silly!" I was allowed to go into a debrief with one of these women and I asked her, did this have any effect? She said, "No. Absolutely none."'

Not everyone in the UK agreed with this verdict. Further research into conditioning techniques, including sensory disorientation and white noise, continued at Maresfield (and then at the Intelligence Corps' new headquarters in Ashford, Kent) into the 1980s. John Hughes-Wilson, who ran the R to I programme at one point, remembers, 'They taught us sensory deprivation was a short cut to conditioning a subject . . . We would run controlled experiments—there's no other word for it—on people who, because of the nature of their jobs as Intelligence or Special Forces operators, needed them. You can just have white noise—shshshsh—very disorientating. We would actually run a Chinese opera loop. Ping-pong! Ping-pong!'

The type of white noise was not the only thing that changed. 'We tried different sorts of methods' he says. 'Have you ever seen the Marzine advertisement for seasickness tablets? It's a round black and white disc with swirly black and white patterns on it, and if you rotate it, it makes you feel really quite queasy. We would project this on a wall, have prisoners sit on the floor with their hands on their heads, and watching the wall, with this noise going, or Chinese opera. And they would fall over.'

According to Intelligence Corps sources the white noise, the nausea-creating visual patterns and the hooding were deployed in response to intelligence that revealed this was the kind of treatment the Russians and Chinese employed and that special forces should expect it if they were caught. The Intelligence Corps had a point: special forces *are* prone to being captured and need to know what to expect if they are. But the reliability of the JSIW's intelligence regarding Soviet interrogation techniques was more contentious. Not everyone agreed with their theories concerning Eastern bloc methods. Cyril Cunningham visited Maresfield a number of times during the 1960s and was appalled to discover what they were up to: 'I went down to Maresfield on a number of occasions,' he recalls, 'and I took part in exercises with the Strategic Air Command. And I was absolutely horrified that the security interrogators, and one or two of the late arrivals for AI9 ones, who were RAF and Army officers, were knocking people about because they said, "This is what the Russians did". And I said, "Well, how do you know that? How do you know what the Russians did?" And they said, "Well, we read it in the papers." '

Cunningham—who had been at the spearhead of the AI9 project to determine what had happened to the Korean prisoners-of-war—thought that these techniques were being used irresponsibly. 'They were just doing it off their own bat,' he says today. 'And you said, "Well, what do you expect to achieve by this?" And they hadn't got a damn clue . . . I was absolutely horrified when I discovered what they were up to. "Who authorised this? What are you doing it for?" "Oh, we've read this, we've read that. We thought it would be a good idea." And none of it had been authorised higher up. Interrogation and interrogation training: nobody authorised it. It just happened.'

Exactly what techniques were being used to train British special forces to resist interrogation might have remained unknown to the wider public, had not the techniques suddenly found an application in Northern Ireland in 1971. As more people attended the Resistance to Interrogation courses, word got round that these techniques were the ones to be used in interrogation situations. So, as Colonel Hughes-Wilson acknowledges, the line between interrogation and *counter*-interrogation training 'got blurred'. By the time of internment, 'They had been training for so long—there was no real interrogation going on—on Resistance to Interrogation methods that they went in [to Northern Ireland] and as far as they were concerned, they treated it as another interrogation exercise using R to I methods.'

In fact, it was rather more deliberate than just another interrogation exercise. Planning for the interrogations had begun following the visit of MI5's director general, Sir Dick White, to Belfast in March 1971; in April, officers from the 'English Interrogation Centre' (presumably Maresfield) held a special seminar for members of the RUC to teach them the methods they were planning to use when internment swung into action. At this seminar the RUC was specifically instructed in the use of what the army termed the 'Five Techniques' (hooding, wall-standing, white noise, sleep deprivation, bread-and-water diet). Their deployment in Northern Ireland in 1971 had profound political ramifications. It was already having profound *physical* ramifications for the twelve interned IRA suspects.

Paddy Joe McClean and Joe Clarke, with the other ten men, were interrogated for six days. During that time they were fed only the occasional cup of water or crust of bread. They were not allowed to wash or use a lavatory. Later investigations revealed that the twelve men were made to stand against the wall for periods of up to forty-three and a half hours. But the actual time they spent against the wall was probably less significant than the *atmosphere* in which they were held. As Hebb and Vernon had theorised (and the CIA's Maitland Baldwin had proved), sensory deprivation is particularly intolerable when it is imposed with no upper time limit. Combined with fear, sleep deprivation, brutality, white noise and restriction of food and water, the fact that none of the internees had any idea how long the ordeal would last made this a unique and terrifying experience.

It is perhaps no surprise, then, that at some point during the process many of the victims wished they were dead. One reported later that he had tried to end it all by dashing his own head against the wall. Paddy Joe McClean, convinced that this was an experiment in torture, persuaded himself that the British Army would not allow news of it to get out, and would dispose of the evidence by killing the twelve men once the interrogation was over. Certain that he was going to die, he prepared himself for the end.

Then, suddenly, on 17 August, it was over. The subjects were put into cells, told to face the wall, and permitted to remove their hoods. They were informed that they were being taken back to Crumlin Road prison. At this point, Clarke recalls, their captors became human again. 'Hopefully,' one RUC officer told him, 'you'll live the rest of your life happily.'

By now, Clarke was in such a state that he could barely stand up. An officer helped him. 'I went to the toilet,' he recalls. 'I couldn't even wipe my own backside because my arms were so sore with standing at the wall. And the [Special] Branch man, or the policeman, or the MI5 guy—whoever it was—actually cleaned my behind for me.'

The twelve men were put into helicopters. Again, Clarke recalls a moment of humanity. Before they got into the helicopter, a Special Branch man told him that he would have to wear a hood for the duration of the flight. Clarke, who had been pushed out of the last helicopter he had been up in, begged him to leave the hood off. The man told him he was sorry but those were his orders. 'But,' he said, 'I will stay with you until you're out of the helicopter. Then I'll be taking the hood off you—and then don't look back.' The RUC man then made a bizarre request: 'If I ever meet you in the street, will you buy me a pint?' Clarke, relieved to be returning to prison and shocked by this sudden kindness, said he would. 'He was a good guy,' he says today. The men were flown to the grounds of St Malachi's College in Belfast. A hole in the wall led into the Crumlin Road Prison. As they were led through it, they were finally allowed to remove the hoods.

McClean, who had a black eye, recalls the reaction of the prison guards to the twelve men's physical condition when they arrived: 'I could see the expression of horror in their faces. So that if I didn't already know—which I already did know by my loss of weight and the marks on my arms, legs and body and so on—I could have worked it out.'

Having lost all track of time during the interrogation, Clarke and McClean asked what day it was. They were told it was Wednesday. Both said that this was impossible: they had been arrested on Monday and kept in the holding centres until Wednesday. It couldn't still be Wednesday. No, said the guards. That was a week ago. Clarke was accosted by a warder called Dickie Elder. 'Where were you?' asked Elder. 'I don't know,' he replied. 'What do you mean, you don't know?' When Clarke told him he had been hooded for a week, Elder patted him on the head. 'He says, "Don't be worrying, son, you're amongst decent people now. Nothing more is going to happen to you." Tears just flew out of me, so they did.'

Clarke, McClean and the other ten were taken to the prison sanatorium, where they were allowed to wash and were fed their first proper meal in six days. When they were weighed it was discovered they had each lost up to sixteen pounds in the previous week. Then an opportunity presented itself. The prison officer in charge of McClean's wing, by chance another old acquaintance, asked if there was anything he could do for him. McClean requested pencil and paper. Although he could barely see, having been hooded for the best part of a week, he managed to scrawl twenty-two lines detailing what had happened to him. He gave the list to the officer and asked him to deliver it to Cardinal Conway, Archbishop of Armagh.

That night the warder, a Protestant, took a taxi from Belfast to Armagh and delivered the note to Conway, telling him it was from Paddy Joe McClean in Crumlin Road Prison, and that it was important.

Cardinal Conway flew to London to see the British prime minister, Edward Health, at 10 Downing Street. Exactly what was said at this meeting is not clear but Heath immediately ordered that the use of the 'Five Techniques' be suspended. At Crumlin Road Prison seven further suspects, who had been isolated, photographed, numbered and told by RUC officers that they were in for 'the horror treatment' were reprieved.

Clearly it wouldn't be long before news of the incident got out. The authorities, realising that when it hit the press there would be trouble, contacted Father Faul. 'When I started to publicise this stuff, they burst out in protest,' he recalls. 'One of them rang me up, said, "You're going to go to the newspapers?" I said, "Of course I'm going to the newspapers! These people have no protection, there's nobody speaking up for these people and they have got to have somebody speaking up for them." '

The incident was downplayed, the Northern Ireland prime minister, Brian Faulkner, stating that 'If any of these things had happened, it would have been public knowledge within twenty-four hours.' But on 31 August the British home secretary, Reginald Maudling, announced the appointment of a committee under Sir Edmund Compton to investigate the allegations.

The Compton Report was an extraordinary piece of work. In the course of their investigations, Compton and his team took evidence from ninety-five soldiers, twenty-six RUC men, eleven prison officers, two regimental medical officers, two civilian doctors and two further medical specialists.

Yet of the 342 men who had been interned and supposedly mistreated, they interviewed just one (other internees refused to speak with some-one they regarded as a British lackey). The idea of a case with one witness for the prosecution but 138 for the defence does not appear to have seemed unbalanced to Compton: he was happy to take the RUC's and the army's word for what had happened. He was also happy to disregard evidence from the Association for Legal Justice and Amnesty.

Despite Compton's impressive sources he made an immediate error, listing the number of men interrogated as eleven, not twelve. Micky Montgomery was forgotten. Meanwhile, in a distressing irony—and despite a specific order from Edward Heath that it was not to happen again—another two IRA suspects were given the interrogation-in-depth treatment, just five miles away from where Compton was compiling his report in October 1971. At one point a subject, William Shannon, was approached by an RUC officer with a syringe and threatened with a truth drug. Shannon had the number '21' written on his hand.

The conclusions of Compton's report, published on 3 November, 1971, were incongruous. Wall-standing, he said, was not a 'stress position': its purpose was not to exhaust the men but to 'impose discipline' and provide 'security'. If the subjects refused to stand correctly, their legs or arms were not kicked but *pushed apart gently*. No one ever had to stand at the wall for longer than four to six hours at a time. Food had been offered at six-hourly intervals—but most of the men had refused to eat it. Likewise, lavatory facilities had been available but the soldiers had found it difficult to know when the interrogation subjects had wanted to go. Paddy Joe McClean, it was stated, had repeatedly soiled himself 'by his own choice'. Beatings were flatly denied, McClean's black eye being explained as an accident 'in transit'.

Hooding was a security measure for the protection of the subjects. In fact, on occasion, 'some complainants kept their hoods on when they could have removed them if they had wished'. White noise, again, was for the protection of the subjects. The fact that hooding and noise together might lead to disorientation was acknowledged but downplayed.

Clearly there were (and still are) good practical reasons for hooding suspects and using white noise in interrogation situations. If subjects can't see, they will be easier to handle; they will not be able to recognise interrogators afterwards; if they can't hear, they will not know when other interrogation subjects in the room are giving information or what they are saying. But to imply that the disorientation experienced by the twelve men in 1971 was an unfortunate side-effect was disingenuous. No one familiar with the Canadian sensory-deprivation experiments in the early 1950s was in any doubt that what had happened in Northern Ireland was a result of that research. At McGill University, Ron Melzack remembers that Donald Hebb was 'really unhappy' when news of 'interrogation in depth' broke in Canada. 'He thought that what had started off as a perfectly reasonable experiment—the effect was appalling . . . Having known all of those people who were involved—they absolutely *knew* it was linked. It had to be linked. I mean, sure, that's what the idea was! They would have been *really* appalled.'

Eventually even Compton was forced to conclude that the Five Techniques constituted 'ill-treatment'. But his job was done: it wasn't 'physical brutality', and it certainly wasn't 'torture'.

Compton's report was famously described by the *Observer* as 'Six grains of truth and a bucket of whitewash'. Roy Hattersley, now Lord Hattersley of Sparkbrook, then deputy foreign affairs spokesman, agrees: 'It was [a whitewash], wasn't it? I don't want to sound too cynical. But it was bound to be the case that the investigators of those facts in those circumstances were going to be sympathetic towards the Army . . . it's very easy defending heroes—but it's very difficult defending the rights of criminals and assumed criminals. The Compton Report was always going to come out that way.'

Six months later, on 3 December 1971 another committee, under Lord Parker, sat to determine how IRA suspects should be treated in future. In his report, Lord Parker noted that the deprivation techniques had been used for some time on the SAS without any harm but admitted that 'The real thing is obviously quite different from the experiment.' He then performed a complete about-face, concluding that it was probably harder for SAS recruits to undergo forty-eight hours of Resistance to Interrogation training than for IRA suspects to endure a week of the same treatment because the IRA has a strong '*esprit de corps*' to help them through the process. The SAS—arguably the finest military unit in the world—is known for its lack of morale, of course.

As proof of the efficacy of the interrogation techniques, Parker cited statistics: more than seven hundred IRA members were arrested, crucial details of the organisation, operations, arms caches, safe-houses, communication lines and supply routes had emerged. More than eighty-five crimes had been solved. 'There is no doubt,' he wrote, 'that . . . these techniques have produced very valuable results.' Parker recommended that, subject to certain guidelines, the techniques were acceptable for use in the interrogation of potential terrorists.

He discovered, however, that interrogation was a murky business: there was not a single official manual detailing how to do it. Techniques used were apparently transmitted orally at JSIW. Consequently the 'Five Techniques' had never been vetted by a government minister, and therefore never specifically authorised.

Once again, this was no surprise to Roy Hattersley: 'If I understand the army,' he says, 'and if I understand ministers, somebody—and I don't know who—would say, "Well, it's just better not to let them know that we're doing it," and ministers would say, "It's just better not to enquire into how they're doing this sort of thing." My guess is that there was a conscious decision to keep some block between the army and ministers.'

Despite the lack of documentation about the Five Techniques, Parker decided that they were not dangerous: while there may have been 'some degree' of mental disorientation, this would disappear within two months (where he acquired this information, since there was apparently no printed matter on the subject, is anyone's guess). In any case, it stood in stark contrast to the evidence of the doctors who examined the fourteen men after their experiences. Dr Pearse O'Malley, who examined three in Crumlin Road prison, estimated that all had developed a psychosis within twenty-four hours of their arrival at the interrogation centre. They had all suffered profound visual and auditory hallucinations. One man shook continually, found it hard to put sentences together and refused to be left alone, even for a minute. Another was 'shuddering spasmodically and complains of violent headaches, insomnia and nightmares when he goes to sleep'. Two of the three men he examined would probably get better eventually, he thought, but one might have 'permanent mental damage'.

Professor Robert Daly of Cork University also examined the men and was later asked to testify concerning their condition. Daly noted anxiety, fear and dread, insomnia and recurring nightmares. Some were so depressed that they 'did not care whether they lived or died'. 'Whether you want to call it interrogation in depth or brainwashing is academic,' he wrote in 1973. 'The aim of the treatment was to cause temporary psychosis—temporary insanity—which was a severe psychological injury liable to have lasting consequences.'

But the authors of the report were unable to agree. Alongside Lord Parker's Majority Report came a second, minority report, by Lord Gardiner. Here, some interesting facts emerged: first, that Sir Edmund Compton was either lying or wrong when he said that no one had stood at the wall for more than four to six hours. In fact, as far as surviving records indicated, they had stood there non-stop for up to sixteen hours at a stretch. The hooding and noise were more than security measures: as one witness told Gardiner, 'Sensory isolation is one method of inducing an artificial psychosis or episode of insanity.' Hebb's experiments at McGill and Smith's at the Moor Hospital were cited in the report, and Gardiner concluded, 'Interrogation in depth as described in the first Compton Report is a form of Sensory Deprivation leading to mental disorientation.'

Gardiner also disagreed with Lord Parker's claim that crucial intelligence had been gained from the interrogations. Clearly there had been a huge increase in arrests: on the first night of internment 342 suspects were marshalled. It would have been surprising if arms dumps and information had not shown up. The entire incident, in his view, was a 'sorry story': 'Forcibly to hood a man's head and keep him hooded against his will and handcuff him if he tries to remove it,' he wrote, 'is an assault and both a tort and a crime. So is wall standing of the kind referred to . . . No Army directive and no minister could lawfully or validly have authorised the use of the procedures . . . The procedures were and are illegal.'

On 2 March 1972 the British Government accepted Lord Gardiner's Minority Report instead of Lord Parker's Majority Report. The same day, prime minister Edward Heath told the House of Commons that the Five Techniques 'will not be used in the future as an aid to interrogation'. Interrogation in depth would continue, he assured MPs, 'but these techniques will not be used'.

Two years later the British were taken to task by the European Court of Human Rights in Strasbourg. By the time the case was heard, there had been a change of government. In the Foreign Office there was some disagreement concerning how best to minimise the damage. Roy Hattersley, by then number two in the department, argued that the British should come clean, apologise and blame it all on the previous administration. He was quickly silenced: 'I remember Harold Wilson, who was prime minister, was absolutely scathing to me' he says. 'Very embarrassing for a young minister—at my decision that we should plead guilty and get away with it. He felt that we had to defend the British reputation by defending ourselves. And that's what we did in 1974, '75.'

Perhaps Hattersley was right. Legal deliberations went on for some time, at the end of which, to no one's great surprise, Britain was found guilty of 'inhuman and degrading treatment'. The subjects were awarded financial compensation.

But there were more serious side-effects than the Strasbourg verdict. The month after his visit to Edward Heath in August 1971, Cardinal Conway attended a senate in Rome. There he passed on what he had heard about 'interrogation in depth' to Cardinal Cooke, Archbishop of New York. Cooke returned home with a mission.

In New York Cooke, a high percentage of whose parishioners were of Irish descent, issued a statement to his fellow Catholic priests. It contained the most forceful denunciation of foreign policy from the American Catholic community since New York's Cardinal Spellman had attacked Hitler's treatment of the Jews in the Second World War. He called for the establishment of relief funds for Northern Irish Catholics, mentioning specifically 'interrogation camps, where Catholic dissidents are interned without trial and are brought to the brink of physical and mental exhaustion during the process of interrogation'.

Word of what had happened in Northern Ireland spread like wildfire across the United States. Alistair Cooke, normally a tranquil correspondent, told the BBC: 'As a reporter, it would be irresponsible of me to the point of callousness not to tell you how widespread in this country is the disquiet—to put it mildly—over the rumour, or report, that torture is being used under the typically twentieth century euphemism of "deep interrogation"'.

American anger at British conduct in Northern Ireland was fuelled in January 1972 by reports of Bloody Sunday. Sinn Fein lost no time in capitalising on the opportunity, flying the interrogation subjects, including Paddy Joe McClean, to the United States to tell Americans what the British had done to them. 'Interrogation in depth' and Bloody Sunday helped to mobilise the huge Irish-American community. NORAID, the American funding organisation for Republican causes in Northern Ireland, stepped into the breach. Suddenly large amounts of money were flowing from Irish Americans into the hands of the IRA.

Publicity about the incident made a splash in the Province too. Paddy Joe McClean, still active in civil-rights circles in 2005, remembers the re-action of the Catholic community in Northern Ireland: ' "You think *we*'re the terrorists? We're not the terrorists! *They*'re the terrorists! These are the terrorists! They are masquerading under the rule of law!" And that caused upheaval. That caused more death.'

McClean is under no illusion about the nature of the consequences. 'That was the greatest recruiting sergeant the IRA ever had,' he told me. 'Internment, the interrogations, Bloody Sunday: August, September, Oc-tober, November, December, January—those six months—*made* the Pro-visional IRA.'

I met Denis Faul—now a monsignor—at his home in Sixmilecross, County Tyrone, in November 2004. I was pretty intimidated: he'd told me on the phone that Britain was a 'nation of shopkeepers' and I got the im-pression that he didn't like the English very much. But after a breakfast of apples and marmalade ('You Brits, you love your marmalade! I know you do!'), he agreed, 'Oh, yes. Recruits and money. It was wonderful for [the IRA], you know.' Likewise Joe Clarke, who admits to having been ac-tive in Republican circles at the time, told me that interrogation in depth was a colossal error: 'They made a big mistake by doing that. *Big* mis-take.'

Part of the mistake was that the RUC and the Army had interrogated the wrong people. Of the twelve original suspects, at least seven were completely unaffiliated to the IRA. This was the RUC's fault: it had handed the list of suspects for interrogation to the army. Its intelligence had been inaccurate.

'The problem,' says John Hughes-Wilson, of the Intelligence Corps, 'was that the interrogators who went in to interrogate those who had been interned had no say over who the subjects were. They were just given these people by the RUC . . . They picked up completely the wrong list, given to them by the RUC. The methods we used in 1971 worked bril-liantly. The irony is that the Army interrogators got the wrong people and sucked them dry . . . The original 1971 internment and the interrogation that followed was a blunder of cosmic proportions.'

Paddy Hillyard, chair of Social Policy Administration at the University of Ulster—not usually a man to go along with the opinions of colonels in the Intelligence Corps—agrees: 'They may have had two or three—I don't know the details—people who were in the IRA at the time but the majority weren't and therefore symbolically it meant that the Catholic community just cohered together and said, "Right, we're going to oppose this."'

'It was completely counterproductive,' he goes on, 'because overnight literally thousands of young men joined up . . . When you take the broader impact of what happened as a result of internment, and the interrogation in particular, you know, you had armed conflict for the next thirty years. And look at the number of people who died. Phenomenal.'

Ironically, there was another side-effect of the incident. Before I said goodbye to Monsignor Faul in November 2004, he smiled resignedly. 'A very interesting fact is that in the 1970s and 1980s the IRA set up torture houses to interrogate suspect informers,' he said. 'There was one in Dundirk, one in Andersonstown . . . They employed nearly all the RUC techniques. But the first thing they did was—they put a hood on you. They *hooded* them! That was one of the ones we reported to the Heath Government in 1971! They imitated it! This was really despicable of the IRA.'

Faul walked me to the door. 'Torture goes on and on,' he said. 'It never stops.' We shook hands. 'And they *love* the hooded bit.'

5

Building the Manchurian Candidate

The telephone, on the desk beside his chair, rang. He picked it up.
'Raymond Shaw, please.' It was a pleasant male voice with an indefinite accent.
'This is he'.
'Why don't you pass the time by playing a little solitaire?'

Richard Condon, *The Manchurian Candidate,* 1959

Palle Hardrup cycled to work at seven a.m. on Thursday, 29 March 1951. Hardrup, a twenty-nine-year-old tool machinist, was supposed to be starting a contract for the Danish Oil Burning Company that day. Instead, he approached his supervisor with a request. He had personal problems at home: if he promised to make up the time later, would it be possible to take the morning off? The supervisor, who had no reason to suspect that he was lying, agreed.

Glancing over his shoulder, Hardrup walked to his clothing locker, opened it and removed a heavy metal object concealed in a tablecloth, then a smaller item, similarly wrapped. He placed both objects in his briefcase, closed it and shut the locker door. He then said goodbye to his boss, climbed on to the bicycle and rode away.

That year, Copenhagen was unseasonably cold. Everyone was waiting for spring to arrive but it was nearly April and there was still a bitter chill in the air; a thick layer of slush covered the streets. As he cycled away from work, though, Hardrup had other things on his mind. Three months earlier, God had told him to save the world. The briefcase on the pannier of his bicycle contained a pistol and a handful of bullets. Palle Hardrup was about to rob a bank.

He cycled to a flat belonging to the aunt of a friend. The aunt, a heavy drinker, would provide his alibi for the bank job. On the way there he stopped at an off-licence and bought a few beers to make sure his cover story would stand up. Together the pair drank them. At ten thirty, he decided that the old lady was sufficiently inebriated not to be able to recall things clearly and told her that he was popping out for more beer. He would only be a few minutes. She agreed.

Hardrup never got round to buying more beer. Instead, he put the briefcase back on to the bicycle and rode to the Landsmandsbanken at number fifty-eight Norrenboro Street. He parked the bike on the pavement, then paused. He was scared; his body would not do what he wanted it to. Finally, realising that robbing the bank was God's will, at 10.45 he took a deep breath, put on a pair of sunglasses and walked in through the double doors.

As he entered the lobby, Hardrup pulled out the pistol and fired a shot into the ceiling. 'Fill up the briefcase!' he shouted, at the nearest cashier. Startled, the cashier did not react fast enough, so Hardrup shot him. He turned to the next cashier. 'Now it's your turn,' he said. 'Fill the case!'

The heist took too long. At the sound of the gunshots, customers in the bank panicked. In the street outside, passers-by approached the doors, cutting off Hardrup's escape route. Then someone tripped the bank's alarm. Hardrup, convinced he was about to get caught, raised the gun again. The second teller tried to run but it was too late. Hardrup shot him dead. Empty-handed he then turned, fled the building, leaped on to his bike and began to pedal furiously. As he pulled away from the kerb another cyclist tried to cut him off. Just before the two men collided, Hardrup put out his foot and fended off his assailant. The other man tried again to stop him so he shoved the pistol into his face. The man backed off, leaving the way clear. As he cycled off, Hardrup congratulated himself on his coolness. When a pedestrian asked him what was going on, he stopped and said he didn't know. 'Why don't you go over there,' he suggested, 'and take a look for yourself?' Then he made good his escape.

Back in the flat, Hardrup told the old lady that someone had robbed the local bank. She wasn't interested. Where was the beer? Realising that he had better firm up his alibi, he changed his coat, to make sure no one would recognise him, and headed back down the stairs to the off-licence. The moment he arrived at the bottom of the stairs, however, he knew something was wrong. The street outside was empty—and silent. Then the police arrived. Hardrup, still armed, was hopelessly outnumbered. Silently, he raised his hands and surrendered.

Initially, Hardrup did not tell the police that God had told him to rob the bank. As a result the arresting officers were jubilant: not only did they have their man, but he had openly admitted the crime. But they soon became concerned. Asked why he had robbed the bank, he answered that he was raising funds for a political party that he had founded, the Danish National Communist Party (DNKP), whose goal was to prepare for the Third World War. Once war had been declared, he told the police, he would use the money from the bank job to charter a fleet of ships to carry Denmark's intellectual élite to a safe haven in Sweden, preserving the country's heritage. In the end, he explained, the DNKP would bring about world peace but in the meantime he was stockpiling guns. Police promptly raided Hardrup's flat, locating uniforms, propaganda, medals and documents relating to the Party.

· Noting that he appeared unusually composed for someone who had just robbed a bank, killed two men and been caught, the police asked whether he felt guilty for the double murder. Hardrup assured them he didn't. Why should he? God had told him to do it. Eyebrows heading for the ceiling, the officers exchanged a glance. 'Come again?' Oh, said Hardrup, God had told him to do *everything*. God had told him to form the DNKP. God had chosen the crime and the bank, and even told him where to hide afterwards. God was always with him. But don't worry—he reassured them—it would all be all right in the end: God would make sure of it.

On 21 June 1951, Hardrup was taken to see Dr Max Schmidt, Copenhagen's chief police psychiatrist. He told Schmidt everything he had told the police: that he had committed the robbery on God's orders and that he felt no guilt about the deaths of the two bank tellers. He believed in 'fate, and life after death'. He was, he said, like Joan of Arc.

Schmidt was intrigued. Murders in Copenhagen were rare, cases like this infinitely more so. The next day, hoping to cut through Hardrup's religio-political gibberish, he gave him an intravenous shot of the 'truth drug' narcodon. Hardrup immediately launched into a convoluted explanation of his anti-Semitic, anti-Fascist philosophy: there was to be a third world war. Denmark must be saved. A 'Northern Kingdom' was to be established. When the drug had taken hold and his subject was fully re-laxed, Schmidt asked the one question he really wanted answered: 'Where did you get the idea to rob the bank from?'

'From "it",' replied the criminal.

'And who *is* "it"?'

' "It" is my guardian angel,' said Hardrup.

Schmidt was suspicious. There had to be more to the case than this. For a start, it was likely that Hardrup had been behind an almost identical rob-bery committed seven months previously in Hvidovre. There were also in-dications that he had not acted alone. The day after the robbery, a known criminal called Bjorn Nielsen had shown up and admitted that he was the owner of the bicycle used in the crime. It was Nielsen's aunt whom Hardrup had been drinking with that morning, and her flat where he was arrested. Cursory investigation revealed that Hardrup had spent three years in Horsens State Prison—as Nielsen's cellmate. Former inmates reported that Nielsen had exerted an unnatural influence on Hardrup; Hardrup did nothing, they said, that had not come from Nielsen.

On 30 March Nielsen was hauled in for questioning. Nothing useful emerged. Yes, he admitted, he and Hardrup had served time together, and they had shared a cell for a while. Nielsen was aware of Hardrup's new political party and had even been involved in the early stages—mainly putting up posters around town—but he had backed out long ago. Other than lending Hardrup his bicycle, he said, he'd had nothing to do with the robbery.

But there were inconsistencies in the two men's stories. Hardrup said he had stolen the bicycle, Nielsen that he had lent it to him. Hardrup said that Nielsen had had nothing to do with the DNKP, Nielsen had admitted he was involved. Nielsen also indicated that he knew more about the crime: at one point he suggested that Hardrup's wife, Bente, was behind the whole thing. In the past, he said, the pair had planned robberies but each time he had persuaded them out of it. It almost appeared that Nielsen was trying to get Hardrup into more trouble. Nielsen, a career criminal, had been in prison more or less continuously since 1933. Hardrup, with his naïve mes-sianic tendencies, and his 'guardian angel', appeared to be a lackey.

Schmidt now began to lean heavily on Hardrup, giving him repeated doses of barbiturates and pushing him to admit that Nielsen was behind the crime. Hardrup refused. When the psychiatrist tried to trick him into revealing that Nielsen and the 'guardian angel' were one and the same, Hardrup stated flatly that this could not possibly be the case: he had first 'experienced God' in January 1947, six months before the two men had met. He was categorical: the guardian angel was *not* Nielsen. Nielsen was released. There wasn't enough evidence to keep him in.

Max Schmidt completed his report on the crime in mid-December 1951. In it he concluded that Hardrup was a paranoid schizophrenic with psychopathic tendencies but that 'the details of what Hardrup believes are influenced by his being together with Nielsen'. There was no doubt in Schmidt's mind that Nielsen had somehow persuaded Hardrup to commit the crime, but that he was still exerting so much control over him that he could not—or would not—admit it. As to the nature of Nielsen's hold over Hardrup, Schmidt could only guess: Nielsen denied it, Hardrup denied it, and there the trail went cold.

That Christmas, however, after he had been told the result of Dr Schmidt's report and assured that he was going to be sentenced to life in an asylum, Palle Hardrup had a change of heart. He picked up a pen and paper and wrote a letter to Roland Olsen, the officer in charge of the investigation. Olsen's 'continual bombardments' of his mind had finally broken him, he said. It was time to come clean. The letter, which eventually covered eighteen pages of a children's notepad, became known as the 'Exercise Book Confession'. As confessions go, it was a weird one.

Hardrup recounted how he had been a Nazi collaborator during the German occupation of Denmark and how, after the war, he had been sentenced to fourteen years in jail. Arriving at Horsens State Prison, he had been extremely depressed until he was detailed to work in the metal shop. One of the first people he met there was Nielsen. Nielsen, who had previously served time for robbery and who had been sentenced to twelve years for collaboration, saw this as another stretch to be endured, but Hardrup, who had not experienced prison before, took the sentence badly. He was an idealistic young man from a good background who had made a foolish choice, and was paying the price. He was vulnerable.

Nielsen soon impressed Hardrup by telling him that he had fought in the Spanish Civil War, regaling him with heroic war stories until it was clear that he had won an acolyte. As the two became closer, he addressed a more important matter: religion. Hardrup had always had a religious bent and Nielsen played on this, portraying himself as an expert on Eastern mysticism. He introduced Hardrup to meditation and yoga, and the pair practised the techniques at night in their separate cells. Eventually Nielsen suggested that Hardrup request that they be allowed to share a cell. He did. Nielsen then went to work on his disciple. Under his tutelage, Hardrup started with breathing exercises. Nielsen suggested to him that, as part of the meditation process, he should practise 'becoming one with the deity'. The powerful feeling that ensued, he said, would become stronger each time he practised the technique, and would lead him to ecstatic religious experience—and to God.

Then came the revelation that would crack the case. In his Exercise Book Confession Hardrup revealed that one of the techniques the two men had experimented with was hypnosis. Nielsen had instigated the experiments, suggesting that Hardrup try to hypnotise him, but the results were unconvincing. The pair soon determined that Hardrup was more suggestible and thus the better candidate. It wasn't long before he was being hypnotised by Nielsen every night. Often the sessions would end with Hardrup drifting directly from a hypnotic state into sleep. 'From the beginning,' wrote Hardrup, '[Nielsen] has been playing with my mind. He has been taking control of me.'

It was at this point that the Danish press went bananas. 'Bank Murder Committed Under Hypnosis?' asked *Politiken*. 'Guardian Angel Made Him Commit Murders,' reported *Berlingske Tidende*, and followed up the revelation with Hardrup's assertion that 'Nielsen Drove Me Insane Through Yoga!'. 'Even nice people can be hypnotised to kill,' claimed a psychiatrist in *Information*.

The reaction of the press can't have come as much of a surprise to anyone who knew anything about journalism. A double murder as a result of a botched bank robbery was news, but that the killer had committed the crime in a hypnotic trance was something else. Coverage soon moved from sensational to lurid. When it emerged that Nielsen had sent Hardrup a Christmas card in jail, the papers concluded that this was an attempt by the hypnotist to stop his charge testifying: 'Christmas Card From Friend Nearly Interrupted Hardrup's Confession' was *Politiken*'s headline on 9 January

1952. It was reported that Nielsen had given Hardrup a sausage, the sight of which had triggered in its recipient some kind of programme that led to mental collapse: 'Received a Sausage—and Withdrew Confession!' reported *Information*.

Public interest in the possibility of a technique capable of making people behave in ways alien to them lingers to this day. At the bottom of our fascination with hypnosis lies a perplexing question that has still not been solved, namely: is it possible to use hypnotic techniques to make people act against their own will? Even at the time of the robbery, the question dated back nearly two hundred years.

From the beginning, hypnotism was regarded with suspicion. The technique surfaced in the late eighteenth century at the hands of German physician, Franz Anton Mesmer. Believing that the hypnotic trance was induced by waving the hands around the body of the subject, he termed it 'animal magnetism'. By 1784, the French Government was so concerned about the power of the mysterious technique that it launched a commission to study the phenomenon. The commission concluded that the magnetism was effective to 'an amazing extent', that it was a 'great power . . . at the disposal of the magnetist' and that it was certainly capable of controlling people.

Following instructions while in a trance was one thing, but could ordinary people be hypnotically programmed to commit crimes? In 1787 the French Academic Commission of Animal Magnetism concluded that they could. A century later the argument was still raging when physician Jules Liegeois suggested 'a number of splendid crimes' to hypnotic subjects in 1884, lined them up in front of a group of witnesses and had them perform 'murders' with wooden daggers and cardboard pistols. Liegeois had his subjects kill, perjure themselves, lie, sign impossibly vast cheques to him and donate large sums of money to charity—all at his command.

Not everyone agreed that it was possible to force hypnotic subjects to break the law. In a landmark experiment at the Salpêtrière Hospital, where hypnosis had been revived in the late nineteenth century, Giles de la Tourette hypnotised a woman named Witt, then instructed her to commit a series of crimes in front of an audience of medical professors and magistrates. Acting under de la Tourette's instructions, Witt proceeded to 'shoot', 'stab' and 'poison' the audience until, as one observer noted, 'the floor was littered with corpses'. When the audience had dispersed, however, de la Tourette's students attempted an experiment of their own. They stood Witt, still in a hypnotic state, in front of them, told her that she was alone in the room and that it was time to take a bath. Then they ordered her to undress. Witt, who had apparently murdered a roomful of people, was suddenly seized with shame, 'threw a violent fit of hysterics' and woke up—convincing de la Tourette that hypnotism could *not* be used to force people to perform anti-social acts. This seemed about right: recognised wisdom held that it was impossible to force unwilling subjects to perform acts alien to them. But no one could prove it.

As academics at the Salpêtrière debated the ins and outs of hypnotism, the technique found a wider audience. By the 1860s hypnosis had become a staple in circus sideshows and theatre revues where, as today, the public wondered at the power of the mysterious phenomenon. From such shows, it soon made its way in to popular Gothic fiction, where it began to exert a powerful hold on the public psyche. Perhaps inevitably, the hypnotist (almost invariably male) was represented as a dark, evil controller, manipulating innocent victims (almost invariably female) to his own ends.

In Dracula (1897), Bram Stoker portrayed the vampire with evil, flashing eyes that mesmerised his victims; Alexandre Dumas later wrote a number of stories dealing with the subject. But it was George du Maurier's *Trilby* (1894) that hammered hypnosis into the public domain. In the book an evil Austrian musician, Svengali, uses hypnosis to control a beautiful, tone-deaf English girl called Trilby O'Ferrall. Svengali programmes her to become an operatic diva, leading her on a tour of Europe's theatres to great acclaim. Her friends try to intervene and are discarded: she has been conditioned to forget them. The message is not hard to discern: '[Hypnotists] get you into their power,' warns one of the book's heroes, Sandy, 'and just make you do any blessed thing they please—lie, murder, steal, anything! And kill you into the bargain once they're done with you!'

Trilby is programmed to waste away and die should she ever be separated from Svengali and, following his fatal heart attack, that is what happens. Her tragic demise, with the novel's none-too-subtle anti-Semitic leanings, propelled hypnotism into the public consciousness. *Trilby* was one of the best-selling novels of all time—200,000 copies were snapped up in the United States in the first year after publication. Such was its popularity that at one point George du Maurier had to retreat into hiding.

In the meantime soaps, songs, toothpastes and even a town in the US were named after his heroine. The hat she wore in the book is still known as a trilby. The novel inspired Gaston Leroux's *The Phantom of the Opera* in 1910, and the term 'Svengali' entered the public lexicon. To some extent, *Trilby* is still responsible for the public perception of hypnosis as an insidious form of mind control.

When Palle Hardrup's 'Hypnosis Murders' reached the Danish press in 1951, hypnosis was back in vogue but for different reasons. With the furore generated in 1949 by the strange confessions of Cardinal Jósef Mindszenty, there were clandestine rumblings about the technique, and whether the Soviets were using it for their own, Svengali-like purposes.

The CIA was at the head of those interested in the phenomenon. Was this what the Soviets were using? Perhaps. An early CIA document on the Mindszenty case reports that 'It is a reasonable certainty . . . that confessors in high-level trials of political or propaganda significance in Russian-dominated areas are prepared by hypnosis'.

The document goes on to state that the hypnotist used in obtaining the Mindszenty confessions was a German Professor Orsós who, with Dr Ferenc Völgyessy ('the best hypnotist in Hungary'), had induced in the cardinal an irrepressible urge to confess to crimes he had not committed. A document a month later concludes, 'It can be said with certainty that the Russians and several Russian-dominated countries are utilizing . . . hypnosis in special and important instances'.

To the intelligence community, techniques capable of coercing people into acting against their own best interests have always been appealing because the actions desired are often—like treason—truly objectionable. Hypnosis held enormous possibilities. In fact, work on the use of hypnosis in intelligence situations had started well before the formation of the CIA, during the Second World War. At one point, according to Stanley Lovell, the Office of Strategic Services toyed seriously with the idea of programming a German national to 'assassinate Hitler in the post-hypnotic state being under a compulsion that might not be denied'. In the course of formulating the plan, Lovell consulted with 'two of the most famous psychiatrists in the country', Drs Karl and William Meninger, along with hypnosis expert Dr Lawrence S. Kubie. They concluded that the plan was unlikely to work: if the hypnotised subject had no motive for the killing, it would be impossible to persuade him to carry it out. The plan might work if they could find a subject suitably bitter towards the Nazis—but if they found such a man, wouldn't it be easier just to *ask* him to do it?

Lovell agreed the plan was flawed until another hypnotist arrived from South Carolina and announced that he might be able to solve the problem. To demonstrate the power of his technique he hypnotised two GIs, giving them a post-hypnotic suggestion that they would return to his office in an hour, whereupon their feet would begin to itch uncontrollably. In the meantime Lovell arranged for the OSS's deputy director of Intelligence, Brigadier General John Magruder, to visit the office and witness the result. The idea was that the soldiers would not dare to remove their footwear and scratch in front of him. An hour after they were dispatched, however, both men came in, sat down, began to look uncomfortable, then proceeded to remove their boots and scratch. When asked why they had done this, they were baffled. Magruder was impressed. Lovell was characteristically blunt. 'Horsefeathers!' he exclaimed. 'What private in the whole US Army wouldn't enjoy taking off his shoes and socks before a general when he knew in advance he couldn't be disciplined for so doing?' 'It's a wonder,' he concluded, 'they kept their pants on!'

Stanley Lovell was not alone in exploring the military applications of hypnosis during the war. A US Army doctor, J.G. Watkins, was also intrigued, and contrived a series of experiments to demonstrate the operational use of the technique. In one, he hypnotised a soldier and attempted to convince him that he was back in the front line. 'In a minute,' Watkins told him, 'You will slowly open your eyes. In front of you, you will see a dirty Jap soldier. He has a bayonet, and is going to kill you unless you kill him first. You will have to strangle him with your bare hands.'

Ten feet in front of the soldier Watkins placed the director of the Neurological Psychiatric Division of his hospital, a lieutenant-colonel. When he was satisfied that the soldier had absorbed the fantasy, he instructed him to wake up. 'The subject opened his eyes' he later reported. 'He then slanted them and began to creep cautiously forward. Suddenly, in a flying tackle, he dove at the Lieutenant Colonel, knocking him against the wall and with both of his hands (he was a powerful, husky lad) began strangling him'. It took three more staff members to prise the soldier off his victim.

In a repeat performance another soldier was given the same post-hypnotic suggestion and nearly killed a colleague. He happened to have a penknife in his pocket, pulled it out and tried to stab his target. Watkins, now convinced that hypnosis and warfare went well together, devised a couple of further experiments that can't fail to have impressed CIA analysts when they read about them later on. They involved interrogations and the results were, frankly, glorious.

In the first experiment a US Army corporal was given a post-hypnotic command to drop into a trance every time he was handed a yellow pencil. He was then instructed not to disclose to Watkins a 'secret' that a Captain S told him. Watkins reminded the soldier that if he did, he would be disobeying a direct order from a senior officer. The soldier, who clearly thought this would be a walk in the park, guaranteed that the secret would be safe. He then went into a huddle with Captain S. Finally, flashing Watkins a defiant expression, he sat down. Watkins handed the soldier the yellow pencil, whereupon he fell into a deep trance. He then gave the man an order:

> **WATKINS:** I am Captain S. I just gave you a piece of information you were not to divulge. I want to see if you can remember it, Corporal. What is it?
> **SUBJECT:** Company B will leave at 12.00 tonight.
> **WATKINS:** [removes subject from trance] Did you divulge the message?
> **SUBJECT:** No, and you can't get it out of me.

Watkins repeated the experiment with an extra incentive:

> **WATKINS:** What is this I'm putting in front of you?
> **SUBJECT:** Why, that's a $10 bill!
> **WATKINS:** I want you to try again. I shall ask Captain S to give you another message. That $10 bill is yours if you do NOT tell me the message. Do you understand?
> **SUBJECT:** It's in the bag.

The corporal was told another secret by Captain S. He returned to his seat and stared intently at the ten-dollar bill on the table. Watkins handed him the yellow pencil. He fell into a trance and revealed the secret. When awakened, he was jubilant: 'The ten-dollar bill is mine, isn't it?'

WATKINS: Let's try it once more. This time you can earn the $10 bill if
you will just stay awake. Do not go to sleep. Fight back and refuse to go
into a trance.

SUBJECT: (belligerently) That's easy. Just try to put me to sleep.

WATKINS: (hands subject the yellow pencil. Subject blinks a moment or
two, then sinks back into a deep trance).

Watkins's greatest coup was a wonderful demonstration of the powers of
hypnosis in interrogation. The experiment took place in an army theatre
in front of two hundred military staff. This time the victim was a member
of the Women's Army Corps (WAC):

WATKINS: If you were captured by the Germans, how would you answer questions asked you?

SUBJECT: With my rank and serial number, nothing more.

WATKINS: You're certain of that?

SUBJECT: Certain.

WATKINS: Let's pretend that I am a German military intelligence officer
and you are a POW. Remember, you will tell me only your name and
serial number.

The WAC rating was put into a trance, whereupon Watkins opened the
interrogation:

WATKINS: I am your First Sergeant. I have a few questions to ask you.
What is the name of the installation where you are stationed?

SUBJECT: The Aberdeen Proving Grounds.

WATKINS: What part are you in?

SUBJECT: The WAC detachment.

WATKINS: About how many are there in the WAC detachment?

SUBJECT: Oh, about 1500 girls.

WATKINS: What do you do?

SUBJECT: I'm assisting with a research project.

WATKINS: What kind of research project?

SUBJECT: We are developing a new secret type of fuel for propelling
rockets.

WATKINS: Do you know how this fuel is made?
SUBJECT: Of course, I have watched them make it.

At this point a senior officer ran onstage and grabbed the microphone. 'I think we've gone far enough,' he announced. 'In the interests of military secrecy, we'll have to stop at this point.' Watkins's conclusion was that it was indeed possible to make subjects reveal sensitive information during interrogation using hypnosis. In fact, once they got going, it was hard to stop them.

The Palle Hardrup case created consternation in Denmark. Quite apart from the press assertion that Hardrup had been hypnotically silenced by a sausage, there was the matter of his exercise-book confession, in which he had stated categorically that he had been coerced into robbing the bank and shooting dead the two tellers by his former cellmate.

Bjorn Nielsen was rearrested, and the police grilled him to prove that he was behind the robbery. But there was some dispute as to whether this was really the case. Nielsen refused to admit it, and Hardrup was rambling like a maniac. When Nielsen and Hardrup were put into a room alone together, their conversation threw up as many questions as answers. In his confession, Hardrup had confessed to robbing the Folkebanken in Hvidovre in August 1950, saying that he gave the money from the robbery to Nielsen. Nielsen took issue with this statement:

HARDRUP: I gave the money to you.
NIELSEN: I'm not going to continue with this conversation if you keep
    on lying to me. You must say that you didn't do this—that I didn't get
    the money and you didn't rob the bank.
HARDRUP: OK. I withdraw that statement. I didn't rob the bank.

Was this evidence of Nielsen's continuing hold over Hardrup? Or was Hardrup just trying to shift the blame on to his friend? Other exchanges demonstrate that, in direct contradiction to the police theory, Hardrup was far from the innocent he was making himself out to be. In fact, on the tape, Nielsen comes across as the less-educated man: he was dyslexic and did not argue well. Hardrup argued fluently. At one point Nielsen became so confused by the conversation that he suggested that he himself might have a split personality and that perhaps he had persuaded Hardrup to rob the bank but couldn't remember it. Not quite the Svengali the press was making him out to be.

The Danish police appear not to have noticed the contradiction.

Nielsen was sent to Max Schmidt, who performed a battery of psychological tests on him, concluding that he was a criminal psychopath 'who bluffs and deceives others' but who was able to get people to trust him without limit. Nielsen denied everything, telling Schmidt that Hardrup's exercise-book confession contained 'the ramblings of a madman'.

Hardrup, meanwhile, had been sent to the Psychiatric Department of Copenhagen Memorial Hospital. There, Dr Paul Reiter, an expert hypnotist, set about trying to break into Hardrup's conditioning to determine exactly how Nielsen had programmed him to commit the crime. But this proved more difficult than he had expected.

Reiter's initial attempts to hypnotise Hardrup were unsuccessful. For two months, in May and June 1952, nothing happened. Tests revealed that Hardrup was unusually suggestible, so should have been an ideal candidate for hypnosis, but he refused to succumb. Yet if he had been put into a trance before, he should have been easy to hypnotise. However, the more Reiter tried, the shallower the trances became. When Reiter pushed harder, Hardrup woke up. Asked why, he explained that as he was going under he became more and more relaxed until the point where he felt as if he was drifting off to sleep. Suddenly a rush of painful emotions would jar him awake.

Reiter drew two possible conclusions. First, his patient was insusceptible to hypnosis. This seemed unlikely: not only had all the suggestibility tests come back positive but Hardrup admitted having been hypnotised, repeatedly, in jail. The second possibility was more disturbing: that Hardrup was indeed highly hypnotisable—but that someone else had got there first.

The idea that one hypnotist could block access to a subject from another hypnotist was not new. In theory it is possible for a hypnotic candidate to be instructed not to succumb to further hypnotic induction. In fact, this was one of the things that had brought the technique to the attention of the CIA.

Credit for the introduction of the Agency to hypnosis is generally given to George H. Estabrooks, professor of Psychology at Colgate University in New York. In his seminal book, *Hypnotism* (1943), he wrote that the technique had numerous applications in the intelligence world. Most were classified but he was willing to expound on a few.

The first was the notion of the 'Hypnotic Messenger'. In this scenario, an intelligence operative was hypnotised and given a secret message. He was then woken and dispatched on a mission, with no recollection either of having been hypnotised or of the message he had to deliver. On arrival at his destination he would be rehypnotised, and the secret message would be released. The advantage of this technique was that if the subject was captured, he could not reveal the message because he had no conscious memory of it. It was also possible to create a 'locking' mechanism in the messenger's psyche so that, should he be captured and his enemy try to hypnotise him, he would prove insusceptible, as was happening with Reiter and Hardrup in Denmark.

In 1971 Estabrooks summarised his theory of hypnotic messengers in an article in *Science Digest*, explaining that he had personally employed the technique in the war. The subject was a Captain George Smith, hypnotised in Washington, DC, and given a classified message to deliver to a Colonel Brown in Tokyo. Estabrooks instructed Smith that he was to forget ever having been hypnotised but told him that if he was given a coded phrase by either Estabrooks or Colonel Brown he would fall into a trance and reveal the secret message:

> I put him under deep hypnosis and gave him—orally—a vital message . . . Outside of myself, Colonel Brown was the only person who could hypnotise Smith. This is 'locking'. I performed it by saying to the hypnotised captain: 'Until further orders from me, only Colonel Brown and I can hypnotise you. We will use the signal phrase "The moon is clear". Whenever you hear this phrase from Brown or myself you will pass instantly into deep hypnosis.'

'The system,' Estabrooks reported, was 'virtually foolproof': the information, locked into Smith's unconscious mind, could be retrieved only by the two people who knew the combination. 'The subject had no conscious memory of what happened,' he wrote, 'so couldn't spill the beans. No one else could hypnotise him even if they might know the signal phrase.'

Other than Estabrooks's own account, there isn't a shred of evidence to indicate that this incident took place. In fact, Estabrooks seems to have been regarded as a joke by the intelligence community. From the mid-1930s he bombarded politicians, military and intelligence staff with his plans to use hypnosis as a weapon. Those with whom he shared his thoughts on the subject included William Donovan, head of the OSS, J. Edgar Hoover, head of the FBI, the US Marine Corps, US Naval Intelligence, the British Embassy in Washington, DC, and Winston Churchill. Churchill appears not to have paid much attention: in *Hypnotism* Estabrooks laments, 'The British are paying a terrible price for refusing to look reality in the face.'

Thirty years after his death it is impossible to prove that Estabrooks was a fantasist, but CIA memos openly disparage his repeated offers of assistance. That he bragged in public to such an extent about his techniques ('I can hypnotise a man—without his knowledge or consent—into committing treason against the government!') and told distinctly tall tales of hypnotic derring-do behind enemy lines indicates that he never got far with them.

But this is not to say that his methods were not investigated by the CIA. As declassified documents reveal, the Agency had been intrigued by hypnosis almost from its inception in 1947. The source of the technique was less than clandestine:

In the September, 1947, issue of Reader's Digest, there is an article entitled 'Do as you're told', which describes the interrogation by the use of hypnosis of a fast submarine captain . . . One of the outstanding features of this method is that when properly used, the person hypnotised has no memory of having done anything but gone off to sleep. There is almost no chance of there being any proof of its having been applied . . . therefore in my opinion we would be safe to use it in this country.

By 1950 the CIA's BLUEBIRD teams were using hypnosis as an adjunct to drug-based interrogations: essentially an offensive form of what in 1936 William Horsley had termed 'narcoanalysis' in the UK. While it was clear that drugs and hypnosis together had some useful effects, it was impossible to determine whether subjects talked as a result of the drugs, the hypnosis, or both. So, as truth-drug experiments continued, the focus of Agency work shifted towards hypnosis as a technique worthy of exploitation.

The CIA's first hypnosis guru was Morse Allen, head of the BLUE-BIRD programme. He took an immediate shine to the technique. Itching to try it himself, he hunted down a suitable tutor, eventually settling on 'a famous stage hypnotist' in New York. This expert regaled Allen with stories that immediately impressed him:

> [Hypnotist] stated he had constantly used hypnosis as a means of inducing young girls to engage in sexual intercourse with him. [Deleted], a performer in [deleted] orchestra, was forced to engage in sexual intercourse with [hypnotist] while under the influence of hypnosis. [Hypnotist] stated that he first put her into a hypnotic trance and then suggested to her that he was her husband and that she desired sexual intercourse with him . . . Many times while going home, [hypnotist] would use hypnotic suggestion to have a girl turn around and talk to him . . . and . . . as a result of these suggestions induced by him he spent approximately 5 nights a week away from home engaging in sexual intercourse.

Well! This all sounded promising! Allen took a four-day course in hypnosis from the expert. Records of his subsequent experiments detail the CIA's gradual evolution from interest in the subject as a means of interrogation, to other, more esoteric goals.

Allen used Agency secretaries as guinea pigs. At first he was cautious, writing about how he had made Miss X or Y's arm feel numb, or having them wander around the room 'performing nonsense movements'. He practised putting the women into a trance and instructing them to forget that they had been hypnotised when they reawakened. He made them ask for a glass of water immediately after waking up. In July 1951 he regressed a CIA secretary to her summer holiday in the Gulf of Mexico, a month earlier. The result was so effective that she relived an experience of falling off a surfboard and woke up choking, having swallowed a mouthful of imaginary seawater. Allen practised putting the secretaries under faster and faster until he could have them in a trance within five seconds. Eventually some became such good subjects that he could merely snap his fingers when they were in the room and they would drop into a deep trance.

Over the next few years the CIA explored the potential of the 'hypnotic messenger'. A 1955 memorandum reports its version of Estabrooks's idea, concluding that it held promise. The unwitting agent 'would not talk because he has nothing to talk about. Furthermore, it is our contention that alcohol, drugs, and/or physical duress would not be successful in recovering the message.'

The same document requests a grant of ten thousand dollars to create twenty such messengers. The idea, reported Allen, was that a hypnotised subject was like 'a blackboard on which a message will endure until erased or blurred by time'. It might be possible, one CIA adviser suggested, to protect the message further by burying it inside the subconscious at a specific date in the subject's past. That way, when the controller wanted the secret to come out, he could regress the subject to that specific date. Any hostile interrogator, even if he was an accomplished hypnotist, would not know which date to search for. But would subjects really be able to protect secrets like this? In 1955 a male CIA officer was hypnotised and given a series of specific instructions:

> During a demonstration with an excellent subject who is still a staff employee of the Agency, the operator suggested 'Any time that anyone asks you any question the answer to which would involve a breach of security, you will immediately fall into a deep coma.' After the subject was awakened, I began to question him about his background, education, where he was employed, what his duties were ('clerical'). I finally asked 'What is the combination of your office safe?' The subject's eyes rolled up, his head fell forward and he entered a deep sleep.

In a later trial, a female CIA officer was hypnotised, given a false codename and told to protect it. She was then woken up and interrogated. She refused flatly to divulge her codename under questioning and, when the word was explicitly stated to her, denied her own false identity in complete innocence, with the statement 'That's a pseudo if I ever heard one!' The technique seemed to work.

Another possibility that emerged early on was the idea of using hypnosis as an aid to learning. Hypnotic subjects appeared to be able to memorise large quantities of complex technical data almost effortlessly. If, as was widely supposed at the time, powers of recall were heightened by the process, it might be possible to programme agents to memorise vast amounts of information while in a trance. This information could then be held in the unconscious memory, inaccessible to potential hostiles unless they knew the correct hypnotic code. It was a neat idea. But would it work?

In July 1951 a group of men was hypnotised and each was instructed to memorise a certain piece of supposedly secret text. They were ordered to release the details only upon receipt of the correct codeword. Subjects were then taken to another room and asked about the document. Every CIA subject proved unable to recall any of the details in the text until the codeword was mentioned, whereupon they regurgitated the entire document, verbatim.

The idea that hypnosis might be used to assist the learning process and to protect secret material from interrogation was shortly superseded by a more ambitious goal. Soon after he began his experiments Morse Allen noted that some exceptional candidates, under hypnosis, could interact normally with other people in the room so that no one other than he would know that they were, in fact, in a trance. If this were the case, it might be possible to turn agents into unwitting 'human cameras'. Hypnotise a CIA secretary and release her into a foreign embassy and she could, unknown to her hosts (and to herself, even), memorise everything she saw and heard. She could also, potentially, be sent in clandestinely to read and memorise classified documents. All the time no one would be able to tell that she was in a trance. 'This test,' he wrote, 'is important in that it would indicate that good subjects under full [hypnosis], could be introduced at cocktail parties, assemblies, and still talk and act normally, yet at all times be in a trance state.'

If hypnosis were to prove useful in intelligence work, Allen realised that the CIA would be hampered by the simple fact that it had few qualified hypnotists. But there was a simple and elegant solution to this problem, as he learned in August 1951, when he managed to hypnotise one secretary and instruct her to fall directly into a trance upon receipt of a codeword from another CIA officer—then do whatever he told her. The secretary went into the next room where she mingled with staff members until the second officer approached and whispered the codeword in her ear. She fell into a trance and, sure enough, followed the second man's instructions. The test, he wrote, was important in that 'it demonstrated that a person having no ability or knowledge of . . . hypnosis techniques can assume control of and run an individual via a codeword'.

When the experiment was repeated in a remote form, the secretary receiving the hypnotic codeword from a stranger by telephone, it proved just as effective. Allen was excited: on the basis of the work done so far, it would be possible for a complete stranger to telephone an indoctrinated individual in a sensitive location, give him a specific codeword, have him fall directly into a trance and follow instructions to the letter. Moreover, if the subject was a good one, the trance state would be undetectable to his colleagues.

Getting CIA secretaries to memorise and protect information appeared simple. The problem was that these women were employees: they could be successfully ordered to do this sort of thing without hypnosis. The real question was whether it was possible to use hypnosis to get foreign agents—*unwilling* foreign agents—to perform acts that they did not want to do. Or, as one CIA memo asks: 'Can we create by post-hypnotic control an action contrary to an individual's basic moral principles?'

In late 1951, Allen decided to find out, encouraging subjects to perform acts they would not normally have agreed to do. It didn't take him long: by the end of September he had got secretaries to flirt with strangers at CIA cocktail parties and to ask nominated individuals to dance. One even approached a complete stranger and sat on his lap. The conclusion was obvious: 'If hypnotic control can be established over any participant in a clandestine operation, the operator will apparently have an extraordinary degree of influence, a control in order of magnitude beyond anything we have ever considered feasible'

For someone with fewer than six months' experience as a hypnotist, Allen was making great headway. Little did he know, however, that while he was working his way through the CIA's secretarial pool, a common criminal had already trumped him in Denmark. Bjorn Nielsen, it seemed, had programmed Palle Hardrup to rob the Landsmands bank, killing anyone who got in his way. But how had he done it? No one knew. That was the problem.

At the Memorial Hospital in Copenhagen Dr Paul Reiter, in charge of assessing Hardrup, was stuck. That Nielsen was behind the crime could only be proved if Hardup revealed what had happened to him before it had taken place. But after two months things weren't going well: Hardup was still 'neurotically tense' and refused to go into a trance. Reiter was convinced that he could be hypnotised, but that Nielsen had given him a 'locking' suggestion to ensure that, should he end up in custody, a police forensic hypnotist would not be able to access their past hypnotic sessions. Reiter called in the big guns.

On 4 July 1952, he instructed Hardrup to stare into the lamp of an ophthalmoscope and sedated him with 3ccs of Citodan. Then he began the hypnotic induction. The result was a 'deep emotional crisis': Hardrup's breathing became fast and shallow and his pulse leaped to 120 beats per minute. He clenched his teeth and screwed his face into an expression of terror. 'No! No! No!' he shouted. 'I can't do it!' Reiter instructed Hardrup to stare back at the ophthalmoscope. Suddenly he went limp and fell into a deep trance.

Reiter had broken into Hardrup's mind; now he had to discover what was in there.

Over the next month Reiter hypnotised Hardrup repeatedly while simultaneously lowering the dose of the sedative he was giving him until Hardrup was falling into a deep trance after an injection of distilled water. Gradually the water injections were phased out. Soon Hardrup could drop into a trance just by looking at Reiter's ophthalmoscope lamp. Eventually this process took under three seconds.

To make him more comfortable with being hypnotised Reiter told Hardrup to imagine small furry animals in the room that approached and huddled up to him for warmth. He seemed to enjoy stroking the imaginary pets. Reiter then told him to imagine old friends and relatives popping in for a chat. Once Hardrup was happy with the hypnotic process, he suggested that together they go back into the past, to explore how Nielsen had programmed him. Hardrup agreed.

Before he started the regression Hardrup was instructed, under hypnosis, that if he were to lie he would feel terror, sweat uncontrollably and that his pulse would race. As a test he was deliberately instructed to say something that wasn't true. His pulse leaped immediately to 132 beats per minute and he gasped for breath. The system seemed to work. Once they were both comfortable, Reiter put Hardrup into a trance, took him back into the past and asked him what had really happened.

Hardrup told Reiter that Nielsen had never mentioned hypnosis. He called it 'magnetic stroking'. Having persuaded Hardrup that the technique was a portal to all sorts of useful techniques, including the ability to pass through keyholes, walk through walls, travel immense distances in no time at all and even be in two different places at once, Nielsen started the experiments by telling Hardrup to imagine that his arm was stiff and would not bend. Soon the arm was performing strange tricks, apparently outside his control. Without warning it would stand up, become hot, cold or impervious to pain. Nielsen explained that these sensations were caused by an ancient life force that Indian mystics called *prana*. Hardrup bought it.

Then, at the start of June 1947, there was a breakthrough. One night, when Hardrup was in a trance, Nielsen apparently made contact with a 'higher plane'. He jolted as if shocked with electricity and assumed a new voice: 'I am your guardian angel,' he announced. 'You believe that what has happened to you is a misfortune for you. But that is not the case. It has all been to strengthen and test you, in order that you may carry out the mission which it is your destiny to fulfil.'

Nielsen introduced another level into Hardrup to confuse the police further. He was, he told him, not the 'guardian angel' but 'X', the mouth-piece through which the guardian angel spoke. (There was little doubt that Nielsen was X: in court the defence produced a number of written messages from X, which were all in Nielsen's handwriting.)

Through X, the guardian angel instructed Hardrup to fulfil his true messianic role. He was instructed to clean up his act with more medita-tion, more yoga and more 'magnetic stroking'. He was warned that if he mentioned X or the guardian angel to anyone else in prison the relation-ship would end immediately. He was then told that his former friends were obstructing his spiritual progress. 'From this moment on,' X told him, 'you will no longer speak to or address your previous comrades. They will be as the air to you . . . *You must not and will not* have any con-tact with them. You know yourself that it is of supreme importance that you follow my instructions implicitly.'

X also instructed Hardrup to perform other spiritual exercises. He was to become a vegetarian, and was to indulge in fasts for up to three days at a time—giving his unwanted food to Nielsen. He was told that all physi-cal possessions were to be discarded, including his wristwatch ('You feel instinctively how it binds you to this world. You feel it like a physical thought'). Hardrup got rid of the watch and, later, a valuable accordion: he gave them to his cellmate. Money, likewise, was dangerous and should be handed over.

X now told Hardrup that contemplating imaginary crimes was a good way of proving his detachment from the physical world. At first the crimes were small, robbing church donation boxes, but soon they escalated. He was instructed by X to imagine burgling properties around Copenhagen, then to visualise himself shooting random civilians. Eventually he was ordered to imagine murdering his mother, a crime justified as an act of charity towards her. 'Your body feels nothing,' X told Hardrup. 'You are absolutely free. You shoot and shoot again . . . you will carry out the task. I know that you will succeed . . . You know you belong to a higher sphere. You cannot possibly fail me.'

As the pair's release date approached, Nielsen began to prepare Hardrup, telling him that if they were separated, he must always seek contact with X through him. X, meanwhile, would communicate with him by post.

Sure enough when they were both released in October 1949 Hardrup contacted Nielsen. Now it was time for the tutor to find out if his lessons had been absorbed. On their first meeting, X told Hardrup that money was needed to set up a new political party to save the world. He should give seven hundred kroner to Nielsen, who would take care of it—suspiciously, this was exactly the amount Hardrup had been given upon discharge from prison. He handed over the money. At the start of 1950 Hardrup got a job earning two hundred kroner a week; X told him that the money should, likewise, be handed over. When Hardrup's family tried to intervene, X told him to cast them aside: in the celestial realm family was nothing.

X then ordered Hardrup to get married and chose him a wife a local girl called Bente. Shortly before the wedding, X told him to prove his devotion to God by allowing Nielsen to sleep with her. Hardrup, initially reluctant, was persuaded after a couple of days of 'magnetic stroking'. After the wedding, when Bente told Hardrup that she thought Nielsen was a bad influence, X told him to ignore her. If she asked where he was going, he was to say that he was meeting his new political friends—not Nielsen. There were frequent, boozy gatherings, at which X always made an appearance, telling Hardrup to buy the drinks.

That summer, Nielsen prepared Hardrup for the Hvidovre bank robbery. Hardrup was reluctant so yoga, meditation and magnetic strokings were ordered. Then, when he was still apprehensive, Nielsen chloroformed him. God wanted him to rob the bank. His guardian angel wanted him to rob the bank. What was the problem? Hardrup agreed. In the meantime, Nielsen showed Hardrup a place in the woods where he was to hide the money from the robbery. The date was set for 21 August.

When the day came, Hardrup took the day off work and cycled round Copenhagen, panicking. He couldn't go through with it. That evening he met up with Nielsen, and X made an appearance, telling him to try again. Two days later, he did. On the morning of the robbery, to ensure that there were no mistakes, Nielsen met up with Hardrup and the pair meditated together. Then he gave Hardrup a large glass of schnapps and bade him good luck. A couple of hours later, Hardrup relieved the Hvidovre Folkebanken of 21,000 kroner (about nineteen hundred pounds). As instructed, he took a taxi to the woods and handed over the money.

Six months later, the money from the first crime was gone. X told Hardrup to move himself and his wife into a smaller flat to keep costs down—so that Hardrup could give more money to Nielsen. When his wife objected, Hardrup was instructed to tell her he wanted a divorce. As if that wasn't enough, X then decided that Nielsen should test Hardrup by sleeping with her again. Bente refused, whereupon Nielsen hit her. Hardrup stood by and watched.

Just after New Year 1951, X ordered Hardrup to rob the Landsmans Bank, and to persuade Bente to make a drawing of the street and the branch in question: if he was caught, it would look as though she had planned it. Finally, if he was arrested he was to tell the police about his plan to unite the Scandinavian nations with DNKP. If he liked, he could talk about his guardian angel. But the names 'X' and 'Nielsen' were never to enter the equation. Then it all went wrong. On 29 March 1951, Hardrup was caught after he had attempted to rob the bank, and shot dead the tellers.

Dr Reiter, wide-eyed, was convinced he was on to the truth. But was it really possible to programme someone so thoroughly through hypnosis? Unfortunately, the only people who might have been able to advise him weren't saying anything. They were working for the CIA.

As Agency officials learned the ins and outs of hypnosis, potential uses for the technique in intelligence work multiplied. In May 1953 hypnosis was incorporated into MKULTRA as Sub-project 5 (it would continue in sub-projects 25, 29 and 49) under Alden Sears at the universities of Minnesota and Denver. According to the sub-project's classified file, the CIA was interested at this point in five main areas:

EXPERIMENT 1   N-18 Hypnotically induced anxieties to be completed by September 1.

EXPERIMENT 2   N-24 Hypnotically increasing ability to learn and recall complex written matter, to be completed by September 1.

EXPERIMENT 3   N-30 Polygraph response under hypnosis to be completed by June 15.

EXPERIMENT 4   N-24 Hypnotically increasing ability to observe and recall a complex arrangement of physical objects.

EXPERIMENT 5   N-100 Relationship of personality to susceptibility to hypnosis.

Deliberately inducing anxiety was thought to be useful in interrogation—or possibly in discrediting exercises; preparing CIA agents hypnotically might enable them to beat a polygraph (lie detector) test if they were captured. Experiment 7 was an afterthought: 'Recall of hypnotically acquired information by very specific signals'—in other words, once the 'human camera' had been loaded with intelligence, they would be presented with a specific sound or codeword that caused them to download their database of memories.

Of all the CIA's work on hypnosis the most intriguing was the idea of hypnotically programming people to break the law. It was a notion that, if the research panned out, would offer 'unlimited opportunities to the operating officers'. But, and this was what the Agency referred to as the '$64,000 Question', could it be done?

Morse Allen's initial experiments had been tentative, rather like elaborate party tricks. But as he explored the possibilities of forcing people to do things they didn't want to do, they appeared more like operationally useful techniques. In September 1951 he programmed two female CIA staff members to fall into a trance upon receipt of a codeword over the telephone, then to follow orders delivered by a stranger.

[Subject] was told that she would go to the small room containing [deleted]'s safe and seat herself at [deleted]'s desk. She was given the combination of the safe. She was told that she would receive a telephone call from an individual . . . who would, during the conversation, mention a codeword to her and she was instructed that upon hearing the codeword . . . she

would proceed to the safe, open it, search the safe, and find a given Top Secret document . . . conceal it on herself and proceed to the ladies' room,
where she would wait for another girl to approach her.

The first secretary waited for the phone call, was given the codeword, and
fell into a trance. She opened the safe, stole the document and took it to
the lavatory where, as instructed, she handed it to another CIA secretary,
also in a trance. Both women then returned to their respective offices and
fell asleep. When awakened after the experiment, neither could recall anything about the incident. The Agency concluded that such operations
might be useful not only for gaining access to sensitive documents but also
for use on foreign individuals who might be 'compromised and black-
mailed'.

By now, stealing classified documents under hypnosis was bread-and-
butter stuff to the CIA. Much of Morse Allen's experimental budget for
1953 was spent on the production of a film, *The Black Art*, to be shown to
Agency employees. In it, an Oriental diplomat is drugged and hypnotised
by a US agent. He enters his own embassy, opens a safe, steals a pile of
classified documents and hands them to the American. 'Could what you
have just seen be accomplished without the individual's knowledge?' asks
the voiceover.

'Yes!'

'Against an individual's will?'

'Yes!'

'How?'

'Through the powers of suggestion and hypnosis!'

A week after the stolen-document experiment Allen upped the ante,
hypnotising one of his star pupils to see how far she would follow instructions:

[Subject] was told to open her eyes and shown an electrical timing device.
She was informed that this timing device was an incendiary bomb and was
then instructed how to attach and set the device . . . the timing device
was to be carried in a briefcase to [deleted]'s room, placed in the nearest
electrical light plug and set for 82 seconds, and turned on . . . She was to return at once to the operations room, sit on the sofa, and go into a deep
sleep. The experiment was carried out perfectly without any difficulty or

hesitation . . . the entire experiment from original instruction to conclusion consumed 27 minutes.

On the same day he programmed a pair of secretaries to enter a room in which they were told they would find an unconscious man. They were to approach him quietly, rifle his pockets, steal his wallet and run away. Once again, both women acted perfectly.

But if CIA secretaries could be made to steal or to plant bombs, what *else* could they be made to do? 'Can we,' asks one memo, 'induce a hypnotic condition in an unwilling subject to such an extent that he will perform an act for our benefit? Could we seize a subject and, in the space of an hour or so, by post-hypnotic control have him crash an airplane, wreck a train, etc.?' Although they admitted internally that the whole concept was 'frightening—a kind of double think Orwellian world', Agency experts now became interested in the possibility of programming agents to kill either themselves or others under hypnosis.

The idea of a hypnotised assassin was interesting not because there was a shortage of killers for hire in the 1950s: CIA conduct throughout the first half of the Cold War indicates that the Agency was more than capable of finding hitmen. The real advantage of a hypnotised assassin was that, if he was caught, he would have no idea why he had committed the crime or who had put him up to it. If the system really worked, there would be no tracing the true source of the hit. An amnesic assassin was a perfect assassin.

Initial thought on the matter of hypnotised assassins was that it might be possible. A consultant told the CIA in 1952 that

> Individuals could be taught to do anything including murder, suicide, etc.
> This would be difficult, but I believe it could be done by a careful process
> of conditioning a person psychologically while under a hypnotic state, set-
> ting the stage for the act, as it were. I do believe that you could carry out
> acts that would be against an individual's moral feelings if they were rightly
> psychologically conditioned.

In reality, however, getting people to perform anti-social acts under hypnosis is a great deal harder than the popular press might have us believe. As Giles de la Tourette's experiment demonstrated, when subjects are instructed to do something genuinely unacceptable (such as when Witt was told to undress in front of a room full of male observers) it is notoriously hard to make them comply. But, analysts reasoned, there might be a neat solution to this problem.

Lloyd Rowland, a civilian at the University of Tulsa, had demonstrated the idea thirteen years earlier. In 1939 he had built a wooden box with a curved glass front and lit it so that the glass was invisible to the observer. He put a large rattlesnake into the box, fitted the glass front and shook it vigorously until the snake was well and truly angry. He hypnotised a number of subjects, told them that there was a piece of rubber tubing inside the box, then instructed them to reach in and pick it up. All of his subjects tried to pick up the snake; one even tried to smash through the glass to get to it. In a follow-up experiment, Rowland persuaded the subjects to throw a glass of sulphuric acid into the face of a lab technician, who was likewise protected by the curved glass shield, by telling them that the glass contained distilled water.

Rowland figured that if the subjects were hypnotised and told to do something dangerous or illegal, they would refuse. But if they were given an imaginary scenario in which the required behaviour was acceptable, they might carry it out. The idea has some merit. If a laboratory subject is instructed, under hypnosis, to fling himself out of a tenth-storey window, he will almost certainly refuse. If, however, he is led to believe that he is on the ground floor and that the building is on fire, he might just do it. A later CIA document posits a similar scenario: 'Suppose that while under hypnosis a subject is told that a loved one's life is in danger from a maniac and that the only means of rescue is to shoot the person designated as the maniac? Three expert practitioners . . . say that there is no doubt that in such circumstances murder would be committed'. It was this notion of creating a 'pseudo-reality' that Morse Allen seized upon for his next experiment.

On 10 February 1954, in Building 13, Allen hypnotised two CIA secretaries. One was told to fall asleep and not to wake until she was given the proper codeword. The other was instructed to try to rouse her. When the sleeping secretary failed to wake up, the second secretary was to become enraged—so enraged that she would pick up a pistol from a nearby desk and shoot the sleeping woman. The shooter, who had previously refused to touch the pistol and expressed fear of all firearms, carried out the 'murder', with no idea that the gun on the desk was not loaded.

★ ★ ★

Although the CIA's early hypnosis experiments were characterised by a certain innocence, they were tempered with a degree of arrogance. In 1955, the Agency examined the case of Palle Hardrup in Denmark to see if they could learn anything from it. It seems that they couldn't: the officer concerned dismissed the hypnotist, Bjorn Nielsen, as a 'rank amateur' for getting caught in the first place, and especially for not burying details of the crime deeper in Hardrup's mind, as any 'experienced operator' would have done.

For an 'amateur', though, Nielsen seemed to have done a pretty good job. Hardrup had fallen under his control, given him all his possessions, including his food, got married on command, and robbed two banks, killing two men. And if that wasn't enough, Nielsen had covered his tracks by making Hardrup believe God had told him to commit the crimes, via his guardian angel. Nielsen was only the messenger-boy: 'X'.

Paul Reiter was impressed. To discover whether Hardrup really could be programmed to such an extent, he now tried to programme him. He told him that the letter P was significant and that whenever he heard him announce it he would fall into a deep trance. It worked. To find out how powerful his programming was, Reiter telephoned Hardrup's prison and had a warder fetch him from his cell. Over the phone, Reiter simply said, 'P.' His assistant, monitoring the experiment inside the jail, reported that 'a far-away look immediately came into Hardrup's eyes'. He released his grip on the telephone and collapsed on to the floor, refusing to wake up until the assistant held the phone to his ear and Reiter instructed him to do so. In a further test, Hardrup was given a closed envelope. Inside, in Reiter's handwriting, was a note: 'Greetings from P—Reiter'. Hardrup fell into a trance.

By October 1952, Reiter had made sufficient headway to demonstrate his programming to police officials and the lawyers preparing to argue the case in court. He gave Hardrup a post-hypnotic suggestion that the next time he woke up he was to ask the first man he saw his name, his age, when he had left school and what had made him choose his current career. In front of all the trial lawyers, including Nielsen and his defence team, Hardrup confronted the police commissioner with just these questions. He was put into trance again and told to experience no pain. Reiter then shoved sharpened matchsticks under his fingernails. Hardrup didn't flinch.

To demonstrate the power of his 'locking' suggestions, Reiter offered a defence witness, hypnotist Dr E. Geert Jorgensen, the chance to hypnotise Hardrup. Jorgensen was unable to break through the conditioning. Reiter even allowed Nielsen to have a go. Nothing happened.

Four months later Reiter's programming was almost complete. He proved it by persuading Hardrup to perform post-hypnotic suggestions a full week after they were given to him. At one point he instructed Hardrup to call the prison warder, complain loudly about the food and throw it on to the floor at his feet, then fall into a sound sleep. Hardrup, reported Reiter, acted 'like an automaton'. Perhaps, after all, the CIA could have learned from the Danish case.

Meanwhile, the CIA had run into problems. The Agency men, intent on using hypnosis to make foreign agents commit treason—or worse— understood that there was a huge difference between getting someone to 'break the law' in a laboratory and getting them to break the law for real. As long as research into this phenomenon was conducted in make-believe situations, there was no way of knowing whether any of their plans would work operationally. This was a problem that the Agency seems to have appreciated early on. A memo in January 1954 requests thoughts on how the CIA should go about testing their techniques for inducing illegal actions: 'In short, how long can we go along these lines and I am not referring to the 'college-type' experiments?' The next month, it was decided to find out.

> As a 'trigger mechanism' for a bigger project, it was proposed that an individual of ***** descent, approximately 35 years old, well educated, proficient in English and well established socially and politically in the ***** government be induced under ARTICHOKE to perform an act, involuntarily, of attempted assassination against a prominent politician or if necessary against an American official.

The individual concerned was a former CIA asset who had recently become uncooperative. The plan, labelled 'hypothetical', was to drug him at a cocktail party, kidnap him and then, in a single session, hypnotise and instruct him to perform the assassination. After the killing was done, 'It was assumed that the SUBJECT would be taken into custody by the ***** government and thereby "disposed of".'

The ARTICHOKE team eventually decided that the operation was probably not possible since the subject would be an unwilling participant and that one session was not long enough to programme him properly. Also, if things went wrong, the guy might go AWOL and spill the beans. They were, however, willing to give it a go. 'Under "crash conditions" and approximate authority from headquarters, the ARTICHOKE team *would* undertake the problem in spite of the operational limitations'.

The problem was still not solved, though, as was noted at a committee meeting later that month. All present agreed that what was needed was not a hypothetical trial but a real one. Money was made available for further research into the plan, which apparently had 'great merit'. While it was acknowledged that there were 'drastic moral problems involved', work was to be carried out to determine whether this would work or not and 'just how far human beings can be controlled . . . using ARTICHOKE techniques'. A year later the committee was still debating, and commented that there was 'no way of obtaining answers which we can trust short of trying our knowledge in operational situations'.

While the CIA doesn't appear to have been reticent about trying new techniques in 'operational situations', in this case there was a further complication that made a practical trial tricky. The target of a hypnotic attack who knew nothing of it would, in all likelihood, be hostile to it. Clearly, such subjects were unlikely to sit still and allow themselves to go through a standard hypnotic induction. How could they be hypnotised? Two immediate techniques sprang to mind.

The first revolved around a method of forcible hypnotic induction utilising a 'magic room'. MKULTRA sub-project 43, under the University of Oklahoma's Dr Louis Jolyon West (who would kill Tusko the elephant a couple of years later) suggested the construction of a unique laboratory containing a 'special chamber' in which all aspects of physical environment could be minutely controlled by the operator.

A later CIA document explained how it worked. In the room, unwilling subjects would be forced to *believe* that they were succumbing to hypnotic induction, even if they were fighting it. 'A number of devices,' wrote West, 'would be used to convince the subject that he is responding to suggestions.' Hidden heaters could be used to warm the man's hand when he was instructed to feel hot. Alternatively he could be persuaded under hypnotism that cigarettes would taste bitter, then presented with a doctored cigarette. 'With ingenuity,' he concluded, 'a large variety of suggestions can be made to come true by means unknown to the subject.'

Once the subject believed that, despite his best efforts to resist, he was indeed under the hypnotist's influence, he would give in and allow himself to fall into a trance. It was a neat idea and might have worked but it was a bit too theoretical for the CIA. The 'magic room' was a complicated piece of kit that couldn't easily be transported into the field where it was needed.

The other idea for forcible hypnotic programming, and the one that showed most promise, was the 'rapid-induction' technique, which brought about a trance state so fast that the subject didn't have time to mobilise his defences against it. To perform this 'peculiar and somewhat dangerous' technique, the hypnotist grabbed the subject's neck with his left hand while simultaneously using the right to push the head back as far as it would go. Then the fun began.

> The operator then presses the right thumb and index finger against the vagus nerve and carotid artery on each side of the Adam's apple, and pressure is exerted with both fingers . . . While the right hand is operating as described above, the left thumb and second finger are pressed firmly against the neck just below the mastoid behind each ear. This is also done to produce a slightly detached feeling. While these pressures are being applied, the operator then 'pours on' the suggestions.

The result was immediate unconsciousness through lack of blood to the brain followed, hopefully, by a trance state. However, if it went wrong, it went really wrong: 'instant death' was a possible side-effect. The doctor who recommended it reported that he had used the technique successfully to cure cases of stuttering, alcoholism, smoking and masturbation.

By the end of 1961 the CIA was convinced that rapid induction was the technique for them. Now, though, they had a new method which didn't involve hampering blood flow to the brain but laying hands on the subject's forehead and shouting at him—ordering him to go to sleep. The technique appeared to rely on the shock of the approach. Sometimes it worked, sometimes not.

In 1963 the Agency finally had a chance to test it for real. In June, counter-intelligence staff sent a cable to Mexico City asking whether there were any potential candidates available 'among station assets'. The next month the Mexico station came up with a low-level informant suspected of working for the KGB. Two CIA men lured him to a local hotel where the hypnotist, who had just flown in from California, was waiting for them. At a given signal, the two agents grabbed the subject's chair and flung it—with him—on to the floor, ready for the hypnotist's grand entrance. Only, there was no grand entrance. The hypnotist had got cold feet and was cowering in the room next door. A later memo reports, unhappily, that the rapid-induction technique needed to be returned to the lab for more investigation: 'A great deal of work and effort by [deleted] staffers and agents was wasted, and a great deal of emotional energy was expended to no purpose.'

Which, as it happens, is a pretty good summary of the CIA's entire Manchurian Candidate programme. From the available documentation, it is not clear when research into hypnotic induction ceased, but a 1975 document concluded that, while there had been extensive work into the phenomenon through the 1950s and 1960s, 'There are no records of hypnosis being used in the field.' After all this research, the CIA says that the project was abandoned before it could be applied.

Is that true?

It's impossible to tell. As one commentator wrote in the 1970s, the CIA is 'in the lying business': if the Agency had succeeded in creating a Manchurian Candidate, there was no reason on earth why it would want to advertise it. But there are good reasons to believe that the CIA was telling the truth. For a start, modern experts generally agree that hypnotising people to break the law, and especially to commit such a serious crime as murder, is not possible.

Laboratory experiments have succeeded in prompting subjects to behave in strange and anti-social ways. Subjects have indeed 'stolen', 'lied', 'become violent' and even 'killed'. But what does this prove? As numerous academic papers have concluded, subjects placed under hypnosis are unusually susceptible to suggestion: that is why they succumb to the technique.

In hypnosis experiments, hypnotists are usually doctors, teachers, or in the case of CIA or military research, senior officers: authority figures. It is not necessary to look further than Stanley Milgram's famous experiments on obedience (Milgram persuaded volunteers to administer 'fatal' electric shocks by telling them simply that it was necessary for the experiment) to discover that most people will do as they are told, as long as the person giving the order is authoritative and appears to know what he is doing.

In addition, candidates selected for such experiments have invariably been hypnotised by the experimenter a number of times before the trial. In the course of the earlier sessions they have learned that nothing bad will happen to them. So, in the Rowland experiment when subjects were told to pick up a rattlesnake, they knew, deep down, that there was no danger. They trusted the experimenter.

To test whether someone under hypnosis might break the law for real, it would be necessary to use a hypnotist unknown to the subject, make them do something illegal, then face the consequences. The chance of any reputable hypnotist agreeing to such an experiment are negligible. Moreover, even if such an experiment were designed, and were to work, there is no guarantee that it would work twice, or that the same technique could be used successfully on another subject.

For the CIA, this was a serious problem. If you're in the business of killing people clandestinely, you need to be sure of two things: first, that the assassination will take place, and second, that the killer will not reveal who put them up to it. If these two factors cannot be established with some degree of certainty, a highly risky operation becomes unacceptably dangerous. It might have been possible to build a Manchurian Candidate and to have them assassinate someone—but what if it went wrong? What if the hypnotic programming wore off? What if a CIA-programmed assassin was caught? The consequences didn't bear thinking about.

There were more prosaic reasons why the Manchurian Candidate programme was never put into active service. The main advantage of a hypnotised assassin was that he would be amnesic and not capable of revealing who had hired him. But as one MKULTRA official commented in the 1970s, the number-one candidate for assassination at the time of the hypnosis programmes was Fidel Castro. Even in the 1960s, everyone on the planet, including Castro, knew that the Agency wanted him dead. A number of CIA assassins had already botched the job, and some had gone public. What was the point? The whole thing was just too much hassle. 'A well-trained person,' recalled another MKULTRA veteran, 'could do it without all this mumbo-jumbo.'

Not everyone agrees, of course. One dissenting voice is that of Milton Kline, an unpaid consultant to the CIA who worked with Alden Sears on various MKULTRA sub-projects. In the 1970s Kline commented that hypnosis *could* be used to create a Manchurian Candidate: 'It cannot be done by everyone. It cannot be done consistently. But it can be done.' Perhaps he was right. Who's to tell?

More than fifty years after the CIA's hypnosis programmes began, no plausible evidence of hypnotic programming of individuals, other than the experiments cited in this chapter, has emerged either from inside or outside the Agency. David Rhodes, a long-serving MKULTRA official, later told an investigator, 'Creating a Manchurian Candidate is a total psychological impossibility, but it is intriguing; and it is a lot of fun.'

'Fun' might not have been the word chosen by either Palle Hardrup or Bjorn Nielsen to describe their experiences in Denmark. When their case came to trial in June 1954, the country's entire press corps was camped outside the courthouse. Inside, Hardrup's lawyers did their best to prove that he had committed the crime under the influence of Nielsen's hypnotic programming. Nielsen's lawyers, meanwhile, argued the opposite. Police and psychiatrists were split down the middle. Dr Reiter, who had clearly taken a shine to Hardrup, gave a seven-hour statement, concluding that Hardrup was indeed a killer but that he wasn't to blame: he had committed the crime without being conscious of what he was doing. Hardrup's lawyer painted Nielsen as a 'limitlessly cynical and deadly criminal'. 'With his eyes,' he concluded, 'Nielsen directed his "friend", who acted like a mechanical doll.'

A month later the judge instructed the jury to consider three key points: whether Nielsen had planned and prompted the robberies; whether he had planned and prompted the murders and whether he had used hypnosis or some other kind of excessive influence on Hardrup. In his summing up, he agreed that Nielsen had indeed exerted a 'systematic influence' over his *protégé* that had been something *like* hypnotism but stopped short of saying either that the control *was* hypnotism or that it had specifically caused the crimes.

The jury was less equivocal. In July 1954 Nielsen was convicted on all three counts. Both men were sentenced to life, Hardrup in a psychiatric institution, Nielsen in a high-security prison. Appeals went on for the next ten years, during which the case was taken to the European Commission of Human Rights at Strasbourg. In 1965 both men applied for a pardon. Their requests were denied. On 24 December the next year, however, Hardrup was released. Six months later, so was Nielsen.

One balmy summer night nine years later, Nielsen telephoned his ex-wife, Titte, and told her he was depressed. The time in prison, the notoriety and the fact that he was more or less unemployable had driven him to desperation. He couldn't stand it any more. It is perhaps ironic that a man supposedly capable of persuading another to rob a bank and kill two men was unable to convince his own ex-wife that he was serious about suicide. Titte told him to get over it. Later that night, Bjorn Nielsen took an overdose of Cyankalium. The next day he was found dead in his flat.

On 5 August 1972, Palle Hardrup gave an interview to Soren Petersen, of the Danish newspaper *BT*. He admitted he had not been hypnotised into committing the robberies or the murders. In fact, when the police had suggested that hypnotism had caused the crimes, he realised he 'might get off the hook' if he agreed. In another interview, Hardrup was asked why he had fingered Nielsen for the crimes. What had Nielsen done to deserve such a terrible fate? 'Nothing,' said Hardrup. 'He just treated me badly.'

6

'Do it': James,
Ray and the Depth Men

HOW MANY TIMES WERE YOU SEDUCED TODAY?
Chances are, you don't know the answer. As far as advertising men are concerned, you're not supposed to know. Their job is to arouse you without you suspecting it.

This very day, every time you looked at a TV commercial, or an ad in print, you very probably were being sexually assaulted by devices your conscious mind cannot detect.

After you read *Subliminal Seduction,* you will see things you never saw before in every ad you look at.

Subliminal Seduction, Dr Wilson Bryan Key, 1973

Christmas 1985 came early for James Vance. He and his friend Ray Belknap were listening to music in Ray's bedroom on 23 December when Ray told him that he had a secret. Silently Ray, a freckle-faced eighteen-year old, reached down behind the stereo and produced an LP record. Grinning, he handed it to James, who flipped it over, examined the cover and matched his friend's grin. Then he frowned: the LP's cellophane wrapper was torn. The record had been played. 'Aw,' said Ray. 'You knew I'd listen to it before I gave it to you!' Then he laughed. 'Merry Christmas, brother!'

The record, which James put on to the turntable immediately, was the 1978 Judas Priest classic, *Stained Class.* James knew it well. A couple of years ago he had owned all of Judas Priest's LPs but, in a fit of madness brought about by love (at the time he was dating a Christian girl who disapproved of heavy metal), he had sold his collection. After the pair had parted company he had regretted the decision, as his friend, Ray, knew. Gradually he had been picking up Judas Priest LPs ever since; *Stained Class* was the last album the two boys needed to complete their collection. James was delighted with the present. After all, The Priest were 'metal gods'.

As the opening track began, James reached for the volume control, and music flooded the room.

Ray was having a good day. That morning he and his mother, Aunetta, had taken his four-year-old half-sister, Christie Lynn, to buy a Christmas turkey. They had then moved on to a local beauty parlour, the Happy Looker, for Christie's first proper haircut. In the chair Christie had looked so cute that Ray insisted on capturing the moment for posterity and rushed home to fetch a camera. Swept up in the emotion of the event, he had decided to have a haircut himself, after which the trio had gone to pick up James from his parents' house at 934 Glen Meadow Drive. Before he climbed into the car, James had left a message for his mother saying where he was going, and the four had headed to Ray's for the afternoon. Aunetta had gone out again, leaving the boys to themselves.

Not that they were entirely alone. On arriving at the house, James and Ray said hi to Ray's pregnant older sister, Rita, who was sitting on the sofa minding her children, then grabbed a couple of beers from the garage and retired to the bedroom. Rita soon noticed that a great deal of noise was emanating from Ray's room. The pair were listening to *Stained Class* at full volume, and singing along heartily. When the album ended, they began working their way through Judas Priest's back catalogue. Occasionally one of the boys would emerge from the bedroom, accompanied by a waft of marijuana smoke, to fetch more beer from the garage.

About ninety minutes after they had come in, James and Ray left the house. When they returned forty-five minutes later Rita noticed that something appeared to have got into them. James asked her whether 'if anything happened' she would name her baby after him. She laughed the comment off: 'Not unless it's a goddamn redhead!' Ray gave her a hug and said he loved her, but added that if she ever told anyone he'd said so he would deny it.

Then James turned to Ray and said, directly, 'Let's go finish it.' Rita wasn't sure what this meant but assumed he was referring to the marijuana.

In Ray's room, the two boys argued. James wanted to listen to *Stained Class* again but Ray wanted Lynyrd Skynyrd, so they skipped some tracks. James's favourite from *Stained Class* was 'Beyond the Realms of Death', a poignant anthem of rejection and teen alienation. In the song a disaffected individual withdraws from everyday life, retiring into the sanctity of his own mind. Friends repeatedly try, but fail, to rouse him from his torpor. Time passes, and the boy begins to vanish from the real world altogether. Eventually he achieves a Nirvana-like state in which the pain and suffering of mortal existence become meaningless. At that very instant he smiles and dies, transcending death itself.

Lyrically, the song is not a million miles away from The Beatles' 'The Fool on the Hill', in which another individual retires to a hilltop eyrie, rejecting the comings and goings of supposedly more balanced people in order to achieve illumination. On paper, 'Beyond the Realms of Death' could be read as an ode to Buddhism. In the light of what happened next, however, the song was to acquire a new, and disturbing, meaning.

By now the pair had worked their way through the best part of a twelve-pack of Budweiser and were getting into the spirit of things. They debated lyrics, played knuckles and, smoking another joint, discussed the future—and the past.

James Vance and Ray Belknap had met at Dilworth Middle School in Sparks, a small suburb next to Reno, Nevada, six years earlier. James, now twenty, was two years older than Ray but had been held back twice in school. In 1979 the boys ended up in the same class. Since then, they had been inseparable. Sick of high school they had dropped out together after their sophomore year and taken a series of menial jobs. This hadn't worked out too well. Ray, who was working for a building contractor, was unhappy because his boss had won fifty dollars from him at pool the night before. He and James decided that the best thing to do was to find the guy, beat him up and recover the money.

James had other concerns. He worked part-time at a local printing press, where the work was dull and the pay worse. The printing ink was filthy stuff that got everywhere and stuck to everything, making employees look 'like you had leprosy'. Neither James nor Ray had a car. Both were flat broke. Neither had a girlfriend. To cap it all, James was due at work at 3 p.m. that day—but the way things were going, that seemed increasingly unlikely.

At three o'clock James's mother, Phyllis, who was due to give him a lift to work, arrived home to find the note saying he was at Ray's. She phoned Ray to see what was up. James had left for work on foot some time ago, he lied; she needn't bother about the lift. Concerned that he might be skiving, Phyllis and her husband drove the route James would have taken to work. When they failed to locate him along the way they stopped at his workplace and discovered, as expected, that he hadn't shown up. They drove to Ray's, where Rita showed them to the locked bedroom.

A shouting match ensued, James's mother and stepfather telling him that if he didn't go to work he'd lose his job, and James replying that he didn't care. He was going to quit: he and Ray were going to work in construction together. Eventually he shouted at them to leave him alone, retreated into the bedroom and slammed the door, wedging it shut with a block of wood.

When James's parents had gone, James and Ray began to plan an alternative future. By four thirty, they were agreed. They turned up the music and began to destroy the bedroom. Ray had a collection of glasses and baseball caps on the shelves above his bed. Everything was swept on to the floor. They screamed and kicked holes in the walls and door. The television screen and mirror were smashed, as was everything else except the stereo—which, of course, they were still using.

At the sound of breaking glass, Ray's sister Rita telephoned her mother, saying that she had better get home fast because the boys were stoned and wrecking the place. Aunetta arrived at five o'clock and, fuming, headed straight for Ray's bedroom.

Ray reached down beside the stereo and produced a Harrington-Richardson twelve-gauge shotgun, a fourteenth-birthday present which the boys had modified by sawing off the barrel. With the weapon in one hand, Ray pulled out a bedside drawer with the other and removed two shells.

Ray's mother shouted for them to open the door and the pair stood, silent for a moment. They embraced. Then, without a word, they opened the window, leaped out on to the street below and vanished into the night.

Convinced that Ray's mother would call the police, or that someone would spot them running down the street with a gun, they ducked into the nearest alleyway, which led to a children's playground behind the Community First Church of God on Richards Way. Ray, who was still carrying the gun, reached the playground first and, breathing heavily, walked over to the roundabout at the south-west end of the yard. James kept lookout at the fence to make sure they hadn't been followed.

Ray stood on the roundabout. 'I sure fucked my life up,' he announced, before sitting down. Ray Belknap—the eighteen-year-old freckle-faced kid who had rushed home to fetch a camera to photograph his sister's first haircut that morning—then placed the shotgun beneath his jaw, wedged the stock into the ground, and pulled the trigger.

Shocked by the sound of the detonation James swivelled round in time to see his friend's body slump to the ground. Then he panicked. What if someone called the police? What if they thought *he* had shot Ray? What was he supposed to do now? Whatever it was, he didn't have long. He walked over to Ray's body, picked up the shotgun, opened and reloaded it. Originally he had planned to put the barrel into his mouth but now it was covered with blood. He put it under his chin. He was shaking. James Vance looked up at the clouds and shot himself.

At 5.13 p.m. in the building overlooking the playground, neighbour Susane Barela heard the first blast and immediately called 911. Someone had been shot, she said. The operator told her to calm down and take her time to explain what had happened. But while she tried to do just that, the second shot rang out.

One minute after the call, patrol officer Dan Kelly was told by the Sparks Dispatch Center that there had been a shooting at the Lutheran church on the corner of First and Richards. He and his partner arrived three minutes later. Seeing the bodies, both officers drew their weapons and searched the playground for the gunman responsible. When the area was secured they turned their attention to the corpses. As they approached the roundabout, they heard a moan. One of the boys was alive.

An hour after the police arrived at the scene, Phyllis Vance received a call from Washoe County Medical Center. Was she the mother of a James Matthew Vance, born on the tenth of December 1965? She was. Well, said the caller, she should come right away. He'd been shot.

Arriving at the hospital, Phyllis was told that the situation was critical. James was in intensive care; he was unlikely to pull through. In the waiting room Detective Sergeant Dave Zarubi informed her that the Sparks police had no idea what had happened. They didn't know who had shot the boys, or even who the second boy was. Phyllis told him he was Ray Belknap, James's best friend, and that his mother lived at 330 Richards Way.

At 7.30 p.m., a police officer and a counsellor arrived at Ray's house and informed his mother that he was dead. Aunetta immediately assumed they had shot him. 'Are you sure? Are you sure it's Ray?' she asked. They explained that Ray and James appeared to have shot themselves. Did she have any idea why they might have done such a thing? In shock, Aunetta was unable to tell the police anything other than how they had left the house: 'They climbed out of the window,' she said.

That evening, police officers searched Ray's room for clues to the mystery. The only thing they found intact was Ray's stereo and, on it, James's early Christmas present: a pristine copy of the 1978 Judas Priest classic, *Stained Class.*

On Boxing Day, police officers David Zarubi and Robert Cowman were finally allowed to see James in Washoe County Medical Center. Face swathed in bandages, he agreed to answer questions by nodding or shaking his head. For answers more substantial than 'yes' or 'no' they gave him a clipboard and a pen. When he was asked if he had shot Ray, he shook his head vigorously. No. He said that they had been listening to music and drinking, and that Ray had been smoking marijuana. They had shot themselves. Asked why, he became animated, waving one arm frantically. Eventually the officers realised he was using his hand to write in the air. They told him to start the message from the beginning: why had they tried to kill themselves? Letter by letter, they deciphered his response: 'L-I-F-E S-U-C-K-S.'

Outside the hospital room, doctors summarised the situation for the detectives. Each boy had wedged the shotgun beneath his jaw, then pulled the trigger. Ray had died instantly but James appeared to have tilted his head at the last moment. When the gun went off, the shot had missed his brain. Instead it had blown off his jawbone, mouth, nose and tongue.

Later that week, Reno attorney Ken McKenna received a call from Ray's mother, Aunetta, who asked if she could come to see him. Assuming she wanted advice on legal aspects of her son's death, he said of course: he'd do anything he could to help. The moment she arrived, however, it was clear that she was after more than advice. Aunetta told him that one of the police officers who had searched Ray's room had noticed the copy of *Stained Class* on the stereo and told her that this kind of music—heavy metal—had been known to cause suicide in teenagers before. Ray's mother held out the LP. 'What do you know about this?' she demanded.

As it happened, McKenna didn't know anything. Heavy metal wasn't his thing. He did know, however, that she was a bereaved mother who needed support. He took the album. 'Let me look into it,' he said.

McKenna stood the LP on his desk and, as he had promised, made some calls over the next week. Originally he had intended to make a few cursory enquiries, then call Aunetta back and tell her that there was nothing in it, that she should let it go. But he soon learned that there was an ongoing court case in California in which heavy metal singer Ozzy Osbourne was being sued by the parents of a nineteen-year-old boy who had shot himself while playing Osbourne's LP *Blizzard of Oz*. There was little doubt that the boy had been listening to the album at the time of his death: when the coroner arrived at the scene, the corpse was still wearing headphones. *Blizzard of Oz* included a song entitled 'Suicide Solution'.

Interesting, thought McKenna. He rang the lawyer handling the Osbourne case, who sent him a pile of information on heavy metal, teenage fans and suicide. McKenna then went to the local university library and did some digging. 'I had no idea what an epidemic teenage suicide is in this country,' he recalls today. 'You start reading stuff on teenage suicide and there's volumes and volumes of material. And it's a terrible thing that teenagers contemplate suicide. There's a ton of professionals trying to figure out why'. McKenna joined them.

The Reno lawyer now began to follow up a theory that heavy metal music could be dangerous. The noise, the rhythm, the image: wasn't it possible that all might combine to create a volatile psychological state in the listener? Eighteen months before the shootings, James and Ray had seen Judas Priest play live in Reno. Afterwards, in James's words, they had 'gone out and terrorised the town'. Together, they had vandalised everything they came across. Couldn't this have been the result of the music?

McKenna researched various other forms of music that caused strange behaviour—African drumming ceremonies and voodoo rituals—looking for common traits. Undoubtedly teenagers used music as a means of escape, often listening to it alone for extended periods. Perhaps prolonged exposure to heavy metal had a psychologically destabilising effect. In the course of his research he discovered a 1940s Czech song about suicide that had apparently provoked a series of deaths. The record had been banned. It wasn't the only precedent. Almost two hundred years earlier Goethe's novel, *The Sorrows of Young Werther*, was credited with a spike in suicides. In fact, to this day, unnaturally high statistics for teen suicides are known as the Werther Effect.

In the meantime McKenna listened to *Stained Class* repeatedly to determine what the lyrics on the album were about. The problem was, he couldn't tell. Like all heavy metal albums, *Stained Class* is extremely noisy, with a great deal of electric-guitar work and wailing going on throughout most of the tracks. McKenna, brought up on the Beatles and the Rolling Stones, found it galling that he couldn't decipher the lyrics on a rock-and-roll LP: he was no prude—but he was beginning to feel like one.

Meanwhile, five miles across town, another Reno lawyer, Tim Post, received a call from James's mother, Phyllis. She suggested that he might like to take on the case for the Vance family. Post, who had misread the newspaper reports, refused—what was the point when both boys were dead? Phyllis put him right: both boys were not dead. James was very much alive, and was now out of hospital. And he was angry. Post told her to bring him over.

Tim Post met his new client in April 1986, by which time James had endured four months of reconstructive surgery. It hadn't made much difference. The lower half of his face was missing and the boy had to hold a towel round his neck so that the continuous stream of his saliva didn't drip on to the furniture.

James's appearance took some getting used to. 'When he came to my office,' Post recalls, 'clients that were coming or leaving all told me the same thing: they said that they had terrible nightmares that night. If he would go to a grocery store or something, the kids would scream and cry and run from him . . . My daughter would panic when she saw him. She would go, "That man! That man!" and she would bury her head in my shoulder . . . He was like the Elephant Man. It was pretty shocking to see in person.'

When James and Phyllis arrived that day, Post didn't know where to look but he asked Phyllis how he could help. She said that the boys had been drinking and smoking before the shootings—but that wasn't why they'd done it. The music, she said, had pushed them over the edge.

Sceptical, the attorney wondered if this was true. 'James,' he asked, 'but for the music would you have tried to kill yourself anyway?' James, who had severe trouble talking, immediately became animated, waving his arms in the air. 'No! No! Something in the music! Something in the music! I didn't want to kill myself!' He began to quote Judas Priest lyrics 'as if they were scripture'. One of the two songs he had listened to before he shot himself, he said, was 'Beyond The Realms Of Death'. The other, 'Heroes End', asked repeatedly why teen idols had to die young. Once again, the song had an apparently innocuous message: the tragic truth that pop stars such as Jimi Hendrix and Jim Morrison burned themselves out, failing to capture the promise of their early careers. In the light of the two shootings, however, the lyrics—together with those of 'Beyond the Realms of Death'—acquired a new, and sinister interpretation. Wasn't it possible that the song could be intrepreted by impressionable fans as advocating early death as a means of achieving immortality?

Post, persuaded, took the case. Now there were two believers: Tim Post, on behalf of the Vance family, and Ken McKenna, on behalf of the Belknaps. McKenna promptly hired another lawyer, Vivian Lynch, renowned as the finest legal brain in the state, and the suit began to move.

The Judas Priest complaint was filed later that year, and designated number 86-3939. The defendants were CBS Records, which handled the band, and the members of Judas Priest. In the complaint it was alleged that suggestive lyrics, accompanied by the music's loud, repetitive beat, had a hypnotic effect on susceptible individuals, especially the largely adolescent audience at whom the music was apparently directed. Judas Priest maintained a 'cult-like' following, so the band's audiences were especially receptive to anti-social suggestions. The combination of all these factors meant that the album *Stained Class*—particularly the songs 'Heroes End' and 'Beyond The Realms Of Death'—led to 'an uncontrollable impulse to follow the suggested behaviour by committing suicide'.

Clearly, CBS Records wasn't going to take this on the chin. The idea that a leading record producer might be putting out LPs encouraging American teenagers to kill themselves was too terrible to contemplate. The company lost no time in hiring representatives of one of Reno's oldest, most respected law firms, Woodburn and Wedge, to defend them. Local attorneys Bill Peterson and Suellen Fulstone took on the case.

Peterson was under no illusion as to the significance of the case for CBS should they lose. 'Oh, the damages would have been in the mega-millions,' he says today. 'The liability in those kinds of injuries—in particular the Vance case, because there was no question but that his pain and suffering was intense and long standing—I think if the court had concluded that [CBS was responsible], the liability would have been many, many millions.'

The CBS lawyers launched a two-pronged counter-attack. First, there was no proof, they said, that Judas Priest's music had anything in it that encouraged anyone to kill themselves. And, second, even if there had been lyrics explicitly advocating suicide, they were protected by the First Amendment, which guaranteed artistic freedom. In addition, they said, Judas Priest was a British band. They didn't work, live or pay taxes in Nevada. It was a frivolous case, which should be thrown out.

Fulstone and Peterson filed papers objecting to everything in the plaintiffs' case that could possibly be disputed. 'They papered us!' recalls McKenna. 'I mean, that's the game. You get corporate attorneys on the other side, they just try to beat you with volume. So this was a paper battle from the beginning. They just came at us with everything they had.'

A year later, the suit was still rolling, and Ken McKenna was still trying to work out the lyrics to the songs. Then, in September 1987, the case took a strange turn.

A chance meeting with a colleague turned up a character who might be able to help. Dr Wilson Bryan Key, a former professor of marketing, had written three huge bestsellers in the 1970s and 1980s about the advertising industry and its use of secret manipulation techniques to make consumers buy things they didn't want. If anyone understood what was going on in the media and how it influenced audiences, McKenna was told, it was Key. When McKenna called, he immediately agreed to help.

Wilson Key's first assignment was to gather together a group of students, have them listen to the album and transcribe the lyrics. When the answers came in, McKenna was relieved: the students hadn't been able to tell what they were, either. He petitioned CBS Records to produce the lyrics.

Then Key did two things that turned the case round. First, he examined the *Stained Class* album cover in minute detail. He immediately found a number of strange anomalies. The record sleeve features a metallic-coloured human head with what appears to be a bullet, or a laser beam, entering the left eye socket and exiting the right temple. A dark red substance flows from the right eye. Key thought that this was suspicious: this album had apparently encouraged two teenagers to shoot themselves in the head, and its cover featured a facsimile of a human head with a projectile passing through it. Then he saw something else and, excited, called Ken McKenna. In the bridge of the nose on the head, he said, was a smaller image of a human silhouette, facing downwards. The laser beam (or projectile) passed directly into the front of this head. The back of the head had been blown away, with what appeared to be fire, or blood, all over it. If this was a coincidence, it was a big one. McKenna showed the hidden image to Tim Post, who made a connection.

On 19 November, 1987, James had been hypnotised and encouraged to relive the suicide. The following exchange took place:

HYPNOTIST: [Belknap] said, 'I sure fucked my life up'?
VANCE: Yes. And then he shot himself.
HYPNOTIST: What happened?
VANCE: Fire came out the back of his head.
HYPNOTIST: His brains came out the back of his head?
VANCE: Fire.

In fact, in two earlier interviews James had said that he saw Ray's brains—or 'fire'—spray out of the back of his head. Tim Post dug out the autopsy report and cross-checked it with James's account. The two didn't match. According to the coroner, Ray's head was a closed wound. No fire, blood or brains had come out of the back. Nothing had come out at all. Why was James saying it had?

Wilson Key suggested that James was not recalling what he had seen that day but a previously implanted image that he had picked up from the album cover. When he was shown the image, James claimed not to have noticed it before. If this was the case, said Key, it was a *subliminal* image, absorbed into James's mind unconsciously. Key might not be an authority on heavy metal or teenage suicide but, he insisted, he was a world authority on the use of subliminal images. And that was what they had here.

The two lawyers were intrigued but didn't think much more of the matter until Key suggested a second link. Were they aware, he asked, that subliminal stimuli were not necessarily only visual but could be auditory? It was possible, he said, that there were messages somewhere inside the album. What kind of messages? asked the attorneys. *Hidden* messages, said Key. *Secret* messages. Hidden messages that might explain why these two boys had shot themselves? Absolutely.

Key passed on the name of a man who might be able to help. William Nickloff was the president of a company called Secret Sounds, Inc., in Sacramento, California. The company specialised in making subliminal self-help tapes. If, he reasoned, Nickloff could put secret messages *into* tapes, he could probably get them *out*. Post and McKenna rang Nickloff and asked what he would need to detect subliminal messages on a rock-and-roll LP. Nickloff said that ideally he would have the twenty-four-track master tape of the album so that each recording track could be isolated and vetted. The lawyers promptly demanded the master from CBS. In the meantime, they hired Nickloff and sent him a copy of *Stained Class*.

By October 1988 the case was in trouble. CBS had filed a motion for summary judgement, which effectively meant that there was no legal basis for the complaint because the album's contents were protected by the First Amendment. If granted, the motion would stop the suit in its tracks. The judge appointed to hear the case, Jerry Carr Whitehead, looked over the submissions and, early in the week of 3 October, rang all the lawyers to request their presence in his chambers on Friday, 7 October. No one was in any doubt that Whitehead was about to grant the motion for summary judgement, and that would be that.

Just in case something had come up, McKenna rang Nickloff in California, 'I think on Wednesday or Thursday,' he recalls, 'and I said, "We're gonna go see the judge on Friday. Do you have anything for me?" He says, "Yes. I've discovered some subliminals." And I went, "REALLY? What have you got?" and he told me. I said, "Put it in writing! Get it to me immediately!"'

That Friday, lawyers for both sides met Judge Whitehead in his chambers. As Whitehead began to read his prepared speech, dismissing the complaint, McKenna stood up. 'Judge', he said, 'excuse me, but it's a different ball game.' He then handed out copies of Nickloff's letter. 'We're not talking about the lyrics any more. We're not talking about the rhythm any more, or the First Amendment. We're talking about subliminal messages.'

Nickloff's document stated that he had found 'below threshold' audio messages in track six of *Stained Class*, 'Better By You, Better Than Me'. The sounds 'resemble human speech and are most noticeable at a center frequency of approximately 50Hz, nominal bandwidth +/−2KHz'. They occurred at 1:30, 1:35, 1:40, 2:29, 2:34, 2:39 and 2:44 of the track and, when isolated and cleaned up, were simple to decipher. The message was the same each time. It appeared to be an instruction: 'Do it.'

The idea of subliminal messages, and their ability to influence people, was not new. The theory had emerged thirty years earlier when an article in the American advertising journal, *Printer's Ink*, announced a revolutionary discovery:

INVISIBLE ADS TESTED:
New Process for TV and Movie
Commercials Stepped up Product
Sales in First Test

The feature, on page forty-four, was the result of a press conference held eight days earlier by a 'motivational research consultant' called James Mc-Donald Vicary. Vicary had invited fifty reporters to a cinema in New York, promising a story. At the conference, he showed the journalists a short film, then turned on the lights and made a sensational revelation. The film, he said, had contained secret messages. Had any of the journalists present noticed them? The reporters exchanged glances. No. They hadn't noticed anything.

Vicary explained that he had modified a piece of equipment called a tachistoscope—essentially a mechanical iris, rather like a camera shutter, that was widely used in psychology laboratories at the time—to flash images at very high speeds on to the movie screen. The flashes, which lasted just thousandths of a second, were imperceptible to the naked eye but were picked up unconsciously. Essentially, the journalists' brains had been absorbing Vicary's messages without their being aware of it. The experiment, he said, had profound implications for the modern media.

He then handed out a press release detailing a similar experiment he had recently completed. It had taken place over a sixteen-week period in a movie theatre in New Jersey. During that time 45,699 unwitting patrons had been repeatedly exposed to the flash-frame instructions 'Eat popcorn' and 'Drink Coke' while watching the feature film *Picnic*. The flashes had lasted just a three-thousandth of a second. In the course of the experiment, he reported, popcorn sales at the theatre had leaped by 57.7 per cent, Coke sales by 18.1 per cent.

Vicary had apparently designed a way of bypassing the conscious, rational mind and plugged directly into the audience's unconscious, creating an artificial desire for popcorn and Coke. He called the technique 'Sub' ('beneath') 'Liminal' ('threshold') perception because it sneaked in under the brain's radar system. Subliminal perception, he explained, was 'a new band in human perception, like FM', the new radio waveband that was catching on at the time. Furthermore, said Vicary, he was already conducting research into the use of subliminal advertisements for a number of major American corporations, including AT&T, Time Inc. and the Ford Motor Company. 'This little technique', he concluded, 'is going to sell a hell of a lot of goods.'

Naturally, the media wanted details. Where were the results? Where was the tachistoscope machine? Could they see it? Vicary reined himself in. Apologising profusely, he explained that full details of the trial and his apparatus were currently part of a patent application with the United States Government. Since the patent had yet to be granted, he had to be careful what he said. The tachistoscope and the exact details of the trial would have to remain secret for now. But, he assured them, 'sound statistical controls' had been employed.

Vicary's press conference was perfectly timed to coincide with a wave of paranoia concerning advertising techniques then in use in America. That same year, the US public had been shocked to read *The Hidden Persuaders*, an exposé of the advertising industry by investigative journalist Vance Packard. In his book Packard explained that recent developments in psychiatry and psychology had been purloined by the advertising industry. The insights of the social sciences were being employed by advertising specialists known as 'Depth Men' not to cure the mentally ill or to learn more about the mind but to sell consumer products. The Depth Men, he said, spent their time identifying and isolating human psychological weaknesses, then working out how to exploit them to peddle more goods. As a result of the use of the new techniques, he wrote, 'Americans have become the most manipulated people outside the Iron Curtain'—and no one had any idea that it was happening.

According to Packard, two-thirds of US advertising agencies were actively using Depth Men to get into their consumers' minds, prise open their psyches and sell more products. The Depth Men, he wrote (of whom Vicary was 'the most genial and ingratiating'), used issues such as sex, death and self-confidence to create needs and wants that the public had never had before, then flogged products to satisfy them. 'The aim,' he wrote, 'is to bypass the resistance of the buying public . . . Man sustains a continual sneak attack on his better judgement.'

In an era when brainwashing was all the rage, this was explosive stuff. Packard's book was at the top of the bestseller lists for most of 1957. So it was no surprise when, receiving news of James Vicary's discovery, the press went for the story. To Vicary's surprise, however, his invention did not receive the positive coverage he had been looking for. When he had told *Printer's Ink* that 'We can take a whole day's commercial effort on one station and boil it down to a five-minute presentation,' he had assumed that viewers would be delighted, since it would give them the rest of the day's TV viewing advertisement-free.

That wasn't how it turned out. *Newsday* called his technique 'the most alarming invention since the atom bomb' and the *New Yorker* declared that, with the technique, 'Minds and not just houses could be broken and entered.' A *Saturday Evening Review* feature by Norman Cousins reported the wider implications of Vicary's invention: 'If the device is successful for putting over popcorn, why not politicians or anything else?' The tachistoscope appeared able to 'break into the deepest and most private parts of the human mind and leave all kinds of scratches'. The best thing to do with Vicary's machine, Cousins suggested, was to take it away, stick it on to an atom bomb and blow it up.

It wasn't only the popular press that was concerned. Aldous Huxley, author of *Brave New World*, saw his nightmares coming true in this new 'horror', predicting that if Vicary's technique was widely applied it would soon become impossible not to buy Coca-Cola or Camel cigarettes, or to vote Republican. 'Within a few years,' he concluded, it would be possible 'to abolish the free-will almost completely'. 'There are no references [in

Brave New World] to subliminal projection,' he wrote, two years later. 'It is a mistake of omission which, if I were to rewrite the book today, I should most certainly correct.'

Of course, if Huxley knew about the technique, his entire circle did too, including the new friend he had recently made, the mescaline, LSD and hypnosis expert Dr Louis Jolyon West ('an extremely able young man, I think'). And, since West knew about it, his sponsors at the Central Intelligence Agency knew about it, too. Naturally, it interested them: might it not be possible to use it to assist with forcible hypnotic induction?

> It might be that in order to lessen the resistance of an individual to the hyp-
> notic induction process, the use of subliminal projection may be consid-
> ered. This technique has achieved success in commercial advertising, as 'Eat
> popcorn' or 'Drink Coke' projected on a screen in certain movie theaters
> for 1/3000 of a second intervals. It may be that subliminal projection can
> also be utilized in such a way as to feature a visual suggestion such as 'Obey
> [deleted]', or 'Obey [deleted]'—with similar success.

The Agency set up a small-scale trial to investigate the possibilities of sublim-inal perception, a fact soon picked up by Vice-President Richard Nixon, who concluded that the technique might be 'politically useful' and de-manded a briefing. According to former CIA officer William R. Corson, the Agency men explained the phenomenon to Nixon, then returned to their laboratories 'content in their beliefs that their efforts were being appreciated'.

While the CIA was running its clandestine trials, America's advertising agencies were milking the subliminal advertising phenomenon for all they could get. In October *Newsweek* reported that 'some 250 advertisers are in-terested in making test runs on theater or TV'. Meanwhile, various broad-casters were trying the technique on their own. WAAF Radio in Chicago ran subliminal ads encouraging listeners to 'Drink 7-Up' and 'Buy Okla-homa Oil', while WCCO in Minneapolis ran subliminal messages warning of ice on the roads, reminders to mail Christmas cards and to promote up-coming broadcasts—when President Eisenhower was due to address the nation, the station ran a subliminal plug, warning 'Ike Tonight!'. Soon, other companies sprang up, selling the technique across the country. One was Precon Process and Equipment, which told a Wall Street reporter that it was designing a new technique capable of teaching schoolchildren their multiplication tables while they were watching TV.

Some saw the technique as a target for satire. US comedian Stan Freberg opened a TV commercial for Butternut Coffee in 1959 with a warning that the advertisement contained subliminal messages. Then, while elephants cavorted around a stage beneath a firework display, 'SUBLIMINAL' flashed on and off the screen in huge letters. The advertisement won a number of awards. This advertising in-joke has been retold, in different formats, more or less continuously ever since.

The net result of all this coverage was that James Vicary's 'experiment' was catapulted into the public domain. By 1958—just nine months after his press release—41 per cent of Americans polled on the subject professed to having some knowledge of subliminal advertising. Awareness of the experiment has stuck with us ever since: ask anyone you know about subliminal or flash-frame advertisements and the chances are they'll tell you about 'Eat popcorn, drink Coke'. So efficient was the rumour mill concerning the technique that by the 1980s, when the 1958 poll was repeated, American public awareness had increased to 81 per cent.

So, it wasn't all that surprising that there was consternation when attorney Ken McKenna said that he could prove that the Judas Priest track 'Better By You, Better Than Me' contained the subliminal message 'Do it'. Judge Whitehead, who was familiar with the 'Eat popcorn' experiment, looked over the lawyer's document and changed tack. 'I want briefing,' he told the attorneys. 'I want your arguments. I want your research. We're going to have a hearing and see what's going on here.'

It now became crucial that the court, and the plaintiffs, got hold of the original CBS multitrack master tape of the Judas Priest album to see if there really was a subliminal message on it. But CBS couldn't find it. McKenna and his team had first requested the tape in November 1987, and CBS had provided a two-track copy of the album, but the plaintiffs, and the judge, now said that this was not good enough. Where was the tape? At nine on the Monday morning after McKenna's bombshell announcement, Judge Whitehead ordered CBS to hand over the master tape within thirty days.

To CBS, this was a real worry. The corporation had tried to find it, at one point even hiring a British private detective to track it down, to no avail. No one could remember where they had put it. 'That,' Bill Peterson recalls, 'was a horrible thing to happen to us.'

The attorneys representing James Vance and Ray Belknap's family didn't see it that way. Multi-track master tapes for big bands are extremely valuable. Once they are completed, they are kept in a locked vault in case the album has to be re-engineered, or in case the band wants to release a greatest-hits album somewhere down the line. They don't just go missing. In their minds there was no doubt. CBS *had* the master tapes. They didn't *want* to hand them over in case they showed that something was there. So they had hidden them.

'I *know* they hid them!' laughs McKenna. 'We didn't get them! Where are they? You lost the *masters* to a multi-million-dollar band? Come on! Everything's possible: I mean it's possible that a fairy will fly through the window and leave fifty million dollars on my desk. It's ridiculous! It's ridiculous that they would lose master tapes to an ongoing band that they produce. Ridiculous. Nobody believed it.'

. A multi-national corporation had been taken on by the families of two suicidal boys, and had lost the one piece of evidence that would solve the case? Nearly twenty years later, it still sounds unlikely. Over a breakfast of pancakes at Marie Callender's restaurant in Reno, I put it to Judge Whitehead that if I had been Ray Belknap's or James Vance's attorney, I would have been suspicious about the tapes' disappearance. 'Yes,' he agreed. 'If you were the trier of fact, it might make you suspicious as well.'

While CBS staff considered how they might go about finding the multi-track master tape within the thirty days the judge had given them, Post and McKenna were busy examining the subliminal contents they had already found. It appeared that the track 'Better By You, Better Than Me' was not the only place where something strange was going on. In an attempt to discover more hidden messages, the album was played backwards. More messages were found.

There was a history of this: from the Beatles onwards, bands have occasionally hidden little messages in their albums for aficionados to find. Some have been recorded backwards. On Pink Floyd's *The Wall*, the track 'Empty Spaces' contains what is clearly a reversed human voice. Looped back, the message is revealed to be: 'Congratulations! You have discovered the secret message! Please send your answer to Old Pink, care of the Funny Farm, Chalfont.' Ozzy Osbourne's 'Bloodbath in Paradise' contains a play on a famously offensive line from *The Exorcist*. Ozzy's version, reversed, becomes 'Your mother sells whelks in Hull'.

Not everyone got the joke. It wasn't long before various authorities were convinced that something sinister was going on. In the 1970s fans had played LPs backwards to find something amusing. In the 1980s, religious authorities played them backwards to find something illegal or offensive. The real threat, they thought, was hidden material inciting violence or, worse, satanism. Heavy metal music seemed part of it. In 1982 Robert K. Dornan introduced a House of Representatives bill stating that all LPs containing backwards messages should be plastered with warning stickers. The next year a US pastor, Jacob Aranza, published *Backwards Masking Unmasked* in which he revealed that Led Zeppelin's track 'Stairway to Heaven', the most notorious of all 'satanic' recordings, contained backwards messages stating that 'There's no escaping it. It's my sweet Satan. The one will be the path who makes me sad, whose power is Satan,' and 'Oh, I will sing because I live with Satan.'

So it was with Judas Priest. On the track 'Stained Class' the lyric 'Faithless continuum, into the abyss' played backwards revealed the message, 'Sing my evil spirit'. In 'White Heat, Red Hot,' the line 'Deliver us from all the fuss' backwards apparently became 'Fuck the Lord! Fuck all of you'.

A month after these messages were found, James Vance became depressed. As the third anniversary of the shooting approached, he was hospitalised and placed on suicide watch. On 24 November 1988 he was found unconscious in his bed, having apparently taken an overdose. Five days later, just before midnight, he died. He was twenty-three.★

Had he lived, James would have enjoyed the day, nine months later, when Judge Jerry Whitehead ruled on the case. On 23 August 1989, Whitehead issued a fifty-four-page order, discussing the nature of free speech, artistic self-expression and the First Amendment. It was true, he said, that speech was protected in the United States. But there were certain exceptions to this rule. The First Amendment did not protect speech, for example, if it incited violence or if it was libellous. He had to decide whether subliminal messages fell into one of these categories.

★ James's lawyer, Tim Post, believes that this was more than just bad luck. 'I'm absolutely positively convinced that there was foul play,' Post told me on 29 June 2005. The authorities disagreed.

Whitehead ruled that subliminal messages, delivered without the knowledge or consent of the recipient, violated the right to privacy. They also violated citizens' rights not to be assaulted with speech when they didn't want it. Most importantly, since subliminal communications did not encourage thought, discussion or the free flow of ideas—which, after all, was the point of speech in the first place—they were not really 'speech' at all. And if they weren't speech, they weren't protected by the First Amendment. CBS's motion for summary judgement was denied.

James would have loved it: his case was going to trial.

When news got out that a British heavy metal band was being sued for putting subliminal messages into one of their LPs, the press had a field day. Washoe County Courthouse was besieged. Outside the front door there were vans full of Judas Priest supporters, demanding that the charges be dismissed. Inside, print jounalists jostled for position, trying to get access to the case's main players. At one point Tim Post was cornered in the gents' against a urinal by a plummy-voiced foreigner. He turned out to be a correspondent for *The Times*. 'This guy pumped me for information while I was in there going to the bathroom!' He laughs. 'It was incredible!'

Shortly before the trial began, CBS's lawyers suggested that it might be easier to have the judge try the case rather than a jury. James Vance, in his horribly disfigured state, would have made a tremendously sympathetic witness so Post and McKenna had originally insisted on a jury, but now that he was dead there didn't seem much point. Besides, since the judge had ruled for them in the pre-trial motion and appeared to be on their side, they agreed.

The absence of a jury left open other possibilities. The jury room was now filled with broadcasting kit so that the entire proceedings could be transmitted live on television; the Judas Priest trial was the first ever transmission for *Court TV*. This made the case even more accessible to the media. By the time the trial began, in the summer of 1990, the world was watching.

Soon after they had taken on the case, CBS's lawyers had decided that the best way to defend the corporation was to rely on scientific evidence regarding subliminal perception. But in the meantime they set out to make a case that James and Ray were disturbed and would have committed suicide anyway. Peterson and Fulstone hired private detectives to dig into the boys' backgrounds. Despite Ray Belknap's mother's assertion in court that 'my son was very well adjusted', it wasn't long before evidence emerged that both boys had a chequered personal history.

Ray had been disciplined at school for 'inappropriate aggressive sexual behaviour' and had been caught shoplifting and sent to a probation officer. He had also previously stolen $450 from an employer, fled the state and been given a thirty-day suspended sentence. Further police charges included citations for truancy and underage drinking, and one for animal torture earlier in 1985: he had taken to shooting his neighbours' cats with a dart gun.

Before his death, James Vance hardly painted his friend in a positive light. He told police that they had discussed getting automatic weapons and 'committing mass murder'. At one point he had told his mother, 'Ray and I are going to go and shoot some people.' Clearly he thought Ray had taken the idea seriously: in his hospital bed three days after the shooting, Jams wrote, 'Thank God he killed himself before he killed someone else.'

Vance himself was hardly a paragon of virtue. He had been expelled from school for breaking another boy's jaw, and his mother admitted that he sometimes became physically violent with her. At one point he had grabbed her by the throat and tried to choke her. On another occasion she had walked into his room to find him lying on the bed listening to music. He had stood up, shoved a pistol into her face and said, 'I'm going to shoot you.' He had punched her, splitting her lip and necessitating hospital treatment. A couple of years earlier, he had broken her nose. 'He was seriously weird,' recalled James's ex-girlfriend, Lisa Davis. 'He talked a lot about killing other people.'

Before his death Vance had also admitted to using drugs extensively, starting with marijuana at the age of just three. At one point, he said, he was using a gram and a half of cocaine every day. Other drugs he enjoyed included LSD, crank, barbiturates, angel dust, amphetamines and heroin. Five months before his suicide attempt, he had checked into a drug rehabilitation centre, complaining of blackouts and flashbacks. When asked by a counsellor if he had a favourite hobby, he replied, 'Doing drugs.'

At the rehab centre, James had given the impression that he saw his predicament as hopeless. When asked what his perfect career would be, he had thought for a moment, then answered, 'Janitorial work.' This wasn't quite true. In fact he had applied to, and been rejected by, the army twice; since then he had decided to become a mercenary. Asked by another counsellor to name something that was good about life, he was unable to think of anything.

This kind of material was music to the CBS lawyers' ears. In an attempt to demonstrate the futility of both boys' lives, they followed up the 'mental-illness' angle as hard as they could. Sometimes they pushed a bit hard. Private investigators had discovered that Ray's sister, Rita, had herself attempted suicide a number of times. Bill Peterson thought that this might indicate that there was a family problem with depression, so he grilled her on it. The moment she burst into tears, he regretted it: Rita made a sympathetic witness. Peterson's children, who were in court watching the proceedings, later gave him a rocketing for being so unkind.

Unfortunately, grilling witnesses under cross-examination was not the limit of CBS's efforts to discredit the plaintiffs. The corporation had also hired private detectives to investigate the lawyers representing the two families—and apparently struck gold. It turned out that attorney Ken McKenna had a brother on Death Row for murder and that his partner, Vivian Lynch, had previously had her licence to practise law revoked. At the start of the trial, this information was leaked to the press.

On the day the news broke, Vivian Lynch arrived at court in tears, whereupon both she and McKenna were summoned to Judge Whitehead's chambers where they explained what had happened. Whitehead, livid, demanded to know who was responsible for the smear operation.

Authorisation appeared to have come not from the Nevada lawyers but from staff at the CBS headquarters in New York. Since a representative from New York was in court, Judge Whitehead decided to even the score. The lawyer concerned was not licensed to practise in Nevada so was not legally under his jurisdiction. At the start of the day's play, Whitehead tried to remedy this, instructing lawyers from both sides to stand up and identify themselves to the court. If CBS's New York lawyer got up, she would place herself under his jurisdiction. Fortunately for her, Bill Peterson realised what was going on. 'Do *not* stand up,' he whispered, 'and if he asks you why you haven't, then tell him that you are the client and not the attorney.'

Wisely, the CBS lawyer did as she was told. 'She saved her butt!' laughs

McKenna today. 'If she'd said that, he would have sanctioned her, he would have turned her in to the bar. He was prepared to unload on her, and she skated. I respect him for trying on our behalf. I thought it was brilliant!'

Judge Whitehead, still fuming, summoned CBS to his chambers and told them he was going to sanction the lawyer concerned anyway. When reminded that this was impossible for technical reasons, he pulled back but made clear to Peterson that this would not be allowed to lie. 'He said, "All right,"' recalls Peterson, '"but I'm going to take care of this after the case is over."' Eventually Whitehead did take care of it; the smear operation proved costly for CBS.

In court, the issue now turned to the subliminals. Did they exist? Since they had been ordered to turn over the multi-track master tapes, CBS had managed to locate the master for one song only. As it happened, the song was 'Better By You, Better Than Me'. It was taken to a series of recording studios where technicians for both sides pulled it to pieces in an attempt to locate the hidden message. But the sound could not be isolated to one track of the tape, implying that whatever was there was the result of a series of noises combining to create something that *sounded like* 'Do it' rather than a deliberately planted message.

No matter. A noise that sounded like 'Do it' was clearly audible on the LP. Even if it had not been put in deliberately, CBS was responsible for the album and had to face the fact that even an accidental subliminal might have caused the boys to shoot themselves. Now the real arguments began.

As suspected from the outset, the case's outcome now hinged on who could provide the most convincing scientific testimony concerning the effectiveness of subliminal stimuli. It became necessary to look back at the history of the subliminal phenomenon, and to separate fact from fiction. It soon became clear that the origins of subliminal stimuli were not nearly as conclusive as they seemed.

In 1957 James Vicary had told the US press that he had managed to increase sales of popcorn and Coca-Cola in a movie theatre in New Jersey using subliminal flash-frame images. In the midst of the media panic that ensued, he was summoned by the Copy Research Council and told to demonstrate his technique for them in New York, under the eye of the US Psychological Corporation. The demonstration was a failure.

Not long afterwards Vicary was again asked to demonstrate his technique by the Federal Communications Commission in Washington DC. In January 1958 his audience included a number of congressmen, representatives of regulatory bodies and journalists. The message 'Eat popcorn' was subliminally flashed over a broadcast, but at the end of the show nothing happened. No one was sure what they were supposed to be eating. The only person who thought he had seen something was a Senator Charles E. Potter, who commented helpfully, 'I think I want a hot dog.'

For Vicary things went from bad to worse. In the aftermath of his experiment, he was approached by a magazine called *Motion Picture Daily*, and asked which movie theatre he had used to conduct his original popcorn experiment. Vicary gave the location of the theatre in Fort Lee, New Jersey. But when a *Motion Picture Daily* reporter rang the cinema's manager, he was told that there had been no increase in popcorn or Coke sales over the last year. Apparently everything was normal.

In the spring of 1958 at Hofstra College, Long Island, psychology undergraduate Stuart Rogers decided to investigate. Having discovered the location of the 'Eat popcorn' trial from *Motion Picture Daily*, he hopped into his 1949 Plymouth Sedan and drove the thirty miles over the Hudson River to Fort Lee. He soon found the cinema and knocked on the door. Rogers, who went on to become clinical professor of Marketing at the University of Denver, immediately smelled a rat: Vicary said he'd flashed the messages to 45,699 people in six weeks. But the cinema wasn't big enough to accommodate so many over that period. Rogers buttonholed the theatre manager. What about the experiment? he asked. The manager shrugged his shoulders. He didn't know anything about it.*

'Eat popcorn', it seemed, was a hoax.

Further tests on subliminal advertising soon indicated that the technique was ineffectual. In one famous trial, the Canadian Broadcasting Corporation flashed the subliminal message 'Phone now' 352 times during the Sunday-night TV show, *Close-Up*. Nearly five hundred viewers wrote in afterwards to say that they had felt either hungry or thirsty. Nobody telephoned.

By mid-1958, the papers were openly reporting there was no proof that

---

* A number of academics have since searched the US Patent Office for Vicary's tachistoscope application. Neither a patent nor an application for one has ever surfaced.

subliminal advertising did anything at all.★ Then, mysteriously, everything went silent. In June that year James Vicary upped sticks and left town.

Four years later, *Advertising Age* tracked Vicary down and persuaded him to talk about the 'eat popcorn' experiment. In the interview he said that there had been a leak in 1957 and that the press's premature coverage had thrown him off-balance, pre-empting his conclusions. Then he made a startling confession: 'Worse than the timing, though, was the fact that we hadn't done any research, except what was required for filing a patent. I had only . . . a small amount of data—too small to be meaningful. And what we had shouldn't have been used promotionally'.

The revelation that 'we hadn't done any research' should have put the story to bed for good. But it didn't. Vicary's experiment had touched a nerve. People liked it. As a result, while debate in professional journals ceased, the story was relegated to the domain of the Sunday colour supplement, the popular-science magazine and, ultimately, hearsay. There, subliminal advertising might have died a slow, unlamented death but for another maverick researcher who emerged ten years later to relaunch it—with an intriguing new twist.

I met Dr Wilson Bryan Key at his home, just south of Reno, in July 2005. It had taken me some time to track him down: of his four books on subliminal advertising, three were out of print, and the publishers of the fourth had no idea where to find their author. One company representative assured me that he was dead. When this proved not to be the case I gave Key a call and we arranged to get together.

Wilson Key is an imposing figure who walks with a bandy-legged gait—the result, he says, of a lifetime spent parachute-jumping. His leather belt sports an impressive MENSA buckle. He has huge hands, a shaved cannonball head, and stands perhaps six foot one; even in his eighties, this

---

★ The CIA agreed with them after a series of trials of its own in a movie theatre in Alexandria, Virginia. According to officer William R Corson, the message 'Buy popcorn' was flashed at civilian audiences over a number of nights. Instead of following the instruction, however, the audiences made a bee-line for the drinking fountain. In the spring of 1958 the Agency concluded that 'There are several mighty leaps in [Vicar's] logic.' Admittedly, it might work sometimes, but at others it might force people to do the exact opposite of what you wanted them to do. Ultimately there were so many variables that 'its operational feasibility is exceedingly limited'.

is not a man with whom you would choose to start a fight. Unfortunately, I suspected that at some point in our meeting I was going to have to.

We headed out to a local restaurant he recommended, which turned out to be Kentucky Fried Chicken. As he drove me there in a car the size of a couple of bolted-together grand pianos, he began to talk about the Judas Priest case. The moment he'd heard *Stained Class*, he said, he had known that something strange was going on. The whole theme of the album was suicide. All heavy metal music, he said, was about suicide. 'The bands were playing with it,' he told me. 'The kids knew about it. Their parents sure as hell didn't!'

In 1985, to learn more about heavy metal, Key had attended Judas Priest concerts in Sacramento and at the University of Texas. He was intrigued at the extent of the satanic imagery. The whole event, he realised, was a 'passion ceremony': the lead singer addressed his 'acolytes' in tight leather trousers with a tail—'Of course, everybody knows the devil has a tail.' Meanwhile the kids in the audience greeted the music by raising their fists in the air, forefinger and little finger extended like horns: the sign of the devil. Band members gathered around a motorbike and whipped it, and there were skulls in abundance.

The moment Key appreciated the scale of the spectacle, he calculated how much it had cost to stage. After a bit of research he concluded that it was in the realm of half a million dollars. CBS, he said, owned twelve bands this size. 'Nobody,' he assured me, 'ever made as much money out of music in the history of the world as CBS Records on the heavy-metal rock thing.'

Hyperbole aside, Key had a point. Judas Priest is employed by CBS for one purpose only: to make money. Lots of money. When you're talking about millions of dollars, it stands to reason that the corporation will do almost anything to maximise the return on its investment. If a band's sales could be increased by slipping subliminal messages into their songs—for this kind of money—*woulnd't they do it?* But Key has been making this point in his books for more than thirty years. He usually uses it as the launching point for his next argument, which is hugely speculative.

Key believes that James Vicary's 'Eat popcorn' experiment only scratched the surface of the subliminal phenomenon. In his opinion, Vicary nearly blew the whistle on one of the great conspiracies of our time: the use of subliminal advertising to generate implausible amounts of money for international marketing corporations around the world. He has expounded this theory in his four books, at least three of which were international bestsellers. He is the reason that we have heard about subliminal advertising—and why a large percentage of the world still believes in it.

Wilson Key first came across subliminal advertising when he was a professor of Mass Communications Studies at the University of Western Ontario, Canada, in the early 1970s. At UWO he lectured on all sorts of things including journalism, art and, occasionally, psychology. One day in the middle of a lecture he had a revelation. 'The first one was, I think, an illustration in *Esquire* magazine,' he says. 'I was lecturing to the class on this particular article—it was on one of the beatnik poets of the day. And I looked at the picture, I think it was of him, a painting of him upside-down. And there on the bookshelf behind him was an erect penis as a bookstand. I walked around the table. "Jesus Christ! That shouldn't be there!"'

Key now began to scour newspaper and magazine advertisements, holding them sideways, upside-down or against the light. He put his eyes out of focus and scanned them: he knew there was something else in there. Where was it? The more he looked for subliminal images, the more he found. Within three months, he had a two-foot pile of magazines in his office. He enlisted his students to help him. 'I got them interested,' he recalls. 'It was almost like participating in a revolution!' Then he made a crucial discovery: 'The S-E-X Business'.

The S-E-X business was so simple it was beautiful. By inserting hidden pictures of sexual images, advertisers made potential customers take notice of their products. An erect penis here, a pert breast there: if they were masked cleverly enough, the magazine readers wouldn't notice that anything was amiss. But their unconscious minds, attuned to such subliminal images, *would*. Subliminal sexual images attracted unconscious attention the way that girls in miniskirts turned men's heads on the street. Readers were biologically programmed to respond.

But advertisers were not only using images of sexual organs in their pictures: they had also discovered that the letters S-E-X, hidden in advertisements, prompted the same response. Although the reader might not be consciously aware of them, his unconscious mind would pick them up and alert him to the fact that something racy was going on. Better buy the product.

Key admits that James Vicary and Vance Packard could have made the same discovery, but they did not have the necessary background. He, however, had been trained by the US Army where he was 'in intelligence for a time'. Working on interpretation of aerial-reconnaissance photographs during the Second World War, he was instructed that if something looked too normal, too perfect, 'somebody is putting one over on you'. Everything was to be mistrusted.

Advertising agencies had reckoned without the likes of Key and his army intelligence training, so they were in for a surprise when, in 1973, he published his first book, *Subliminal Seduction*. In it he stated that each year $20 billion was spent in the US on advertisements alone. Of this, an 'enormous proportion' went into subliminals. Everyone was a victim of subliminal manipulation.

Key's presentation was extremely effective. He was a professor at a reputable university and knew how to write convincingly. He had, he said, tested hundreds of advertisements on students in laboratory conditions, and proved that subliminal advertisements worked. An ad for Gilbey's Gin, for example, originally featured in *Time* magazine, made unwitting students in laboratory experiments feel emotions ranging from 'uncomfortable' to 'somewhat loathsome' to 'hideous, like a monster'. Only after the experiment was over were they encouraged to look at the ice cubes in the gin glass, where there was concealed, cunningly, a full-on orgy featuring three women and two men. Every ice cube in the advertisement featured the word S-E-X.

But Key's real masterstroke was to include photographs in his book. Readers buying a copy of *Subliminal Seduction* could examine real advertisements for Cinzano, Playboy, Sprite, Chivas Regal, Bacardi and Camel cigarettes and try to locate the breasts, penises and S-E-Xs for themselves. When they failed, he told them where to look.

Subliminal Seduction was an immediate bestseller. As a result, he says, it generated extraordinary jealousy on his university campus. Academics weren't supposed to be writing bestsellers. They were supposed to produce weighty tomes that no one read. Shortly after the book came out he was told that the faculty wanted him to leave. This created a problem. Key had recently been awarded tenure, effectively meaning that he wasn't sackable.

It's hard to know exactly what went on behind the scenes at the University of Western Ontario. Perhaps Key is right and his colleagues were jealous. Quite possibly, however, a prestigious academic institution didn't want its reputation sullied by a man who was, by now, seeing pornographic images in everything he came across. By his own admission, one of his classes involved taking students outside and making them lie on the grass to examine the clouds for smutty pictures. 'You'd be astonished,' he laughs today, 'at the filth that's floating around up there!' Key was eventually paid $64,000, tax free, to leave. Despite the fact that Key recognised that the 'filth' concerned was entirely in the minds of the beholders, this was all a bit too much for the university authorities.

Subliminal Seduction was followed up by *Media Sexploitation, The Age of Manipulation* and *The Clam-Plate Orgy*—this wonderful title came from an advertisement at a Howard Johnson's restaurant featuring a plate of fried clams. Key concluded that the picture contained nine human figures engaged in an orgy—with a donkey. All told the same story but some took the argument further. Kent cigarettes, for example, were successful because you have only to substitute the E in the name for a U and you have another word; teenage boys are aroused by *Playboy* magazine not because it contains photos of curvaceous nudes but because it is laced with subliminal images, and the Sears catalogue apparently contains 'fascinating perversities'.

As Key sensationally discovered in the course of his research, subliminal images were nothing new; neither were they exclusively the preserve of advertising agencies. Michelangelo had used them, as had Picasso, Rembrandt and Titian. The US five-dollar bill contained the word SEX embedded in Abraham Lincoln's beard. Most famously, Key discovered that Nabisco's Ritz crackers contained the word SEX baked into each side twelve times. All of these, of course, were scientific discoveries.

In the Judas Priest trial, Key was the first expert witness to come on board. It was Key who noticed the subliminal images on the record sleeve, and Key who recommended scouring the LP for audio subliminals. In court, he showed his video of the Judas Priest concert—in which he demonstrated that the musicians were masturbating their guitars while the enraptured audience made satanic signals—and presented some of his examples of subliminal advertisements. In them he pointed out hidden death's heads, fellatio, Christ figures, screaming men, testicles and the penis on the Camel cigarette packet. The judge was not persuaded.

To Wilson Key, Judge Whitehead's scepticism was proof that the court was against him. 'The judge showed prejudice against our side almost from day one,' he recalled, over lunch. 'Me particularly! I've been in court quite a few times as an expert witness, and I won't take any shit from these people. They . . . kept trying to get me to answer yes or no, and I said, "Look, I'm a psychologist, I don't work like that, I don't know any question about human behaviour that I can answer with a simple yes or no. It's not that simple." So at one point, or a few points, he threatened me, citing me for contempt of court.'

It's perhaps not surprising that there was friction. At one point, according to Key, he was asked what religion he was. He refused to answer. When asked why, he said that it was none of the court's business and pleaded the Fifth Amendment. This apparently, did not impress Judge Whitehead. In Kentucky Fried Chicken Key recalled, bitterly, that Whitehead was a 'sonofabitch'. (Whitehead was reluctant to go on the record about his impression of Key. When pushed, he paused and thought for a moment before declaring, 'I remember Dr Key.' Then he sat silent, eyebrows raised.)

With such an expert witness, it was clear that the Vance and Belknap families were going to need further scientific support in court. Their alternative expert was everything that Wilson Key was not. Dr Howard Shevrin, a professor of Psychology at Michigan State University, was one of the world's foremost experts on the subject of subliminal perception. In court, Shevrin explained that although there was a lot of bunkum in the popular press about the phenomenon, subliminal cues really *could* produce certain effects and that there was a long and reputable scientific literature to prove it.

Shevrin argued that subliminal commands were effective because the recipient was unable to work out where the order was coming from. If a command is given to us overtly, we can decide whether or not it makes sense, whether it's a good idea and thus whether to obey it. But if the order appears out of nowhere, it sneaks up on the unconscious and bypasses our logical thought mechanism. To the listener, subliminal suggestions appear to be the results of decisions that he (or she) had made themselves.

While CBS's lawyers recognised that Shevrin's credentials were unassailable, they had little trouble in gathering a triumvirate of well-respected psychologists to demolish most of what he said. Tim Moore, of the University of Toronto, testified that a lot of experiments purporting to prove the powers of subliminal suggestions were scientifically flawed, and that those that weren't showed that the suggestions didn't have enough impetus to make anyone do anything concrete. Anthony Pratkanis, of the University of California, likewise testified that subliminal suggestions were highly suspect. To prove it he cited experiments in which he had given laboratory subjects subliminal self-help tapes, misleading them about the tapes' content. Ultimately, volunteers who thought they had been listening to self-confidence boosters testified that they felt more confident, even though the tapes they had heard were supposed to enhance memory. Testing afterwards showed that neither memory nor self-confidence had been boosted.

Finally Don Read, of the University of Lethbridge, addressed the question of backwards speech. He described an experiment in which he had played backwards messages to university volunteers, who were invariably unable to understand them. In fact, volunteers could not tell if they were statements or questions, or even whether a sentence contained real words or just nonsense. In another experiment, given a multiple-choice test that should have increased their chances, students were unable to tell whether the backwards messages they were hearing were Christian messages, satanic messages, pornographic messages or nursery rhymes.

Of all the expert witnesses, though, Shevrin was the one the judge took to most. And he seemed to have a point. OK, subliminal suggestions might only have a weak effect—possibly unpredictable, and possibly minute. No way could they force people to kill themselves. But these two boys were *already* suicidal. What if that tiny push of the 'Do it' had been enough to nudge them over the edge? It was, he said, technically possible.★

Looking back, lawyer Tim Post explains Shevrin's theory: both boys were clearly profoundly psychologically disturbed. This was not Judas

---

★ In the trial, Shevrin testified that there were 'hundreds' of experiments showing that subliminal commands could induce concrete actions, citing a number of academic papers in support of his statement. Other experts were not convinced. 'None of [those papers] demonstrated anything remotely close to subliminal commands influencing motives,' says Tim Moore today. In fact, Moore says that Shevrin's testimony 'raised eyebrows' in the academic community at the time because 'it was not in line with what we knew about the potential influences of subliminal stimulation'. He declined to be interviewed for this book.

Priest's fault—but what happened next was. 'James and Ray were up on the bridge, thinking about jumping,' he says. 'They were in the "zone". And at this point, hopefully, your priest, your rabbi, your mother, a policeman, whoever, comes by and says. "No. Don't do it. There's so much to live for. Come on down. Don't jump." The *last* thing they needed was someone coming up from behind saying, "Do it." '

When put like that, doesn't it sound possible? Despite the alleged falsity of James Vicary's popcorn experiment, and the expert testimonies of Read, Moore and Pratkanis, the problem for CBS was that, on the face of it, the case sounded eminently believable.

In court, a further piece of evidence emerged. Immediately after his release from hospital in 1986, James had spoken with a school counsellor called Susan Rusk. In court Rusk revealed that, immediately before the shooting, the two boys had been listening to *Stained Class* and chanting, 'Just do it.' 'I very specifically remember him saying it because he said it over and over again,' she recalled.' 'It was one of those themes that got repeated a number of times . . . I said, "Why, why did you decide to commit suicide? What were you thinking about? What was going on?" And he described that day: "And then we got a message. It told us to just do it." '

Rusk's conversation with James had taken place in 1986, two years before the question of subliminal messages had emerged. There was no way James could have known at the time that there was apparently a subliminal message on the LP yet here, apparently, was evidence that he had picked one up.

To the Vance and Belknap families and their lawyers, this was proof that the message was there and that the boys had heard it. Unfortunately, while it sounded convincing, there was a fatal flaw in their reasoning. Their own expert witness, Howard Shevrin, had testified that subliminal suggestions were effective precisely because they were subliminal: you couldn't hear them. But if, as James appeared to have told Mrs Rusk, he had *heard* the message, it wasn't subliminal. His brain should have been capable of judging it in the same way that he made normal conscious decisions, and rejected it. Subliminal messages that you *hear* are not subliminal messages.

Did James and Ray really hear 'Do it' or, as Mrs Rusk had testified, 'Just do it'? It's pretty hard to think how anyone could prove this either way. If they said they'd heard it, it wasn't subliminal, and it wouldn't have done anything. If they hadn't heard it, they would never have known what hit them—so there would be no evidence that the subliminal suggestion had caused them to do anything. Either way, both boys had been drinking and taking drugs and both were now dead, so who knew what they had really heard that day?

In court, no one appears really to have understood the importance of the argument surrounding Mrs Rusk's testimony, but her statement sounded convincing, and furthered the impression that CBS was losing the PR war and stood a good chance of forfeiting the case, too. CBS had a secret weapon left, though, in the figure of the plaintiffs' expert witness: Wilson Bryan Key.

As the trial approached, McKenna and Post became less and less inclined to put Key on the stand. It was obvious that the judge didn't find his arguments convincing. Post wanted to have nothing to do with him: 'Key,' he recalls, was clearly 'out there'. CBS would make mincemeat of him. McKenna agreed, but knew that he was hugely in Key's debt. It was Key who had got him on the right track in this case. He decided to put him on the stand.

Judge Whitehead, unimpressed, summoned the lawyers and told them he was not going to let the trial degenerate into a circus. Whatever Key said as an expert witness would be disregarded. He then summoned CBS's lawyers and informed them that Key would appear in court but that they needn't bother cross-examining him: everything he said would be ignored. But Bill Peterson, handling the CBS case, was not going to miss the opportunity to score a few points. 'Accusing the government of marketing dollars with S-E-X symbols on them?' He laughs. 'And the Ritz cracker company of putting S-E-X symbols on their crackers? It was so far out that we *wanted* to cross-examine him basically to even the score in the publicity. And to show the world that—this is a nutty case! We're dealing with a bunch of nuts here!'

Key himself was spoiling for a fight, having decided that the judge and the court were against him (he also had a new book out). Told that Whitehead was going to disregard his evidence, 'I said, "Hell! That's suppressing evidence!"'

By the time he took the stand on 29 March 1990, Key was raring to go.

He had a few things he wanted to say about this case. He never got the chance. He was cross-examined by Bill Peterson. Here is the transcript of that examination, almost in its entirety:

PETERSON: You have seen subliminal messages, Dr Key, in the paintings of Michelangelo in the Sistine chapel, haven't you?

KEY: Yes.

PETERSON: You have seen subliminal messages, specifically 'SEX' painted by Rembrandt in the museum in Amsterdam?

KEY: Yes.

PETERSON: Same with the artist Titian?

KEY: Yes.

PETERSON: You have seen 'SEX' embedded in Lincoln's beard on a $5 bill?

KEY: Yes.

PETERSON: And you believe that to be done purposely by the US government, the Mint, the Department of the Mint?

KEY: Yes.

PETERSON: The same is done in Canada with Canadian money?

KEY: Oh, yes.

PETERSON: You know that the words 'SEX' are baked on Ritz crackers, both front and back, by the bakers at Nabisco?

KEY: Yes.

PETERSON: You believe that the cover of *Time* magazine, the publishers, use subliminal messages?

KEY: Yes, yes.

PETERSON: Hilton Hotel menus?

KEY: Yes.

PETERSON: Howard Johnson menus?

KEY: Yes.

PETERSON: Elementary school textbooks?

KEY: Yes, yes.

PETERSON: Sears catalogues?

KEY: Yes indeed.

PETERSON: . . . NBC evening news . . . ?

KEY: Yes. Some time ago.

PETERSON:... and on the cover of your own book, *Subliminal Seduction,* there are also what you believe to be subliminal messages embedded there?

KEY: Oh, yes, indeed.

MS LYNCH [FOR THE PLAINTIFFS]: Your Honour, I think we are now going a little far afield . . .

THE COURT: I think it's a proper cross-examination, Ms Lynch.

PETERSON:That's all, Your Honour.

There may be a legal term for this. Perhaps it's 'filleting'?

On August 24 1990, Judge Whitehead reached a verdict. While he agreed that he had initially heard a sound on the song 'Better By You, Better Than Me' that resembled the instruction 'Do it', he deemed that since the instruction could not be isolated in the studio, it was probably accidental. Moreover, while he accepted that subliminal stimuli could have effects in some cases, he concluded that science had not proved that they could have an effect as concrete as pushing someone to kill themselves. Thus he was unable to accept that in this case the 'message had proved a significant cause of the two boys' suicide pact.' 'It was a step,' he told me over breakfast, 'that I couldn't take.'

One step he could take, and did, was to punish CBS for messing around during the trial. The corporation had been ordered to hand over the multi-track master of the album, and had delayed for years. Eventually they had come up with the master tape for just one song. This was unacceptable. In addition, there was the matter of the private detectives and their smearing of the plaintiffs' lawyers. As a result Judge Whitehead imposed a Discovery Sanction on CBS—a fine for suppressing evidence and not being candid or forthright—of forty thousand dollars.

Over lunch at Kentucky Fried Chicken, Wilson Key was vocal. Whitehead, he said, was 'deaf, dumb and blind' and had been 'paid off by CBS' (there is no evidence whatsoever that this is the case). Key's verdict on the judge was disparaging but, then, he was pretty disparaging about everyone in the case. Tim Post, lawyer for the Vance family, was 'unskilled'. Reno courts were corrupt. Ken McKenna, the Belknap family lawyer, was 'not very bright or very perceptive . . . and lazy'. Meanwhile CBS's expert

witness, Tim Moore, was 'A joke! . . . A complete phoney! A fruitcake!'
As for the band members—well! Key had sat behind them in court and
watched them playing the fool. He strongly suspected that the lead singer,
Rob Halford, was on drugs. 'They were,' he said, 'making a charade of
the whole thing'.* In fact, it was quite hard to find people in the case that
Key wasn't willing to take a swing at.

Twenty years on, lawyers Post and McKenna are philosophical. McKenna
feels that they won the battle: there *was* a message, and messages like it *can*
have effects. OK, science can't prove that James and Ray killed themselves
because they listened to Judas Priest but 'How do you test whether people
given subliminals will kill themselves?' he asks. 'Put a bunch of them in a
room and subject them to the subliminals and see who kills themselves?
You can't perform that experiment! So we will never be able to prove scientifically that you can make someone kill themselves with a subliminal.
You can't prove it scientifically. That's where we failed.'

McKenna's right, of course. It would be unconscionable to take a group
of suicidal teenagers and play them subliminal messages to see whether
they killed themselves. But there is an error in his reasoning. To assume
that something is true because you can't prove that it's *not* demands a leap
in logic. The vast majority of scientific evidence regarding subliminal
stimulation indicates that it simply does not have the power to produce
this kind of effect. Why should we assume, because an individual experiment has not been done, that it would prove something that contradicts
everything else we know about the phenomenon?

Lack of scientific proof that subliminal stimuli lead to powerful actions
does not seem to have deterred the trade in subliminal products. In the decade after the Judas Priest trial, the market for subliminal self-help tapes in
the US was estimated at $50 million per year. The tapes worked, appar-
ently, 'like a dog whistle going straight into your brain'. Listening to them
helped people recover their self-confidence, enhance their memory, beat

---

* Key's recollection of Judas Priest's behaviour contrasts with that of the judge, who recalls that they were 'charming'. Although heavy metal music was not his cup of tea, he
was terribly impressed that they attended the entire trial, and by their demeanour in
court. A dignified Rob Halford told a press conference that all the band members were
'upset and concerned'. 'You must understand,' he said, 'we all have families.'

acne and win girlfriends. One company even offered subliminal self-help tapes for unborn foetuses, to be played through the mother's stomach. Babies, an 'expert' reported, 'come out more intelligent and walk sooner'.

In 1992, in response to popular coverage of these products, the British Psychological Society published a report to set the record straight: 'They simply do not work. There is no evidence that commercially available subliminal auditory tapes have any genuine utility for enhancing human performance . . . We do not recommend purchasing them.'

A decade on, the self-help cassette market appears to have waned, to be replaced by a more modern phenomenon: subliminal computer software. Subliminal programs flash messages on your computer screen that, according to 'experts', can give you a photographic memory, supreme confidence, business success, a fantastic love life, or 'the razor sharp memory, quick wit and confidence of 007'. Messages, flashed eight million times a day, can even be adjusted to synchronise with your brainwave patterns. The software, says one ad, is '28 times more powerful than subliminal tapes'.

It all sounds terribly impressive. But isn't twenty-eight times zero still zero? Fifty years after a bogus experiment persuaded a gullible American public that subliminal advertising had miraculous effects, we still seem to believe that it works.

Occasionally someone applies the technique to see what happens. Warner Bros have admitted that *The Exorcist* contains a subliminal image of a death mask at various moments in the movie and *Mad Max* utilised a similar technique; on both occasions the inclusion of the images appears to have been an attempt to heighten tension. Meanwhile, in 2000, the Republican National Committee ran a subliminal TV advertisement. Over pictures of Democrat statesmen was flashed the word 'RATS'. There was no evidence that the subliminal advertisement caused anyone to change their vote, but the result was a huge wave of publicity, ensuring the Republican campaign gained top billing in the newspapers.

Meanwhile, for every genuine subliminal image, there are ten examples of cases where people have spotted subliminals that weren't there. In *Who Framed Roger Rabbit?*, Jessica Rabbit appears without underwear for three frames; in the sky above one scene in *The Lion King*, the word 'S-E-X' is spelled by the clouds. Disney's *Aladdin* contains a line that, when played backwards, reveals the secret message 'All good children take off your clothes.'

Is this really true? Or is it the result of some overactive paranoid imagination? As psychology professor Tim Moore reported in a seminal article on the Judas Priest case, a woman in Georgia saw the face of Jesus in a bowl of spaghetti in a Pizza Hut advertisement in 1991. Dozens of others soon reported seeing it, too. Was this a miracle? Did someone deliberately put the face there? Or was it, perhaps, just a plate of spaghetti?

Looking back at the Judas Priest case, it's not hard to track the roots of the scare. In 1985 heavy metal music was nasty, noisy and dangerous-looking. It collided with a religious panic that children were godless, which soon escalated into an unfounded belief that they were worshipping Satan. Parents were afraid. Then, tragically, two boys shot themselves. At this point, the pseudo-science of subliminal perception stepped in, offering an apparently plausible explanation. It all sounded so believable. Only it wasn't.

Of course I didn't expect Wilson Key to agree with this point of view. But as we drove back to his house, I was beginning to become sceptical about what he was telling me. He had, he said, been employed by US Special Forces in 1990, designing subliminal tapes to be blasted into the papal nunciate in Panama City to force Manuel Noriega to come out. The same techniques were used, he said, during the Waco siege—he knew this because he saw his Delta Force contacts wandering around the compound disguised as Drug Enforcement Administration (DEA) agents just before the place went up. The subliminal message at Waco was apparently an order to surrender, read by the actor Charlton Heston, on the basis that his voice resembles God's. I asked Key for the names of his special forces contacts so I could verify his story. He refused to divulge them.

Key was good company and a genuinely nice guy, but I felt that his subliminal paranoia was spiralling out of control. Besides, I suspected he wasn't being entirely truthful with me. He had told me that he was trained by the army; actually he was in the Air Force. He said he had worked 'in intelligence', when his CV cited him as an expert in 'public relations'. The same CV stated that he held qualifications in aircraft engineering and was an 'electrical and power-plant specialist'; no mention of aerial photographic reconnaissance. He also told me—twice—that he had a Ph.D. in psychology; actually it's in journalism and mass-communications science. Admittedly, it was quite possible that these seeming inconsistencies were the result of misunderstandings on my part. But they didn't fill me with confidence.

Back at his home, I asked Key if people sometimes accused him of being crazy. He conceded that they did, but explained that this was because they were scared of confronting the truth. I put it to him that James Vicary's 'eat-popcorn' experiment—cited in his books numerous times as fact—was fantasy. 'Bullshit!' he replied. He then instructed me to look at a poster on his sitting-room wall of Picasso's, 'Le Rêve' (The Dream) and pointed out that the subject had six fingers (which indicated, apparently, that she was masturbating) and that the top half of her head was actually a huge penis. I told him I still didn't buy it and asked what he would say to people who were, like me, sceptical. He pointed to the Picasso again. 'The thing you cannot deny,' he barked, 'is that that's a prick on the top of her head and that she is masturbating! It's clear! And you didn't know it was there before I told you! Thirty years from now you will look at that painting and your eyes will go straight to the top of her head.'

I'm not so sure they will.

7

Sleep

'He that sleeps feels not the toothache'

Cymbeline, Shakespeare

There's a great ghost story about Ravenscrag. I know because my guide, Paul, told it to me when I visited in June 2005. Head of the building's security, Paul had a ponytail, a big smile and, the day I arrived, a shocking hangover—'We'll just talk quietly, shall we?' he suggested. Wherever he went, jangling an unfeasibly large bunch of keys, he told people, 'Hey, I'm with this guy from England. He's writing a book about the place.'

At that point everyone turned to me. 'Did you hear the ghost story yet? Wait till you hear it! Paul tells it real well!'

Of course, we got to the ghost story in the end. The wing of the building that had been Lady Marguerite Allan's sleeping quarters, he told me, was haunted: the heavy dead-bolt on the external door at the end of the corridor had a habit of unlocking itself when no one was watching. Even the security guards refused to go in there alone at night. When they did their rounds, in pairs, flashlights sweeping through the darkness, they locked and secured the door, then scuttled away down the corridor to safety. No sooner had they turned the corner than there was an ominous 'click'. Returning to investigate, they invariably found the bolt drawn, the door swinging listlessly in the breeze. Paul leaned towards me and dropped his voice: it was almost, he said, as if someone was trying to get out. Someone. Or some*thing*.

One night a couple of years ago, two of Paul's colleagues were patrolling the wing when they accidentally surprised Lady Marguerite, standing outside her bedroom in a dressing-gown. Since she had been dead for fifty years, this came as something of a shock. 'This is my house,' she told them. 'Get out.' First thing the next morning, both men resigned. 'One of them was a former Para,' Paul laughed. 'Built like a brick shithouse!'

Sitting in Ravenscrag's basement, laughing about the two terrified security guards, I cast my mind back to something I had heard the morning before, and the relationship between the two stories.

I'd met Janine Huard in her lawyer's office in Montréal just round the corner from the Ritz Carlton Hotel where Sir Henry Tizard had discussed brainwashing techniques with his Canadian and American intelligence counterparts in June 1951. Somehow, the location seemed appropriate: after all, Janine's story was related to that meeting. Over a cup of tea she told me what had happened to her at Ravenscrag. It was a great deal more frightening than the ghost of Lady Marguerite Allan.

The story began when Janine attended a dance at the Victoria Hall in Montréal in 1947. She was just seventeen, loved jazz and was a regular visitor. The occasion was to prove memorable because of the two men she bumped into that night. The first was jazz legend Oscar Peterson—'I shook his hand! Can you imagine? Oscar *Peterson*!' The second, more important still, was the man Janine would marry.

Bob, a friend of a friend who lived in Ottawa, ran a factory that made cleaning products. The friend offered to set Janine up with him. She was ambivalent and more interested in Oscar Peterson—until she saw him. 'He was *very* good-looking,' she told me, 'and very nice with his manners: a very nice man.' She leaned forward and whispered conspiratorially, 'I had a crush right away!'

Five years later in the winter of 1952, Janine and Bob were married in a small church in northern Montréal. The pair took a short honeymoon at Lake Placid—'Yes, it was cold. But when you're in love, you don't mind!' No doubt the newlyweds found a way to ward off the chill because immediately after the honeymoon Janine discovered she was pregnant. One thing followed another and shortly she was a housewife with three young children: Michelle, Pierre and François. But that was where the fairytale ended.

After Pierre's birth Janine went deaf in one ear. Her doctor diagnosed otosclerosis—immobilisation of the bones in the inner ear—and gave her a cumbersome hearing-aid. Afraid that she might not hear the baby cry-ing, she wore it in bed at night. Soon lack of sleep, combined with the un-comfortable hearing-aid and the fear that she might not be there for Pierre when he needed her made her anxious. She stopped sleeping, lost her ap-petite and became depressed.

In March 1958 Bob encouraged Janine to consult a doctor at the Royal Victoria Hospital, who in turn sent her to the department's chief psychia-trist, Dr Ewen D. Cameron.

Cameron was an eminent figure in Canadian psychiatry. A Scotsman by birth, he had emigrated in 1929 and, at the request of Wilder Penfield, moved to Montréal's McGill University in September 1943. His mission was to found the Department of Psychiatry and his base was Ravenscrag, the imposing family seat of the wealthy Allan family, donated to the Royal Victoria Hospital by Lady Marguerite Allan in 1940.

During the next three years the beautiful mosaic floors were covered up, the pillars knocked down, the high corniced ceilings lowered, and the building was converted into a psychiatric hospital. By the time it opened for business in July 1944, the largest and most opulent private house in the country was no more; in its place stood the Allan Memorial Institute.

Janine's depression was successfully treated there and she was sent home in May 1958. Then a series of tragic events laid her low again. In 1960 she had a miscarriage, then produced a fourth healthy baby, Martine. Ex-hausted by the birth, Janine was told to rest for a week while Martine was temporarily admitted to a childcare centre. There, however, Martine con-tracted a viral infection. Janine became convinced that it was her fault.

This time the depression was more serious. Once again, she went to the Royal Victoria Hospital and once again she was referred to the Allan Memorial Institute. On 30 October 1961, six weeks after Martine was born, Janine began treatment, and was admitted as an in-patient in February 1962. Once again, her doctor was Ewen Cameron. This time the results of her treatment were less satisfactory.

Cameron was an ambitious man, who dreamed of developing a blanket cure for psychiatric illness, and of winning a Nobel Prize in the process. To this end, since his arrival at the Allan in 1944 he had tested new and often controversial physical treatments for psychiatric illnesses there. He practised medicine with an evangelical zeal: there was little he would not try to solve his patients' problems. Regrettably, as time went by, his cures became every bit as terrible as the diseases they were designed to remedy.

Cameron was especially enthusiastic about electro-convulsive therapy (ECT). Widely used at the time to counter depression, bursts of electricity to the human brain led to unconsciousness and *grand mal* seizures, like those associated with epilepsy. Although the mechanism by which ECT worked was not understood, sometimes when the patients came round afterwards they were noticeably better. It was rather like switching off the power to a computer after it had crashed so that it could restart properly.

Unfortunately, each time the brain was switched off and restarted there was a price to pay: memory loss. For this reason ECT was generally administered as infrequently and in as low a dose as possible. Then there was time for patients to recover from each shock, and for doctors to monitor how much memory had gone. No one wanted to remove people's past.

No one, that is, except Ewen Cameron. Quite early in his time at the Allan, Cameron became convinced that the side-effect everyone else was trying to avoid was the most important aspect of the treatment. If, he theorised, it was possible to eradicate memories with electricity, it was also possible to eradicate the unhealthy, repetitive thought patterns of the psychologically disturbed. Chemotherapy targeted sick cells; Cameron targeted sick thoughts. The objective, he wrote, was to 'destroy pathological behaviour patterns held in the memory storage systems'.

In order to induce maximum memory loss, Cameron adopted a method of ECT that nobody else in the world was using. Instead of administering a single electric shock to his patients to induce a single seizure, the Page-Russell technique involved giving six shocks in a row, one directly after another. Cameron also increased the dosage: most doctors gave ECT to a maximum dose of about twelve shocks over three or four weeks; Cameron gave two Page-Russells per day, every day, for an initial thirty-day period—and, in many cases, much longer.

The result was substantial, and sometimes complete, memory loss. Cameron's patients were shocked until they no longer knew who they were, where they were, or why. In this 'third stage' of post-ECT amnesia, he told his students, patients lost all sense of 'space-time image'.

'The method' he wrote, 'consisted essentially of the administration of 2–4 electric shocks daily to the point where the patient developed an organic brain syndrome with acute confusion, disorientation and interference with his learned habits of eating and bladder and bowel control.' Only after the old, sick thought patterns had been obliterated could 'reorganisation set in'. Regressed to the state of pre-school children, Cameron's patients became incontinent, sucked their thumbs, cried and had to be fed. Aware that this intense ECT was obliterating their memories and personality traits, he called the technique 'annihilation'.

It was into this regime that Janine Huard, depressed mother of four, was admitted in October 1961.

No one explained to Janine what ECT was. They called it 'treatment'. All she knew was that one morning she wasn't allowed to eat breakfast, was laid on a stretcher and wheeled into a strange room. She was given something to clench between her teeth to stop her biting her tongue once the seizures started, and the stretcher was surrounded by men to restrain her. She thought they were trying to kill her. 'It was like they were going to put me on the electric chair, you know. That's what I had in my mind.'

Janine didn't feel the shock. You never did. But she felt the effects when she came round a couple of hours later, and vowed that this was not going to happen again. The next day it did. When she tried to complain, no one listened. 'I used to be a fighter,' she told me, clenching her fist, 'and I used to resist! Resist! Very much!' To Cameron, the fact that Janine was uncooperative was of no consequence. Her mind was not working properly; the sick thought patterns had to be destroyed. She looked into her empty teacup, silent for a moment. 'So they held me down,' she said.

Terrible as it may sound today, 'annihilation' was not the true goal of the procedure. Cameron knew that you couldn't just turn people into vegetables and send them home. The real trick lay in *replacing* the sick thought patterns with healthy ones. And this was where his treatment became really revolutionary.

Ewen Cameron, a naturally impatient man, viewed conventional psychotherapy as time-consuming and frequently unproductive. Why did the psychiatrist need to spend so many hours listening to patients' ramblings? There had to be a better way. Then he had a brainwave. Why couldn't a tape-recorder do the listening? Thinking that any method of accelerating the process would allow him to cover more ground, he bought an early 'floor-model' reel-to-reel machine and began to tape his patients' therapy sessions. Tape-recorders, he decided, would revolutionise psychiatry. If the idea panned out, the psychiatrist might not even need to be present for the therapy session: he could simply record some standard instructions and have patients listen to the tapes. Automated psychotherapy was at hand.

The first recipient of the new technique was a forty-year-old French-Canadian woman. In 1953 Cameron recorded an assertion she had made during a therapy session that her mother had threatened to abandon her as a child, then snipped out the relevant passage and made it into a loop that would play on his tape-recorder for ever. He sat the patient down and told her to listen to what she had said.

After nineteen repetitions, the woman became irate. 'Does it go on all the time?' she asked him. 'I hate to hear that. It upsets me. Look at me shaking!' Twenty repetitions later she became argumentative and begged him to stop the tape. He refused, and after forty-five repetitions she broke down completely and poured out all her problems. Further experiments revealed that when patients at the Allan were played their own voices repeatedly, they experienced 'discomfort, aversion and resentment'.

When another patient who had been forced to listen to his own voice told Cameron that he was having trouble stopping himself thinking about it, the psychiatrist became excited that he had, at last, 'got my hands on something that really *did* something'. Exactly what it was doing, he didn't know. But he was determined to find out.

Clearly, he thought, it was something to do with the number of repetitions. Patients hearing their own voice once didn't react much at all: the dose had to be increased to see a significant result. 'If this thing worked after thirty repetitions,' wrote Cameron, 'it was only common sense to see what would happen if the repetition was increased tenfold, a hundredfold, or even more.'

He concluded that while the repetitions were breaking through to the unconscious mind, the patients didn't like hearing the sound of their own voice repeated incessantly—and it was at this point that fortune played a hand. In March 1948 he came across a magazine advertisement about 'sleep teaching'. According to the advertisement, it was possible, by playing repeated messages to a sleeping person, to force their unconscious mind to absorb new information.

The notion had originated in the world of science fiction, making its début in 1911 in a short story, 'Ralph 124-C41+' by Hugo Gernsback. In it, subjects were fitted with headbands that passed electrical impulses directly into their brains. The machine responsible was called a hypnobio-scope. 'While in a passive state,' wrote Gernsback, 'the mind absorbed the impressions quite readily and mechanically.'

The technique was soon picked up by other writers, most famously Al-dous Huxley, who portrayed it as a way of indoctrinating human babies in *Brave New World*. Soon, he speculated, all hospitals would be fitted with pillow speakers broadcasting messages to be absorbed during sleep. The technique, which he called hypnopaedia, was potentially 'the greatest moralising and socialising force of all time'.

Shortly after *Brave New World* was published in 1932, an American businessman called Max Sherover contacted the British Linguaphone company—and science fiction became science fact. Linguaphone sold gramophone records teaching foreign languages but Sherover had other plans for the technology. What would happen, he wondered, if Lingua-phone records were played overnight while the student slept? He bought the US rights to the company and went to work building himself a sleep-teaching machine by fitting a timing device to a standard gramophone so that it could turn itself on or off without human interference during the night.

Sherover's machine was tested at a boys' summer camp in New York in 1942. Over a month, the phrase 'my fingernails are terribly bitter' was played to twenty compulsive nail-biters six hundred times a night. By the end of the summer, reported Sherover, eight of the twenty had given up the habit.

Concluding that this was a breakthrough in human learning, Sherover rapidly renamed his invention Cerebrophone and launched it on the US market, accompanying it with a wave of publicity attesting to the miracu-lous effects of sleep learning, which he called Dormiphonics. According to the publicity, a Spanish opera singer had taught himself fluent Italian with the machine, later performing all over the world without a single audience member noticing his Spanish accent. A German woman eradicated her ac-cent when speaking English by listening to the song 'The White Cliffs Of Dover' while she slept. No effort was required to learn like this. 'The les-son is repeated automatically' Sherover opined, 'Lulling . . . [the listener to sleep] and sinking deeper and deeper into the subconscious mind.'

Since Ewen Cameron was a science-fiction fan it is quite possible that the idea of sleep teaching was not new to him. But it was only when he read

Sherover's Cerebrophone advertisement that he became intrigued and asked a member of his staff, Lloyd Hisey, to look into it. Hisey contacted Sherover, who confirmed that anything could be taught during sleep, from music to languages to Morse code. The sleep-learning machine, he said, cost $120.

The idea clearly struck a chord. Perhaps, Cameron figured, it might be better to play the tape loops to his patients while they were asleep. That way he would be killing two birds with one stone: the patients could sleep through the repetitions, and could listen without supervision. The hard graft of the technique would be over before they even got up for breakfast.

Instead of forking out $120 for a Cerebrophone, Cameron asked his assistant, a British engineer called Leonard Rubenstein, to build him a machine in the stables workshop at Ravenscrag. It was quite a simple procedure: Cameron highlighted phrases he wanted repeated to the patients and Rubenstein cut them out of the tape and made the loops. 'Rubenstein twisted [the tape] around,' says Dr Peter Roper, who worked with Cameron at the time, 'so there was an endless tape. So Cameron could have them playing endlessly—because they kept on going and going . . . It would go on saying what you had recorded.'

Dr Maurice Dongier, who worked at the Allan in the early 1950s, recalls the early experiments with automated psychotherapy. 'He had the microphones in the pillow of the patients and during their sleep he would have suggestions made by a recorded speech, so he would have the patient say, "No. It's not true that my mother-in-law is trying to poison me. She is a very nice woman." And that would go on and on all over the night.'

To determine whether the repeated suggestions had any effect, Cameron and his colleagues devised an experiment. According to Peter Roper, a patient was played a repeated message warning, 'Your hand is getting hotter and hotter.' As this happened, a probe strapped to the subject's hand measured the physiological effect. No rise in temperature was noted. But then, suddenly, all that changed: 'I remember that this patient was listening to this, and he tore the headphones off and rushed out of the hospital!' laughs Roper. 'We couldn't understand why, but he said, "The place is on fire!" So there was *some* effect.'

Now convinced that he was on to something big, Cameron worked on new ways of making the treatment more effective. First, he theorised, the mind should be 'annihilated' with ECT before it was saturated with messages from the therapist to replace the eliminated sick thought processes. The messages were to be played during the day when the patients were awake as well as at night while they slept. He christened the technique 'psychic driving'.

The messages were varied. Initially it was deemed best that the patients were played recordings of their own voices ('autopsychic driving') but when they found this unsettling, Cameron and his staff recorded suitable messages for them ('heteropsychic driving'). Then the technique was honed further. 'He had what he called a negative tape,' recalls Roper, 'which was, "There's something wrong with you, nobody likes you. You've got serious problems." Then there was a positive one. "People like you. You like people." He had a programme where he would sometimes play the negative tape first and then the positive one.'

Examples of the messages are somewhat baffling. Val Orlikow, admitted to the Allan in late 1956 for postnatal depression, received the negative-driving message: 'Do you realise that you are a very hostile person? Do you know that you are hostile with the nurses? Do you know that you are hostile with the patients? Why do you think you are so hostile? Did you hate your mother? Did you hate your father?'

Montréal businessman Lou Weinstein, admitted for panic attacks and breathlessness the same year, was administered the positive-driving message: 'You feel friendly towards people. You like to feel intimate with others. You can get along with people by being yourself. You feel neat and tidy. If you see paper on the floor, you pick it up.'

To Cameron it was clear that the more times the messages were repeated, the greater the beneficial effect would be. Soon the messages were being played for up to twenty hours a day non-stop. Patients' records indicate that some had to endure the same messages for up to half a million repetitions. The result was a saturation of the brain with information, leading to catharsis: 'If [the senses] are continually overloaded,' wrote Cameron, 'their breakdown is to be expected. Analogous to this is the breakdown of the individual under continuous interrogation.'

Lou Weinstein seemed to prove the point. In 1954 he was played his driving messages for fifty-four days, at the end of which staff found that he was hallucinating wildly, looking under the blanket on his bed and instructing imaginary animals to 'come out of there'. When the nurse asked whom he was talking to, he told her he was addressing the dogs and birds that lived in his room. Then he went silent and turned to the animals. 'Are you watching her?' he asked suspiciously.

As the technique proved more useful, so the experiments were boosted. In the stables at Ravenscrag, Leonard Rubenstein designed a system capable of playing eight separate tape loops to eight patients simultaneously, each listening in a different room. By 1955 Cameron was going great guns with his new technique, boasting that 'in the past two years, more than a hundred persons have thus been successfully brainwashed—Canadian style'.

Admittedly, there were a few teething problems. For a start, there was the question of how to coax patients to listen to boring, repetitive messages when they were awake. At first they were told to sit still and listen to the tapes in their rooms, but if everyone was listening to a different message the corridor became noisy. More importantly, they tended to get bored and wander off after a couple of hours.

Perhaps, wondered Cameron, headphones were the answer. Not only were they quieter but they had the advantage that they made the messages sound like they were coming from inside a patient's head. The idea worked, up to a point: there was still the issue of patients removing them and refusing to listen. To combat this, Rubenstein fitted sets of headphones inside leather American-football helmets, which were strapped on to the patients' heads. Soon wings of the Allan were filled with the bizarre spectacle of patients, their memories obliterated by ECT, strapped into leather helmets so that they couldn't escape the sound of their own voice.

For some reason the patients were still reluctant to take their medicine. When they tore off the helmets, Cameron decided that the only way to get them to listen to their psychic-driving messages was to immobilise them forcibly, and that the best way to do this was with drugs.

Over the next fifteen years, he immobilised his patients with any number of chemicals, including the 'truth drugs', sodium amytal and pentothal, LSD, mescaline, PCP, Largactil, psilocybin and just about anything else that came his way. Val Orlikow, the post-natal depressive whose negative-driving message asked her why she hated her parents, was given a cocktail of amphetamines mixed with LSD on fourteen separate occasions over a two-month period. On no occasion was she told what the drugs would do. Left unsupervised after the injections, she became convinced that her bones were melting and tried to climb the walls of her room. 'It was terrifying,' she later told investigator John Marks. 'You're afraid you've gone off somewhere and can't come back.' Another compound Cameron combined with psychic driving was the African poison curare. In the right dose, curare immobilised the body, leaving the patient paralysed but awake—so that he or she could not escape the recorded messages.

Janine Huard was in her room when her psychic driving began. 'They had this machine on top of the bed and I said, "What is that?"' she remembers. 'The nurse said, "You have to listen to that." I said, "No, no, no! I'm not in Russia! I'm not going to listen to anything!"'

But she was. Fifty years on, she still can't forget her negative-driving message: 'Janine', the voice admonished her, 'you are running away from responsibility! Why? You don't want to take care of your husband! Why? You don't want to take care of your children! Why? Why, Janine? Why?' After a number of weeks she was given her positive message, essentially a reversal of the negative one but with the added instruction 'If you see paper on the floor, you pick it up.'

To force her to listen, she was immobilised by drugs including—on at least one occasion—curare. Several times the drugs used on her were not named, only given numbers. Records show that she received RO-41038, G-2235, chlorpromazine and sodium amytal—but the favourite seems to have been nitrous oxide, administered via a mask that was strapped to her face so that she couldn't remove it.

'I tried not to listen, but it was so hard,' she says today. 'When you have something in your ears . . . It was so loud! I don't know if I was asleep with the pills but you cannot think of anything else, even if you want to. I was trying not to think. In my mind I said, "I will not listen to that." But how can you be strong enough?'

Janine was also played the messages in conjunction with LSD. Convinced that she was going insane, she crept round her bedroom and tried to hide in the corners. When nurses came in to check on her, they assumed ghastly proportions and she cowered in the corner like a frightened child. At one point, she remembers, a nurse left her a sandwich, then locked the door again. The sandwich made her paranoid: since she didn't want to eat it and couldn't bear to look at it, she lifted up the mattress and hid it. And all the time there was the message: 'You *like* to take care of your children, Janine! You *like* to take care of your husband! If you see paper on the floor, you pick it up!'

'I thought they wanted to drive me crazy,' she recalls. 'I found myself looking for paper on the floor and didn't know why.'

Sometimes when she was alone Janine tried to get out of the room but it was often locked. On one occasion she escaped and made her way down to the cafeteria on the ground floor for a cup of coffee. Cameron found her in the hallway. 'Janine!' he said. 'Go back there! Go back and listen!' When she remonstrated, he put his arm round her shoulders and became paternal. 'Janine!' He sighed. 'Don't you *want* to get well?'

Faced with the problem of intransigent, uncooperative patients, Cameron soon discovered that the best way to make them listen to their driving messages was to put them into a deep chemical sleep. Sleep served two functions: not only did it immobilise the patients effectively, it also seemed to enhance the effects of the ECT, further confusing them and making them more susceptible to the programming. What he was after, he wrote, was the eradication of the mind's contents, followed by the insertion of new, healthy thought patterns, which he referred to as the 'dynamic implant'. The result was a nuclear version of Max Sherover's sleep-teaching technique, as Cameron attempted to pour his opinions into the hamstrung minds of his patients.

Having made this discovery, Cameron established sleep rooms in which groups of patients were sedated for weeks, or even months, so that they could listen to their driving messages without interruption. Patients were put to sleep with a cocktail of powerful sedatives for between fifteen and thirty days, during which they were played their driving messages continually through small speakers beneath their pillows. They were only woken for a couple of hours a day to be given ECT, to be taken to the lavatory and to eat.

Others were put to sleep for longer. Charles Pagé was left in a sleep room for thirty-six days; during thirty-one he was played driving messages. Others were put to sleep for up to sixty-five days non-stop. If the drug doses were wrong and the patients woke up, they might get out of bed and try to escape, as Janine had done. Periodically there was a panic at the Allan as one of the patients would disappear and be found stumbling along the corridors, lost, incontinent, looking for a way out. They were put back to bed, sedated and tucked in tight.

A few unfortunates had other experimental techniques tested on them: at least one man had copper wires wrapped round his legs and linked up to a battery, which gave him a small electric shock at the end of every driving message. This ensured that, although he was sedated, he could never go to sleep and escape from the messages.

In his original papers, Cameron advocated the use of driving messages for fifteen minutes per day. This was soon extended to fifteen hours a day. Negative messages were played ceaselessly for up to sixty days, and there are records of positive-driving messages being played to patients for over three months. In the case of Mary C., a fifty-two-year-old depressive, who received the treatment for 101 days, Cameron noted that 'No positive results were obtained.'

But the treatment continued. After all, reported Cameron in July 1959, the technique clearly demonstrated 'that reorganising of the personality may be brought about without the necessity of solving conflicts or abreaction or the reliving of past experiences'. It was a breakthrough.

The single most sinister aspect of the entire affair, however, was not the treatment that Cameron was doling out but the people who were paying for it.

Ewen Cameron was an assiduous user of the popular press. Author of hundreds of scholarly articles in various academic journals, he never missed the opportunity to plug himself, his hospital and his new theories in magazines and newspapers—and even hired himself a PR man, Fred Poland, to ensure that the Allan received plenty of coverage. In 1955 he gave an interview to the Canadian magazine *Weekend* in which he admitted that what he was doing to his patients was essentially the same as the new Soviet technique of 'brainwashing'. The doctors at the Allan, he told the reporter, 'face many of the same problems as professional brainwashers. Prisoners-of-war resist attempts to interrogate them—and almost every patient tries to defend himself against the unpleasant impact of his own recorded voice by deliberately not listening to it.'

'Brainwashing' versus 'psychiatry' was an interesting analogy, and Cameron used it for the rest of his life. It piqued the interest of all kinds of people not usually concerned with psychiatric illness. Perhaps predictably, the Central Intelligence Agency was at the head of the queue.

For some time, the CIA had nurtured an interest in the kind of work that Cameron was doing. Of particular interest was amnesia. It would be convenient, thought the Agency, if it were possible to find a means of making people forget secret things. The CIA had a perennial problem with agents it no longer needed. These people couldn't just be released on to the streets: they knew too much. Unfortunately the only alternative to releasing them was to incarcerate them. But where? For how long? And how much would it cost?

In March 1951 a request went out for suggestions on how to solve this tricky problem. The memorandum, entitled 'Disposal', warned that certain categories of people including 'blown agents, exploited agents, [and] difficult defectors who may wish to re-defect' posed a great threat to the Agency. There was a clear need, said the memo, for 'some method of treating such people in a way that would cause semipermanent amnesia for a period of approximately one year'. The request was fired into the ARTICHOKE system for comments.

For a little while Agency staff debated the idea of silencing former agents by lobotomising them but the technique was shortly dismissed as too complicated to be practical—'any operation requires cumbersome equipment . . . expert, neurosurgical knowledge . . . and an anaesthetist and nurse attendant'. Not only was lobotomy impractical, it was also immoral: 'War is a grim business,' reported one officer, but 'other means should be found and could be found.'

In July 1953 the issue became more pressing when a former CIA officer, now a chronic alcoholic, had to undergo a brain operation in Texas. Worried that he might reveal sensitive information under the anaesthetic, he asked that another Agency man be present. As he had warned, during the course of the operation he talked 'extensively', revealing a number of 'internal problems of the Agency'. Luckily the CIA had been prepared, vetting the doctors and nurses in advance, but the incident raised an issue: what if Agency men—even reliable ones—talked under anaesthesia? They couldn't all be monitored for the rest of their lives.

'Some individuals in the Agency,' pointed out one officer at an ARTI-CHOKE meeting on 15 July, 'had to know tremendous amounts of information.' Perhaps it might be possible to find a way to make them forget that information after they had left the CIA. 'If any way could be found to produce amnesia for this type of information,' concluded the officer, 'it would be a remarkable thing.'

One way of making people forget things, it was reasoned, was to hit them hard on the head. In January 1956, in an attempt to work out how best to exploit this discovery, the Agency established MKULTRA Sub-project 54, dedicated to inducing concussion in targeted individuals. It yielded a couple of inventions, including 'a pancake-like blackjack [leather-encased lead truncheon], giving a high peak impact force' and 'concealed or camouflaged spring-loaded impacting devices that trigger upon contact with the head'. There was a distinct problem, however, when it came to testing the items. Strangely, there were no Agency volunteers. Eventually the systems were tested on fluid-filled skulls, on a 'blast range'. When these experiments were complete, the equipment was tested on human cadavers.

The problem was, the line between clubbing someone on the head and making them forget something, and clubbing them on the head and making them dead was just too fine: even the most ruthless optimists had to admit the technique had the capacity to go horribly wrong. Higher-tech solutions were followed up but they had their flaws, too. The use of ultrasonic blast and radar waves was investigated. In 1977, Charles Geschickter told a Senate committee how the idea worked:

> GESCHICKTER: The other [technique] was . . . the use of radar to put monkeys to sleep, to see if they could be, should I say, instead of the Mickey Finn, they could put them under with radar directed towards the monkeys' brains.
> SENATOR SCHWEIKER: Did they?
> GESCHICKTER: Yes, sir. But, Senator, it showed that if you got into too deep a sleep, you injured the heat centre of the brain the way you cook meat.

Since killing former CIA officers or cooking their brains was not part of the remit, it wasn't long before a group of consultants came to the conclusion that the work was probably best left alone: 'Our professional consultants emphatically support the ARTICHOKE view,' a 1956 document summarises, 'that short of cutting a subject's throat, a true amnesia cannot be guaranteed.'

But there was one further possibility: electricity. In December 1951, ECT had been suggested as an adjunct to interrogation when an Agency expert informed his handler that low doses of ECT, insufficient to cause fits, caused excruciating pain, as if the recipient's 'whole head was on fire'. The procedure apparently 'had the effect of making a man talk'; there was, suggested the helpful expert, a portable ECT machine on the market that might be suitable for such a purpose.

At the end of the discussion the expert warned his handler, in no uncertain terms, that caution was to be exercised with electricity and the brain. A little might help interrogation. A lot, however, and an individual would be reduced to 'the vegetable level'. This information, coupled with another request in 1956 stating that amnesia-inducement was 'of extreme importance', seems to have galvanised officers, who began to investigate the idea of using electricity not to force people to remember but to forget.

It wasn't long before the officers discovered that someone in Canada was deliberately inducing amnesia with ECT. In early 1956, the year after Ewen Cameron's interview on 'beneficial brainwashing' appeared in *Weekend*, CIA officer John Gittinger read a piece on psychic driving in the *American Journal of Psychiatry*. Intrigued, he instructed a colleague, Colonel James Monroe, to contact Cameron and find out what was going on. Monroe telephoned the Allan saying that he was a representative of the Society for the Investigation of Human Ecology, and suggested a meeting. Following a conference that spring, he reported back to the Agency that this guy was for real. Cameron was encouraged to write a research proposal and submit it to the society.

News of outside interest in his techniques was music to Cameron's ears. Since he had started psychic driving, outside funding had more or less dried up. Originally he had received support from the Canadian Mental-health programme but that had stopped when its officials discovered what his research entailed. He had applied for funds from the Defence Research Board of Canada, headed by Ormond Solandt (who was then funding sensory-deprivation work under Donald Hebb at McGill University) but was turned down: Solandt had a friend whose wife had been 'depatterned' by Cameron and never fully recovered. The more he and his colleagues looked into psychic driving, the less worthwhile it appeared: not only did they consider the project bereft of scientific value, they also thought it ethically dubious.

Cameron's application to the Society for the Investigation of Human Ecology, submitted in January 1957, requested financial assistance to monitor the effects on human behaviour of the 'repetition of verbal signals'. The goal of the research, he said, was to explore his patients' reactions to repetition, which depended on their stress tolerance, the number of repetitions and their capacity for 'desensitisation'. Research was also to be conducted into 'finding chemical agents which will serve to break down the ongoing patterns of behaviour', as well as better ways of 'inactivating the patient' while he or she was listening to the psychic driving.

Stress tolerance, desensitisation, drugs that deconstructed patterns of human behaviour: this was right up the CIA's street. In Cameron, the Agency had found someone who was investigating many of the techniques that interested them, and was clearly happy to take his research to levels that other scientists were not willing to touch. Already he was apparently wiping his patients' minds clean and attempting to reprogramme them. Who knew what he might be capable of, given the right funding? Through the Society, the CIA offered to plough money into the project and Cameron accepted, becoming MKULTRA Sub-project 68. Over the next three years, from April 1957 to June 1960, Cameron received nearly $75,000 from the Agency.

There is little doubt that he would have continued his research with or without the CIA's help, but the organisation's money and support certainly gave him an added impetus to crank his experiments up a level. And not only in the field of sleep and psychic driving.

Cameron was always on the lookout for new techniques that might help him to wipe the minds of his patients. One day Janine Huard was summoned from her bed and led to the stables, where Leonard Rubenstein— who had made the tape loops and other psychic-driving equipment—was waiting. He wired her into an elaborate polygraph (lie detector) machine, then Cameron appeared and interrogated her. She was never told why this was happening or what she was supposed to gain from the experience.

On another occasion she was taken back to the stables, given an injection and made to wear large plastic glasses with opaque blinkers. Standing in the darkness, she had no idea what was going on until a doctor lifted one of the blinkers and pointed what appeared to be a gun at her. He fired a jet of high-pressure air directly on to the surface of her eyeball. Janine screamed and tried to get away. 'How much can you take?' he asked her. 'Just say when you can't take any more.' When he fired another jet of air into her eye she begged him to stop. He took away the gun and shut the blinker, leaving her in darkness again. 'OK,' he said. 'Now the other eye.'

'It hurt!' Janine says today. 'I don't know why they did it. They said, "It's a test." To me, it was an experiment.'

One area that Cameron was keen to explore was sensory deprivation. The Allan Memorial Institute was part of McGill University, where Donald Hebb had run his experiments into the physiological effects of isolation on the human mind in the early 1950s. Ever on the lookout for techniques that might depattern his patients more efficiently, Cameron decided to try sensory deprivation, and soon he was locking people into dark rooms for days at a time. At McGill, Hebb had discovered that healthy postgraduate students were unable to tolerate isolation for prolonged periods. Fifty per cent had backed out after just a day, and the longest anyone lasted inside the chamber was 139 hours. Cameron didn't care about this: he locked patients into chambers for up to thirty-five days.

One early recipient of the Allan's sensory-deprivation regime was the middle-aged Mary C., who suffered from depression and anxiety attacks. Having been told that she needed 'a rest', Mary C. was fitted with goggles and cuffs and locked inside a sensory-deprivation chamber in the stable building. Daily progress reports reveal that she was hallucinating by the end of the first day, when she told a nurse that she could hear her sisters calling to her. Aural hallucinations soon became visual ones and by day three she appeared to be regressing to childhood, asking for candy and whining like a toddler. The next day she tore off the goggles, threw them down the lavatory and tried to escape.

Led back to the chamber, the treatment continued. By the end of the next day Mary C. had apparently forgotten how to talk and was eating only small portions of food, which had to be chopped up for her. Eventually she refused to eat anything other than puffed rice. For two meals she was fed milk from a baby's bottle. She wet herself at night. The result of this treatment, reported one doctor, was that she was 'much calmer'.

When Donald Hebb heard what Cameron was doing with his technique, he was appalled. For some time, Hebb had been unhappy with goings-on at the Allan. Now he refused to attend conferences chaired by the psychiatrist. 'Cameron was irresponsible,' he later told an investigator. 'Anybody with any appreciation of the complexity of the human mind would not expect that you could erase an adult mind and then add things back with this stupid psychic driving.' The work, he said, was 'criminally stupid'.

Hebb was also concerned that Cameron, who was inclined to brag to the press, might publicise his sensory-deprivation experiments at McGill, blowing the whistle on the university's brainwashing work. In December 1952, shortly after Cameron had begun to use the technique, Hebb wrote to his sponsors at the Defence Research Board (DRB), warning that the story was about to leak. 'Let's not forget,' he told Whit Morton, head of DRB's Division D, 'that Cameron is now undertaking some work with this method, and he'll talk about it freely.'

Arguments raged until the end of 1953, when Hebb sent Morton a letter formally requesting permission to let the cat out of the bag and control the public-relations explosion that was bound to ensue. 'I have worked hard for you,' he wheedled, concluding the letter with a little picture of himself on his knees, begging. Morton refused permission.

Less than two months after this exchange, news of Cameron's experiments with sensory deprivation indeed hit the press. While efforts were made to control the story, the genesis of the technique was immediately traced to Hebb at McGill. There would eventually be protests outside the university, and a number of his colleagues came under fire from their students for taking part in work that led to interrogation and 'torture'. One later committed suicide.

Although Janine Huard was never subjected to sensory deprivation, it didn't take her long to realise that she didn't like being an inpatient at the Allan, and that she wanted to go home. 'It was like they were trying to take everything away from me,' she says, 'making me become a dummy.' But when she told Cameron this, he wasn't having any of it. 'Come on, Janine! You want to get better, don't you?' he asked. When she nodded, he sedated her and sent her back to listen to her driving messages again.

Every other day Janine's husband, Bob, left the factory early and came to visit her. 'I remember he was very sad,' she recalls. 'He didn't stay long. If I was awake we would talk for a few minutes. To see me like that was very bad for him, too: it must have been terrible.' More often than not when Bob arrived, she was unconscious. He used to leave notes for her beside the bed, 'I came to see you. But you were sleeping . . .'

Sometimes Janine was allowed home for the weekend to see her children and her mother, who had moved in to care for them while she was in hospital. One weekend, in a lucid moment, she told Bob what they were doing to her at the Allan, and begged him not to send her back.

Although he had no idea of what Janine's treatment entailed, Bob realised that she was miserable, and called the hospital to tell the staff that she would not be returning on Sunday night. He was put on hold. Eventually Ewen Cameron picked up the phone and told him that if he didn't bring her back, the Allan would have no alternative but to tell the police to bring her in. That evening, Bob put her into the car and drove her back in tears.

In March 1962, Janine's treatment was deemed complete and she was sent home. But she seemed worse than she had been before. Terrified of her children, unsure how to hold them or what to say to them, she became convinced that she might harm them. This was only natural: thanks to her treatment at the Allan, she had become a child herself.

In her lawyer's offices in downtown Montréal, Janine explains, 'I became so lost. I was afraid of everything—afraid to cross the street, afraid my mother wouldn't stay with me. My mother had to be with me all the time. I couldn't cook any more. I was just sitting there and watching her. I had to sleep with my mother, even. I had to tell my husband, "Please, go and sleep in the other bed." She couldn't leave me, or I panicked. That's *after* the treatment,' she reminded me, 'not before.'

Unable to cook, clean or take her children to school, she sat at home, watching her life pass by. One day she went out for a walk carrying an umbrella. When someone pointed out that it wasn't raining, she became confused about what she was doing and where she was. In the end, Janine's mother stayed with the family for a decade.

Janine was filled with guilt about how she had let her family down. She felt worse when her children tried to ask what was wrong. 'I remember my daughter, she was clever, and she used to come to me and say, "Mummy, why don't you smile any more?" I was always like that. I didn't smile, I didn't laugh. I couldn't play with them. That made me very sad. I knew—I was conscious of what I was doing to them.' Years later she asked her elder daughter, Michelle, how the family had survived. 'We thought you didn't care for us very much,' she replied.

Of course, the children weren't the only ones to suffer. Janine's husband, Bob, found the strain intolerable and stayed out late at night, drinking. To make matters worse, the treatment Janine had received at the Allan was private, which meant it had been very expensive, and he was going broke. Eventually Bob lost his factory and his job, spent more time drinking—and the family slowly disintegrated.

The loss of her marriage remains a source of great sorrow to Janine. 'Although there was a lot of love, a man cannot last for so many years alone all the time. Now I understand that. My poor husband! I loved him to the end but he lost the business, he lost everything and he became very alone.'

Hard though it may be to imagine, Janine was one of the lucky ones. She was never fully 'depatterned' with ECT, and most of her memory returned. For others, the past became a mystery; the present a dream.

Linda McDonald, who received over a hundred ECT treatments and eighty-six days of sleep therapy, was unable to recall anything that had happened to her before her admission to the Allan. She was also unable to recognise either her husband or her children. Robert Logie, originally admitted for a leg infection, got lost when he was discharged from the Allan. When he was eventually found sleeping under a bridge in Vancouver—he lived in Toronto—the police had to place a picture of him in the newspaper to ask if anyone knew who he was, because he didn't. Lou Weinstein, the Montréal businessman, was discharged from the Allan addicted to two separate drugs, had lost all sense of personal hygiene and awareness of others, was unable to remember anything for the decade around his admission, and was incapable of stopping himself humming. He spent the rest of his life getting lost in his own home and asking for his mother, who had been dead for a number of years.

According to MKULTRA documents, Ewen Cameron and his staff were never aware that their research was being bankrolled by the CIA. Not everyone believes this. Cameron himself seemed pretty clear that what he was doing related to recent events in Korea and the strange happenings behind the Iron Curtain. 'It was definitely related to brainwashing,' Leonard Rubenstein later told the *New York Times*. 'They had investigated brainwashing among soldiers who had been in Korea. We, in Montréal, started to use some of the techniques, brainwashing patients instead of using drugs.' Laughlin Taylor, the Allan's resident psychologist, also recalled there being no doubt about why they were applying these techniques: 'We were told that this was to prepare for a war effort', he said. '[Cameron] was involved in brainwashing and made no bones about it.'

The idea that the political significance of the work went undetected is laughable. The Institute was visited on a number of occasions by military personnel who lectured staff on the ins and outs of brainwashing—how often does that happen in civilian hospitals? Over dinner in a fashionable Chinese restaurant in Montréal, Dr Peter Roper told me about a mysterious colonel, apparently from the US Army, who arrived at the Allan in 1959, gathered all the doctors together and gave them a talk about the Korean confessions. 'It was interesting from a psychological point of view', he said. 'How you could change someone's behaviour and attitude. That was quite interesting.' Then Roper dropped a bombshell: 'And then, of course, we had William Sargant, too. Do you know him?'

I nearly dropped my chopsticks. *William Sargant?* What was the British brainwashing expert doing at the Allan Memorial Institute?

Lecturing. According to Roper, Sargant, whom he knew quite well, visited the Allan in 1964 to give a talk on brainwashing and modern psychiatric techniques. But there was an ulterior motive: the visit, says Roper, 'was really to show Sargant what the Allan was like. And also for [him] to be vetted, because they were looking for Cameron's replacement.'

The idea of William Sargant as chief psychiatrist at the Allan Memorial Institute was intriguing but it begged the question: why would Sargant—probably the most famous psychiatrist in Britain at the time—consider associating himself with a man like Ewen Cameron, whose theories had spiralled so far out of control?

The answer is that the two men had a great deal in common. Both were eminent figures in the world of psychiatry. Cameron was a former head of the American Psychiatric Association; Sargant, meanwhile, was physician in charge of Psychological Medicine at St Thomas's in London—one of the pre-eminent hospitals in the world. Both men were powerful, opinionated, and maintained a healthy disregard for psychoanalysis. As Sargant and Cameron knew, mental illnesses were not cured by talking: they were cured by aggressive medical intervention. Unpleasant, sometimes, but there it was.

In addition, the two men were friends. One interviewee for this book recalls them meeting 'like long-lost brothers' at an academic conference in the early 1960s. In 1961 they had co-founded the World Psychiatric Association together (Cameron was president, Sargant, associate secretary).

Sargant and Cameron spoke the same language: it led them both into brainwashing, and the therapeutic possibilities of erasing and reprogramming human minds. For Sargant, as for Cameron, the key weapons in the war against mental disease were electricity, drugs and chemically induced sleep.

William Sargant himself was an intriguing character. Born in 1907, he attended Leys School and St John's College, Cambridge, which he represented at rugby. Prodigiously talented and possessing an extraordinary amount of self-confidence, social networking presented no obstacle to the young Sargant, who seems to have spent much of his time as a medical student travelling around introducing himself to the most famous medical men of the age. Among the mementoes in his personal papers are a pair of lobotomy picks presented to the young doctor by their inventor, Walter Freeman, and a restaurant menu signed by Ugo Cerletti, who developed ECT. In December 1938, aged thirty-one, Sargant managed to get himself invited to dinner at the White House with the Roosevelts.

Some have attributed Sargant's tremendous drive to his Wesleyan upbringing: a classic example of the Protestant ethic in action. Perhaps some of it was bluster: his energy, immense self-confidence and his habit of barking at patients made him appear physically larger and more intimidating than he was. Dr David Owen (now Lord Owen of the city of Plymouth), who worked with him in the 1960s, recalls Sargant as 'a human dynamo . . . a giant both physically and clinically'. Dr Henry Oakeley, his registrar in the late 1960s, considers Sargant 'a big man—with a big head! A real alpha male. If he'd been a gorilla, he would have been one of those huge male silverbacks.'

If he hadn't been a doctor, Sargant would have made an excellent adventurer or soldier, carving out swathes of territory for the British Empire, or holding off cavalry charges against impossible odds by sheer dint of determination alone. He was that kind of man—and it was that kind of energy that he brought to British psychiatry when he entered the discipline in the 1930s.

Sargant's extraordinary drive is perhaps best illustrated by his bedside manner. Dr Henry Rollin, emeritus consultant at the Horton Hospital in Epsom, recalls the standard Sargant approach: 'He was a showman. A wonderful man to watch perform. He would say'—Rollin banged the flat of his hand on the table—' "You're BETTER! I bloody well WON'T ALLOW YOU to say you're not better! YOU'RE BETTER! AREN'T YOU?" He'd bang and bash until they gave in and said, "OK, I'm better." '

According to Owen, such was Sargant's confidence in his techniques that he could diagnose a patient's mental state before he examined them. 'You would sit in the consulting room with him and the doorknob would turn, and Sargant would say, "HE'S BETTER!" And I'd say, "He hasn't even walked through the door yet!" ' Owen laughed. 'And he'd say, "Aaah, but did you see the way he turned the doorknob? That would have been very slow a week or a fortnight ago. HE'S BETTER!" '

While his energy, self-confidence and drive marked out Sargant as a leader from an early age, many chose not to follow him: as he told the *Sunday Times* in 1977, 'Some people think I'm a marvellous doctor. Others think I'm the work of the Devil.' Having interviewed more than forty of his former colleagues, I can testify to the accuracy of this statement. So, while Owen holds that Sargant was 'the sort of person of whom legends are made', another interviewee—an eminent medical figure—told me, 'I don't think he should escape hellfire for all the damage he did.'

The root of the amazing antipathy that Sargant generated lay in his rejection of standard psychoanalytical methods. For him, talking to patients was all well and good but it was actually unlikely to cure anyone. For the treatment of complex, debilitating illnesses such as schizophrenia and depression, *physical* intervention was essential. Anyone who thought otherwise he deemed a 'sofa merchant'.

In the course of his crusade against mental illness, Sargant proved himself eager to embrace all kinds of new physical treatments that others regarded as unwarranted, untested or dangerous. At the top of the list was the practice of leucotomy (lobotomy), which he prescribed with a frequency that appalled other psychiatrists. Dr Henry Rollin recalls that when he prepared his junior doctors for their Diploma of Psychological Medicine examinations, he instructed them that if Sargant asked how they would treat any chronic psychiatric illness, they should always respond 'leucotomy'. This tactic worked for a number of his students: 'Chronic depression, chronic schizophrenia, chronic whatever it was, when he asks, "What treatment should you give?" they should say, "leucotomy." "GOOD!" Sargant would say. "GOOD! GOOD! And what if they *relapse*? What should you do *then*?" They should say, "*Another* leucotomy!" "*GOOD!*"'

Sargant's enthusiasm for physical treatment might have resulted from his own experience of long-term depression: he attacked psychiatric illnesses head-on, with no quarter; in fact, many colleagues believe that he chose psychiatry as a career specifically because of his own experiences with depression.

David Owen remembers him explaining that all the pain he had witnessed as a neurologist was nothing compared to that of chronic depression. 'How often have you seen somebody commit suicide because of pain?' Sargant asked Owen one day when they were on the wards, then answered the question himself: 'Answer: practically never. Occasionally but very, very rare. But how many times,' Sargant continued, 'have you seen somebody commit suicide because of *depression*? Frequently.' Owen concludes, '*Ipso facto*, according to Sargant, that explains why depression is such a bloody awful illness. That is what people forget, what they don't understand. This is a terrible, terrible thing.'

To counter this suffering, Sargant was willing to pursue treatment beyond the levels at which other psychiatrists would admit defeat. If a low dose of antidepressants didn't work, it must be doubled. If that didn't work, it should be doubled again. If it still didn't work, the drug should be combined with other treatments. The trademarks of Sargant's zeal became the combination of various physical treatments, and the steady increase in doses of drugs and ECT.

His maverick tendencies ensured that Sargant became the man to whom other psychiatrists around the UK referred their intractable patients. Faced with such cases he was forced to treat them with still higher doses. It was this, along with his wholesale rejection of psychoanalytic techniques, that alarmed his colleagues, to whom such wholesale prescriptions were frequently irresponsible and occasionally downright dangerous.

One junior anaesthetist at St Thomas's in the 1970s recalls an occasion when a patient taking monoamine oxidases (MAOIs) for depression needed an anaesthetic before general surgery. Since the combination of MAOIs with the current anaesthetics was deemed potentially lethal, the anaesthetist rang Sargant to arrange for the patient to be taken off the drugs before the operation. Sargant wasn't having any of it. 'She has to stay on them,' he barked down the telephone. 'I'm not going to make any compromise.' Well, asked the anaesthetist, what would happen if the patient died on the table? 'Just tell them Dr Sargant said it would be all right,' was the reply. The anaesthetist, deciding that he was 'not in the business of killing people', put the phone down, took the patient off the MAOIs and the operation went ahead.

Anne Dally, who set about writing Sargant's biography shortly after his death, is unsurprised by such stories. 'He used to give huge doses and he was known for that . . . He was very lucky—he had a very lucky streak about him . . . He did a lot of very dangerous things with his patients but they never seemed to die on him or anything like that. Had they died, he would have got into real trouble. But they never did!'

Malcolm Lader, now professor of clinical psychopharmacology at the Institute of Psychiatry, gave me the best description of Sargant: 'There was a whiff of sulphur about him.' I quoted this to a number of interviewees, who all agreed it was appropriate; I suspect that Sargant himself might have chuckled.

Over the last couple of years, reports in the press and on the Internet have linked Sargant directly to Ewen Cameron's CIA-funded experiments at the Allan. While this is not entirely fair, there are clear similarities between the two men, as Sargant's treatment of one patient demonstrates.

In the winter of 1969 Anne White, a long-time sufferer of depression, hit rock bottom. In the previous three years she had had three children. Following the birth of each, she had become depressed but each time the gloom had lifted with the next pregnancy. After the birth of her last child, however, there was no escape.

White and her family lived in Zambia, where doctors didn't know what to do with her. She was sent to Johannesburg, in South Africa, where she received ECT, to no avail. 'It went on and on,' she remembers. 'I could sit down for days and days and not want to do anything. You could have told me that one of my kids had been run over by a bus . . . or that I had won the lottery, and there was no feeling. Nothing. Almost like a hibernation state.'

When her life became intolerable, Anne attempted suicide, slashing her wrists. Now that the situation was critical, her husband's medical insurers took charge. On New Year's Eve 1969 she and her children were flown to Britain where, on 9 March 1970, she left the children with her parents and reported to St Thomas's Hospital. She had been told that she would be treated in Scutari Ward, in St Thomas's itself, but when she arrived she was told to report instead to the Royal Waterloo Hospital for Women and Children, overlooking the Royal Festival Hall. There, she was given a check-up and a gown, and led to Ward 5, on the top floor.

Ward 5 was Sargant's domain. With twenty-two beds, most of them in single or double rooms, it was where the most serious psychiatric cases were treated. The ward was essentially one long corridor with doors off either side. There was a communal area, a dining area and a nurses' station, near the door. And it was in Ward 5 that Anne White's treatment became controversial.

According to his own papers, Sargant came up with the idea for his new technique in 1964. After leucotomising patients suffering from chronic anxiety states he noticed that they tended to become depressed and wondered whether their problem hadn't been depression in the first place. In order to avoid such errors in the future, before any leucotomy was performed the patients were given 'a long full course of combined antidepressant drugs and ECT'.

Since the combination of drugs and ECT frightened the patients, Sargant wondered if it might not be more humane to put them to sleep throughout the process. That way, they need not consciously endure the weeks of treatment. The unexpected result was that when they were woken up, the patients were noticeably better. Many no longer needed a leucotomy. 'We had accidentally found a way,' he reported, 'of giving a prolonged anaesthetic to a person going through a long painful psychiatric treatment just as one gives an anaesthetic for a surgical operation.' 'Modified narcosis' was born. The basic procedure was simple. Patients were put to sleep with a cocktail of barbiturates. While asleep, they were also fed antidepressants. Two or three times a week, they were woken and given ECT.

Narcosis, originally a procedure that involved putting patients to sleep to allow their minds to rest, usually lasted a few days, or possibly a couple of weeks. By the time of Sargant's report to the 5th World Congress on Psychiatry in 1968, however, he had increased the period to three months. 'Undoubtedly,' he concluded, 'what we're doing is we're breaking up long, set patterns of behaviour, which don't respond to so-to-speak quick treatments.'

Sargant was trying to cure his patients, and he wanted only the best for them. But his comments about 'breaking up' patterns of behaviour through the use of ECT, drugs and prolonged sleep were more than a little reminiscent of work taking place across the Atlantic. In Canada, of course, Ewen Cameron had a word for this technique. It was 'depatterning'.

Anne White had no idea about any of this. When she arrived in Ward 5 she was examined by Dr John Pollitt, who told her that her brain needed rest, that the feelings that were making her depressed would vanish once she was asleep. Then she was shot full of drugs. She was placed in the Narcosis Room with another three women. Like Cameron's sleep rooms, the ward was in semi-permanent darkness, with blinds over the windows and the lights off. At the foot of her bed was a small desk, at which was permanently stationed one of St Thomas's Nightingale nurses.

Many of the Nightingales who monitored the sleeping patients in the Narcosis Room were students, on their rotation of different hospital wards. Every fifteen minutes the Nightingales' job was to record the patients' sleep patterns—how deeply they were sleeping, if they were having nightmares or resting quietly. For this purpose they had a book of graph paper, which they were told to shade in different colours: white meant awake, grey half asleep and black fully asleep.

The Nightingales also had to wake the patients every six hours to feed them, wash them, check their blood pressure and take them to the lavatory. Since they were still heavily medicated, they were hard to wake, and frequently reluctant to eat or drink anything.

Thirty years on, Nightingales recall the experience of working on Ward 5 differently. Some say the experience was fascinating, that they regarded it as a great honour to be working for Dr Sargant, that the patients were happy to be sleeping and never complained. Others, however, hated the experience.

One of the latter group, Jane, recalls, 'I very nearly gave up nursing because of [Ward 5].' Her job was to sit at a desk in the darkened room facing the sleeping patients, listening to their breathing. There was a small Anglepoise lamp on the desk with a special shade to stop light reaching the sleeping patients but otherwise the room was dark. She sat in that room for three months. 'It was horrible. Horrible,' she says. 'Being shut up with these ladies for hours on end and seeing them in a vegetative state . . . It didn't take a lot of brainpower to realise that this wasn't the norm.'

In the morning, when the new shift of young Nightingales arrived for work, their duties were assigned: 'We all hated it. It was like, you'd go on duty in the morning to be told, "You're in the Narcosis Room," and there would be a sort of awful, "Oh, no! Not again!" feeling.' Jane didn't like waking the patients up, trying to get them to communicate, and especially disliked giving them their pills to put them back to sleep, which, she says, they often fought against.

Mo Harvey, Ward 5's sister for four years, agrees that some of the junior Nightingales disliked working in the Narcosis Room. 'Several of them were unhappy,' she says. 'But I think they were generally unhappy and certainly the ones that I remember as being the most unhappy didn't actually finish their nurses' training—so it wasn't particularly Ward 5 and the narcosis that upset them.'

On the contrary, according to Harvey, working on Ward 5 was a hugely rewarding experience since it was at the cutting edge of mental-health therapy. In contrast to the unhappy, sleepy patients that Jane remembers, Harvey says that they were pleased to be helped and quite willing to take their drugs. 'You wouldn't just be doing this in silence,' she says. 'You would be interacting with the patients all the time, and sometimes there would be quite a bit of laughter in the Narcosis Room at lunchtime. They weren't zombies!'

But 'zombies' is exactly the phrase that most of the nineteen Nightingales I interviewed used to describe them. When they were woken up, the patients had to be assisted to walk, were unable to recognise the nurses they had seen the day before, and were frequently unable to recall where they were, or why.

Dr James Birley, a past president of the Royal College of Psychiatrists, recalls the theory in terms alarmingly reminiscent of Cameron's psychic driving: 'It was the idea that the brain's circuits that were fuelling the psychotic ideas, or the neurosis, or whatever it was, could be sort of turned off and something else could take their place as people recovered and were reassured. This was the idea. All his forms of treatment like that were related to this idea of "breaking up the circuits"—that was the sort of phrase he liked to use—and replacing them with more healthy views of themselves.'

That's one way of putting it. Others came up with more disturbing analogies. Jane, who says she still feels traumatised by her time on Ward 5, felt that 'They were trying to take over these people, and almost infiltrate them, change their personalities, change who they were. Almost acting like a god—if that makes sense? . . . The sort of thing you'd expect in Hitler's time.'

In Anne White's case, the situation was worse. Naturally tolerant to the drugs she was being given to make her sleep, she needed higher doses, which caused her blood pressure to drop drastically. The moment she was woken up, she felt unwell. 'They woke you up and poured a jug of water down you,' she says, 'and as soon as I got upright I passed out because my blood pressure was down in my boots . . . If I stood up, I just passed out.'

Worse, as White became habituated to the drugs she found herself unable to sleep in the Narcosis Room. So she lay there, sedated, awake. 'For day after day, with no sensory input, really—and not sleeping!' As might be expected of a patient immobilised in a silent, darkened room, White began to experience a form of sensory deprivation. 'Everything is a blur,' she says. 'You're desperately tired and want to go to sleep but for some reason you're up, couldn't get to sleep and watching the hours go by—but you can't do anything. You can't turn the light on, can't do anything, and you're just lying there . . . It just went on for day after day. It was almost like I was being abused, or tortured.'

Of course, sleep and drugs were only two-thirds of the treatment. Three times a week, patients in the Narcosis Room were given ECT. To many, this was the most worrying part of the process.

The trainee anaesthetist who conducted the ECT sessions recalls the Narcosis Room as 'very scary' and says that ECT duties there were regarded as the 'punishment rota' for the anaesthesiology department. 'You didn't upset the secretary,' he says, 'because somebody had to go—and if she was cross with you that was where you went.' The young anaesthetists nicknamed Ward 5 'The Black Hole of Calcutta'.

'You'd end up waking them,' says the doctor, ' "Hello, dear, I'm Dr so-and-so, I'm here to help you", talk to them perfectly—they were not ill-treated in a kind of Bedlam fashion—put a needle in the vein, you always did, to give them the anaesthetic. Give them the ECT. Then you'd have to wake them up because you couldn't leave a patient anaesthetised . . . It was just horrible to go into this room of sleepy people, wake them up, put them back to sleep again, zap their brains, wake them up again, then put them back to sleep.'

Finally, once the patients were back in bed and sleeping soundly, 'We'd turn the lights out—and go and do something less spooky.'

The doctor says that because none of the anaesthetists was happy about the procedure, they all went out of their way not to get chosen for the ECT sessions. 'None of us wanted to be involved,' he says. 'It was easy work—it wasn't that—and safe, let's not be unfair: it was perfectly safe in a physical sense, perfectly conducted and easy. But we hated it. And there was a feeling that this is—odd.'

To Anne White, the regime was worse than 'odd', and she soon began complaining that she wanted to be taken off it. At first the doctors encouraged her to stay longer but when she insisted they became angry. Finally they took her out of the Narcosis Room and put her into a single room where, she says, they simply stopped giving her the drugs.

Normally when patients came out of deep narcosis they were treated gently and shown newspapers to let them know what the date was and how long they had been asleep. Most importantly, their drugs were not simply terminated: large doses of barbiturates over two or three months meant that their bodies had become used to the drugs; simply stopping them would have been dangerous.

But according to White, this was what happened to her. The result was that she went through a form of cold turkey. The experience was horrific: 'Just lying there on the bed, with nobody really caring that much, and the bed shaking because you get muscle aches,' she says. 'It's like if you see people having the chills or shakes with malaria—the whole bed is shaking. Plus the fact that you are confused because you are gradually coming out of this drug regime.' White felt that she was being punished for not agreeing to more narcosis. To counter the shakes, she says, Dr Pollitt gave her Artane—a drug used to treat Parkinson's disease.

Since all medical records from Ward 5 have been destroyed, it is impossible to verify this story. Understandably, having been depressed and heavily sedated for a number of weeks, White cannot recall exactly what happened to her in Ward 5 or for how long, so it is possible that her memories of the period are unreliable. She does know, however, that she was admitted on 9 March 1970 and that she came out on 11 May.

She also knows that, after discharge, her memory failed to return. When she went to see Dr Pollitt about this, he told her that she had received twenty-six bilateral ECTs—between two and five times the usual dose. The result, she says, was substantial memory loss. 'Some of my memory functions pretty well but I really can't recall my teen years. I can't remember my children when they were babies at all. I can't remember, you know, the things that people rejoice in: first steps and all that. I can't remember any of those things. First words. Nothing. It's gone.'

White has nothing against ECT ('It's really a very good treatment') but she is extremely angry about her time in Ward 5. Since, however, there are no records and Dr Pollitt refused to speak to her about her treatment afterwards (he has since died), there appears to be no way of working out exactly what happened during her time there.*

Thirty years later, psychiatrists tend to shrink at the mention of Sargant's modified-narcosis regime. Apart from anything else, keeping people asleep for long periods of time is dangerous—Sargant admitted that four of his patients died as a result of this treatment. Then there is the matter of the ECT.

As is common knowledge, ECT can lead to memory loss, and for this reason it is administered in low doses so that patients can be monitored afterwards. But in Ward 5, where the patients were asleep all the time, it is hard to determine how effective the monitoring could have been. Mo Harvey says that it was possible to tell how the patients were because they talked when they were woken for their meals, exercise and baths. She would know when to stop the regime, she says, because 'they would begin to loosen up'.

Others disagree. Dr Desmond Kelly, who worked with Sargant at St Thomas's, remembers the procedure as 'a bit hairy'. 'When people are having a course of ECT,' he says, 'if their memory gets really bad, one would stop it. But with narcosis, they weren't able to tell you that, and so

---

* Painful though the loss of her early memories may be, it must be acknowledged that, since the treatment, Anne White has learned to play a number of musical instruments, qualified as a doctor and become a full professor of medicine. On the basis of these impressive achievements, it would be hard to argue that her ability to function successfully has been damaged. I suspect that Sargant and Pollitt would be proud of the outcome of narcosis treatment in this case.

there were some people whose memories were worse than they might have been as a consequence of it.'

This problem was highlighted by Sargant's habit of pursuing therapies until they worked: Anne Dally recalled, 'He'd give ECT sixty times.'

'What's normal?' I asked.

'Three or four,' she replied.

It should be noted that while there are similarities between Sargant's deep narcosis and Cameron's depatterning techniques—and while Sargant was and is regarded by many of his contemporaries as a quack—deep narcosis was nothing like as intensive as psychic driving. The true nature of the two men's relationship, however, is more contentious.

When news of what Cameron had been doing at the Allan broke in the 1970s—and former patients began filing legal complaints—his reputation went into a nose dive, from which it will almost certainly never recover. At this point it appears that Sargant went out of his way to distance himself from his Canadian friend. His personal papers do not contain a single piece of correspondence between them.

Over dinner in Montréal, Allan Memorial psychiatrist Peter Roper recalled visiting Sargant in the UK in the 1970s to discover that his old friend suddenly regarded him as *persona non grata*. 'Sargant had changed completely. At one time he was very friendly, advising me, but now he was distant. He didn't really have much to talk about.'

To Roper, the fact that Sargant was recoiling from Cameron became clear during a phone call when Sargant denied point-blank ever having corresponded with him about Cameron's treatments. But Roper had a letter in front of him, signed by the man himself. 'Why did Sargant deny the connection, and to similar treatment to Cameron?' he asked. 'I wonder if Sargant's estate, or Sargant himself, might worry about being sued, even at this late date.'

To conspiracy theorists, however, there is another, more intriguing reason for Sargant's silence on the matter: that he was a spy.

If we are to believe certain sources, Sargant's work at the Royal Waterloo was part of British secret involvement in the CIA's MKULTRA project. And if this is so, what happened in Ward 5 is not an example of a misguided attempt to combat mental illness but a terrible, criminal piece of human experimentation.

How close was Sargant to British Intelligence?

According to the writer Gordon Thomas, just before Sargant died he admitted that he worked for MI6. This seems unlikely. One psychiatrist who did work for MI6—but who declined to be named—recalls that Sargant 'loved doing things for the Government' but was never 'part of the official group of psychiatrists who saw sick spies and things like that . . . he wasn't on their list of official people.'

He does seem, however, to have done some work for the British Security Service, MI5. According to intelligence historian Nigel West, Sargant was MI5's in-house psychiatrist for a long time, and Mo Harvey, Sargant's ward sister, remembers that her boss—indiscreet at the best of times— liked nothing more than to hunker down in Ward 5 and tell tales about his cloak-and-dagger exploits. 'On a Friday afternoon he would sit down and be quite expansive about what he'd been doing,' she says.

In the course of his anecdotes, Sargant revealed that he had been employed by a British intelligence organisation: '[It was] one that had a house somewhere for debriefing people.' The psychiatrist's opinion of his employers, it seems, was not positive. 'He thought that the people there were "in need of treatment"!' says Harvey. 'He would say, "I've been doing some work—and oh dear! They're such funny people!" I asked Harvey if she had known at the time that Sargant was MI5's in-house psychiatrist. 'Oh, yeah!' she replied.

Sargant alluded to his clandestine work in his autobiography. '[On] one or two occasions,' he wrote, 'I confess to having been so scared by information given me that I have preferred to burn the records without delay.' But it's hard to see how this comment—or any other information that has emerged since his death—points to any involvement of MI5 (or the CIA) in his controversial treatment in Ward 5 at the Royal Waterloo. 'I don't think so!' says the MI6 psychiatrist. 'Sargant wasn't like that. That would have meant setting up special . . . No. I don't think Sargant would have done that.'

On the contrary, all indications are that, after their initial dalliance with truth-drug research, MI5 and MI6 were disparaging about brainwashing in general. It's hard to imagine them sanctioning experiments on civilian mental patients without their consent.

Cyril Cunningham, the MoD's in-house brainwashing expert, makes this point pretty clearly: 'I had pressure put on me—even the highest levels of the US Army and US Air Force . . . were very excited about it. But we British were a bit more serious than that.' Apart from anything else, brainwashing research was terribly expensive: 'I was inundated when I was at AI9 with various recommendations from America,' he said, 'none of which we could tinker with in any way, partly because we didn't have the funds or the facilities to do anything about it.'

The true extent of Sargant's clandestine advice to the British Government on brainwashing will probably never be known—a fact which he appears to have found rather galling. 'Most of us are expected,' he noted in his autobiography, 'to leave instructions that when we die all our notes will be destroyed.' This was rather sad, he said, since future investigators would have no idea what had happened: 'I sometimes regret it. Perhaps it should be the duty of those who possess explosive secret information to ensure at least that the record does not die with them.'

Perhaps he really felt that way. On the other hand, since his correspondence with Ewen Cameron has been destroyed and he refused to speak to Peter Roper about the links between the two men, it appears that his reputation meant more to him than future reconstructions of what he had been up to in his long, controversial career.

Posterity certainly seems to have been a motivating factor in Sargant's reaction when news broke in the late 1970s that deep narcosis had also been prescribed in a small hospital in Chelmsford, Australia. This time the perpetrator was a maverick psychiatrist and self-publicist named Harry Bailey, who saw Sargant as something of a mentor. Tragically, it turned out that without the expertise of the St Thomas's Nightingales to care for the sleeping patients it was impossible to conduct the therapy safely.

Starting in the mid-1960s—when Sargant discovered the uses of deep narcosis—Bailey put depressives to sleep for long periods, sometimes without their consent, and shot them full of drugs and ECT. In the first six months, he killed five patients with the technique. In the next two years another five died and by the end of 1974, deep-sleep therapy, as he called it, had been responsible for at least twenty-four deaths.

In an attempt to legitimise what he had been doing, Bailey went out of his way to link himself to the famous St Thomas's psychiatrist, claiming that Sargant had been a friend on and off for about thirty years. There was more than a little truth in this: one of Bailey's nurses recalled that he often spoke of a macabre competition between the two psychiatrists to see 'who could keep their patients in the deepest coma without killing them'. Like his correspondence with Cameron, however, Sargant's letters to and from Harry Bailey have been destroyed. All that remains is his reaction when he was asked to testify at Bailey's trial. He could come and testify, he said, but if he did, 'I should have found myself supporting the prosecution and not the defence.' In 1985, when Bailey heard that his old mentor felt this way, he committed suicide.

It's hard to know what to make of William Sargant. Almost all the doctors I interviewed thought that he had gone too far in his treatments, and that he had actively damaged patients. This notion is hard to dispel: one Nightingale who worked with him in the early 1960s recalled his work in Ward 5 in ambivalent terms. Two hours later, she rang me back. 'I've just talked with my husband,' she said, 'who has reminded me that I had no time for William Sargant or his treatments at all.' That's what you deal with when you ask about Sargant, a man whose entry in *A Century of Psychiatry* opens with the statement that he was 'both one of the best loved and most hated of twentieth century psychiatrists'.

At the same time as they were telling me about Sargant's excesses, however, almost every doctor I interviewed acknowledged that he was an important psychiatrist, whose ruthless pursuit of cures for psychiatric illness had transformed numerous lives, and psychiatry itself. 'At the time there were appalling patients in mental hospitals with no treatment whatsoever,' recalled Dr Henry Oakeley. 'Sargant was the man who said that these people were suffering from medical illnesses that needed treatment in hospital wards, with proper medication. He put physical brain psychiatry on the map.' Without him, said Oakeley, 'We'd still be sending schizophrenics off for psychotherapy.'

Today, whether you regard William Sargant as 'a dominating personality with the therapeutic courage of a lion' (David Owen) or 'autocratic, dangerous, a disaster' (a senior psychiatrist who declined to be named) depends entirely on where you stand with regard to psychotherapy, psychiatry and modern medicine.

Notes currently proliferating on the Internet refer to Sargant as a 'right-wing scumbag MI5 psychiatrist'. This is both ill-informed and unfair. Sargant wasn't an MKULTRA operator, brainwashing patients to see what happened—as David Owen is keen to make clear: 'He wasn't a Dr Sinister, you know. He really wasn't.' Even deep narcosis, although regarded as dangerous these days, is double-edged. 'There were some deaths with it,' recalled another colleague, Desmond Kelly, 'but it must have saved a hell of a lot of lives.' No doubt the debate will continue in the years to come.

The case is slightly clearer when it comes to Ewen Cameron. His successor at the Allan, Robert Cleghorn, stated the problem succinctly: 'In Cameron's book [*Objective and Clinical Psychiatry*], the key words "sympathy", "patience" and "insight" stood out like beacons. Unhappily, he was unable to bring these magic words to bear prominently on his dealings with disturbed people.' The result, he wrote, was 'therapy gone mad, with scant criteria'.

Donald Hebb had an interesting take on his former colleague. In his zeal to prove that he was a great scientist, he said, Cameron had ploughed ahead with radical and dangerous therapies, ignoring all the warning signs. 'Cameron,' he concluded, 'was a victim of his own kind of brainwashing: he wanted something so much that he was blinded by the evidence in front of his own eyes.'

Even the CIA wasn't impressed. At one point a group of officers visited the Allan to see how things were going and Cameron offered to demonstrate the results of psychic driving. He paraded a patient before them who had listened to the same driving message over half a million times but, when questioned, the patient's mind was so scrambled that he was unable to recall any part of it. Sid Gottlieb, in charge of the MKULTRA operation, later admitted that 'we never got any payload out of [Cameron's work]'. In 1960 the CIA pulled the plug on the research, and Cameron's funding dried up. John Gittinger later told a Senate hearing that supporting Cameron was 'a foolish mistake. We shouldn't have done it. I'm sorry we did.'

Back at the Allan Memorial Institute in June, 2005, security guard Paul relived the sordid details of the CIA affair with relish. As he led me through the building's basement—a labyrinth of corridors and former treatment rooms—we stopped from time to time so that he could point out various remnants of the Cameron era. 'These were the patients' rooms,' he told me, 'or "torture chambers", as I call them.' He paused for a moment. 'They were here in the basement to kill the sound of the screams. Jeez, those poor guys! It must have been like waking up inside a concentration camp!'

Deep beneath the building, rooms PO-051 and -052 were still fitted with the two-way mirrors Cameron had installed so that doctors could monitor patients' reactions to various drugs. LSD and curare were administered there to people like Janine Huard and Val Orlikow: kindly, middle-class ladies who had somehow got lost in life and come looking for help. Not that they received it. 'Sometimes', said Paul, 'they were tied down.'

The basement corridors, waxed to a high sheen, were overhung by a dense network of heating pipes in the ceiling; wandering around was rather like exploring the belly of an old warship. The morgue was now the staff smoking room, the ECT room, fitted with two-way glass to allow observation from next door, the laundry.

Servants' stairs from the basement, leading nowhere, were now walled in behind an office where Cameron's eleven-digit safe remained. 'This was where he used to keep his LSD,' said Paul. Around the hospital, further relics of the era abounded. I pushed one door open to find it jammed against a huge bookshelf of rotting psychiatric journals from the 1940s and 1950s. Up in the building's attics we found further remnants: old medical papers and manuals lurking among the heating ducts and air-conditioning systems. Paul said that he had once found one of Cameron's old golf clubs up here. 'Only odds and ends are left now,' he told me.

In the conference room there was a series of framed photographs of former heads of the Allan. Ewen Cameron was among them, austere in his tweed suit and tie-pin. I wondered what he'd think if he were there today. Would he apologise, or attempt to justify his work? 'I don't think he looked upon them as *experiments*,' Peter Roper told me over dinner. 'I mean, he was an intelligent, thoughtful, considerate man . . . His ideas on therapy did make sense at the time because he was trying to help people.'

On the ground floor was the library, with its impressive gargoyle-fronted mahogany bookshelves, preserved exactly as they were when Lady Marguerite Allan donated her home to the Royal Victoria Hospital in 1940. Just outside was the coffee bar—the same coffee bar to which Janine Huard had headed on that day in 1962 when she couldn't stand the psychic driving any longer. Cameron had stopped her, of course. He always did. 'Janine,' he had entreated, 'don't you *want* to get well?'

Forty-five years on, the Allan was full of ghosts; Lady Marguerite was only one of them.

We ended our tour in the stables where Leonard Rubenstein had built Cameron's equipment: psychic-driving loop-players, pressurised airguns for blasting human eyeballs, polygraphs and sensory-deprivation boxes. Today the building is the hospital's Human Resources Centre, staffed by polite, smartly dressed executives on orthopaedic swivel chairs with mouse mats and flat-fronted PC screens.

On a noticeboard was a sign: 'Great minds discuss ideas. Average minds discuss events. Small minds discuss people.'

Perhaps that's the message of the Allan Memorial Institute, where Ewen Cameron forgot about events and people, casting himself instead into the world of ideas—to prove that he was, indeed, a great mind.

8

Jesus Loves You

CLARKE WANTS TERRORISTS TREATED LIKE VICTIMS OF
CULT BRAINWASHING
The Home Secretary has told colleagues that anti-brainwashing techniques
used to 'deprogramme' cult members could be used to fight the sort of
fanaticism behind the July 7 bombings.

The Daily Telegraph, 2 October 2005

It was only natural that Ford Greene was nervous. This was his first kidnap. Not that the operation hadn't been well planned: in fact, preparations
had been under way for over a month and Greene, the leader of the
fourteen-man team, had ensured that everyone was properly briefed. The
two heavies hired to perform the snatch had been equipped with a blindfold and handcuffs to immobilise the victim and a length of rope to tie her
legs. A van had been borrowed for the getaway. Greene was the driver.

The plan was straightforward. Greene knew that his victim was due to
visit her parents in Ross, California, at ten a.m. on Wednesday, 13 April
1977. All he had to do was grab her as she arrived, bundle her into the van
and drive her to a safe-house thirty minutes away in San Geronimo.
Preparations had been made there, too: over the last week, Greene had selected a basement bedroom in which to incarcerate the subject and examined every inch of it meticulously, hiding anything that might help her
either to escape or to harm herself. He had removed all glass objects that
could be smashed and deployed as weapons. Content that the room was
sanitised, he had then nailed boards over the windows to ensure that she
couldn't break them and that no one could see in from outside.

As the team waited, Greene checked his watch. Perhaps all kidnappers got pre-snatch nerves. But perhaps their nerves were worse when they, like Ford Greene, were about to kidnap their own sister.

Events leading up to the kidnap were set in motion nearly three years earlier when Catherine Greene wandered into San Francisco's Sproul Plaza looking for something to do. A tall, vivacious eighteen-year old, she had led a privileged life. Her father, Crawford, was one of the city's leading attorneys and the family lived in some affluence. Virtually all of her relatives were Yale graduates; while studying there her father had struck up what was to be a lifelong friendship with a James Buckley, who went on to become a New York senator—and the godfather of his first son, Ford. The Greene household was full of comings and goings when the kids were young. It was that kind of home.

Catherine, who had recently graduated from high school and gained a place at the University of California at Berkeley, was talented, attractive, popular—and lost. All her life she felt that she had been searching for something but couldn't put her finger on what it was. Like a lot of teenagers growing up at the tail end of the 1960s, she was convinced that somehow, things should be better.

Catherine didn't want to condemn her parents' values but she didn't especially want to live by them either. She found her inspiration elsewhere: in Hermann Hesse's *Siddhartha*, for example. She had been intensely moved by Franco Zeffirelli's film *Brother Son, Sister Moon*, about the life of St Francis of Assisi, immediately identifying with the hero who, like her, had come from a privileged background and struggled to come to terms with his mission in life. She'd hung a picture of St Francis above her bed.

Nobody seemed to know what was wrong with Catherine. Most people didn't even realise that something *was* wrong. The few times she tried to tell adults about her spiritual concerns, she'd received the same answers: 'You'll grow out of it' or 'All young people think like that'. In an attempt to sort out her life, Catherine had deferred her entrance to Berkeley and taken a year off. In November 1974, she took a trip into town with her mother, Daphne, and found herself alone in Sproul Plaza.

At the time, the plaza was a bustling market for alternative lifestyles. Vegetarians, Marxists, Jesus freaks, hippies—they were all there, peddling their various lifestyles. Having grown up around San Francisco, there wasn't a lot that Catherine hadn't seen before. But then, on the corner of the plaza, something caught her eye.

The stall consisted of a single desk and a pinboard covered with Polaroid photographs of a farm. In the pictures, young people tended crops, held hands, played guitars and listened to lectures. They all looked happy. A well-groomed young woman sat at the table with a sign above her head: 'Creative Community Project'.

Catherine had heard of the project but wasn't sure what it was, so she walked up to the stall, confronted the young woman and asked. Delighted at the interest, the girl told her that the Creative Community Project was a non-profit organisation that advocated a better life through philosophy, communal living and spirituality. The pictures of the happy-looking people, she said, had been taken at the organisation's retreat in northern California, not far from Berkeley. Catherine was fascinated: here was a group of people who, like her, felt that life was missing something and were trying actively to work out what it was. What really attracted her, however, was not what the girl said but the way she *listened*. As Catherine shared her spiritual doubts, she knew instinctively that her new friend was taking them in and understanding.

The next Tuesday, after choir practice, Catherine visited the project's headquarters, an imposing building on the north-east corner of the Berkeley campus, at 2717 Hearst Street. Inside, she was surprised to find that, in contrast to purveyors of alternative lifestyles hanging around the west coast at the time, the project's members were all smartly dressed and clean-shaven. They seemed to be completely out of touch! She was taking all this in when an official stood up and started to talk.

The man told a parable: 'The Blind Men and the Elephant'. Each blind man feels a different part of the elephant's body—its tail, its tusk, its leg, and so on. From this limited experience of the animal, each concludes that it resembles something completely different: a rope, a snake, a tree, and so forth. There follows a heated argument. None of the blind men can agree on what the elephant actually looks like. Of course, they are all wrong. An elephant doesn't resemble a rope or a snake or a tree. It only resembles an elephant. Life, said the speaker, was like that. You had to open your eyes! Perception was everything; true power came only from *understanding*. And that, he said, was what the Creative Community Project was all about.

At the end of the lecture there was a slide-show about the project's retreat to the north of San Francisco, just outside a town in Mendocino County called Boonville. All present were invited to visit for the weekend to learn more about the group's goals, to play sports, sing songs—and have a lot of fun, too.

Catherine wasn't sure. These guys were pretty weird. Besides, the girl she had met in Sproul Plaza wasn't there. But when a polite young man came up and asked her why she was worried, she eventually agreed to go along. That Friday, Catherine caught the Creative Community Project's bus to Boonville. And vanished.

Two days later, she phoned her mother and told her she was with the Family (the name by which project members referred to the organisation) and that she wanted to stay a week longer. Daphne Greene, who had never heard of either the Creative Community Project or the Family, assumed that her daughter was staying with a friend's family out of town, and agreed.

Catherine's next phone call, exactly a week later, came in the middle of her grandfather's birthday dinner. 'Mom! Guess what?'

When Daphne asked what a torrent of words poured down the line. Catherine said she had discovered what she wanted to do with her life. She had joined the Family and she wasn't coming home. At all. Flummoxed, Daphne asked what was going on: what *was* the Family? 'Well', said Catherine, excited, 'there was this lady, and she came from Korea . . .' Daphne narrowed her eyes: 'Is this anything to do with Reverend Moon?'

Catherine's heart leaped: her mother knew about Reverend Moon! That was fantastic! 'Yes!' she said 'He—'

But her mother cut her short again. '*Oh, shit.*'

What neither Catherine nor her mother had realised at the outset of her recruitment was that the Creative Community Project was one of a number of front organisations for the Unification Church or, as they were dubbed in the press, the Moonies. Catherine had joined one group offering spiritual and lifestyle advice, and ended up belonging to another. This didn't bother her: she had been looking for a spiritual organisation and, as her phone call made clear, she was happy. But it certainly bothered her mother. Over dinner that night, Daphne asked one of her guests, Albert Johnson, what he knew about the Moonies. Johnson, a Jesuit priest, told her that the Unification Church 'exploits young people's spirituality'. Daphne Greene had no idea whether or not that was true so she started reading up on the subject. What *was* the Unification Church, anyway?

As she soon discovered, the Unification Church was one of a number of new religious movements flourishing in the United States at the time.

The Church—like the brainwashing allegations that were soon to plague it—had emerged from Korea in the Cold War. When it was introduced to the United States in 1959, Unificationism struggled. In the mid-1960s, however, with the burgeoning interest in alternative lifestyles, word began to spread. Over the next decade, the aftermath of the liberal 1960s, the floundering war in Vietnam and the Watergate scandal, led to an increasing dissatisfaction with 'conventional' authoritarian organisations, and young people reached towards more 'authentic' ones. The Unification Church was one of a number of movements to benefit.

In the public mind, this was bad news. Hippies smoking pot in the 1960s was one thing. But running away from home to hook up with bizarre religions was something else. And the religions! Moonies, Children of God, Love Israel, Hare Krishna, the Love Family, Divine Light Mission: they multiplied like rabbits, each weirder than the last. To them you could add the new self-help programs that were springing up everywhere. Scientology, Synanon, Erhardt Seminars Testing, Life-spring, Mind Dynamics, and so on. The explosion of new groups across the country terrified parents everywhere. As Flo Conway and Jim Siegelman reported, in their study of the phenomenon:

America has been gripped by an epidemic of sudden personality change. The college student leaves school without warning and is discovered by his parents selling flowers on a street corner. The wealthy executive, taking full responsibility for his fate, quits his job at a moment's notice to sit on the bench and play the flute. A young mother abandons her children after having a 'personal encounter with the Holy Spirit' . . . Are these changes good or bad? Are they permanent? What's really behind them? Who's susceptible? Me? My kids? Everyone?

Worst of all, when the runaway kids were eventually tracked down by their parents, they weren't the same any more. They had a funny look in their eyes, as if they were focusing on something a long way off. They wore false smiles and spoke in a monotone. Their sense of humour and spontaneity were gone. Outwardly they were healthy, but inside something was missing, like apples that had been cored. 'There was something eerie about them,' wrote Conway and Siegelman, 'but it was nothing you could put your finger on'.

It was no surprise, then, that when Catherine Greene told her mother that she was now a Moonie and that she wasn't coming home, the result was consternation. Not knowing what to say, Daphne passed the phone to her eldest son, Ford. Thirty years later, Ford says at the time it struck him that Catherine was struggling to reconcile conflicting loyalties—to her biological family and her new ('real') family, the Moonies.

That Wednesday night, Ford and a friend, Jim, clambered into his BMW 1600 and drove up Highway 128 to Boonville to check on Catherine. They arrived early the next morning and were unimpressed. The Church compound consisted of a couple of rather ramshackle buildings and a few trailers in the middle of a field. Greene was even less impressed with the people he found there. 'There were maybe fifteen people,' he recalls, 'whose behaviour right away was strange. They were strange because they appeared to me guarded and suspicious. They wouldn't allow me any one-on-one time with Catherine. They were strange because when I, in curiosity, asked them what it was they were studying, what their books were about, they wouldn't tell me. Fuck! They were just weird!'

When Ford spoke to Catherine, she was distant. He thought she was saying what her companions wanted her to say, not what *she* wanted to say. After half an hour of trying unsuccessfully to get through to her, he and Jim climbed back into the car and drove off. They arrived at the coast off Mendocino at about nine a.m., cracked open a couple of beers and sat silently, watching the waves roll in and wondering what was going on.

Staring at the kelp, watching it ebb and flow with the tide, Greene decided that the reason Catherine had become involved with this group was that she was unable to trust other people. The Greene children's upbringing had been unconventional, and they regarded it as traumatic. Perhaps joining the Moonies was her way of coming to terms with her childhood. Filled with this revelation, Ford leaped back into the car and barrelled back to Boonville. This time he cornered Catherine without her chaperones and asked her if she was with these guys because she didn't know how to love people. According to him, she burst into tears and admitted that she was.

Ford thought he'd made a breakthrough. But no sooner had she said this than a number of Unification Church authorities stepped in. This

time, instead of being cagey, the Moonies asked if Ford and Jim would
like to come and learn more about the movement. If so, it would be best
if they returned at the weekend, when they could join the next course.
The boys agreed.

Sure enough, that Saturday morning Jim, Ford and a cousin, Oliver,
rocked up in the car at three a.m. Since everyone was asleep, the trio gathered some wood, built a huge bonfire in the middle of the Boonville compound and sat by it, drinking beer. 'It was not,' Greene laughs, 'a standard
Moonie wake-up that morning!' The three boys had shown up on the right
day but it was pretty clear that they were not taking the religious angle of
the organisation entirely seriously.

Not that the Unification Church instructors were discouraged. The
first thing they did when they found the three boys was to give them
a hearty welcome, feed them some breakfast—and separate them. They
were put into classes with the other new recruits in groups of ten.

It wasn't long before all three noticed how *incredibly friendly* everyone
was, wanting to hold hands all the time. Everywhere they went they were
followed by spiritual guides, who made sure that they were never unhappy or needed anything. Everyone said they loved each other. And they
were extremely busy! Every now and again, the three would exchange a
glance as their different groups passed each other, heading in different directions. But they didn't have time to get together and really talk about
what was happening. It was the same when Greene saw Catherine. There
just wasn't time to say any more than 'hi'.

The three boys heard the same lecture about the elephant and the blind
men. Greene thought it seemed reasonable. Afterwards the groups were
encouraged to sit in a circle so that each member could tell their story:
where they were from, how they came to be there and what their goals
were. When it was his turn, he decided to be honest. 'I'm really here,' he
told his group, 'to rescue my sister.' Without a moment's delay, the leader
of the group began chanting, 'We love you, Ford! We do! We love you,
Ford! We do!' The entire group joined in. Greene, who had been clinically depressed for eighteen months, was saucer-eyed. Was it *really* possible
that these people loved him? The holding hands, the singing, the uncon-
ditional love: he wasn't sure what it was all about—but it felt good.

Further lectures on philosophy were likewise intriguing. Greene and his
friends heard that humans were flawed and had to work hard to be pure.

God and man had a covenant. God did 95 per cent of the work. It was man's job to do the other 5 per cent but that 5 per cent took 100 per cent of his energy. Love was a goal, and a real possibility. Science and religion had been at odds for too long. It was time they were unified. 'It made big sense,' he concedes today.

After a busy day meeting people, attending lectures and playing dodge-ball, the recruits were bedded down in sleeping-bags in a communal dormitory. At eight the next morning, a young man with a guitar charged in, singing at the top of his voice, 'When the red, red robin goes bob-bob-bobbing along!' Everyone in the dormitory leaped out of bed, jumped into the air and shouted, at the top of their voices, 'Good morning, Heavenly Father! Good morning, brothers and sisters!' Greene thought it was pretty 'out there'—and the guy couldn't play guitar.

By the end of the second day, though, he was on his way to being persuaded. Oliver and Jim were not: throughout the day they had been gesturing at him, trying to get his attention to tell him they wanted out. To their horror, when Sunday night came he said he was staying. Apart from anything else, there was a lot of live music, and it was fantastic. They told him he was an asshole, and left.

And so it was that Ford Greene, the twenty-one-year-old who had gone to rescue his little sister from the Unification Church, became a Moonie, too.

Ford and Catherine's mother was now extremely concerned—and extremely angry. Daphne called everyone she thought might be able to help her to learn more about the Unification Church. In the course of her investigations she bumped into other parents whose children had vanished, then made mysterious calls from Boonville to tell them they weren't coming home. Clearly, she thought, something weird was going on. And something had to be done about it.

Parental concern from all over the United States eventually led to the formation of the Citizens' Freedom Foundation, dedicated to learning about strange cults and finding out how to go about extracting their children from them. The way the CFF saw things, the Moonies and their other weird religious companions were exploiting American kids for financial purposes. Children who joined the organisations were expected to donate to them their personal possessions, including stereos, musical instruments and cars. These items were then redistributed or sold to raise cash.

In some cases recruits were fed badly and kept in poor conditions—at least one 1970s group encouraged acolytes to forage in the garbage cans behind fast-food outlets. Once they had gone through their initial training, moreover, they were put to work for up to twenty hours a day raising further funds. Popular fundraising activities in the early 1970s included selling flowers, peanut brittle, American flags, fortune cookies, homemade candles or vacuum cleaners. These items, hawked on the street or door-to-door, were sold with the assurance that the profits would go to charity. All too often, however, the 'charity' turned out to be the religious group itself. In fact, that was the most suspicious thing of all: many of the 'cult' leaders appeared to be running multi-national corporations on the backs of the young adherents' efforts, while living lives of luxury. The groups, concluded the CFF, were parasites, feeding on American kids' idealism.

Children not involved in selling shabby products on the street were sent out to make new recruits. As Daphne Greene and her colleagues soon learned, there were few lengths to which new religious movements would not go to hook in punters. The most common was lying. At various points the Unification Church lured new recruits under the names New Educational Development Systems Inc., the Collegiate Association for the Research into Principles, The Family, Creative Community Project, 3L Associates, and International Family Association. In this way, even young people who were careful to avoid the more notorious of the new religious movements could be suckered in and not realise where they were until it was too late. It was scandalous.

Catherine, of course, didn't see it that way. She was having a ball. After receiving her basic training she was dispatched with a mobile flower-selling team to raise funds for the Unification Church. She turned out to be one of the best flower-sellers the organisation ever had. Her team rocketed around the west coast in a battered Dodge van, hawking flowers in the street, in bars, restaurants and clubs. They would travel for up to a month at a time. Anywhere that anyone might want to buy a bunch of flowers, Catherine and her team were there with a smile. 'It was such a blast!' She laughs. 'We used to pile into the van, we used to head off to Oregon and Washington selling flowers! I had so much fun! It also filled that St Francis wanderlust thing. It was really kind of an adventure because you got to go everywhere, you met everybody.'

Sometimes they got into trouble. Various areas of the US had been allocated to different Unification Church groups for fundraising. In their evangelical zeal, Catherine's team ignored the boundaries and sold as much as possible, wherever possible. They nicknamed themselves the Oakland Raiders and set about breaking all records for flower-selling 'We're the greatest, there's no doubt!' they would chant as they drove from venue to venue. 'Heavenly Father, we'll sell out!' At the time, the star performer on the team was an attractive young Moonie called Barbara Underwood. Eventually she honed her technique to the level at which she could personally sell five hundred dollars' worth of flowers a day. Catherine, in her typically determined way, became the first person to beat her.

Ford, though, was not doing so well. He didn't like flower-selling. From the beginning he had been wary of Moon and his teachings, especially his political leanings (at the time Moon was encouraging his followers to stage pro–Nixon rallies, and was actively promoting the war in Vietnam). He also resented not being given enough time to himself to think. In the Unification Church, you always had to be doing something. 'Whenever there was the slightest threat of downtime,' he recalls, 'when somebody could actually have a conversation, the leader of the moment would say, "Time for some entertainment!" Group entertainment or individual entertainment! Some kind of entertainment! So the dead spaces, which otherwise would provide the opportunity for independent communication, were filled up with fucking songs!'

In fact, Greene had so many issues with the organisation that it was hard to know where to start. They used communal toothbrushes; the food was terrible; there was too much chanting and singing; the work was boring; they weren't allowed enough sleep (new recruits were allowed six hours a night, staff members just three; tiredness was generally attributed to evil spirits). He soon began to suspect that the displays of affection he was getting from his 'brothers and sisters' were phoney, that love was withdrawn the moment he started asking awkward questions.

Then there was the matter of the Moonies themselves who, he says today, were 'pussy people'. Ultimately, the whole thing was just no fun: 'Being a Moonie sucked! It was boring, it was stupid, there was no sex, there was no fun! . . . Just no juice—nothing!' He lasted seven months, and walked out in the summer of 1975.

It's not hard to imagine that the Unification Church was pleased to see the back of Ford Greene. Unfortunately for the organisation, however, they had not heard the last of him.

Ford spent a year coming to terms with the fact that he was no longer a Moonie, then teamed up with his mother and declared war on the Unification Church. By now, Daphne Greene was advising parents all over the world on the organisation and how to get their kids out of it. One course of action she recommended was a technique that had emerged a couple of years earlier.

The technique had its roots in an incident that took place in San Diego on Independence Day 1971 when Ted Patrick, California Governor Ronald Reagan's Special Representative for Community Relations, lost his teenage son, Michael, at Mission Beach. When Michael showed up at the family hotel later that night, he told his father that he had been accosted by some young evangelists with guitars. They had told him that if he came home with them he wouldn't have to go to school any more and that he would never have to do any work. He shouldn't go home, they said, because his parents were evil. The evangelists were so persuasive, Michael said, that he had almost had to drag himself away. They had called themselves the Children of God.

Patrick didn't give the matter much thought until, back at work a week later, he was contacted by a woman who claimed she had lost her teenage son at the same beach on the same day: the boy had wandered off, been accosted by the Children of God and never returned. When he began to collect information about the organisation further reports emerged. The stories were identical: a teenager vanished and then, a week or so later, called his parents and told them that they were evil; the Children of God were his family now and he wasn't coming home. Sometimes, in the background, the parents heard their child being told what to say by another group member. After just two days' research, Patrick had allegedly collected near-identical reports from twenty-six separate families.

At the end of July Patrick went under cover on Mission Beach, deliberately getting himself recruited by the Children of God to see what they were up to. He was driven to a hot, crowded house where he was en-couraged to hand over his car and various other possessions. Then he was lectured to, prayed over, made to sing religious songs and hectored. Luke 14:26 ('if anyone comes to me and does not hate his own father and mother . . . he cannot be my disciple') was cited and the recruits were told that this proved they should reject their parents in favour of the organisa-tion. Exhausted, Patrick was finally allowed to sleep only at four a.m. on his third night in the compound. Three hours later he was woken up and the process started again. The next day, desperate to escape, he told staff that he was ready to give all his possessions to the group and, under the pretext of going to fetch them, took a taxi home. He was shaken by the experience: another twenty-four hours in the compound, he thought, and he would have been converted himself.

Convinced that something deeply sinister was going on, Patrick and parents like him turned to the brainwashing literature and, in particular, the work of a psychiatrist called Robert Jay Lifton. Lifton, who had served in the US Air Force in the 1950s, was one of a handful of doctors allowed access to prisoners-of-war returning from Korea. In 1961 he had written a seminal study of the brainwashing phenomenon, *Thought Reform and the Psychology of Totalism*. In Chapter 22, he described eight specific techniques that could be used by an ideological group to disorient anyone. Ranging from 'loading the language' (introducing technical jargon that limited, rather than enhanced, the ability to think critically, thus stifling dissent) to 'milieu control' (restricting communications to ensure that doubt and dis-sent couldn't get in from outside) the eight techniques of 'ideological to-talism' seemed to offer potential brainwashers a means of controlling virtually anybody.

Patrick and the other parents concluded that the new religious organi-sations were using all eight of Lifton's techniques simultaneously, together with food and sleep deprivation and sensory overload to brainwash their recruits. The method, wrote Patrick, was 'the same as the North Koreans used on prisoners-of-war'. If toughened US soldiers in Korea couldn't fight it in the 1950s, what chance did fresh-faced American teenagers have in the 1970s?

Patrick now began his own crusade against the Children of God. He developed a technique called 'deprogramming' to fight them. It involved sitting new religious converts down and telling them a few hard facts about their chosen religion. He would engage in religious debates until, finally, the acolyte would break down and realise that he had been misled.

That was the theory, anyway. In fact, things worked out rather differently. As might have been predicted, persuading religious converts to take part in a deprogramming session proved impossible. Invariably they had to be lured into a room under some pretext, then forcibly prevented from leaving. When this proved difficult, they were snatched on the street when they were least expecting it—and kidnapped. Patrick persuaded parents that this kind of treatment was necessary since their children were 'beyond reason'. They had, he said, been turned into 'zombies'.

Even when the youths were kidnapped, though, Patrick faced the problem of getting them to listen to what they were being told. Many religious groups taught recruits to combat doubt by focusing their minds on repetitive and meaningless activities as a means of distracting themselves. The result was that Patrick frequently found himself facing glassy-eyed automatons who sat cross-legged and rocked backwards and forwards, chanting. How could you get through to people in that state? His solution was to bully them into listening using repetition, forced incarceration and, on occasion, physical force. But this had repercussions. Although Patrick denied it vociferously, deprogramming seemed to involve applying the same techniques that had been used to 'brainwash' religious devotees to 'unbrainwash' them. It was quite hard to see where the techniques differed, except in objective.

As Patrick took to kidnapping young people from religious groups, so more and more parents called and asked for his help. Soon he and the other key deprogrammer of the early 1970s, Joe Alexander, were dealing with hundreds of cases a year. Meanwhile, other deprogrammers started to copy him. But as kidnaps and deprogrammings multiplied, the religious groups got smarter. The Unification Church, which saw itself as under attack from bigoted outsiders, put up fences around the Boonville compound and stationed a guardhouse at the gate. According to the Church, the fences, the defensive stance towards outsiders and the secrecy surrounding the organisation would not have been necessary if people hadn't kept busting in, sometimes armed, and snatching their members. Wasn't it allowed to protect itself?

To the deprogrammers, the fact that the groups were now walling themselves in made them even more suspect: if the kids who joined were really free, as they purported to be, why were they locked in? Why weren't their parents allowed to visit them? What did they have to hide? As the organisations took more and more precautions to stop kidnaps, the kidnaps became more elaborate and imaginative. The situation escalated.

Inside the Unification Church, tales began to multiply about 'deprogramming'. There were rumours that the process involved beatings, degradation, torture and sexual abuse. According to various sources, two members of the Tucson Freedom of Thought Foundation had deprogrammed an Old Catholic priest because his Episcopalian parents objected to his choice of religion. Ted Patrick, say some reports, had apparently deprogrammed two Greek Orthodox girls because their parents were upset that they had resisted the traditional Greek custom of living at home until their parents had found them suitable husbands.

Deprogramming even assumed a macabre sense of the absurd. New York deprogrammer Galen Kelly—who was sentenced to seven years in jail in 1993 for staging a kidnap on a Circle of Friends devotee, and mistakenly snatching the wrong girl off the street—apparently told a story about how a deprogrammer 'snapped' a young girl out of her 'cult mind' and returned her home. 'You'll be glad to know,' crowed the triumphant deprogrammer, 'that your daughter is a Christian again.'

'But,' gasped the parents, 'she used to be *Jewish*.'

It was no surprise that when Unificationists failed to return home, troops were immediately dispatched to find them. Where had they been snatched from? Where were they being held? Had they been taken to their parents' address for the deprogramming? Pickets were sent out to spy on possible locations and try to snatch back the Church member before it was too late. When they found the building, they surrounded it and Moonies stood at the windows, chanting messages of love and support to their incarcerated brother or sister inside. For the deprogrammers, being in a building surrounded by chanting Moonies was pretty spooky.

Meanwhile, once the press got hold of the fact that young people were being kidnapped from weird religious groups and 'unbrainwashed', deprogramming became a hot story. Both religious groups and deprogrammers played the media for all they were worth. 'I believe firmly,' Ted Patrick wrote in his autobiography, 'that the Lord helps those who help themselves—and a few little things like karate, mace, and handcuffs come in handy from time to time.' He later boasted, 'I could snatch a kid from Alcatraz if I had to.'

After a successful mission, the newly deprogrammed subject was paraded in front of the cameras to prove that they were happy to be free and glad to have been kidnapped. In press conferences tales were told of military-type extractions and how truth had triumphed in bringing the children back to their families. If the deprogrammings were unsuccessful, meanwhile, the returned believers would tell stories of horrific abuse and how truth had triumphed in bringing them back to their True Family.

Initially, there was so much antipathy regarding new religious movements that the deprogrammers won this press war. After all, if *your* children were recruited by a wacko cult, persuaded to hand over all their possessions, then sent out on to the streets to sell shoddy products for twenty hours a day without rest, proper food or shelter, wouldn't *you* do everything in your power to get them out? So successful were the deprogrammers at the start of Ted Patrick's crusade that even when the police were alerted to ongoing kidnappings by the screams of the victims they frequently looked the other way. In at least one case, when a devotee actually managed to escape his kidnappers and fled to the police seeking protection, they put him into a squad car and returned him to Patrick for more treatment.

This attitude did not last. For many people, the kidnapping and incarceration of young Americans to remove their chosen religious beliefs was deeply unsettling. In 1973 a *Time* magazine feature likened deprogramming to the horrific 'brain-blowing' Ludovico technique used on Alex, the hero of Anthony Burgess's *A Clockwork Orange*. Ethically, the issue was fraught with problems, and it wasn't long before it became obvious that kidnapping people because you didn't agree with their religious beliefs was illegal. Although he always made sure that at least one parent of the child concerned was present throughout his operations, it wasn't much longer before Ted Patrick was serving time for kidnapping.

Having realised that he was fallible, the Unification Church and other religious movements began to follow up the issue with lawyers. Kidnapping by parents—even if well-intentioned—could not be condoned. And once deprogrammers such as Patrick had been sent to jail for their antics, it was easy to portray them as criminals. The ensuing legal battles between new religious groups and the various different incarnations of the Citizens' Freedom Foundation continue to this day, and have become extraordinarily acrimonious.

Ford Greene got into deprogramming more or less as soon as he was over his experience with the Unification Church. Not for him the handholding of distressed parents: he liked the combat of the deprogramming itself. If you wanted to snap someone out of their religious belief, you had to be able to engage him in debate on the subject closest to his heart—and best him. Someone who knew nothing about the Unification Church could not persuade a Moonie to leave it. But someone like Greene, who had been a Moonie, stood a far better chance. He knew how Moonies thought. He knew the points where pressure was best applied to crack their faith.

It didn't matter to Greene how the subject was brought to him—he left the kidnapping to others—only that he or she was in a secure place. Arriving at the location of a deprogramming, his only question was 'Can I lock the door?' If the parents said yes, Greene knew he had a fighting chance. He could continue battering at the subject until he or she had to listen. If the parents decided that the kid was allowed to leave when he wanted to, the game had to be played more carefully. 'It was a lot harder if you didn't lock the door,' he says today, 'because they could run and say, "Fuck you! I'm not talking to you."' Without forcible incarceration, deprogramming was 'like fly-fishing: set the hook and keep the line taut. But not too taut.'

Deprogramming without incarceration may have resembled fly-fishing but deprogramming with it was more like a war. As Ted Patrick had discovered, Greene found that Unification Church members refused to listen to reason, either sitting there in a trance or chanting perpetually to avoid having to confront the issues he was raising. It was like talking to a brick wall. What he needed, he realised, was a means of snapping the subject back into reality for a moment so that he could start a dialogue. The split second when they reacted would be the thin end of a wedge that could be driven home over time. 'I would do it by either scaring the shit out of them,' he says, 'or making them really angry until something broke. I was as rude and aggressive and insensitive and nasty as I could be. High-level, high intensity: I'd degrade them until they'd snap and come close to punching me out. Then we'd have something to talk about!'*

Once the subject was talking—for whatever reason—Greene would be open with them, telling them that they both had their beliefs, which were contradictory. They were going to debate who was right and who was wrong, and neither of them would leave the room until the argument was resolved. Greene—who is a man I wouldn't like to take on even if I was pretty sure of my ground—would then batter the subject intellectually until they made a small concession. He would then change tack until he prised out another, then another. Gradually the walls came down, and the citadel collapsed.

A wonderful first-hand account of Greene's deprogramming technique features in Josh Freed's book *Moonwebs*—filmed in 1981 as *Ticket to Heaven*. It covers the farcical, but ultimately successful, attempts of a group of Canadian students to extract their friend, Benji, from the Unification Church. After a successful kidnap Greene shows up wearing an eye-patch and covered with cuts from a recent car accident. In the book his eyes stare 'hypnotically' and his presence is 'so electric his words crackled when he spoke'. There is, writes Freed, 'a primal sense of power about him'. Apart from anything else, at six foot three, and with his surgical stitches, he looks terrifying. Greene demands to be left alone with Benji, and when Freed peers through a crack in the door to see what's happening, he and the terrified Moonie are face to face, foreheads pressed together. Greene has removed his eye-patch to reveal a hideous mass of bruises and is staring into the Moonie's eyes, whispering, 'Love me, Benji! Love Satan!'

From this portrayal I wouldn't have recognised the Ford Greene I met in 2005. In reality, he's a tall, floppy-haired, funny, charming man with an easy Californian drawl. But he swears that the account is accurate. What happens next, he says, was typical.

After scaring Benji half to death to get him to start talking, Greene

---

* One technique Greene used to get subjects to open up was to denigrate the Unification Church and its leader. When I met him in 2005, news had recently broken about the treatment of suspects at Guantanamo Bay in Cuba, and the apparent desecration by military interrogators of the Qur'an in front of detainees. 'That,' he said, 'is a deprogramming technique if I ever saw one!' I asked if he would have done that back in the 1970s. 'Flushing the Bible down the toilet?' he asked. 'Fuck, yeah! No problem! Right away!'

engages him in a debate on Unification Church theology. From time to time he is so offensive that Benji breaks down in tears. Periodically Benji's friends stick their heads round the door to see how things are going, only to be told to get out: when the deprogramming is successful, they are told, they'll know it. Then, suddenly, Benji's friends are startled by a high-pitched wail 'like a newborn baby's first scream'. Ford Greene walks out of the bedroom purposefully. 'Get in there fast,' he tells them. 'He needs you all.'

Thirty years on, Ford recalls the moment of success fondly. 'It's *awesome*,' he says, 'when it happens. There's a point where, all of a sudden, instead of eyes that look like a shark's, that are fucking dead, that don't see anything—the eyes light up like a Christmas tree! And the mind lights up like a Christmas tree! And all of a sudden there's just this *torrent* of questions . . . It's crystal clear. It's awesome!'

The deprogramming in *Ticket to Heaven* took place in late 1977; Ford Greene had undertaken the deprogramming of his sister Catherine just a few months earlier. For various reasons, the outcome of the operation was rather different.

In the spring of 1977 Catherine, who had been a Moonie for two and a half years, spent a weekend with her mother on the coast. Daphne was so shocked by her daughter's demeanour that she came back convinced that intervention was necessary. The Greenes had a family pow-wow to determine what to do. For months, Ford had been advocating a kidnap; to him, Catherine's situation was analagous to 'a whore . . . being pimped' by the Unification Church. The family finally agreed and concocted a trap. Daphne was the bait.

At the start of April, Daphne called Catherine and told her she was worried. She had been having dreams about Reverend Moon, she said, and was coming to the conclusion that she might be wrong about the Unification Church. What should she do? Catherine fell for the story and agreed to visit her on Wednesday, 13 April. In the meantime, Greene assembled a team of fourteen people, including two private detectives to carry out the kidnap, a bunch of family and friends to take care of Catherine when she was in their custody, a doctor and a registered nurse in case something went wrong. When the day came, the team arranged for Catherine to be picked up downtown at nine a.m. by her mother's secretary, Judy, and driven to the family home where the snatch squad was waiting.

Since there was a drought in northern California that spring, Catherine decided to do her mother a favour. She stopped on the way and picked up a two-gallon container of water, bought two dozen roses and made the rendezvous with Judy. On the way up to the house, they pulled over at a post office. Judy had an errand to run, she said. Would Catherine mind nipping in and picking up the post? Catherine walked into the post office, collected the mail and wrote a note to her aunt. In the meantime, Judy went round to the back of the building, picked up a pay-phone and rang Ford and Daphne at home: 'We're on our way,' she told them. 'Five minutes.'

In the house, mother and son now went to the living room: Ford to hide, Daphne to lure her daughter into the trap. The private detectives were stationed out of sight behind the door frames on either side of the corridor. Just before ten a.m., Catherine walked in through the front door and turned right to see her mother waiting in the living room. She took another step forward, raised the flowers and the water container and smiled. 'Hi, Mom,' she said. But she got no further than that.

Catherine realised what was happening the moment the first man hit her. Kidnap! This was what she had been warned about. As the two private eyes threw their arms round her and wrestled her to the ground, she also realised that if her faith was going to survive, she had better get smart. Suspecting that her captors would expect her to scream and fight back, she decided to do the opposite. On the floor she went limp. One of the private detectives held her arms behind her back while the other blindfolded her. As everything went dark, Catherine began to pray. 'At that moment,' she recalls, 'I remember the library clock striking ten. So I told God, "OK. I'm fasting for seven days from this moment. Ten o'clock. Only water." Like that. I did not speak, did not say, "Mom, why are you doing this?" Nothing. Just nothing. It's like I took all my energy. The battle lines are drawn!'

Still holding her down, the two private eyes handcuffed Catherine, tied her feet together and picked her up. She was bundled into the back of the waiting van and thrown on to a foam-rubber mat on the floor. Someone checked her pulse and felt her forehead, then threw a blanket over her. The doors slammed, Greene jumped into the driver's seat and the crew sped off. Although she was blindfolded, Catherine guessed immediately that they were heading to her uncle and aunt's ranch in the country. She lay on the floor, silently mustering her energy. With her brother in charge, she knew she was in for a long ordeal.

On arrival at the ranch, the kidnappers opened the back of the van and carried her into the basement bedroom they had prepared for her. Still tied, blindfolded and handcuffed, she was thrown on to the bed. When the exits were safely secured, one of the private detectives sat down beside her, removed the handcuffs and blindfold, and untied her feet. 'Sorry for the inconvenience,' he told her. 'We just wanted to share a few things with you about Reverend Moon.'

Catherine almost laughed. Well! she thought. You sure picked a hell of a way to do it!

Huddled in a foetal position, head down, Catherine tried to recall what she had heard about deprogramming. According to the lectures she had received, the process involved a group of people ganging up to remove your faith. Sleep deprivation, food deprivation and possibly even sexual harassment might be involved. The only way to fight it, she had been told, was to refuse to engage with anyone. Name, rank and number: that was all they would get out of her.

When Ford tried to engage her in conversation, she stared at the wall. She refused to eat, only breaking the silence to ask for a drink of water. If they wanted to play hard, she could play hard, too. Ford, who had been through this procedure a number of times before, refused to let up or to leave her alone: he knew the attack had to be relentless. At one point, when he tried to accompany her to the bathroom, her patience snapped. 'Oh, God,' she said, shutting the door in his face, 'give yourself a break, Ford!'

At various points, different family members came in to have a go, too. Her sister tried appealing to her sense of the past: 'Catherine,' she begged, 'think of all the talks we've had. Think of everything we ever shared about growth and stagnation.' Her father was frustrated: 'Where *are* you?' he shouted. 'Wake up, girl! Where *are* you? Can't you see that I love you?' But it seemed that she couldn't. In an attempt to get through to her, he slapped her face.

Eventually, when the family took a break and left her alone, Catherine got up and scoured the room for possible escape routes. On the bookcase she found a box of matches. For a moment she seriously considered setting fire to a pile of books and burning the place down but as she was locked in a basement room and the windows were boarded shut, she thought better of it. She might not make it out of the building alive. There had to be another way.

* ★ *

When Greene deprogrammed Moonies, he usually attacked hard on all fronts. The only way to break into the Unification Church's 'programming,' he knew, was by being savagely aggressive. But this was his sister and he didn't want to hurt her. So he reined himself in. It didn't matter too much, he thought: they had all the time in the world. It might take a while but she'd break eventually. They always did.

Two and a half days into the deprogramming, things seemed to be going well. Catherine began to talk about her beliefs, giving Greene the opportunity to put her in the picture regarding some aspects of the Unification Church's existence she might not be aware of: its multimillion-dollar investment empire, for example, and its links to the Korean Central Intelligence Agency. Catherine seemed to take this in and, at a few points, even agreed with her brother. 'It's true,' she conceded. 'I've been deceived.'

Greene, thinking he was making good headway, took a break, headed upstairs and told his mother he was nearly there. Daphne told him that Catherine was made of sterner material than that: she was faking it. Ford ran back downstairs and confronted his sister. He'd tried to be nice but now it was time for the gloves to come off. Guessing from his tone that things had changed, Catherine looked up at him: 'You think you're really big, don't you?' she sneered.

He flew into a rage. 'Yeah,' he said, 'and you've got to deal with me *right now!*'

Realising that she was now in serious trouble, Catherine suffered a crisis of faith. Her brother knew her too well. She couldn't take this. She wasn't going to burn the place down. She wasn't going to get out of here. As he launched a tirade of abuse at her, she began to scream. And that was where the operation came unstuck.

Hearing the screams, Catherine's father and a family friend, Ron, ran in and tried to reassure her. Greene, disgusted by their weakness, stamped out of the room. If you wanted to fight the devil, he knew, you couldn't be nice. They were going to have to start again.

In the bedroom, Catherine saw an opportunity. A few minutes earlier, when she had been pretending to be deprogrammed, Greene had asked for a drink. One of his team had brought him a paper cup and a half-gallon bottle of Welch's grape juice. The bottle was still sitting beside the bed. It was made of glass. Catherine leaped off the bed, seized the bottle by the neck and smashed it on the edge of a table.

Exactly what happened next is disputed. The two men in the room with Catherine swear that she tried to plunge the broken bottle into her chest. She says she tried to slash her wrist to force them to take her to hospital. Either way, the men grabbed her arms in time to stop her and shouted for help. Realising that she had seconds before the cavalry arrived, Catherine held the broken bottleneck in her right hand and squeezed it with all her might. Upstairs, Greene heard the scream. 'It was the most scary, marrow-curdling thing I have ever heard in my life,' he recalls. 'It was a combination of pain, sexual ecstasy and triumph all wrapped in one. I came in the bedroom and saw Catherine being held down on the bed on her stomach, hands behind her back, blood all over the place.'

Catherine had severed the main tendon and nerves to her right thumb—and she was still squeezing the bottle. As the team tried to peel open her fingers to make her release it and her mother emptied a pack of sanitary napkins and started mopping up the blood, she saw that the balance of power had swung in her favour. The deprogrammers were scared. At that moment she received an incredible sense of inner peace: she was going to make it. Standing over her on the bed, Greene caught her eye. 'The smile!' He shakes his head. 'That was the scariest bit in the whole thing. That's when you see the goddamn fucking demon—it was the grim fucking smile. It was just like "Oh, my God, man!" I just wanted a machine-gun to blow away every fucking Moonie in the world . . . I looked at that and I went, "Pffft! Game over."'

When the family arrived at the Ross Hospital and tried to usher Catherine quietly into the emergency room, she freaked out. 'I'm being held against my will!' she screamed. 'I've been kidnapped!'

'But why would they want to do that to you?' asked the nurse.

'Because,' said Catherine, 'I'm a *Moonie*!' Led into a treatment room, she refused to open her hand for the doctor to treat unless he allowed her to use the phone. He promised that this would happen, whereupon she unclenched her fist and allowed him to put in nineteen stitches. Taken to a pay-phone straight afterwards and given a dime, she immediately called the Unification Church centre on Hearst Street and told her friends where she was.

Downstairs, realising that the battle was lost, the Greene family called the police chief and turned themselves in.

That night on the news, Catherine Greene, the sister of famed deprogrammer Ford and daughter of anti-Moon campaigner Daphne, told reporters how she had been tricked, betrayed and kidnapped by her own family but had ultimately outwitted them. She then changed her name and moved to a different state so that her family could not find her again.

Did the Unification Church brainwash Catherine? If so, how?

One person who believes that the organisation was using unduly coercive techniques in the 1970s is Gary Scharff. During his four years in the Church, from 1972 to 1976, part of his responsibility was to lead the workshops for new recruits. Looking back, Scharff says that although there was no specific 'brainwashing' or recruiting manual, the process was designed specifically to keep people isolated, pressurised and both psychologically and emotionally off-balance to remove their natural defences. They were intensively 'love-bombed'—surrounded by adoring people who held their hands and simpered to make them feel good about the movement—then persuaded to join the group in small increments so that they didn't grasp how enmeshed in it they were becoming.

At the end of their initial weekend, recruits were still being treated like royalty and were encouraged to stay for the next, seven-day, course. After that was over, they were encouraged to stay for the next one. By then, they were pretty much converted. Within the initial twenty-one-day period, says Scharff, 'they were really hooked. The claws were pretty tightly wrapped around them . . . It was remarkable. Extraordinary!'

Since it was crucial to make recruits stay for the initial ten-day indoctrination period, instructors pulled out all the stops. If male recruits were uncomfortable, pretty girls were sent to try to persuade them to stay; if anyone looked like they were about to back out, they were cornered and reassured. Love-bombing was continual. If necessary, sceptics were removed from the meeting and taken for a walk by a devotee so that positive messages could be reinforced and to stop their doubts contaminating other recruits. In fact, throughout the recruitment process all instructors, says Scharff, were 'constantly scanning the faces of the members to find points of discontinuity with what we were presenting'. Any signs of discontent led to immediate intervention and further love-bombing; recruits were kept extremely busy with repeated activities, meetings and sports. As Ford Greene recalls, any threat of downtime was met with exhortations to shout, scream or sing at the tops of their voices and further exhaust themselves. In the meantime, new recruits were heavily discouraged from talking to one another, to prevent them sharing 'negativity'.

Recruits were also encouraged to distance themselves from their parents, who were portrayed as well-intentioned but misguided. They were told that friends outside the movement would not understand and would try to persuade them to leave. Contact from the compound at Boonville was via telephone or mail. In her book *Hostage to Heaven* former flowerseller Barbara Underwood states that new recruits' mail was censored if they were considered 'not solid' enough, and that there was a master key for switching off the pay-phones so that no one could call out of the compound. When they were turned off, the phones were declared 'out of order'. Underwood—who was herself deprogrammed and is no longer a Unificationist—also recalls supervising phone calls made by new recruits to their parents, and telling them what to say.

Shocking though this might sound, it's not a great deal further than any established religious group might go. All sorts of groups use similar techniques to make converts. The Church of England's Alpha Course, for example, embraces loud singing, being extra-friendly to potential recruits, and keeping very busy—and warns that outsiders may not agree with new-found beliefs. For centuries, Christians have fasted, given away all their possessions, flagellated and put themselves through all kinds of ordeals to prove their devotion. Recruits joining the military, meanwhile, have their heads shaved, are forced to wear identical clothing, deprived of sleep, verbally abused, physically exhausted and endure all kinds of hardships. Yet there's nothing wrong there, apparently.

But there is a key difference. When the Church of England or the military make recruits, they are upfront about who they are, what they are doing and how they will go about it. As Kent Burtner, a former Catholic priest and long-time watcher of the Unification Church, puts it: 'When Jesus approached James and John, he was very straightforward about who he was and the claims he made for himself. He did not say, "Hey, James and John, I've got this really great new way to do business! Why don't you come over here and learn how to make wonderful new fishing nets?" and then sneak in the fact that he was the messiah later on.'

But that is exactly what the Unification Church did in the 1970s. On the west coast of the United States, the organisation made a habit of recruiting

potential members under false pretences. 'Witnessing' was deliberately carried out at train and bus stations to catch new arrivals in town; young people with rucksacks were deemed particular targets. They were told that they
were the guests of a number of different organisations—the Collegiate Association for the Research into Principles (CARP), New Educational Development Systems Inc., the Creative Community Project *et al.* It was quite
possible for subjects to get ten days into their recruitment without realising
that this was the Unification Church. Scharff recalls that, while the early indoctrination was going on, the group's identity and its relationship to Reverend Moon were 'very carefully disguised'.

Only once recruiters knew that, in Scharff's terms, 'the claws were in'
would the true identity of the religious organisation be revealed. The practice of disguising it was even given a name: Heavenly Deception. Thirty
years on, Catherine Greene admits that this happened, and that it was a
mistake. At the time the technique was even controversial in the movement and was not used on the east coast, only the west, where recruitment
was perceived to be more tricky. Numerous Church members, she recalls,
were 'livid' at the practice. The decision to use deception was made, she
says, by over-enthusiastic young Moonies, who thought that the end justified the means. 'Was it wrong?' she asks today. 'Maybe so. Was it insidious,
was it evil? I don't think so. The intention was good. Now, they say the
road to hell is paved with good intentions, so—and it did come and back-
fire in our faces. You know? And I think we paid the price.'

The price to be paid for Heavenly Deception was high. Not only did it
generate extremely bad press and feeling towards the group, it also left the
way open for numerous court cases against it. One of the lead attorneys
behind such cases was Ford Greene.

When his sister vanished for the second time, Geene went to law school.
Deprogramming was too risky. He didn't fancy going to jail and, anyway,
the real battles were being fought in the courtroom now. Since then he has
fought a relentless battle against the organisations, taking them to court repeatedly and, in turn, being taken to court by them. Scientology is his main
bête noire and he appears to be theirs—check out the anti-Ford Greene site:
www.friendsofsananselmo.org.

In the case of the Moonies, the starting point for his arguments has
tended to be that recruits did not know what they were getting into. It's

one thing to allow yourself into a manipulative environment if you know what that environment is about. But if you've been lied to, by the time you realise that the group you've joined is the Moonies, they may have been working on you for two weeks and Lifton's eight techniques will have done their work. In 1988 Greene obtained a settlement from the Unification Church on behalf of one of his clients, David Molko, for the alleged use of coercive techniques applied after Molko was (according to the lawsuit) sucked into the organisation under false pretences.

While the Unification Church appears to admit that it made mistakes in the 1970s, the question remains as to whether deprogramming was any better. Subjects were frequently treated with the same indoctrination techniques as those endured by recruits. Moreover, at the start of the operation they were kidnapped and held against their will. Religious recruiters might be breaking normal bounds of acceptable behaviour but deprogrammers were breaking the law. Modern deprogrammers—they call themselves 'exit counsellors': those still practising have distanced themselves from the term 'deprogramming' because of its criminal connotations—say that the techniques used were never as severe as those employed by the new religious movements. Besides, deprogrammers were in the business of saving souls: the measures used were justified by the end result. Funnily enough, this was exactly the same argument used by the Unification Church for its doctrine of Heavenly Deception.*

Occasionally, evidence emerged that deprogrammers were up to no good: in 1976 a mysterious organisation called POWER (People's Organized Workshop on Ersatz Religions) published a booklet in Britain entitled *Deprogramming: the Constructive Destruction of Belief*. It purported to be a handbook for prospective deprogrammers and advocated a plethora of techniques that will immediately ring bells with anyone familiar with the allegations levelled against American interrogators at Abu Ghraib and Guantanamo Bay. Methods recommended included 'food termination', 'sleep withdrawal', 'physical correction', 'shame inducement through nudity', 'verbal stress' ('maximum volume, minimum distance') and 'the destruction of holy works', including 'having the subject voluntarily defecate

---

* Deprogrammers will take issue with this statement. They were trying to force acolytes to think for themselves; religious groups were trying to get them to accept answers thought up by somebody else. Clearly, there is an important difference.

upon photographs of the cult leaders, copies of the holy gospels of the cults, and other sacred artefacts'. Under the heading 'Sex and Deprogramming Techniques' the author recommended 'the application of aggressive sex by the Technician'.

British psychiatrist William Sargant, who believed that what the Russians and Chinese were up to was duplicated most accurately in religious conversion, told the *Guardian* that the booklet was 'An absolutely correct account of a devastating technique, first elaborated by the Russians and the Chinese, which could very likely work. It horrifies me to see my theoretical work carried to the ultimate degree like this.'

Intriguingly, the POWER booklet was a forgery, circulated by a certain new religious movement to discredit deprogrammers. This was an indication of the way the battle for publicity between the cults and the anti-cult campaigners was heading. In the late 1970s, the 1980s and 1990s everyone took everyone else to court, alleging brainwashing and forced coercion. Sometimes the cults won, sometimes the anti-cult campaigners won. Meanwhile, both sides flung abuse at each other.

In court, the argument turned academic. Were the cults the brainwashers? Or the deprogrammers? What *was* brainwashing, anyway? Did such a thing exist? Both sides drafted in scholars to bolster their legal arguments. The anti-cult organisations hired psychologists headed by the University of California's Margaret Singer, who had evaluated US prisoners-of-war returning from Korea in the 1950s and later testified on behalf of Patty Hearst following her kidnap by the Symbionese Liberation Army. The religious groups, meanwhile, sponsored forums for groups of academics, often sociologists, to debate the nature of religious conversion, new religious organisations and faith itself.

The sociologists argued that anti-cult academics were waging an irrational war against groups that stood for anything outside their own narrow-minded, conservative world-view. They also alleged that, in their desperate efforts to discredit the cults, anti-cult campaigners had become every bit as evangelical as their enemies. They had, in fact, *become* a cult. In response, the psychologists stated that anyone who had accepted cult hospitality, like the sociologists, had been paid off. 'Bad science' was alleged by both sides. At one point the arguments became so heated that a group of academics took another to court for apparently disproving their particular theories and depriving them of future earnings as expert witnesses.

In the meantime, the anti-cult movement was bolstered by such atrocities as Jonestown (912 members of the People's Temple committed suicide in Guyana in 1978), the siege at Waco (eighty in 1993) and Heaven's Gate (thirty-nine in 1997). Clear proof, apparently, that religious cults can lead to suicide. 'How do you explain the mass suicide at Jonestown, the willingness of parents to execute their own children?' asks Rick Ross, one of America's leading anti-cult campaigners. 'Two hundred and eighty of them [children]. How do you explain that? You could say that they were just very religious. But I don't see that as a meaningful explanation. I think they had basically surrendered their ability to make their own judgements, and essentially they stopped thinking. And they allowed Jim Jones to think for them.'

The movement was further boosted when a small Japanese religious sect, Aum Shinrikyo, released the nerve gas sarin on the Tokyo subway in 1995, killing twelve and injuring five thousand: this was just the kind of thing the anti-cult boys had been trying to warn the world about all along. Now the anti-cult movement could assimilate itself into that other great cult of the early 2000s: the anti-terrorism cult. Since then, of course, the advent of Muslim suicide-bombers has reinforced the trend. According to cult-watchers, the techniques used to persuade suicide-bombers to blow themselves up are simply a modified version of those used to recruit Catherine Greene back in 1974. 'The suicidal atrocities perpetrated by Bin Laden's Al Qaeda,' writes Margaret Singer, 'the Palestinian suicide-bombers, and other horrific terrorist acts . . . do appear to be the result of techniques . . . perfected over the years by cultic organisations.'

Steve Hassan, one of the most influential exit counsellors still operating in the United States, agrees: 'Terrorist cults' he says, 'employ many of the same mind-control techniques used by destructive cult groups. These in-clude isolation, hypnosis, sleep deprivation, dietary manipulation and the programming of phobias into the minds of members.' Recalling his own 'cult' experience in the Unification Church in the 1970s, Hassan claims, 'I was trained to obey my superiors without hesitation, including being will-ing to die or even kill.'

Spooky stuff. But as any new religious organisation will point out, these guys have a history of using hyperbole. Any time you speak to an anti-cult operator, he will tell you that the situation is critical: if you're in the busi-ness of combating new religious movements, things just get worse and worse. 'I've been watching cults since 1982', Rick Ross told me, in 2005, 'and I can't recall a time that there have been more of them, that they have been more active than they are *this week*. I am receiving constant enquiries, emails, phone calls, et cetera, about these groups and there are new stories breaking around the world about them every day. The Kabbalah Center, Scientology, Transcendental Meditation, Unification Church. I think the difference is that they are richer, more sophisticated, more powerful and entrenched than they used to be.'

In response to the constant attack from what they saw as narrow-minded, anti-religious campaigners, the new religious movements counter-attacked with a vengeance. Tragedies such as Waco were not, they said, the result of religious cults, but the consequence of meddling anti-cult op-erators urging the federal authorities to step in when such advice was ob-viously likely to be counter-productive.

Two anti-cult experts in particular, Drs Margaret Singer and Louis Jolyon West, came into the firing line. West, according to a Church of Scientology document, was 'a bigot' while Singer was 'out of touch with reality'. In the smear campaign that followed, it was pointed out that both had been connected to the CIA's MKULTRA brainwashing programme during the Cold War.

In 1996 the US anti-cult movement's vanguard, the Cult Awareness Network (CAN)—a direct descendant of the Citizens' Freedom Founda-tion, which Ted Patrick had helped to establish in 1974—having been sued repeatedly, was bankrupted by the Church of Scientology. CAN was characterised in a Scientology document as a 'hate group' that participated in kidnappings and some of whose leaders had criminal records. Depro-grammers, stated the Scientologists, were nothing more than ruthless prof-iteers. In October 1996, CAN was forced to auction its remaining assets, including trade name, post-office box, help-line number and all confi-dential files relating to new religious movements. The highest bid came from Steven Hayes, representing the Church of Scientology. To this day, CAN's website, which is supposed to be an information site for parents worried about the influence of new religious groups, is run by one of the most powerful of the new religious groups.

The simple fact is that, when it comes to religion and brainwashing, both sides, while claiming to be impartial, have an agenda. The anticult cam-paigners claim that brainwashing is a reality and is taking place all over the world. The religious groups, meanwhile, deny that brainwashing exists but argue that if it did the deprogrammers should be in jail for it. The situation is even murkier in the world of religion than it is in the world of intelligence.

Thirty years after her recruitment, Catherine Greene is still a member of the Unification Church. Eight years ago, she flew to Korea where, in a mass ceremony, she married a stranger. Her husband, who had been se-lected for her by Reverend Moon, was Japanese and did not speak a word of English. She did not speak Japanese. Personally, I find this pretty weird. I don't subscribe to the beliefs of the Unification Church and I certainly wouldn't agree to marry a stranger on the advice of anyone—let alone someone who claimed to have received visitations from Jesus. Where I come from, that's pretty strange behaviour.

Catherine spent a long time working out whether she wanted to meet me. Was I going to attack the Unification Church? Was I going to set the record straight? Clearly I was addressing some potentially embarrassing material. In return, I wasn't sure what to expect of her. I wanted to know whether she had been brainwashed. But when the time came, I wasn't sure how to tell.

We eventually met at a Harvard coffee-house in June 2005. I suppose it would be flippant to remark that Catherine didn't *look* brainwashed. She didn't walk like a zombie, her eyes weren't glazed, she didn't try to con-vert me and we didn't spend the morning bashing tambourines. On the contrary, she appeared alert, witty, intelligent and happy. She produced a photograph of her two pretty daughters and showed it to me proudly. When I asked if she was brainwashed she burst out laughing. No, she said, she didn't think so.

'But there *was* some strange stuff going on in the early 1970s,' I said, 'at Boonville . . .'

Catherine explained that the ratio of people who had come to the ini-tial recruitment dinner, compared to those who had stayed for the courses and those who had made a final commitment, was pitiful. The vast major-ity of new recruits checked out before joining the Church. Of those who made the commitment, the majority left soon afterwards. 'If we were brainwashing people,' she concluded, 'we were doing a pretty lousy job.'

Doubtless this is true. All the techniques applied by the Unification

Church, combined with Heavenly Deception and love-bombing, weren't that effective. Perhaps it was possible to trick people into the movement for a while, but they almost invariably left when the novelty (and the programming, if there was any) wore off. If the group was brainwashing people, the practice doesn't appear to have worked on most of them or, if it did, only for a relatively limited period. 'If brainwashing was so effective,' asks former recruiter Gary Scharff, 'why weren't more people being drawn into it?'

It also seems reasonable to assume that, although Catherine walked into the Unification Church unwittingly and was subject to all the manipulative techniques they could throw at her, she has had ample time to leave since then. Instead, she has chosen to stay. Now, it is possible that she has been so heavily programmed that she is terrified to leave. But, having met her, I doubt it. Catherine is no shrinking violet; I suspect that she'll do pretty much what she wants to do.

Ford Greene, of course, is of the opposite opinion. To him, Catherine represents the battle he lost, and that he couldn't save her from the Unification Church evidently rankles. I put it to him that, regardless of what he thought of her choice of religion, Catherine appeared to be living a happy life, so what did it matter? He disagreed violently: it wasn't a happy life, he said. It was only the *appearance* of a happy life.

'I can't sit down and have a conversation with Catherine,' he told me, 'because what comes out is Moon's ideology—but she thinks it's her own personal character . . . She sits down and all that Moonie crap comes out of her mouth and she expects to be respected as if it's her personal identity. I can't, I won't and I don't want to do that. It's too nasty! It's horrible. And that's the thing that breaks my heart.'

Last winter he sent Catherine an email in which he wrote that, after thirty years, all he wanted for Christmas was his sister back. 'Oh, Ford!' She sighed. 'The only bars are in your mind.'

When they start out, all religions are incomprehensible to outsiders, and especially to the families of those who become adherents. Joseph and Mary were probably none too happy the day Jesus came home and told them what he'd decided to do with the rest of his life. But the situation in the 1970s was a bit different: Jesus wasn't building a multi-national business empire and banking millions of dollars each year.

Without doubt there are legitimate questions to ask about the self-help and new-religion industries. To many, the money raised by such organisations makes them look like seedy manipulators, in the business not of saving souls but of milking them financially. This was partly what drove the brainwashing scare of the 1970s: if the new religious movements were crooked, as parents soon came to believe, then any conversion to them had to be the result of manipulation.

For most parents, the news that their child had converted to an alien religion that professed strange and esoteric beliefs would be a cause for concern. In the 1970s what made the issue explosive was that there was a spate of such conversions, that this had never happened before on such a scale, that manipulative techniques were employed to recruit new subjects, and that the religions concerned were apparently industries, making a lot of money—which appears incompatible with conventional religious notions. Faced with such information, parents could only assume that their kids were being conned. Why would they do this? They had been so well balanced and intelligent.

But does this mean that they were brainwashed? Or just naïve?

The interesting thing about the cult 'brainwashing'/deprogramming issue is that, in the belief that the end justified the means, both sides applied coercive techniques. The Unification Church put pressure on new recruits not because it was evil but because the young recruiters sincerely believed they were saving them from hell. Parents, meanwhile, tried to get their kids back not because they were satanic disbelievers but because they loved them. 'I swear to God,' Greene said, that day in 2005, 'it's a spiritual battle against evil.' He was justifying deprogramming but I suspect that the same words might have come from Catherine's mouth as justification for joining the Unification Church. Which side of the dispute you fall on relies entirely on which side of the religious divide you stand.

In the coffee-shop in Harvard, I asked Catherine what would happen if her two little girls grew up to reject the Unification Church and joined some weird cult that she thought was dangerous. She insisted that, whatever path they chose, she would accept it. 'At some point,' she said, 'my kids are going to have to choose for themselves.'

Which, I suspect, is exactly what her mother, Daphne, would have said if she had been asked the same question back in 1974.

9

Believing the Impossible

'I can't believe that!' said Alice.

'Can't you?' the Queen said in a pitying tone. 'Try again: draw a long breath, and shut your eyes'.

Alice laughed. 'There's no use trying', she said. 'One can't believe impossible things'. 'I daresay you haven't had much practice,' said the Queen. 'When I was your age, I always did it for half-an-hour a day. Why, sometimes I've believed as many as six impossible things before breakfast.'

Through the Looking Glass—
And What Alice Found There, Lewis Carroll

If you think you were abused and your life shows the symptoms, then you were.

The Courage to Heal, Ellen Bass/Laura Davis, 1988

Five miles south of Olympia, Washington, Black Lake Bible Camp offers children a wealth of outdoor activities: canoeing, fishing, archery, wakeboarding, horseshoes and ping-pong are all on the syllabus. But the fun, as programme director Craig Piefer notes in his introduction to prospective parents, 'is merely the ketchup on the corndog'. The main goal of the camp and its staff is to celebrate 'Christ's love and His plan for a restored relationship with God'. To this end, visitors are requested to leave their cell phones at home, to wear 'modest' swimming trunks and to bring a Bible. Charity is at the heart of the operation. 'If you don't have a Bible,' notes the camp's website, 'we will provide one for FREE!'

According to camp publicity, Black Lake is the perfect place to turn off the distractions of the outside world and 'seek out the Father's Will'. To search, perhaps, for some still, small voice, or personal revelation.

One thing that Craig Piefer is careful *not* to mention in his note to prospective parents is the extraordinary revelation that took place at Black Lake in the summer of 1988, and the catastrophic sequence of events it set in motion.

The revelation was received by an evangelist from the International Church of the Foursquare Gospel called Karla J. Franko. That summer Franko, a minor sitcom star and stand-up comic, had been invited to address sixty girls on the Church's annual Heart to Heart camp.

On Heart to Heart's final day, Franko was half-way through her lecture when, unexpectedly, she felt the hand of the Lord upon her. A moment later she told her audience that she had been touched by God, and shared the revelation she had received. Franko had been sent the image, she said, of a little girl hiding from her father. The terrified child, who could hear footsteps approaching in the hall, hid deeper and deeper behind the clothes in a closet. A light came on, and there was the sound of a key turning in the lock.

Suddenly a member of Franko's largely adolescent audience sprang up and announced that she was that little girl. Then, in the highly charged atmosphere, Franko received another revelation: someone else in the audience, she said, had been abused by a relative. Another little girl stood up and fled the room in tears. Soon several Heart to Heart campers had come forward and claimed that they, too, were victims of parental abuse.

At the back of the auditorium one member of Franko's audience sat silently, taking it all in. Ericka Ingram, an attractive twenty-two-year-old from nearby Olympia, had attended Heart to Heart some years previously but this time she had returned as a camp counsellor. Unlike the younger, more impressionable girls, she did not become hysterical when Franko shared her revelation. It was only later that she reacted.

There are two versions of what happened next. According to police records, when the meeting broke up the kids dispersed, leaving Ericka in the conference centre—where she was found some time later, sitting cross-legged on the floor, sobbing. When her fellow counsellors gathered around and asked what was wrong she revealed that Franko's speech had hit a nerve: 'I have been abused sexually,' she whispered, 'by my father.'

Karla Franko tells a different story. Finding Ericka sobbing in the meeting room, she says, the camp counsellors sought her out and asked for help. She rushed to Ericka's side where, standing above the weeping girl, she felt the hand of the Lord again: 'You have been abused as a child,' she announced. 'It's by her father,' she told the assembled counsellors. 'And it's been happening for years.'

It doesn't really matter which of these two stories you accept: whether the message came from Karla Franko or from Ericka Ingram, the secret was out. It was a secret that was to destroy Ericka, her family and her community.

Perhaps strangely, Ericka did not tell her mother what had happened when she got home. The police were not summoned. Instead of an investigation there was an uneasy silence, like the lull before a storm. But news of the events at Black Lake began to seep out in other ways.

Shortly after Ericka's revelation her eighteen-year-old sister, Julie, started behaving oddly at school. Asked what was wrong, she broke down in tears and refused to speak. A teacher, Kristi Webster, tried to get her to open up but noted that she just lay on the floor in the foetal position, sobbing. She suggested that if Julie wasn't happy talking about her problems, perhaps she would find it easier to write them down.

At the start of October Webster received the first of a series of handwritten notes. Julie was afraid, she said, and wanted to move away, to 'start my life over'. 'There are time [sic],' she wrote, 'when I want to cry but I can't, I've build [sic] a wall and I don't want to let anyone in because I [sic] afraid.' Without warning, the notes then moved from adolescent *angst* to something infinitely more sinister. According to Julie, her father would creep into her room at night and climb into bed with her. Every night, she said, she would lie in the darkness, waiting for his footsteps in the hallway. 'I just wait in my room for my dad,' she wrote. 'I hate it. It hurt so bad and it makes me feel very dirty.'

Further notes followed. When she was four years old, Julie wrote, her father had taken to inviting work friends to the house for poker evenings. When they were drunk, the men would come into her room and molest her. 'One or two at a time would come into my room a [sic] have sex with me they would be in and out all night laughing and cursing.' Ericka remained safe, wrote Julie, because she slept on the top bunk: 'I think my dad and his friends were afraid the bed might break'.

Realising that she was out of her depth, Kristi Webster sent Julie to a school counsellor, who immediately advised her to speak to experts at the local rape crisis centre, Safeplace. Julie agreed. 'I wonder what will happen to my family,' she wrote plaintively to Webster on 27 October. 'Will my dad be lock up [*sic*] and my mom left behind? . . . Mrs Webster I'm very scared.'

When they met Julie Safeplace's counsellors were appalled. Understandably, she was severely traumatised: her father had told her he would 'cut her up' or 'burn her and make her very ugly' if she told anybody what he had done to her. Other perpetrators included her uncle, a neighbour and a family friend. The last time Julie had been abused, she told them, was on one Wednesday in October, just a month earlier.

Then more horrors emerged.

By mid-November, the revelations Ericka had received at Black Lake had reached their full term. The Sunday before Thanksgiving she called her mother, Sandy, and arranged to meet her after church at Denny's, off Martin Way, in Olympia. Over mugs of tea, Ericka told Sandy that her father had repeatedly abused her sexually, often with his friends from work at their poker parties. Not only that, but her brothers, Chad and Paul Junior, had also molested her. Aghast, Sandy asked why she had never mentioned this before. Ericka replied that she had tried to but it had proved impossible. 'You wouldn't listen,' she said.

That night Sandy Ingram confronted her husband, Paul, with Ericka's allegations. He denied them. Unsure whether to believe him, she rang John Bratun, the assistant pastor at her church, who told her that he already knew about the abuse: he'd heard about the incident at Bible camp six weeks earlier. Unfortunately, Bratun told her, there was every chance that the story was true: after all, why would Ericka make it up? Kids just didn't lie about this kind of thing.

The next morning Sandy drove to Julie's school and pulled her out of class to ask if she had heard about any of it. Julie confirmed Ericka's story and informed her that she had been a victim, too—until about five years earlier. Only last week, she said, she had been at Safeplace receiving counselling.

By sheer bad luck, Paul and Sandy Ingram were due to take their youngest son, Mark, on a week's vacation to the Oregon coast, departing that day. Unsure how to react to the allegations, they decided to go ahead. Paul said he needed time to reflect on what to do next. Sandy, in the meantime, was advised by Pastor Bratun to get away from it all and try to clear her head. Paul, an evangelical Christian, spent the holiday pacing the beach and reading his Bible; Sandy remained inside their chalet, crying.

The moment Paul and Sandy had departed for Oregon, officials from Safeplace took Julie to the Thurston County Sheriff's Office, where she was interviewed by the head of sex crimes, Joe Vukich. The abuse had started, she told him, when she was in the fifth grade and only stopped when she was about fifteen. Typically her father would undress, climb into her bed and rape her. At the end of the ordeal, he would threaten to kill her. Also, Julie said, Ericka had been a victim.

Immediately after this interview Vukich visited Ericka, who told him what had happened at Black Lake Bible Camp and confirmed everything. Her ordeal, she said, had started at the age of five, when her father had taken to climbing into her bed and touching her. The next morning, 'wet and yuckey,' she would hide her pyjamas in an attempt to avoid getting into trouble with her mother. She specifically recalled the last time her father had raped her, in 1987, because he had given her a sexually transmitted disease and driven her to a clinic in San José to have it treated anonymously.

That weekend, police received a note from Julie, revealing that at one point she had become pregnant by her father. When he had found out about her state he had tried to persuade her to have an abortion: if she had the baby, he told her, she would lose her friends at school and he and her mother would stop loving her. Besides, he said, the baby would be born unhealthy and would die anyway. Julie had agreed to the abortion, after which he had forced her to engage in oral sex with him.

When Paul and Sandy Ingram arrived back from their holiday at the end of the week, the allegations had acquired an unstoppable momentum. On the morning of Monday, 28 November, Paul woke up, ate breakfast, suffered an attack of diarrhoea and vomited violently. The week's reflection on the coast had not helped: he was in serious trouble, and he knew it.

Part of his fear was related to his work. Paul Ingram was not some ordinary Joe. He was chairman of the local Republican Party and chief civil deputy of Thurston County Police Department, fourth in charge of the law-enforcement community. The men taking statements from his daughters were his friends.

When Ingram arrived at work at eight fifteen, he was summoned to the sheriff's private office where two men, Sheriff Gary Edwards and Under-sheriff Neil McClanahan, positioned themselves on either side of him. Edwards told him that there was a problem. He nodded: he knew. Paul Ingram was then formally read his rights and arrested.

Moments after his arrest, Ingram said something strange. 'I know that if this did happen,' he told the two officers, 'we need to take care of it.' Asked what he meant by this, he replied, 'There may be a dark side of me that I don't know about.' Twenty years later, Neil McClanahan remembers thinking that this was a weird thing for an accused paedophile to say: 'The sheriff and I went like "Huh?" Why would he say that? Why would anybody say that? You know, he and I were in law enforcement. I've never heard *anybody* say, "There's a dark side to me."'

Stranger things were to come. According to the police report of the interview, when Ingram was told that his daughters were receiving counselling, he interjected that it wasn't only his daughters who were going to need help but his sons, too. McClanahan couldn't believe what he was hearing. When Ingram had left the room for a break he exchanged a glance with his boss: 'We were, like, brains sucked dry!' he recalls. ' "*What* did he say? What are we *dealing with* here? Who *is* this guy?"'

Of course, the only person capable of answering these questions was Ingram. Unfortunately, he appeared to be every bit as mystified as his interrogators. Asked whether he had repeatedly raped his daughters, he seemed genuinely unable to remember. 'I don't know,' he told McClanahan and Edwards. 'I can't see myself doing this.' The detectives asked him why his daughters would tell such horrific stories if they weren't true, and Ingram agreed that they had a point. 'I taught the kids not to lie,' he mused.

Ingram now found himself caught in a contradiction. Either his daughters were lying, or he was. Unsure of his own ground he seems to have begun to appreciate the implications of his predicament. Perhaps he really was guilty? 'I've never thought about suicide before, and I can handle just about anything,' he told McClanahan, 'but if this turns out that I have done something, I want you to get all my guns out of the house just in case.'

To the police, virtually everything Ingram was saying pointed to his guilt. What kind of man didn't know whether he had raped his own daughters? And what kind of man, if he was innocent, would fail to deny allegations like this? Neil McClanahan knew that if *he* had been accused of abusing his kids, his response would have been explosive: ' "Fuck you! I'm not talking to you! This is bullshit!" And that would be that! But [Ingram] never did that.'

Faced with such behaviour, the detectives concluded that Ingram was playing a game common to guilty suspects when they are finally arrested. 'I would say ninety per cent of the time,' McClanahan observes today, 'maybe more, they will confess to the main bulk of it but leave out twenty-five to thirty per cent. "Look, I killed this person and, yeah, maybe I slit her throat, or something like that—but it wasn't me who cut her head off and dumped her body in the river! Yeah, I'm bad but I ain't *that* bad." That's common. Very common.'

If Ingram wanted to play this game, the detectives figured, they would just have to beat him at it. They had to replace the conditional 'I might have' with a solid 'I did'.

At two forty-five p.m. sex-crimes specialists Joe Vukich and Brian Schoening interviewed Ingram again. Immediately he became snagged in the issue of his daughters' honesty versus his own. 'I would never do any-thing like that,' he told the two officers, 'but I also know that my daugh-ters have been taught not to lie, that they tell the truth.' Less than a minute later, he accepted that it was possible he was guilty. 'I really believe that the—the allegations did occur and that I did violate them and abuse them and probably for a very long period of time . . . I had to have done these things.'

Vukich asked Ingram what had made him change his mind. 'Well,' he responded, 'number one, my girls know me. Uh, they wouldn't lie about something like this, and, uh, there's other evidence, uh, that would point out to me that these things occurred.' For the last couple of years, he said, his daughters had treated him rather distantly and he had found it hard to hug them or tell them that he loved them, which he knew was 'not natu-ral'. Asked if he had touched either Julie or Ericka inappropriately, Ingram hung his head. 'I'd have to say yes,' he responded.

Once again, however, the interview wandered infuriatingly into the conditional tense. Ingram was asked to describe an incident that Ericka said had taken place last September, and he launched into an account that was clearly couched in speculation. The officers pounced. 'You've talked about this in the third party. I'm going to ask you directly: is this what happened?' asked Vukich.

But Ingram didn't seem sure: 'I'm having trouble getting a clear picture of what happened,' he replied. 'I know in my mind that these things had to have happened, and I'm still having trouble getting a clear picture.'

The detectives let the matter lie, and Ingram continued. In the story, he entered Ericka's bedroom, removed his bathrobe and climbed into bed beside her. After lying down on the bed, he said, 'I would've removed her clothing, uh, at least the underpants or bottoms to the nightgown.'

Once again Vukich interrupted: 'OK, you say *"would've"*. Now do you mean *"would've"*, or *did you?*'

'I did,' replied Ingram. Once again, however, he was unsure. After the abuse was over, he continued, 'I would've told her to be quiet . . . and threatened her to say that I would kill her . . .'

'OK,' Vukich interrupted again. 'You said *"would've"*. Is that *"would've,"* or *did you?*'

'Uh, I did,' he responded.

The interview continued in this vein, with Ingram recounting what he 'would have' or 'might have' done, followed by the officers asking for clarification and him responding meekly, 'I did'. When further allegations from Julie and Ericka were put to him he was unable, or unwilling, to re-call them. He knew, however, that they had to be true: 'It happened,' he told the officers. 'My kids don't lie. They tell the truth, and that's what I'm trying to do.' Asked whether he had ever had anal intercourse with Julie, he responded, 'I believe that she said she did, so I'm sure that I did.' Likewise, although he couldn't remember a thing about abusing his sons, he agreed that this had probably happened, since his daughters had said so and they had no reason to lie. 'I can't think of anything,' he told Vukich, 'but I—I'm sure it must have happened.'

While Ingram seemed unsure as to why he was confessing, or what tenses to use, the actual confessions themselves were damning. He agreed that Julie had indeed become pregnant, and that he had driven her to a clinic in Shelton when she was fifteen for an abortion. He also agreed that the abuse had been taking place with both daughters for at least ten years. At the end of the interview when the two men enquired if there was any-thing he wanted to add, he asked his daughters, his wife and the rest of his family for forgiveness.

That night, Thurston County officers Schoening and Edwards had the unpleasant duty of informing Ingram's wife, Sandy, that Paul had con-fessed to abusing both of her daughters over a ten-year period. When

Sandy heard the news, she was so shocked that she had to be physically supported. Schoening and Vukich stayed with her until her pastor, Ron Long, arrived with his assistant, John Bratun, then crept out.

Baffled by Paul Ingram's inability to recall his crimes, Thurston County officers requested that a professional psychologist, Dr Richard Peterson, assist with the interrogation the next day. Peterson was regarded as something of an expert in situations like this. He had dealt with a number of abuse cases in the recent past, and was a firm advocate of the theory of repressed memory: that if a situation was traumatic enough, the mind would effectively shut down and isolate it. The memory was then locked up in the unconscious mind, where it could only be accessed later by careful psychological probing.

Of course, there was nothing new or revolutionary about this theory: it had originally been propounded by Freud and was later used to explain the condition of shell-shocked soldiers by, among others, William Sargant in the UK (it was also the theory that had led to the evolution of the so-called 'truth drugs') What was really exciting to Peterson was that people with repressed memories were usually those who had suffered trauma or abuse. This was the first case anyone had ever come across where the *perpetrator* appeared to have blanked out his actions.

The issue of repressed memory—how much Paul Ingram could recall, how much his children could recall, and how all this could be verified—now came centre stage.

With Peterson observing his next interrogation, Ingram once again had problems recalling what crimes he had committed. It was obvious that he was trying to remember but simply couldn't get things clear in his head. 'I'm not consciously trying to hide anything,' he assured his interrogators. 'I really want you to believe that I'm telling you the truth.'

This time, however, the detectives were less understanding. They wanted answers, and the time had come to exert a little pressure to get them. The police told Ingram that it was time to stop couching his confessions in flowery terms that effectively neutered them so that they became, as one officer termed them, 'non-admission admissions'. 'It's time,' Schoening told him, 'to poop or get off the pot.'

The detectives began to cajole and threaten Ingram alternately. If he talked about his crimes, he was told, the case might not make it to court.

What he needed was treatment, not punishment; there were places where he could go. Even Sandy might forgive him for what he had done. Everyone wanted the case to go away—but the truth had to come out first.

But if the carrot was the possibility of clemency, the detectives also wielded a number of effective sticks. The first was that if Ingram did not confess he would end up in prison, where ex-cops and child molesters were beaten, or worse, by fellow inmates. The second, even more effective, was that Ingram's children would be harmed, or even killed, if he refused to confess.

The logic was simple. According to Ericka and Julie, other men had been involved in the abuse. Even though Paul was in custody, the others were still out there somewhere, no doubt preying on his kids while he was in his cell wasting time. '[Julie's] real intimidated and she's in real fear right now because that person is still out on the street,' Schoening told him. 'We need to protect her, Paul . . . How do you know that this person won't go ahead and go after her now, figurin' that she might say something?'

Finally, after some traumatic soul-searching, Ingram came up with the name of a friend, Jim Rabie, whom he thought might have been involved and the police helped him to piece together a picture of how the abuse had occurred. All sorts of ideas started coming into play. 'In this picture, Paul,' asked Vukich, 'do you see ropes . . . some kind of bondage, maybe?' Ingram promptly agreed that Julie must have been tied up.

To the police the ropes weren't that important, but Jim Rabie was. Like Ingram, Rabie had also been a police officer at Thurston County. Why had he been named? Was Ingram having a homosexual relationship with him? Ingram, as usual, was bewildered. 'I don't think so,' he said. 'I'd just hate to think of myself as a homosexual.'

There followed a Pinteresque barrage of questions designed to prise out irregular sexual behaviour. Did Ingram wear his wife's underwear? Had he ever tied up a partner during sex? Did he sniff the family's dirty clothes? Had he ever fondled a corpse? The police were baffled by his ability to answer these questions negatively yet remain unable to recall whether he had abused his daughters.

But they didn't give up. Following these denials, the detectives resumed their most effective technique: reminding Ingram that Julie's life was in jeopardy. 'You gotta help if you want this stopped,' Schoening told him, 'or you may have either a suicidal daughter or a dead daughter . . . She can't take much more of this, Paul.'

Ingram put his head into his hands and began to pray, 'Oh, Lord! Oh, Lord!' while the police reminded him that he had taught his children not to lie. 'Oh, yes!' he agreed. 'My kids are honest.' When he asked for the officers to call his church and get Pastor Bratun over to help him force out the truth with prayer, Schoening picked up the phone right away. The other officers poured on suggestions that might trigger a confession. Ingram now began to cry, exhorting them to help him remember. 'Just keep talkin', he begged. 'Just keep talkin.'

Realising that they were finally getting somewhere, the psychologist and the detectives increased the pressure.

'Choose life over death,' Peterson instructed him.

'That's your responsibility as a father,' Vukich agreed.

'Dear God! Dear God!' cried Ingram. 'Jesus! Merciful Jesus! Help me!'

At this point Dr Peterson silenced the room with a new approach. 'One of the things that might help you, Paul,' he suggested, 'is if you'd stop asking for help and just let yourself sit back, not try to think about anything.' Paul went limp in his chair. 'Just let yourself go and relax. No one's gonna hurt you. We want to help. Just relax. Try not to think about anything . . .'

After a minute or so Vukich chimed in softly, 'Why don't you tell us what happened to Julie, Paul?'

Suddenly Ingram broke, and his memory returned. 'I see Julie lying on the floor on a sheet,' he said. 'Her hands are tied to her feet, she's on her stomach. I'm standing there looking at her. Somebody else is on my left . . .'

The detectives' main objective now became to discover who the 'somebody else' was so that they could arrest him, too. To this end they fired questions at Ingram in the hope that something might trigger a memory and enable them to identify the other abuser. 'What's he smell like?' asked Peterson.

'Yeah,' said Schoening. 'What's he smell like?'

'All you have to do is just look to your left and there he is,' said Vukich.

Ingram focused on his memory and saw the man: 'Broad-shouldered, hairy . . . curly, uh, body hair.' Then came a key detail: the man had a gold watch on his right wrist. The detectives noted that the abuser was probably left-handed. Jim Rabie, whom Ingram had already named, and who had dark curly hair, was indeed left-handed. In his memory, Ingram watched Rabie abuse Julie, who was tied and gagged on the floor. As he watched his friend touch his daughter, he distinctly heard her pleading, 'No!'

Then another abuser hove into view: Jim Rabie's best friend, Ray Risch. Risch was kneeling in front of Julie, photographing the scene.

That afternoon, after Ingram's arraignment, the interrogation continued and the police pushed him to recall more details of the incident. Initially Ingram had stated that the abuse took place when Julie was twelve or thirteen. Now he recalled that she was five or six. Perhaps, the detectives suggested, he was recalling two separate incidents of abuse. He agreed. There must have been many such occasions; his mind was confusing them. Another figure, a former police reservist now made an appearance, and Ingram recalled that the incident was the result of a poker bet that had gone horribly wrong. The stake was Julie, and when Ingram objected, Rabie had pulled a short-barrelled stainless-steel revolver on him.

The day after Ingram had named Jim Rabie, Ray Risch, and the reservist as accomplices, Julie was shown a series of driving-licence photographs and asked if she could identify any of them. Out of a total of fourteen snaps, she picked the very men Ingram had named.

Jim Rabie was an old friend of Ingram's—in fact, Ingram had been best man at his wedding. A former Thurston County detective, Rabie had headed up the sex-crimes unit until his retirement, when he was relieved by Joe Vukich and Brian Schoening. Ironically, this unit now began targeting him.

Detectives Schoening, Vukich and McClanahan, alerted to the fact that Rabie might be a paedophile, watched him closely. They soon found plenty to feed their suspicions. From the start of the investigation, 'Rabie came up [to the police station] during the time frame when Ingram was being interviewed,' McClanahan recalls, 'sat on a chair with his back to the door against the office! Trying to listen to what was happening when Ingram was being interviewed! It was sort of like "Why are you here?"'

On another occasion, Rabie specifically asked investigating officers what Ingram was confessing to, whether he was being 'totally truthful' and offered to help with the interrogation. Rabie's voice, notes the police report, 'was quivering, he appeared to be notably shaken, and his eyes appeared to be watery and bloodshot'.

At eight p.m. that Thursday, under the pretext of dropping off a slide projector he had borrowed for a series of lectures that he was giving to law-enforcement associations, Rabie visited the sheriff's office again. He was taken to one side by Vukich and Schoening. 'They said, "Your name's come up in this and so we've got to talk to you about it,"' recalls Rabie. '"Gee! I don't know what you're talking about!" They said, "Well, here, sign the form." They read me my rights.' Rabie was arrested. Meanwhile Ray Risch was picked up at his home. As the police approached his house, they saw him looking out of the window—as if he was waiting for them. When they asked him why he thought they had come, he didn't need any prompting: 'Is this about Paul?' he asked.

Rabie and Risch were installed in separate interview rooms and told that both Paul and Julie Ingram had named them as paedophiles. They were also told that there were photographs of them abusing the girls.

There are two accounts of what happened next. Neil McClanahan says that both Rabie and Risch's reactions were incongruous. 'When Rabie was arrested, Risch was arrested separately: all three [Rabie, Risch and Ingram] separately. All three said, "I don't think I did this, I don't remember doing this—but maybe there's a dark side of me." You know, the separate detectives came out and said this, and it's kind of like "Where does this come from? Why would anybody say this?"'

Nearly twenty years later Rabie denies saying that he had 'a dark side'. 'That was a quote from Paul!' he says. 'I did not say that! That is not something that would even have crossed my mind.' Since his first interrogation was not recorded, we will never know the truth.

Transcripts of Rabie's second interrogation later that night, which was recorded, reveal that even after the theory of repressed memory had been explained to him, he wasn't admitting much. 'I honestly do not have any recollection of that happening,' he told detectives, 'and I do not believe that I could've done it and blocked it out.'

He had agreed to be interviewed without an attorney present because, as he says today, 'I know, as a cop, that as soon as somebody says, "I want an attorney," they're guilty.' Late that night, however, he realised he was out of his depth and asked the police to call him a lawyer.

Olympia attorney G. Saxon 'Sax' Rodgers, had just returned from a party when he received a call from his friend and fishing partner Detective Tommy Lynch. 'I've got Jim Rabie down here,' Lynch told him, 'for rape.' Rodgers immediately assumed that there had been a mistake: 'I'd known Rabie for years. He was the sex detective! . . . Why would this guy be a child molester, who's put hundreds—probably thousands—of people in prison for that sort of thing? . . . A retired cop that's got a good reputation in the community is arrested for rape? That is *very* unusual.'

Since Rodgers had been drinking wine, he smoked a cigar on the way to the sheriff's office, hoping to disguise the smell of alcohol on his breath. Once he arrived he took charge, telling his client, in no uncertain terms, 'Shut your mouth till I can figure out what's going on. OK? Be quiet!'

Sax Rodgers was a professional criminal attorney with plenty of experience in handling situations like this. The same was not the case, however, when it came to Paul Ingram's lawyer. Instead of hiring an attorney with a proven background, Ingram had turned to a friend from his church, Gary Preble, who had little criminal experience. Unlike Rodgers, Preble didn't know what to say to the police, and he didn't know what to tell Ingram. As a result, both sides ignored him.

One good example of the Ingram–Preble client–attorney relationship emerged in Ingram's second recorded interview, when he recalled images of a woman with her head blown off by a shotgun. Even Preble recognised that this material might get his client into trouble. 'Paul,' he interrupted, as Ingram started the story, 'this is the time I'd advise you not to answer any more questions.'

But Ingram wasn't listening: 'Jesus, help me here. Give me—give me something to see, Lord. Where am I at? Have I seen bodies?'

Once again Preble tried to silence him: 'Did you hear me, Paul?' Oblivious, Ingram continued with the story.

It was no great surprise that Ingram did not acknowledge his attorney's questions. He was now on a crusade to discover the truth about his daughters. His key goal was to remember as much as possible, as fast as possible. His kids needed protecting—and he needed to discover what, exactly, he had done.

Ingram's religiosity was not the only unusual aspect of his behaviour. Throughout his interrogation, he tended to hang his head in silence for long periods while he attempted to recover memories. During these sessions, which lasted for up to ten minutes at a time, he was apparently lost to the outside world, so far away that one detective described the condition as a 'trance-type thing'. To the cops it was weird—but what mattered was emptying Ingram's mind of memories so that they could find the other perpetrators.

As his interviews continued over the next week, Ingram encouraged the return of his memory with fervent prayer: 'Lord, give me a picture! Give me a picture . . .' Repeatedly he entreated his interrogators to be silent so that he could listen to his heart: 'Let me relax and get a picture. The Lord will give me a picture.' Prayer was almost continuous. 'Uh, Jesus, just let me settle down, Lord, help me, Jesus. Help me, Jesus. Help me, Lord. I got a vision!'

'I've got to bring it out!' he chanted to himself on 1 December. 'So, dear Jesus, just bring the picture. Bring the picture close, dear Lord!'

Ingram's interrogators recognised that his religious bent constituted an effective means of getting him to open up. It might be unpleasant, but if leaning on his beliefs produced confessions, they were more than happy to do it. 'I know you really want to cleanse your soul, don't you?' Vukich asked him. 'You don't want to go to hell. Let's be honest, that's something you don't wanna do. You know you want to go to heaven.'

As religion played an increasingly important role in Ingram's confessions, it became clear to him that what he needed was spiritual guidance. Another player entered the investigation. And it was at this point that the events prompted by the strange revelation at Black Lake Bible Camp in August spiralled hopelessly out of control.

Since the Ingram case, a number of articles and at least one book have been written about the events that took place at Thurston County Sheriff's Office over the winter of 1988 and the spring of 1989. In all of these accounts, two characters have merited particular attention. Both were present by special invitation, one at the request of the Sheriff's Office, the other at the request of Ingram. The first of these two men was Dr Richard Peterson, the psychologist. The second was John Bratun.

Bratun's actions might have been funny, had the results not been so tragic. From the outset, his qualifications to advise anyone on their spiritual well-being were dubious. He was not an ordained priest and did not have a degree in theology, religious studies, counselling or any of the social sciences. In fact, he had completed a couple of years of art college and worked as a teacher. But his standing as assistant to the pastor at Ingram's church meant that Ingram regarded him with respect.

From the beginning of his involvement, Bratun assured Ingram that the memories he was recovering came from God, and were thus to be trusted. He told him that while normal people were a combination of mostly good with a little evil, with him it was the other way round. When Ingram asked if it was possible that he was possessed by an evil demon, Bratun said no. There was no demon, he concluded, but there were 'several spirits'.

Just four days after Ingram's arrest, Bratun came up with a plan to help. 'We've got to get this evil spirit out of you,' he told Ingram, before explaining that the only way to go about this was that he—a pastor's unqualified assistant and art teacher—would perform an exorcism. Bratun instructed Ingram to stand on the other side of the room facing him. After they had prayed together, he explained how this was going to work: 'I want you to get over this garbage can,' he said, 'and I want you to *cough*'. Bratun then commanded the evil spirits to come out while Ingram retched unproductively over the bin. When the procedure was over, Ingram looked into it to see if it contained an evil spirit, but it was empty. No one was sure whether this had achieved anything but Ingram said he felt a bit better.

Of course, it would be unfair to blame the derailing of the Ingram investigation on Bratun's 'exorcism'. As it happens, he had a crucial further role to play, which we will come to later. In the meantime, though, the other irregular player was complicating things, with results that no one could have predicted.

Dr Richard Peterson had told the Thurston County detectives that Ingram's inability to recall his own crimes was the result of his repressed memory. It was Peterson who had stopped the interview on the second day at just the right point, instructed Ingram to calm down and relax, and successfully put him into a state in which he was able to retrieve his memories. But Peterson had a more controversial theory than that of recovered memories.

In the mid 1980s, a variety of factors combined to persuade various counsellors, therapists and psychiatrists that satanic cults existed all over the United States. They worshipped the devil in secret and performed all kinds of unspeakable acts, including, significantly, child abuse. When he arrived at the sheriff's office, Peterson told the investigators that he had recently worked on a case where satanic ritual abuse had been a factor. The phenomenon, he assured the detectives, was real, and Ingram's case carried many of the tell-tale signs. Sure enough, the moment the psychologist

warned the detectives that satanism might play a role, Ingram began to recall events in which it had. 'I see black, but not a coat,' Ingram told Joe
Vukich on 29 November. 'It's like there's a fire—lots of smoke blockin'
the light, weird shadows . . . There's a bunch of tombstones in a circle, lots
and lots of tombstones . . . It's like a horror movie.'

These images were shortly joined by other tantalising clues. On the
morning of 1 December, Ingram recalled a series of abuses perpetrated by
Jim Rabie, Ray Risch and others. In the memory, Rabie ordered Ingram
to turn off the Christian music in his house. When Ingram complained,
Rabie told him that he 'didn't believe in God, didn't believe in Jesus, no
more of this crap', then launched an invective against Christianity: 'God
doesn't help pagans,' he told Ingram. 'Jesus can't help anybody. He's a lie,
he's a fraud.'

Ingram could find only one explanation for such views. Terrified, he
turned to Joe Vukich. 'I see evil,' he said.

In retrospect, knowing that Ingram was a fundamentalist Christian who
believed in the physical reality of Satan, it was probably no great surprise
that he would choose to portray the repeated rapes of his own children as
the work of the devil. Perhaps, at the time, he was speaking metaphor-
ically. He soon changed his mind.

On 5 December, Ingram returned to the event he had recalled six days
earlier. He had been praying in his cell, he said, and now things were
clearer. The 'tombstones in a circle' were not really tombstones but people in robes kneeling round a fire. Some kind of ceremony was under
way. There was a masked person in a red robe—'maybe the devil'—and
there was wailing and moaning. Ingram himself was dressed in an apron
emblazoned with an inverted cross. He then detailed his initiation into a
satanic cult. He was expected, he said, to sacrifice a grey cat, which was
tied down on its back. He was handed a stiletto knife, which he used to
remove the animal's heart, then held it up for all to see. At the end of the
ritual, he was rewarded by two of the ringleaders' wives with sex.

As the detectives' eyes widened, Ingram made another, even more startling confession. He and Jim Rabie, he said, had visited Seattle in the early
1980s, where they had picked up and murdered a prostitute, dumping her
body on a stretch of wasteland surrounded by alder trees. Inspection of
police records soon revealed that in April 1984 Ingram and Rabie had indeed travelled to Seattle together to conduct a series of salary negotiations.

This was a huge revelation. For some years a serial murderer, known as the Green River Killer, had been targeting prostitutes in the Seattle area. Was it possible that the killer was two men: Rabie and Ingram? Thurston County detectives alerted the Green River Taskforce, and officers arrived to see if Ingram's confession tallied with any of the evidence on the forty-odd bodies that had so far been recovered.

While Ingram was making this last confession, Rabie's attorney, Sax Rodgers, was trying to arrange bail for his client. Eventually it became clear that this would not be possible, a fact that he found surprising until he discovered that Rabie had been fingered as the Green River Killer. Rodgers nearly fell off his chair: 'My guy is the *Green River Killer*? *Jesus Christ*!' he recalled, in 2005. 'We were just blown away. We couldn't figure it out.' If this was true, Rodgers concluded, Jim Rabie was 'the Ted Bundy of all time'.

Police interviewed Ingram's children again and again to see if what they remembered tallied with what their father was saying. Unfortunately it seemed that much of it did. Worse, it became increasingly clear that the kids' mother, Sandy, had been involved, too.

At the start of December, Ericka began to implicate her mother, telling a friend that Sandy would sometimes sit in on the abuse sessions, or even 'prepare' her for them. On 8 December, both Ericka and Julie confirmed to separate detectives that Sandy had been present. 'She would stand and watch,' Julie later explained, 'or join right in.'

This had bothered the officers from the start: if the abuse had been going on for so long, how could the girls' mother *not* have known about it? When Sandy realised she was coming into the sights of the sex-crimes investigators, she consulted her husband's spiritual adviser, John Bratun.

Having sat in on many of the interrogations, Bratun confirmed that Sandy was indeed a suspect and warned that it was likely she would end up serving a jail sentence. Already an anonymous caller had informed Child Protection Services that her youngest son, Mark, was not safe. She'd better confess, he said, or he'd be taken into custody. In Bratun's expert view, he told her, Sandy was 'eighty per cent evil'.

To confirm that Sandy had indeed been involved in the abuse, the detectives turned back to her husband, who now remembered an incident that had taken place one evening in the mid-1970s. Ray Risch and Jim

Rabie had been abusing two of his sons, he said, when Sandy had returned home early from a shopping trip and caught them. The two men had dragged her downstairs, tied her to a bed and raped her. They had then told her that if she so much as uttered a word about this, her family would be killed. When they left, Ingram had apologised. 'I signed a contract with them where I promised secrecy,' he told her, 'and I said I wouldn't reveal anything about the group or what it did.'

Sandy beat a hasty retreat with Mark, heading off to stay with relatives and ponder how to react to the news that she had been the victim of a violent gang rape she couldn't even recall.

Less than a week after Sandy had left, Ingram's memory improved again and he recalled more details about her rape, and what had led to it. At the heart of the operation, she said, was Ray Risch's ex-girlfriend, who 'had some witchcraft ritual that we got involved in and . . . I signed a contract with them where I promised secrecy and said I wouldn't reveal anything about the group or what they did and the only way out of this was by death'.

The ring involved the use of drugs, he said, and if anyone so much as murmured a word to the authorities, Rabie and Risch would 'sacrifice' the Ingrams' youngest daughter, Julie. 'She was about five or six then,' Ingram recalled, and 'it would be a torture type killing'. He hadn't meant to keep this fact from the investigators, he assured them. It was only now, with the help of the interrogators, the psychologist and 'Pastor' Bratun, that the true facts were emerging. 'My memory is becoming clearer as I go through all this. It's getting clearer as more things come out.'

The satanic-abuse story now began to ferment violently. Questioned about satanism at the end of December, Ericka recalled a vivid account of a ritual that had taken place in the barn on her parents' property, where there was a high priestess and a series of satanic worshippers wearing gowns and helmets with horns on them. There was chanting, she wrote, and 'a lot of blood everywhere'. Like Ingram's ceremony, it had climaxed with a sacrifice but this time the victim was not a cat. It was a human baby. 'The baby would be put on the table,' she wrote, 'and all of the people, including my mother and father, circling the table would stab it with knives until it died. They continued to do this for a long time sometimes even after it was dead . . . The baby was a human baby, about 6–8 months old.' Once the ceremony was over, the corpse was wrapped in a sheet and buried.

After the sacrifice, Ericka recalled that she had been subjected to a form of mind control to ensure that she would never reveal what she had seen. This involved the adults repeatedly chanting, 'You will not remember this,' and assuring her that the incident was a dream. She was then given a red drink that apparently contained Valium—'There may have been other drugs,' she speculated. 'I remember my dad talking to my mom about getting me different drugs so I wouldn't get hooked.' She had seen around twenty-five babies murdered like this, she said. At the end of the statement Ericka drew a map of her family's house, indicating where the bodies were buried.

Faced with such explosive revelations, what could the police do but follow them up? At the start of the second week in December, Detective Schoening and Dr Peterson interviewed Ingram's middle son, Chad, to see what he knew about all this. Unfortunately, Chad's memory seemed to be as repressed as his father's. He contradicted himself repeatedly and had the same habit of couching his recollections in terms like 'would've' or 'could've'. Most annoyingly, he seemed to go into the same comatose state as his father when faced with a difficult question, clamming up entirely, as if he had passed into a trance. 'Sometimes,' noted Schoening, 'he would go for 5–10 minutes without saying anything, and at one point, drool came out of his mouth onto the floor.'

Although the interview was like pulling teeth, the psychologist thought it might be possible to salvage something. In an attempt to help Chad recover his lost memories, Peterson encouraged him to recount a nightmare he had experienced repeatedly as a child.

In the dream, Chad recalled, a straggly-haired witch would come into his bedroom and sit on his chest, restricting his ability to breathe or to cry out for help. She would speak in a strange language and the next morning, when he woke up, he would have a sick feeling in his stomach. For Peterson and Schoening it was immediately clear that Chad had sublimated his fears: it wasn't a witch sitting on his chest but one of the abusers. Asked why he was unable to shout for help, Chad replied that something was in his mouth. What was it? asked the psychologist.

'It's not cloth,' Schoening told the boy, who immediately stifled a laugh.

'You just made me think,' he said. 'Oh, gollee!'

'What is it?' asked Schoening.

'I thought that it was a penis, okay? It could be.' Shown a series of mugshots, Chad selected one he recognised. Jim Rabie.

Isolated in his cell, Rabie was perplexed. On the instructions of his attorney, he was no longer talking to the police but rumours of what was coming out of the Ingram interrogations reached him regularly. He knew that the abuse of the Ingram children was supposed to have taken place during poker parties at their home. But since Ingram was a cop it was only natural that the majority of his friends were cops, too. Some of the names of people who had attended the poker evenings were familiar.

'Three of the primary poker players at that time,' he recalls today, 'were Neil McClanahan, Tom Lynch, and Raymie Hanson. They were, in the 1970s, the primary instigators of the majority of the poker games.' Yet McClanahan, Lynch and Hanson were also the primary investigators on the case. Rabie couldn't for the life of him understand how they could be working it when they had to be among the prime suspects.

Besides, during the 1970s Rabie had often worked the night shift, so had seldom been able to attend the poker evenings. Not only that, but his friend Ray Risch—also currently in jail—didn't play poker. It didn't add up.

The situation was made worse by the fact that before his retirement Rabie had been in charge of sex crimes. Of all the pictures in the press, Rabie's was the most frequent: 'Sex Cop Arrested For Sex Crimes' made a great headline. His wife, Ruth, worked at Thurston County Jail, where inmates took sadistic delight in baiting her. 'You,' they chanted in their cells at night, 'are married to a child molester.'

In a way, the situation was easier for Rabie than it was for Ruth. Rabie had retired because he suffered from sleep apnoea, which led to narcolepsy. In jail, he simply went to sleep and stayed that way. 'They put me on suicide watch,' he says, 'so they had to check on me every fifteen minutes. And every single one I saw later was "He's asleep!" "He's asleep!" "He's asleep!"'

The same escape was not available to his friend, Ray Risch, who lost forty pounds in weight and whose hair went white almost overnight.

While Rabie and Risch languished in jail, Thurston County officers did their best to prise more information out of Ericka and Julie. For the detectives, extracting information from the girls was an extraordinarily laborious process. Ericka liked to communicate in writing and Julie frequently refused to talk. She would curl up in a chair and say nothing for long periods, hiding her face behind her fringe and picking at her shoes—virtually anything, in fact, to avoid direct eye-contact with an adult. The detective who spent most time with her, Loreli Thompson, concluded that 'she had behaviours that were significantly less than that of an eighteen-year-old. She would giggle inappropriately as though extremely nervous . . . questions would evoke responses of hiding her head, looking the other way, or further giggling.' The girls' strange behaviour was put down to trauma.

Trauma notwithstanding, over the next few months both recalled further details of the abuse they had suffered, including a number of truly horrific satanic rituals. In February, Ericka told the police about another ceremony she had been forced to attend, this time in a candlelit haybarn. She had become pregnant, she said, and her parents had not known what to do. Eventually when she was five months down the line, they had decided to perform an amateur abortion on her. Ericka was drugged, placed on a table and held down. Then a group of adults gathered. Although she did not remember the exact procedure, she knew that it had been performed with a coat-hanger.

> I don't know who performed the abortion. It only happened once. I remember after the abortion them putting the cut up baby on me and leaving it for a long time on my chest. It was bloody & I remember hearing a cry before they cut it up. All of them took turns cutting it and then placing it on me.

It's easy to imagine the police officers' disgust when they were confronted with evidence like this. At a number of points, some were instructed to hand in their side-arms for fear that they might take justice into their own hands and murder Ingram, Rabie or Risch. A number of detectives were treated for post-traumatic stress disorder.

Unfortunately for the police, it was just such accounts that were to lead to the disintegration of the vast majority of their case. As the accusations against Ingram and his fellow abusers became increasingly elaborate, so they became decreasingly plausible. No sooner had they taken the statements and begun to cobble them together into a big picture of the abuse than the picture began to crumble before their eyes. Something very strange was going on.

Repellent as the news of Ericka's enforced abortion might have been, for defence attorney Sax Rodgers it was crucial. In the course of their statements to the police, both girls had claimed that they had been physically abused, cut with knives and burned—at one point Julie told detectives that her father had nailed her left arm to the floor. Now both had claimed that they had undergone forced abortions. When asked whether they had physical scars, both girls agreed that they did. Julie's scars were so bad, she said, that she was unable to wear a swimsuit, or even to change for sports in the school locker room in case the other girls noticed.

To Rodgers this was a way of finding out what, if anything, had really happened. When he heard Ericka's new story, he called Detective Loreli Thompson. 'It's a no-brainer!' he told her. 'If they had abortions, we ought to be able to figure this out. The gynaecologist ought to be able to tell . . . Let's take her to a doctor, see if it's there!'

Ericka and Julie were taken to Providence Medical Center, Seattle, to see staff physician and gynaecologist Judith Ann Jacobson. Jacobson was informed about the sensitive background to the case and asked to give both girls a thorough physical examination. The results were revealing.

Other than an appendectomy scar, Jacobson noted that there was no evidence of cuts or burns. Ericka denied ever having had an abortion. She also denied that she had been pregnant, and told the doctor that she was not even sexually active. According to Jacobson's report, her only scars were the result of 'mild acne on back'. She was likewise unable to discover any signs of abuse on Julie but she did confirm something that the police had already learned. Julie's behaviour was 'very abnormal for an eighteen-year-old girl'. In fact, she told Detective Thompson, it was infantile: she couldn't stop giggling.

Not sure what to make of this, two months later Thompson asked Ericka to lift her sweater to show her the scars on her stomach. Even after stretching the skin at the location indicated, Thompson was unable to see anything, let alone the residue of the three-inch knife wound she had been assured was there. Later the day, she repeated the routine on Julie. 'I saw no marks or scars,' she wrote.

Attorney Sax Rodgers was hugely relieved. 'To me, that's pretty simple,' he says. 'If they've been cut with knives, there's gonna be some scars. If they've had an abortion at their age, obs-gynae is probably going to be able to tell us if there's evidence that might be able to corroborate that, you know? *Nothing!* There was none! Zero! There was no physical evidence to corroborate the stories. None.'★

In their search for corroborative evidence, Thurston County officers now came up with the idea of excavating the Ingrams' property to locate the remains of any sacrificed animals or babies. To conduct the search, they contacted Dr Mark Papworth, chief deputy coroner for Thurston County. Papworth, who had a degree in human biology and was a trained archaeologist, had worked for law-enforcement agencies in five different counties in the state. Among other grisly assignments, he had examined the remains of the Green River Killer's victims around Seattle.

Papworth dug up the Ingrams' backyard and an adjoining field where the bodies were supposedly buried. Specifically he looked for evidence of human activity, which tends to last for a long time. 'I've dug people out of pits that I could follow down that were twenty-two thousand years old,' he said, in an interview in January 1996. 'Pits don't go away.'

Once again, the results were revealing. 'The fields around the Ingram house had no pits. There were no holes. No one had ever dug a hole there.' Papworth did find one piece of evidence—an elk toe bone—but that appeared to have been buried by a dog. According to his interview—he has since died—Papworth confronted McClanahan with this news. 'I said, "Neil, there's no evidence. None at all. Zero." And he said to me, "If you were the devil, would you leave evidence?" . . . My hair stood on end!'†

The lack of physical evidence of sacrificed animals or babies does not

---

★ Under-sheriff Neil McClanahan recalls things differently: '[Julie] had evidence that she had given birth to something—physical evidence,' he told me, when we met in June 2005. 'She had a baby at some point . . . There *were* some scars,' he said, before admitting that they were 'not consistent with what she [was] talking about'.

† Once again, McClanahan takes issue. He and Papworth had been friends, he said, until the archaeologist set out 'to make a name for himself'. The fact that there were no graves on the Ingram property was suspicious in itself. 'If you go out to the majority of these farms, they have cattle or horses or whatever, [and when they die] they dig a hole and bury them. They don't get rid of them. So you're gonna have animal bones on these farms. And there wasn't any.' His opinion seems to have fluctuated over the years: in a lecture in 1993 he stated that 'we found many different holes, but very few bones . . . some type of activity took place there.' According to Lawrence Wright's excellent account of the Ingram case, *Remembering Satan*, McClanahan's explanation for the lack of bones was that the soil was acidic and they had dissolved.

appear to have deterred the Thurston County Sheriff's Office. The detectives continued to take statements from Ingram and his daughters. Hard to imagine though it might be, they became increasingly bizarre.

In March 1988, Ericka told Joe Vukich that her father had made her have sex with a variety of farmyard animals, including goats, which were then butchered and buried in the garden. She had also been forcibly penetrated with a variety of objects including poles, wire coat-hangers, 'bondage items' and a knife.

Not to be outdone, the next month Julie repeated the allegation that her mother had been involved with the abuse, writing that Sandy had applied a pair of pliers to her vagina, before watching and laughing while three men gang-raped her. Her mother, she said, had been present 'most of the time' throughout her ordeals. Once when she was about eleven, her mother had opened her vagina with a pair of pliers and put the arm of a dead baby into her. Julie had removed the arm later on, she wrote, because 'if I left it in there, I thought maybe I would die or something'. As if that wasn't enough, Julie added that when she was '5, 11 and 16' Jim Rabie, Ray Risch and her parents had held her down and inserted spiders in her vagina.

Was this even possible? Did devil worshippers really do this kind of thing? The Thurston County officers didn't know. They needed an expert.

The expert they called was Dr Richard Ofshe, a professor of social psychology at the University of California at Berkeley. Ofshe was an expert on cults and religious indoctrination. Among other accolades, he had won a Pulitzer Prize in 1979 for his exposé of the Synanon cult. To the Olympia detectives, he was perfect. Surely he could get to the bottom of it. 'This prosecutor called me up,' recalls Ofshe, '[and] wanted to know if I was an expert on satanic cults.' Somewhat guardedly, he replied that there was no such thing as an 'expert' on satanic cults because no one had ever successfully observed one in action. Most academics believed they didn't exist. 'Well,' he was told, 'we've got one.' Ofshe replied that if this was the case, he was extremely interested, and agreed to fly up to Thurston County.

The moment he arrived in Olympia at the start of February, Ofshe had misgivings. He was picked up by Brian Schoening, who filled him in on the details of the case in the car. 'I knew that something was very wrong,' he says. 'At first I thought that the problem was they just didn't know how to talk to people who had been involved in strange things . . . [but] I knew that this was not adding up . . . that there was something peculiar here.'

Ofshe's major concern was the way that the Ingram family appeared to be recovering their memories. The way it was explained to him, Ingram had a perfect memory—like a strip of cine film—of forty-two years, with the exception of a series of short, specific periods, which had apparently been snipped out. 'It just didn't make any sense,' he says. 'Human memory simply doesn't work that way.'

A number of aspects of the process rang further alarm bells. As he recovered his memories, Ingram sometimes saw 'stick' people whose faces and clothing fleshed themselves out later on. That didn't happen with normal memories either, Ofshe reckoned: you recalled someone's face, or you didn't. You didn't see them as an outline and remember the details later.

In addition to Ingram's ability to forget things that most people would remember, there was his uncanny ability to remember things that most people would forget. In one of his first recovered memories, Ingram noted that Jim Rabie was wearing a watch on his right wrist. 'What time is it?' Schoening asked him, upon which he apparently managed to dredge through his memory and summon a close-up image of the watch. 'Two p.m.,' he replied. On other occasions he was able not only to note the presence of a calendar on the wall as his children were being abused, but to focus on that calendar at his interrogators' request and read a specific date.

To Ofshe, the idea that someone could forget he had abused his children, yet recall the exact time on the watch of another man raping his daughter was implausible. Then there was the matter of the contradictions in Ingram's stories. On his first day under arrest, Ingram recounted an incident of Rabie molesting Julie. She was, he said, tied up and gagged. Yet he specifically heard her say, 'No.' Was that possible? How, Ofshe wondered, was he recovering these memories?

Ingram usually recovered his memories through prayer. Detectives would feed him a snippet of what one of his daughters had said whereupon he would disappear into his cell, close his eyes and, with the help of John Bratun, 'pray on' them until images of the abuse became clear in his mind. Informed of this, when they first met on 2 February, Ofshe decided to try a practical experiment to see if Ingram was really recovering lost memories or inventing them to order.

Without warning the detectives accompanying him, Ofshe told Ingram that he had already met with Paul Junior and Ericka, and that they had told him how he had forced them to have sex with one another while he watched. Neither of these statements was true: Ofshe had not met any other members of the family, and—so far as he knew—there had never been any allegation that the Ingram children had been forced to fornicate with each other for their father's pleasure. 'I wanted to see what would happen if I deliberately misled him,' he recalls. 'I made it up on the spot. It was the least probable thing I could think of.'

When Ingram said he hadn't really thought about the incident before, Ofshe applied a little pressure. 'This really did happen,' he told him. 'Your children were there. They both remember it. Why can't you?' He then instructed Ingram to 'pray on' it. Ingram lowered his head, was silent for a few moments, then said he was beginning to recall something. Ofshe told him to go back to his cell and pray on it further; he would come back later for the full details of the incident. The two men departed the interview room in opposite directions.

While Ingram was 'praying on' the false image he had been given, Ofshe visited Ericka to confirm that the scenario he had suggested was fiction. The next day he returned to Ingram, who confirmed that it had, indeed, taken place. Before further details emerged, Ofshe told him once again to return to his cell and pray on it some more.

That evening, Ingram arrived looking pleased. He had managed to retrieve the memory. He handed Ofshe three pages of paper.

> Daytime. Probably Saturday or Sunday afternoon. In Ericka's bedroom . . . I ask or tell Paul Jr + Ericka to come upstairs + then we go into Ericka's room. I close the door and tell them we are going to play (a game?). I tell them to undress. Ericka says 'but dad', I say 'just get undressed and don't argue' . . .

Two and a half pages of single-spaced writing then detailed an extremely explicit encounter between Ingram, his son Paul Jr, and his daughter, Ericka—none of which had ever happened. 'He was quite proud of it,' says Ofshe.

Ofshe then played his trump card. 'I told him that I spoke to both his son and his daughter and they had both reported that it hadn't happened,' he says. 'He got progressively more upset. He kept begging and saying that he was sure it was right because he remembered it in exactly the same way he remembered everything else.' After interviewing Ericka and Julie again and trying (unsuccessfully) to persuade them that their stories were fabrications, Ofshe returned to California to write up his report.

In the meantime, with a lengthening list of increasingly unlikely crimes, the prosecution's chief expert clearly doubting the veracity of the case, and not a shred of physical evidence, the investigation pressed on.

By February, Sandy Ingram—facing the threat of losing her youngest son, Mark—was retrieving her own memories of abuse. Attorney Sax Rodgers arranged to meet her to discuss them. 'Rick Cordes, who represented Risch, and I met with Mrs Ingram in the courthouse library to talk to her,' he recalls. 'So we were interviewing her about something and she went into this hypnotic trance and started speaking in tongues. I'm sitting as close to her as I am to you. And she started telling these satanic stories.'

In the library, Sandy recovered a memory of attending a satanic meeting with her husband, Rabie, Risch and an ex-girlfriend, who performed a salute with a sword. In the middle of the ceremony Rabie put one hand on a Bible and the other round Sandy's shoulders. The Bible then began to bleed. Blood flowed out of the book, up Rabie's arm, across his shoulders and over on to Sandy until she was drenched. 'Then when they got done,' Rodgers recalls, 'they tied her to a table, and took turns raping her, Rabie, Risch and all these other guys. They were eating little foetuses and—I was about ready to vomit! I couldn't work out what was going on because I *knew* her! And she was sitting right there two feet from me, telling this story. You could tell she was in some sort of a trance or something: she was in a monotone, just kind of spilling this stuff out.' Rodgers and Cordes were flabbergasted. 'I'm sitting there and looking at Cordes, saying, "what the fuck is *this*?"'

By now it was clear to everyone concerned that Ingram's confession about his and Jim Rabie's involvement in the Green River murders was a fabrication. It was also rapidly becoming clear to Rodgers that the entire story was a fabrication, too. The stranger the accounts became, the more certain he was that his client was innocent. 'They were talking about having foetuses ripped out of their vaginas, and vaginas full of spiders and all that kind of goofy shit!' he says. 'At first it scared us, when Mrs Ingram did that. It perplexed us because we'd never been exposed to anything like this . . . but once this started, yeah! Of course! The more the merrier! We started encouraging it! Because it was obviously—I mean, a little girl wouldn't have a hundred spiders coming out of her vagina!'

Rodgers began pestering the police, telling them to be reasonable. 'I kept telling [Detective] Lynch, 'You guys are *cops*! There's gotta be evidence! There's gotta be bones! There's gotta be *something*! Babies missing or something!'

But there were no babies missing. There were no scars. And there were no bones. Instead, there was a wife and her children alleging that they had been abused, and a father agreeing that he was responsible. The more memories that surfaced, the crazier the case became.

In February 1988, Julie Ingram received a letter from her father. 'How's my very special little girl?' it began. 'Do you miss me?' Then it became threatening. Satan, apparently, was 'very upset' with Julie. 'You are going to burn in hell. And all those babies you've killed and the animal [*sic*] boy you'll surely be in trouble down there killing babies is gross you fucken [*sic*] murder [*sic*] you I can't believe you'd do something like that you are no longer my daughter or my special little girl no one will ever love you again you've done so wrong you are very very Bad and Dirty.' Ingram's sign-off was memorable: 'You are a slut, hoare [*sic*] . . . you'll never make it you'll never be any thing [*sic*] to any one [*sic*] you fucking hoare [*sic*]. Your ex-Father Paul'. At the request of the Thurston County Sheriff's Office, the letter was passed on to two separate graphologists, both of whom agreed that it had been written by Julie. On 9 March, she admitted that she had, indeed, been the author.

That one of their main witnesses had fabricated evidence was more than a little disconcerting for the police. But not as disconcerting as what happened next.

From the beginning, the case had implicated members of the Thurston County Sheriff's Office: Paul Ingram was an active police officer, Jim Rabie was a former police officer, Ray Risch had worked for the department as a mechanic and another reservist had been named. But by March 1988 the case had deteriorated so far that the officers conducting the investigation were themselves sucked in.

Over the course of four days in March, Ingram named ten more employees of the Thurston County Sheriff's Office as having been involved in the abuse of his children. The officers were all hauled in and polygraphed.

On 13 April accusations reached a peak when officers in charge of the canine unit were accused of bringing their dogs into Ingram's home to abuse his wife and children. Sax Rodgers remembers the atmosphere inside the sheriff's office becoming explosive. 'There's a guy named————. They started telling stories about how————would come over in his patrol car, with his dog, throw Mrs Ingram down and have the dog fuck her in front of the kids . . . ————got so pissed off, he was going to get a gun and go down to the jail and kill Ingram!'

Eventually the hue and cry had to stop. When Ingram accused another Thurston County detective, Jesse Maynard, of having been involved and it was demonstrated that Maynard had been in Atlanta the entire time that the abuse had supposedly taken place, it did. Rabie and Risch were released. They had spent 158 days in jail.

Just before his case was heard, Ingram received a phone call from Richard Ofshe, who tried to persuade him that his confessions were not memories but fantasies. Ingram told him that he had originally confessed because 'Joe [Vukich] kept saying, "Paul, once you admit that this happened then it will all come out" . . . This went on back and forth . . . and at some point I just went, "Well, okay, I will admit that it happened." It really didn't help me, but it certainly helped them.'

'So you are saying,' asked Ofshe incredulously, 'that at some point . . . you simply decided to confirm to see what would happen if you did it?'

'I think that's a fair way to put it,' responded Ingram. Even if he was wrong and the crimes had never happened, he said, he was going to maintain his 'guilty' plea because he couldn't bear the thought of putting his daughters through a court trial.

The transcript of the conversation makes heartbreaking reading:

OFSHE: Paul, I think your daughter is lying.

INGRAM: I know that is what [your] report says.

OFSHE: I don't know why she is lying, but I think she is lying. And I think you are about to go to prison for something that you probably didn't do.

INGRAM: (laugh-laugh-laugh) I don't know but the memories that I am getting are very real to me and I, I believe that they are true . . .

OFSHE: I know that. I am telling you that I don't think that they are.

INGRAM: Well (laugh) only one of us is in jail (laugh).
OFSHE: Yeah. Only, you are the one in jail.

Ofshe became increasingly frustrated. 'Paul, I will tell you that I can't—don't—know what else to do at this point other than to tell you I feel very sorry for you. I wish I could help you.'

But Ingram was resigned to his fate. 'Well, we will wait and see what happens . . . I am just trusting the Lord to take care of me in all this.'

Ofshe tried one last time: 'Your confession isn't worth the paper it was written on!'

By now, Ingram's mind was elsewhere. 'Well, they are trying to lock me down here, Doctor,' he said, 'so I appreciate the talk and we will be in touch.' Then he hung up.

Despite the fact that there was no physical evidence whatsoever, that Ingram's daughters were never put on the stand, that Richard Ofshe submitted a report on his 'experiment' to the court, and that Rabie and Risch—supposedly the main perpetrators—had been released, on 1 May 1989 Paul Ingram pleaded guilty to six counts of statutory rape.

Ingram had been assured that each count of rape merited a five-year sentence but that, since he had co-operated with the police and was pleading guilty, these sentences would be served concurrently. But he had not taken into account the tenacity of his own daughters, both of whom wrote personal letters to the judge requesting the maximum penalty for their father. 'Please see that I will not have to live in fear of ever having to see or be victimized by him again,' Julie begged, while Ericka warned that if Ingram was ever set free he would continue to 'destroy and kill' innocent people. 'Many lives are in your hands,' she wrote. 'Please do what is best for *all* of *us*.'

In April, 1990, Paul Ingram was sentenced to twenty years for rape. He was released in April 2003, having served fourteen and a half.

Everyone who reads about this case is appalled, but for different reasons. The extraordinary accusations levelled by two young girls, and the nourishment of those accusations by a fecund compost of religious fervour and misguided psychological 'expertise', raise uncomfortable analogies with the Salem witch trials. The actions of the police, meanwhile—swallowing a series of utterly implausible stories, hook, line and sinker—raise further questions about the nature of the American justice system. For these reasons the Ingram case has become a cornerstone of the false-memory movement.

At the same time, for those who believe in recovered memories and satanic ritual abuse, this remains the only case where an individual has actually been caught, forced to confess to committing such crimes and sentenced. Bizarrely, Paul Ingram has become a case study for both sides of the argument. But who is right?

One man who believes that Ingram got what he deserved is Neil McClanahan. Still under-sheriff of Thurston County, McClanahan says that he and his colleagues never believed the satanic-abuse stories. The Sheriff's Office, he says, behaved with complete propriety, fighting 'tooth and nail' against the satanic allegations and rejecting them for what they were: outright fantasy. 'We wanted no part of it,' he says. 'This isn't what the crime is. The crime is not ritual satanic abuse. The crime is *rape*. That's the issue.'

Not long after he said this, however, McClanahan appeared to relent: perhaps there *was* something in the satanic angle after all. Why did the stories from the children, the mother and the father all appear to fit together so well? Why was it that the moment one interviewee started talking about a particular aspect of abuse, everyone else corroborated it? You could almost sense him being sucked back into the story—the Ingram case, where logic ran backwards, so that the more the police learned, the less they knew. The Ingram case, which produced more questions than it ever did answers.

Why did the Ingram children make these allegations if they weren't true? Where did the satanism come from? And why, if the accusations weren't true, did they all confirm each other's stories? 'There's gotta be something to it!' McClanahan concluded. 'Because why is everybody talking about this stuff? I mean, where does it *come from*?'

Unfortunately there is no shortage of potential answers to these questions.

If we ignore the satanic angle for a moment and ask why the children might have alleged that they had been abused, it soon becomes clear that alarm bells should have rung from the start. Julie's accusations emerged at the beginning of October 1988, when she behaved uncharacteristically, curling into a foetal position and crying. What the police either did not know, or did not consider important, was that immediately before exhibiting this behaviour, Julie and a friend had been caught using school

telephones to make long-distance calls: she was in trouble. It was only after she was caught that the symptoms emerged.

In the meantime, allegations of sexual molestation had emerged from her
sister, Ericka, at Black Lake Bible Camp. As it happened, she had been having problems, too. Just before her first 'recovered memory' Ericka, who had
taken and lost a number of jobs, had been told by her father that the time
had come for her to start fending for herself. In particular she had a car that
he had bought her, and Ingram had told her, immediately before her accusations, that if she didn't start paying for its upkeep, he was going to sell it.

Another aspect that the detectives apparently failed to consider important was that this was not the first time that such allegations had emerged
from Black Lake Bible Camp. Jim Rabie, sex-crimes expert for a number
of years and one of the key defendants in this case, recalls that even before
he retired from the police 'That camp was noted with Thurston County
officials as having an extreme number of unsubstantiated or unproveable
accusations.'

Both girls had a history of crying 'rape', too. Before 1988 Ericka and
Julie had separately alleged sexual abuse by different men, immediately after attending camps at Black Lake. In 1983 Ericka had claimed that a man
had tried to abuse her after offering her a ride in his jeep—it later transpired that he had placed his hand on her knee; no charges were filed.
Julie, meanwhile, had alleged rape by Ingram's tenant, Isidro Archibeque,
two years later. Once again, charges were not pressed.

In addition there was the matter of the girls' stories, which meandered
and shifted continually, contradicting each other and themselves. Perhaps,
reading this account, you have noticed some of the contradictions? In case
you haven't, here are a few.

In the first week of the investigation, Julie informed Safeplace counsellors that the last time she had been molested was earlier that month. Later
that week, however, she told her mother and Detective Vukich separately
that her father had stopped abusing her five years earlier; she explicitly told
her teacher, Mrs Webster, that Ericka had never been abused. But when
she was first interviewed by Vukich, she knew that Ericka had indeed
been abused; initially, she had told officers that her mother was not involved in the abuse, but then she suddenly remembered that Sandy had
been present 'most of the time', participating and, among other macabre
abuses, inserting spiders and a dead baby's arm into her vagina.

Meanwhile, after her revelation at Black Lake Bible Camp, when Ericka had decided to blow the whistle on her abusers, the first person she chose to tell was her mother, at Denny's, off Martin Drive. She had tried to warn her before, she said, but 'you wouldn't listen'. Within three months, she was telling police that her mother had abused her, drugged her, held her down and helped a group of satanists perform an abortion on her. If that was indeed the case, it's hard to imagine why she would have wanted to drink tea with her and open her heart that day in Denny's.

Looking back, it's hard not to conclude that both girls were playing the police for fools. Not long after Julie had told officers about the abusive letter she had received from her father, detectives discovered that she had written it herself. Ericka was no saint, either. One of the reasons her mother had felt forced to start recalling satanic abuse was that she was terrified of losing her youngest son, Mark. As 'Pastor' Bratun had told her, Child Protection Services had received an anonymous call warning that Mark was in danger and suggesting that he be removed from his mother. The 'anonymous' call was later shown to have been placed by Ericka—who had decided, it seems, that she wanted custody of her younger brother.

Doubtless the police should have noticed, and explored, these contradictions. But how many of them did *you* pick up on? All of them? Any of them? Or were you, like the Thurston County Officers, too swept up in the horrific nature of the allegations to notice that something was wrong? All you had to do was read a chapter in a book. No-one was relying on you to rescue them. No lives were at stake.

When it comes to the first mention of satanism, it may have originated not with the Ingram family but the Thurston County Sheriff's Office psychologist, Dr Richard Peterson. In 1988 satanic abuse was all the rage in child-welfare circles. It had taken off following the publication of a number of revelatory books about child abuse in the 1970s and early 1980s including *Satan's Underground*, in which a young woman detailed her experiences (now discredited) as a 'baby breeder' for a satanic cult, and *Michelle Remembers*, an account of a girl supposedly abused by a satanic cult in Canada in the 1970s. (Under therapy Michelle 'recalled' being confined in a cage of snakes, the mutilation of babies and kittens and an operation in which cult members surgically attached horns to her head and a tail to her spine.)

Hot on the heels of these lurid accounts came a series of self-help books catering for individuals who now decided that they, too, had been abused. The most famous of these, *The Courage to Heal* by Ellen Bass and Laura Davis, won infamy thanks to its tenuous multiple-choice self-diagnosis technique. According to Bass and Davis, individuals who felt different from other people, who were afraid of success, who felt alienated or lonely, who lacked motivation or who couldn't trust their instincts were exhibiting classic symptoms of abuse. (Later authors on the subject added further 'warning signs' including headaches, palpitations, neglected teeth, lack of sense of humour, arthritis and obesity.) *The Courage to Heal* preached the heady theory of repressed memories, encouraging potential victims to accuse family members of abuse, even if they were unable to recall any specific incidents.

The book, which sold 750,000 copies, famously included the statement that 'If you think you were abused and your life shows the symptoms, then you were.' This was echoed later by another proponent of the recovered-memory movement, Renee Frederickson, who stated that 'The existence of profound disbelief is an indication that memories are real.' With this advice, readers entered a hall of mirrors: the point where *lack* of evidence for something becomes a reason for believing it is the point at which most normal people should have got out some time ago. By the mid–1980s, it was rumoured on the abuse circuits that satanic cults were responsible for the disappearance of 50–60,000 human babies every year.

As psychologists familiar with the work of Frederickson, and Bass and Davis knew, the key symptom of ritual abuse was repressed memories, a diagnosis that Dr Richard Peterson embraced whole-heartedly. But the theory itself was highly suspect. 'Retrieving' lost memories, using barbiturates, hypnosis or regression techniques such as guided visualisation, is a practice that should only be attempted (and many psychiatrists argue that it should *never* be attempted) with extreme caution. It is not reliable. Sigmund Freud had fallen foul of the technique in the 1880s, concluding that a high percentage of children were sexually abused by their fathers before it dawned on him that 'These scenes of sexual seduction had never taken place, and that they were only fantasies which my patients had made up, or which I had perhaps forced on them.'

The CIA had come to the same conclusion following its experiments with 'truth drugs' in the 1950s and 1960s, and even William Sargant, who had overseen the reintroduction of abreaction for the recovery of memories in the Second World War, recognised that it was fraught with danger. Fifty per cent of recovered memories, he wrote, were pure fantasy. In 1944, Sargant specifically warned of the dangers of accepting them at face value: caution was necessary on the part of the doctor, he wrote, to 'save him from swallowing all of his patient's hokum, hunting snarks and exploring mare's nests'.

Unfortunately, William Sargant was not present at the interviews of Paul, Sandy, Chad, Ericka and Julie Ingram. Instead, there was Dr Peterson.

Less than twenty-four hours after Ingram's arrest, Peterson stepped in and pointed him in the direction of a huge mare's nest. 'Before your conversion to Christianity', he asked, 'were you ever involved in any kind of black magic?' Ingram, who had no idea what he was talking about, wondered if reading horoscopes in the newspaper qualified. But the detectives were already running with the idea: Schoening asked if he had ever been involved in 'the satanic cult kind of thing' and Vukich specifically enquired about 'sacrifices, that kind of stuff'.

Within two hours of this exchange Ingram, who was not only highly suggestible but also steeped in the rhetoric of his evangelical church, was talking about fires and tombstones. Informed by the psychologist that repressed memories were genuine, then encouraged by police officers and his spiritual adviser, John Bratun, to retrieve them after he had been asked leading questions, all he had to do was nod and extemporise on the theme. Satanic ritual abuse became a self-fulfilling prophecy.*

The extent of Dr Peterson's eagerness to link 'repressed memories' to sexual abuse is demonstrated by his interview with Ingram's son, Chad, in December. When nothing of any great interest showed up, Peterson suggested that they examine his childhood dreams. The first that he recalled was a nightmare in which a group of dwarfs gathered outside his bedroom window, trying to get in. A harmless bad dream, many psychologists might say. Not Peterson. 'Those,' he concluded immediately, 'are dreams of being invaded.'

---

* The Thurston County officers accepted the diagnosis. In a 1993 lecture at Evergreen State College, Neil McClanahan commented that 'A giant bell—BONG!—was rung across the state . . . Repressed memory is understood . . . Now you have the law enforcement community saying repressed memory is a real thing . . . That bell will never, ever, be unrung.'

Having made his diagnosis, the psychologist was willing to go to some lengths to confirm it:

PETERSON: I'll tell you something. You'd have a—you have the right to
    sue these fuckers [*Chad's parents*] and get as much as you want from 'em.
CHAD: That'd be nice.
PETERSON: Pay for a nice car. Get you started in life.
CHAD: Well, I've already got a nice car.
PETERSON: Yeah, do you have a BMW?

It's hard to imagine how an interviewer could be more influential than by suggesting that a BMW might be a possible reward for implicating someone. Chad later agreed that his parents had abused him.

Thurston County detectives might have reined in their questioning but for one key factor: satanic allegations seemed to be surfacing from all angles of the investigation simultaneously. Since there was a complete lack of physical evidence, the case's only strength lay in the fact that the stories seemed to verify each other. How could this have happened unless they were true? Surely it couldn't simply be a coincidence.

It wasn't.

In this case, a possible conduit was John Bratun. Bratun was present at the interrogation of Paul Ingram and paid regular visits to both daughters. His boss, Pastor Ron Long, was certainly in contact with all major participants other than Ingram himself. In this way, accusations made by one family member may have been carried to the next, and the interviews allowed to contaminate each other. No great surprise, then, that all the interviewees, asked to 'relive' abuse experiences, aped each other.

When I suggested to Neil McClanahan that the interrogations of key suspects and witnesses might have cross-pollinated each other, he denied that this could have been the case. According to him, all the interviewees were strictly isolated. 'There was no way,' he said emphatically, 'that they could have been contaminated in that way during the investigation.'

Jim Rabie's attorney, Sax Rodgers, recalls things differently. 'You've got a go-between communicator between the family and the suspect, which was the minister,' he recalled. 'I don't think [Bratun] meant to, he seemed like a nice guy, but it was obvious what was going on: it was getting communicated back and forth by the minister. I mean, it wasn't the cops doing it.'

Rodgers seemed to have a pretty good take on what had derailed the investigation. 'You've got cops investigating their own, you've got shrinks suggesting cult activity . . . you've got the minister running back and forth every day from the jail to the family,' he said. 'In fact, a couple of times when we interviewed the girls, the minister would come with them . . . The whole thing stank,' he concluded. 'I've *never* seen an investigation like that.'

While he was on the subject, Rodgers also pooh-poohed Neil Mc-Clanahan's assertion that the police had largely ignored the satanic allegations, focusing instead on the rape charges. 'I remember many times going into [the prosecutor]'s office and seeing all these satanic books in the bookcase and saying, "What the hell's this stuff doing in there?" "I got that from Mr Peterson." '

McClanahan himself seems to have become pretty interested in the satanism angle, creating a large wall chart making links between reports of satanic activity all over the United States, and becoming something of an expert on the phenomenon. When we met, he denied it. He was never an expert, he said, because there was no such thing as an 'expert' in satanic abuse. Videotapes of lectures he gave in the 1990s, however, present rather a different story. In a seminar at Evergreen State College in November 1993, he told his audience that abusers created multiple personalities in their victims 'by design' so that the children would be unable to recall what had happened to them during their abuse. The youngest case he had come across, he said, was a woman who had abused her daughter while she was still in the womb. Apparently she had deliberately taken ice-cold baths 'to begin the process of conditioning her, begin the process of breaking up this individual'. The goal of such abusers, said McClanahan, was to split the personalities of their victims to ensure subservience and secrecy. Paul Ingram, he said, 'is proof that this exists.'

A number of times in his lectures McClanahan quoted Albert Einstein's adage that it is the theory that will determine what we observe. When we met, he used the quote on me a couple of times, too. He applied it to Richard Ofshe, who, he said, had clearly decided what he was going to conclude before he even visited. He also applied it to media reporting of the case: the media heard the crazy satanic stuff, made up their minds that the police had screwed up, and dumped on them. It was obviously a quote that meant a lot to him.

But when I bounced the quote back at him and suggested that perhaps the police's theories about Ingram had determined what *they* observed, causing them to ignore the inconsistencies in the case, he changed his mind about its usefulness. 'I have never, ever seen a case,' he said—incongruously, 'where the theory determines what the people observe.'

The one thing that McClanahan was certain of, though, was that Ingram was guilty of *something*. Otherwise why would his daughters have accused him? Kids just don't lie about this kind of thing, do they?

Unfortunately, a cursory perusal of the literature reveals numerous cases where kids *have* lied about it. In the famous McMartin Pre-school case, for example, nearly four hundred children testified that they had, among other things, been forced to sacrifice and eviscerate animals, been flushed down lavatories, flown around the country in aeroplanes, drank blood and eaten chocolate-coated faeces. The children said they had been abused in planes, tunnels, a local carwash and in hot-air balloons flying high over the desert. When asked to pick photographs of potential suspects, one child picked an image of the action-film star Chuck Norris, and another selected a picture of a group of nuns that had been taken forty years earlier.

Crazy. But were Ericka and Julie's allegations any less crazy? Sacrificing twenty-five babies? Nailing an arm to the floor? Inserting spiders and a baby's arm into a vagina?

Whatever you think about the case, there is no doubt that Paul Ingram was retrieving false memories. He *wasn't* the Green River Killer. Neither was he sacrificing babies in his backyard. Thurston County officials say that there was a 'core of truth' at the heart of the allegations. But why should we believe it? With so much material from all of the participants that was simply untrue—and sometimes maliciously, deliberately so—why should we believe anything any of them said? Unless we are willing to agree that there are indeed active bands of roving satanists that routinely kidnap, abuse, programme, kill, and insert spiders and babies' limbs into American children (and the FBI and Interpol have failed to locate any of these groups), we have no alternative but to agree that, sometimes—for all kinds of reasons—kids *do* lie about this kind of thing. When they do, there are casualties.

Jim Rabie's time in prison cost him his job, fifty thousand dollars in legal fees and an estimated three-quarters of a million in lost earnings for the rest of his career. His reputation was destroyed. Today he is in no doubt that kids lie—the Ingram kids especially. To the former sex-crimes expert, the case was absurd, a fact that any police officer with half a brain should have recognised from the outset. 'I cannot visualise,' he says, 'groups of law-enforcement officers, especially from different jurisdictions, collectively molesting kids. It's not the type of thing that you let a whole bunch of people in on, especially when they're cops! It's illogical!' He sighs. 'But there wasn't a whole lot of logic in this case. If there was any, it was thrown out the window.'

Rabie's wife, Ruth, is particularly angry with Neil McClanahan who, she thinks, used the case to make a name for himself. 'When my time on earth gets done,' she told me, 'I hope that the Lord keeps me in this one little spot so that when McClanahan goes down the hill—and he's gonna go!—I'm gonna be waiting with a big stick, and he'll burn in a million pieces!'

It's not hard to identify with what she said. But, then, how often have you opened a newspaper, read about the death of a child, and wondered why Social Services or the police hadn't acted sooner?

Jim Rabie is angry, too—with Julie, Ericka and Sandy. In fact, the only person he isn't angry with is Paul. This is partly because, of all the people who dragged him in, wrecked him financially and ruined his reputation, Ingram is the only one who has had the courage to apologise. 'I feel sorry for Paul,' he says. 'I think he got a real screwing.' Ingram was 'brainwashed. I cannot come up with any other term. He was brainwashed completely.' Understandably, however, Rabie's sympathy is limited: 'I could never completely trust him [again] because he has really shafted me once. And I'm not gonna give him a second chance. I think that this is something that will never happen again. But I don't want to be close enough to prove that.'

Two days after I left Olympia, I finally made it to the small town in Oregon that Paul Ingram calls home. A level-three sexual offender, recently released from prison, he was remarkably sanguine for someone who had spent more than fourteen years incarcerated, whose parents had died while he was inside, who had lost all his possessions and life savings and—most of all—his family.

I offered to take him out for lunch but he declined. Instead we had a barbecue. As we ploughed our way through a pile of ribs, steak and chicken,

Ingram blamed his situation on the fear that had hit him once he heard that his daughters had made their first accusations. 'It's kind of like you're numb,' he said. 'You're not in the right frame of mind: that fear! It's almost like you're in a cocoon and they're pressing on you from all sides.'

The fact that the officers interviewing him were his colleagues didn't help. 'I worked with these people. They were my friends. And I didn't trust myself at all. But to me, the only way I can explain it to myself is the fear: fear just overwhelms everything and you can't think straight . . . I figured something *must* have happened at some point. All the people I trusted were saying the same thing. It really comes back to the girls wouldn't lie about something so serious.'

Even as late as May 1989, Ingram was still being told by the police that the moment he pleaded guilty, the truth would come out and his doubts would be demolished. 'I couldn't really remember it but they still said, "Well, once you get this over with, the guilty plea, then the memory, you'll know for sure that the memories are true."'

In the end, the opposite happened. Once he had pleaded guilty, Ingram's interrogators left him alone. He returned to his cell where, with the pressure relaxed and plenty of time to think, he went down on his knees and prayed. 'I don't like "messages from God",' he says, 'but the message I got was "You know what's true and what's not true—in your heart of hearts." And at that point I knew that none of it was true. I had suspected it all along and I couldn't figure out how it had all happened, but now I knew.'

After lunch, Ingram and I went for a stroll along the creek next to his house. I told him that if I had spent the best part of fifteen years in prison for a crime I hadn't committed, I would be bitter. How could he be so calm about it? He shrugged. 'How else can I look at it? If I dwell on it, I get bitter. So I try not to. Everybody has unique opportunities, and you make the best of every situation. You can eat that lemon sour, or you can put some sugar on it and make lemonade: you decide what you're gonna do. I decided that lemonade was best.'

For obvious reasons, Ingram is not allowed to contact his family. But every now and then he hears titbits of information about them. No one seems to know where Ericka is now. Her last appearance was on a TV chat show during the course of which, to her obvious delight, her attorney alleged that Dr Richard Ofshe was 'probably a satanist' (challenged by Ofshe to repeat this allegation, the attorney refused to comply). In a lawsuit she filed against the county in 1991, Ericka also reportedly characterized her supporter Neil McClanahan as a satanist.

Julie kept in contact for a bit longer and actually visited her father once, in jail. According to some family and friends, she has said—off the record—that she has had doubts about the accuracy of her memories. Neil Mc-Clanahan, who attended her wedding not so long ago, says that this is a lie: Ingram's family tried to make her retract the allegations and she refused. Apparently Julie's husband is a pastor and they are starting their own church. She now has a little girl of her own.

I asked Ingram about his daughters. What did he think of them now? 'I don't bear them any ill-will,' he said. 'I hope they have a good life. I'd like to see them again . . . If they want to get in contact with me, they certainly know how to do it.' He paused for a moment. 'I still love my kids.'

10

The Monster Plot

'Where are you going in such a hurry?' asked Foxy Loxy.

'Haven't you heard?' said Chicken Licken. 'The sky is falling down. We're on our way to tell the king!'

'Well' said Foxy Loxy, 'I know a short cut. Follow me!'

And he smiled.

'The Story of Chicken Licken', Anon

On 8 June 1962 Tennant 'Pete' Bagley, second secretary at the American Embassy in Berne, received a telephone call from a colleague in Geneva. Something strange had happened, he was told: at the recent disarmament conference a Soviet official had slipped the diplomat a note requesting a private meeting with 'a representative of the US Government'.

Both Americans knew exactly what this meant. Soviet officials *didn't* slip notes to Western diplomats at disarmament conferences: the man was trying to defect. Since Bagley was deputy head of the CIA's Soviet Bloc Division at the time, he instructed the diplomat to send the man a return note containing a time and a location for a rendezvous, then stepped on to a plane for Geneva.

Bagley arranged for a fluent Russian speaker, George Kisevalter, to accompany him, and the pair traipsed off to a small apartment in an anonymous block of flats, where they waited. An hour and a half late, in walked a tall, confident Russian with a square jaw. He apologised for having kept them—he had, he said, taken extreme measures to make sure he wasn't followed—then introduced himself: Lieutenant Colonel Yuri Ivanovich Nosenko.

Nosenko told the two Agency men that his job was to ferret out spies within the Soviet Union, and that he worked from a desk in the KGB's Second Directorate. Bagley and Kisevalter exchanged a glance. If this was true, they had a real catch on their hands. So far, the CIA had not managed to recruit a single agent from the Second Directorate; the Agency had only learned it existed a couple of years earlier.

Nosenko offered a deal. He had a wife and children in Moscow so he didn't want to defect, and he didn't want to spy for the Americans. Unfortunately, however, he had lost nine hundred Swiss francs on a drinking binge and if he didn't replace it he was going to be in trouble. In exchange for the money he would hand over a secret KGB surveillance manual. The Americans took a punt, giving Nosenko the money and telling him to return with the book. They also cultivated their new contact, assuring him that if he were to bring more sensitive material with him next time, he could expect a lot more. The reward for unmasking a Soviet mole in the United States, they said, was twenty-five thousand dollars.

Nosenko was noncommittal, a sign that both CIA men thought augured well: most agents needed time to think about this sort of thing. But he was clearly a mine of useful information, and in the course of their two-hour meeting he revealed the location of a number of bugs in the US Embassy in Moscow.

Three days later, Bagley met Nosenko again. As promised, the Russian brought along the surveillance manual, which detailed techniques that the Americans had never thought of, including one method of following subjects by spraying the soles of their shoes with a chemical that attracted dogs, dispensing with the need for risky tailing operations. Bagley, impressed, gave Nosenko the codename AE FOXTROT, before dispatching him back to Moscow with equipment that would enable him to contact the CIA if he had further information he wanted to share. He then flew to Washington to consolidate his victory: if Nosenko was who he said he was—and he certainly appeared to be—he was 'the biggest fish yet'.

Then things went wrong.

Upon his arrival at Langley, Bagley was summoned by the chief of the CIA's counter-intelligence staff, James Jesus Angleton, who told him there was a problem. When Bagley asked what it was, Angleton handed him a dossier containing information from another Soviet defector, Antoly Golytsin. Golytsin, who had defected six months earlier in Helsinki, had provided the Agency with a wealth of information pointing, among other things, to a Soviet spy ring code-named SAPPHIRE high in the French Government. In addition to this invaluable intelligence, Golytsin had educated his handlers about the way that the Soviet intelligence machine worked. The KGB, he said, knowing the damage that his information would wreak, should be expected immediately to launch a damage-control operation to confuse the Americans. The first stage would involve sending over a false defector who, while appearing to give useful information, would actually muddy the waters. The CIA must not fall for this ploy: the appearance of such a false defector, contradicting everything he had said, should serve to confirm, rather than deny, the veracity of his information.

When Bagley read the Golytsin file, it was clear to him that something was wrong. Much of the information Nosenko had handed over in Geneva was, indeed, the exact opposite of what Golystin had said. He and Angleton concluded that Nosenko was 'painting false tracks'. It was entirely probable that he was still working for the KGB, staging a provocation exercise or, worse, trying to get himself deeper into the game, offering himself as a 'dangle': false bait for the hungry, gullible Agency to gobble up. Either way, the CIA was being played. The men now had a tricky decision to make: what should they do with their new friend?

The Nosenko issue sat on the back-burner for a while, until something happened that changed everything. In November 1963 President John F. Kennedy was shot. His assassin, Lee Harvey Oswald, was a former US Marine who had, crucially, defected to the Soviet Union some years earlier before redefecting to the United States. What had happened to him during his time in Russia? Had the KGB got to him? Were the Soviets behind the killing?

The CIA couldn't answer these questions but they knew one man who could. In Geneva, Yuri Nosenko had told Bagley that he worked in the Tourist Department of the KGB's Second Directorate, where part of his job was to monitor the activities of foreigners in the USSR.

Two months after Kennedy's death, Bagley and Nosenko met again in Geneva. Aware that his agent was probably spinning him a line, Bagley was sceptical this time but Nosenko told the CIA man outright that he now wanted to defect. Then he added an irresistible morsel of information: he knew all about Lee Harvey Oswald. Not only was he the case officer who had evaluated Oswald when he had arrived in the Soviet Union, he said, but he had also run the Soviet investigation after JFK's assassination. The Russians were so concerned that they might be implicated in the murder that they had provided Nosenko with a military plane to ferry files, equipment and himself around the country as he conducted his research. He was the only man in the KGB, he said, who knew the truth about Oswald.

Offered this bait, Bagley bit hard. Nosenko was put on to a US military plane and flown first to Frankfurt, then Washington. To his Russian bosses it would appear that their man had vanished off the face of the earth.

It was a textbook crash defection but when Nosenko arrived in the United States on 12 February, the CIA didn't know what to do with him: was he for real, or a *provocateur*? Could he be trusted? Golytsin had specifically warned that there would be a false defector. Now, out of the blue, a man had arrived who had worked on the Oswald case. Nosenko was too good to be true.

Smelling a rat, the CIA bosses debated their next move. Angleton, a legendarily tricky character, thought that Nosenko should be unwittingly doubled again and fed only false information, leading the KGB to believe that they had pulled the wool over the Americans' eyes when in fact they were the ones being played. Other disagreed. If there was any chance that the Soviets had had a hand in the assassination of the President, this wasn't the time for smoke and mirrors. The information was needed now: who *was* Nosenko, and what did he really know?

The ultimate decision fell to the future Director of Central Intelligence, Richard Helms, who concluded that the Kennedy killing had to take priority. At the start of April he authorised a hostile interrogation: one way or another, the Russian was going to talk.

On 4 April, Nosenko was told he was going to be medically examined and was strapped into a polygraph machine with Nick Stoiaken behind it. Even before the process began, Stoiaken and his colleagues knew that this would be tough. If Nosenko was really a double agent, he would have been trained to withstand prolonged interrogation. It was time for the Agency, once and for all, to determine what really worked in the interrogation business.

At the heart of the operation was theatre. When the polygraph test was complete, it was announced to Nosenko with 'intense shouting' that he had failed. The Russian had realised that something was up because of the strange way in which he had been treated over the past few weeks, but he had not expected this. He demanded to see his friend Pete Bagley, who came in, examined the polygraph results and immediately became 'enraged', ordering him to be arrested on the spot. A couple of huge guards swept in and grabbed him. He was stripped, manacled, blindfolded and bundled into a car.

Nosenko was then driven to a CIA safe-house in the Washington suburbs. His head was shaved and he was installed in a ten by-fifteen-foot bedroom in the eaves of the house. The room was sparse: the windows were boarded up and the only furniture was a single iron bed bolted to the floor. The bedroom door had been sawn in two, the bottom half shut, the top replaced with chicken wire so that he could be monitored at all times.

Nosenko was fed under a dollar's worth of food each day, was allowed to shave and shower only once a week, and was denied the use of a toothbrush. There was no human contact, no radio or TV, no reading material, and his guards were not permitted to talk to him. A lifelong smoker, he was not allowed cigarettes. The bathroom door had been removed: when he needed to use the lavatory, he had to do so while his captors watched, a process he found unnerving. Worse still, Nosenko's new home featured no temperature controls. In summer the roof of the house absorbed the heat and the attic was sweltering; in winter, it was freezing. 'It was hot,' he later recalled, 'no air conditioning, cannot breathe; windows—no windows, closed over . . . the conditions were really inhuman.'

Periodically, he was interrogated. Usually the questioning was conducted by two officers simultaneously to disorient him; often these officers were Pete Bagley, who had recruited him, and another CIA man, Tom Ryan. They took to screaming and abusing him at the same time, trying to scare him. In one interrogation, Ryan didn't even ask any questions, simply bellowing, 'Homosexual!' repeatedly into his face. Nosenko was told that his story didn't stand up, that there were inconsistencies, that he was a spy. The interrogations went on day and night for up to twenty-four hours at a time. He was told that this routine would continue until he finally admitted his guilt, even if it took twenty-five years.

After seventeen months of this treatment, Nosenko was moved to a new interrogation site that had been specially constructed for him on the CIA's 'Farm' at Camp Peary, two hours south of Washington. The prison, codenamed Loblolly, consisted of a windowless ten-by-ten-foot concrete cell with a bed and a bare lightbulb protected with a glass screen so that he

couldn't reach it. The bed, deliberately too small for its occupant, was fitted with an uncomfortable mattress and no pillow. Like his old accommodation, there was no heating and no air-conditioning. Food was atrocious
but his captors had thoughtfully ensured that smells from the guards'
kitchen were routed through his cell so that he could continually smell
proper food, which was perpetually out of reach. Behind the lightbulb,
monitoring everything he did, was a CCTV camera.

Nosenko was allowed half an hour outside each day but his tiny exercise
yard was fenced in so that he couldn't see anything other than a wall. When
he was taken outside, it was the first time he had seen the sky in two years.

Conditions inside Loblolly were even tougher than they had been in
the Washington safe-house. Nosenko was still not allowed a toothbrush.
His teeth began to rot. He was interrogated ruthlessly. Once again, since
the agents didn't know how to get him to talk, they resorted to threatening and abusing him, repeatedly telling him that he was a spy and that
eventually he would confess. In 1966 he was given another polygraph test,
prior to which he was examined by a doctor. But even this process was
designed to humiliate him. The doctor insisted on performing a rectal examination, inserting a gloved finger into his anus and wiggling it about for
ten minutes. 'I could not understand what he was doing,' Nosenko reported. 'Later I realised it was done for the purpose simply to get me mad.'

During the polygraph test that followed he was once again assured that
he was a homosexual and was grilled about his deviant sexual practices. In
the middle of the examination, the interrogators decided it was lunchtime
and wandered off, leaving him alone, strapped to the machine for ninety
minutes. Altogether he was there for more than five hours. Whatever he
said, he was told he was lying. At the end of the test he was handed a confession and told to sign it. He refused.

Back in his cell, Nosenko's jailers continually played with his sense of reality to stress and disorient him. Clocks were modified and lighting conditions altered so that he would have no idea what time of day or night it was.
He was woken up and put to bed at irregular intervals and meals were served
at strange times, often directly after each other, to confuse his body clock.

Desperate to maintain his sanity, the Russian tried to distract himself
from the regime by creating things to do. At one point he used old matchsticks and paper napkins to make an impromptu deck of playing cards; no

sooner had he finished it than it was confiscated. Another time he collected pieces of lint from his own clothing and attempted to use them as chess pieces on the floor. When his jailers realised what he was up to they swept the cell and issued him with new clothing, made of nylon this time so there was no more lint.

Nosenko began to lose touch with reality. He went on hunger strike and lost nearly twenty kilos. When he was eventually given toothpaste and a toothbrush to halt the damage to his teeth, he discovered a scrap of the toothpaste-tube wrapper, which featured a list of ingredients, and hid it, treasuring it and reading it over and over again until that, too, was confiscated. The Russian 'broke' repeatedly, telling his interrogators anything and everything he thought they wanted to hear. But no one knew whether to trust him. Was he lying? Was he mad? Or was he speaking the truth? How could they tell?

The CIA officers now found themselves in a situation of some delicacy. They had applied all of the tried and tested interrogation techniques but they didn't know which, if any, had worked. Richard Heuer, who later reviewed the case papers, wrote that all the interrogation had achieved was to have 'muddied the water'. Pete Bagley later agreed. 'There was no intention,' he told journalist Tom Mangold, 'to hold him for a long time. But the results were nil. The truth is, we were stuck.'

For the Agency, the situation was a great deal more important than simply a KGB man who wouldn't break. Following the defection of MI6's Kim Philby in 1963, counter-intelligence chief James Angleton became convinced that the CIA had been penetrated at a high level, and that Nosenko's refusal to speak was part of what was later dubbed the 'Monster Plot': a vast Soviet conspiracy to infiltrate and undermine the entire Western intelligence network. Those who suggested that he was exactly who he said he was, and that the Monster Plot did not exist, lost their jobs and the CIA began to tear itself to pieces. Nosenko *had* to talk.

There were arguments within the Agency for the best part of a year over whether to drug Nosenko, and what drugs might be suitable. But nobody seemed able to decide which ones, or how to use them. David Murphy, a senior CIA officer on the case, later told a Senate committee that 'There were many, many conversations all the time about various things that could be done—all the techniques that are known—to get him to talk,' but said that drugs were not administered because 'none of them appeared to be likely to produce results and they all would be very harmful'.

There are indications that this testimony is not true. At one point MKULTRA psychologist John Gittinger spent five weeks interrogating Nosenko. Gittinger, who had experimented with LSD for the Agency a number of times, including at the CIA safe-house in Marin County, California, later stated that he had been ordered to administer the drug but had refused.

Nosenko himself says that this is nonsense: he was drugged many times. On one occasion a new doctor came in to take blood samples. The next thing he knew, he found himself lapsing into unconsciousness, unable to breathe. Guards rushed in to revive him. 'On me were used different types of drugs and sleeping drugs, hallucination drugs, and whatever I do not know,' he recalled. 'And I don't *want* to know . . . I passed through hell.'

If drugs were used, they weren't effective. At the end of Nosenko's time in Loblolly, Angleton and his boys were no closer to proving the existence of the Monster Plot than they had been at the start. Lost in a world of contradictions, they were more confused than ever. In 1967 Pete Bagley compiled a vast report on Nosenko concluding that he was a liar, and was awarded a CIA medal for his work on the case. Not long afterwards his successor, Bruce Solie, was awarded a CIA medal for concluding the opposite.

Yuri Nosenko was eventually released in October 1967, after 1277 days in solitary confinement. He was offered a salary by the CIA, which was thoughtfully backdated to cover the three and a half years he had been incarcerated. He was given provisional security clearance by the Agency and, until recently, lectured new recruits at Langley. Not everyone was happy about this: twenty years after his defection, various CIA officers were still trying to reopen the investigation to discover, once and for all, whether he really was telling the truth.

The Nosenko case sheds an interesting light on the brainwashing story. It is telling that drugs and other MKULTRA techniques, such as electricity and hypnosis, were not authorised immediately for his interrogation, the Americans choosing to rely instead on more traditional methods. Even once drugs were used (if they were used) they were not effective. At the end of the day, the Agency could not determine whether one of the most important agents of the Cold War was lying. The CIA, which had been looking into truth drugs and brainwashing mechanisms for over a decade, was apparently no closer to discovering one.

By the time of the Nosenko affair it was fairly clear to everyone concerned that the BLUEBIRD/ARTICHOKE/MKULTRA projects had cost a great deal of money without yielding much useful information. Moreover, the year after his defection, the CIA's inspector general had stumbled upon the projects and ruled unfavourably on them. There was a risk, he noted, that the Agency would be caught if it continued dabbling in this sort of thing, and it was an unjustifiable one. The projects were running out of steam.

Following the inspector general's damning report of 1963, there was a wholesale reorganisation of the CIA's brainwashing projects. Sidney Gottlieb gave up control of most of the research contracts while keeping a handful of his favourites, including drug-testing in safe-houses, various conduits for the production of biological and chemical poisons and a certain amount of hallucinogen research. The rest were shifted to the CIA's Office of Research and Development.* To signal the change in Agency policy, in June 1964 MKULTRA was officially shut down. Gottlieb's new project—with an almost identical remit—was codenamed MK-SEARCH. But by now funding was steadily decreasing. In 1964 MK-SEARCH was worth less than a quarter of a million dollars annually, and after that funding dropped steadily. Eventually, the axe had to fall.

In June 1972 Gottlieb, realising that brainwashing research was 'less and less relevant to clandestine operations', closed down the programme altogether. The materials he had been testing were too unpredictable to be

---

* Work was under way, elsewhere, on other means of control. The Office of Research and Development seems to have been especially interested in the idea of implanting microchips into the mammalian brain. By November 1961, 'feasibility of remote control activities in several species of animals' had been demonstrated. Six years later the Agency actually produced a cat ('Acoustic Kitty') that could be guided via remote control. The idea was that the cat, which contained hidden microphones, could be steered close to surveillance targets. Results were not good. A memo detailing plans for the first test, to take place on Monday, 20 February 1967, explains that the cat's operators should beware of traffic and that the team should 'secure gear and remove animals before rush hour'. They didn't. On its first field test the cat was run over by a taxi.

useful in the field. Anyway, operations officers had always been reluctant to use them.

The next year both Gottlieb and his mentor, CIA director Richard Helms, resigned. Before they went, the two men met and decided that if the BLUEBIRD, ARTICHOKE and MKULTRA material was found at a later date, it might be 'misunderstood'. It would be best, they decided, if the evidence of their activities went away. Gottlieb ordered that every scrap of paper relating to the brainwashing experiments be incinerated. By the time he left Langley after his last day at the office, twenty years of research had gone up in smoke.

And that should have been the end of the brainwashing story. But it wasn't. Because not long after Gottlieb's retirement things began to move.

One day in June 1975, a former State Department employee called John Marks read a newspaper article about the Rockefeller Commission. Established after the Watergate break-in, it was investigating various questionable activities of the US intelligence services. Unexpectedly Vice-President Nelson Rockefeller had stumbled on a host of CIA misdeeds, which were now being owned up to and forgiven.

One of the misdeeds reported in the newspaper that day was a botched CIA drug test that had taken place in the early 1950s. An unnamed employee of the US Army, said the report, had been unwittingly fed LSD by a CIA operative. Things had gone horribly wrong. It soon transpired that the employee concerned was a biological-weapons specialist called Frank Olson. At a conference on 18 November 1953, Sidney Gottlieb had spiked a bottle of Cointreau with LSD, poured everyone a glass, then asked the recipients, half an hour later, if anyone felt strange.

As it turned out, they all did. But none felt as strange as Olson, who became psychotic. While the others went home the next morning with hangovers, Olson refused to get better. Chronically depressed, he told his boss that he would have to resign because he had done something terrible; he told his wife he was a failure. God knows what he told himself.

What to do now? Take him to a doctor and reveal that he had received a top-secret brainwashing drug? The CIA wasn't keen. In a panic, they shuffled Olson between Washington, DC, and New York to see a series of Agency-friendly experts, none of whom was a qualified psychiatrist, hoping that someone might make the problem go away.

In the end Olson solved the problem on his own, flinging himself from the tenth floor of New York's Statler Hotel at two thirty a.m. on 28 November 1953.★

John Marks was intrigued by what he read. According to the Rockefeller Report, the Olson LSD experiment 'was part of a much larger CIA program to study possible means for controlling human behavior'. Instead of chasing up the Olson family directly, like other journalists, he took a much smarter route: he filed a Freedom of Information Act request with the CIA, demanding all the files that the Rockefeller Commission had seen as part of their investigation. A year later, he received fifty documents on the brainwashing programme. This was apparently all that had escaped the destruction that had preceded Helms and Gottlieb's retirement. Marks, who didn't believe for a moment that the Agency had no records of its research, lobbied for more.

A year later, his lawyers received a letter from the CIA. There had been a mistake: Helms and Gottlieb had indeed ordered the destruction of all MKULTRA documentation but the clerks responsible had apparently forgotten that there were *two* depositories for this kind of information. Seven boxes of programme documents remained. Marks was invited to a nondescript office block to inspect them, where he sat, supervised, leafing through piles of ageing paper. He was gripped. 'The documents had been redacted with crayons,' he says today. 'I have to admit that I scraped some of the crayon off with my finger to see what was underneath.' Eventually, the Agency supplied him with hard copies of all sixteen thousand pages.

Marks hired a handful of researchers and started to plough through the material. Most of it consisted of financial records—receipts, contracts and so forth—which might have been easy to decipher but for the fact that almost all of the names in the documents had been blanked out by the Agency's censors. He and his team began the excruciating process of assembling a

---

★ Olson's suicide may not be the most shocking example of the misuse of hallucinogens by US government agencies. Eleven months earlier Harold Blauer, a tennis professional suffering from schizophrenia, was forcibly restrained at the New York State Psychiatric Institute and given a shot of a synthetic mescaline derivative, codenamed EA1298. The experiment, conducted without Blauer's permission, resulted in his death. One of the doctors who administered the drug later commented that the death was not his fault because he had been given the drug and told to administer it by the US Army. 'We didn't know,' he said famously, 'whether it was dog piss or what it was we were giving him.'

twenty-year jigsaw with no idea how big it would be, or what picture he was working towards. 'The documents had been heavily redacted,' he recalls. 'Our job was to put the names back in and to find the people . . . It was a real puzzle putting it all back together.'

Sometimes the team hit gold. When it became clear that much of the CIA's brainwashing research had been carried out at the behest of the Society for the Investigation of Human Ecology, Marks called up financial records for the organisation and cross-checked money transfers with the CIA documents. They matched. Other times, censored names were legible when documents were held up to the light. In the case of the mushroom expeditions to Mexico, one of his researchers, Rich Sokolow, managed to decipher the imprint that a typewriter had left on the backs of the project's pages. 'It was written on one of those hand typewriters and I had the documents,' says Sokolow. 'I had the places, but not the names . . . I guessed at the name "Wasson".'

Once names started surfacing, Marks, Sokolow and the team began to make calls, filling in the gaps one by one. Some were easier to verify than others. In the case of the Mexico trip, says Sokolow, 'I just looked up the names of all the mycologists and experts.' By a process of elimination, it wasn't long before he stumbled on the name of the CIA operative who had accompanied Wasson to Mexico: James Moore.

Sokolow called Moore at the University of Delaware and arranged to meet without telling him what he wanted to talk about. 'Moore was a very strait-laced guy, short hair,' he says. 'I had the documents and I just showed them to him. And he just confirmed that he had been on the trip. He wasn't too pleased to see me.'

Other CIA men were harder to pin down. Sidney Gottlieb, perhaps the only man who could have told the whole story, refused numerous requests to talk about his work. CIA psychologist John Gittinger went on the record only about hypnosis experiments and his work on a personality-assessment system that the Agency had sponsored.

But there was one shining light: a CIA man who had worked on the brainwashing programmes almost from the beginning. This character, whom Marks refused to name, was dubbed 'Deep Trance'; meetings with him took place in Italian restaurants and became known as the 'Pizza Hut Interviews'. Unfortunately, while Deep Trance was willing to verify information that Marks already knew, he was unwilling to bring new characters into the investigation. '[Deep Trance] was the only person who ever talked to me openly,' says Marks, 'though he would not tell me stuff until I already knew it.' The way the information changed hands, it was clear that the Agency had more or less decided to help with his investigation. 'They thought that since I was writing this book, and nothing could stop that, it was better if things weren't totally out of context . . . I think they had made the decision that they were going to bite the bullet on this one.'

On a number of occasions Deep Trance came to the rescue. For nearly a year Marks and his team agonised over the name of the CIA researcher who had offered to conduct a 'terminal' sensory-deprivation experiment in 1955. All they knew from the documents was that he had a seven-letter surname beginning with B and ending with N. Eventually a combination of painstaking research and detective work yielded a name, which was cross-checked with the CIA source. 'Have you ever heard of Maitland Baldwin?' Marks asked him.

'I thought,' sighed Deep Trance, 'you'd *never* get him!'

The result of Marks's work, *The Search for the Manchurian Candidate*, was published in 1979, winning accolades from reviewers and investigative journalists alike and collecting the Best Book of the Year Award for Investigative Reporters and Editors.

But while the reviewers raved, the public was unexpectedly ambivalent. 'There were some nice reviews and stuff like that,' says Marks, 'but it didn't take off . . . I was disappointed.' The book didn't vanish, though. It went underground, where it found a resting place among other esoteric accounts of spy tradecraft and conspiracy theories. And fermented.

When *The Search for the Manchurian Candidate* was published, the United States was in a quiet panic about brainwashing. New religious organisations such as the Moonies and the Children of God were recruiting all over the country. In 1978, the year before the book came out, 912 people had committed suicide at Jonestown in Guyana. In 1969, Charles Manson had persuaded members of his 'Family' to murder seven people, including Roman Polanski's wife, Sharon Tate. In 1974, heiress Patty Hearst had been kidnapped by the Symbionese Liberation Army. She was later offered the chance to leave the group but she chose to stay, adopting the outfit and persona of a revolutionary fighter and robbing a bank with an M1 carbine.

Why were these kids behaving like this? Why would *anyone* behave like this? To the public, the answer was simple: they had been brainwashed. What other explanation could there be?

There was nothing particularly surprising about this conclusion. For generations, people had been fascinated by the idea that one individual might be able to control the mind of another. Starting with George du Maurier's *Trilby* in 1894, a number of novels had catered to this fascination, featuring hypnotism as a means of external control. The flames were fanned, and the story began to mature. As popular fiction evolved through the early twentieth century, so the targets of the hypnotic attack became not fey heroines but more manly types.

In John Buchan's *The Three Hostages* (1924) Richard Hannay, hero of *The Thirty-Nine Steps*, encounters a fearsome opponent in Dominick Medina—'an uncommon fine poet . . . and the best shot in England after His Majesty'. Medina uses his startling blue eyes to entrance victims, kidnapping heirs and heiresses and wiping their minds. So effective is his technique that Hannay soon finds himself doing Medina's bidding. In 1945, that master of hypnosis—and self-publicity—George Estabrooks published *Death in the Mind*, specifically advocating the use of hypnosis against the Nazis. 'Tamper with their minds!' concludes the book's hero, Johnny Evans. 'Make them traitors. Make them work for *us!*'

Serious novels about Soviet repression, such as George Orwell's *1984* and Arthur Koestler's *Darkness at Noon*, with studies of coercive techniques by such scientists as William Sargant, Robert Jay Lifton and Joost Meerloo gave the Tom Clancys of the 1940s and 1950s material to work with. No sooner had psychology come up with a new method that might be useful in controlling the mind than it was incorporated into a story. As more and more accounts of the scary, secret process began to appear in print so brainwashing—rather than simply hypnotic programming—began to pass into the collective public consciousness.

With the Mindszenty trial and the Korean confessions, popular fiction collided with current affairs, and the boundary between the two became blurred. The story of Cardinal Mindszenty's arrest and interrogation was eventually made into a feature film starring Alec Guinness and Jack Hawkins. Len Deighton's hero, Harry Palmer, was brainwashed in the film of *The Ipcress File*. Even that most British of secret agents, James Bond, succumbed. In *The Man with the Golden Gun* Bond was captured by an evil Russian, Colonel Boris, and brainwashed at the Institute on Leningrad's

Nevsky Prospekt; 007 made it back to London where he confronted and tried to kill his boss, M.

According to Cold War literature, brainwashed people had a strange, faraway look in their eyes, moved like automatons and talked in monotone voices that sounded like recordings. Bond was eventually recognised to have been brainwashed, thanks to his 'odd sort of glazed, faraway look' and 'distant smile'. Richard Hannay repeated words 'as if my voice belonged to an alien gramophone'. It was known that these were the symptoms of brainwashed people because they had shown up in the Moscow Show Trials, the Mindszenty trial and the Korean confessions. What made the brainwash stories sell was the same thing that made them scary: that they were based on reality.

The book that really gave the story resonance, however, was 1959's *The Manchurian Candidate.* In the novel an American, Raymond Shaw, is captured by the Communists in Korea and taken to the 'Research Pavilion', where he is subjected to intensive Pavlovian conditioning and a 'deep control plant'. Repeatedly hypnotised and drugged, Shaw is eventually programmed to return to the United States and assassinate a presidential candidate. By transferring the action from Korea to the United States, the book's author, Richard Condon, brought the story home to roost. The victims were no longer errant Communists, or servicemen in foreign prison camps, but Americans in America. Now that the threat was on everyone's doorstep, there was plenty of reason to be alarmed.

Frank Sinatra was so concerned about the plot of *The Manchurian Candidate* that he asked President Kennedy whether he should accept the leading role in the film. Kennedy, who had enjoyed the novel, encouraged him to go ahead—but after he was assassinated in 1963, Sinatra pulled the film from circulation for fifteen years: the story was just too close to fact to be comfortable fiction.

In retrospect, it is clear that brainwashing's appearance in novels and movies of the early Cold War was a sublimation of popular fears of the time. In the same way that science-fiction movies such as *War of the Worlds* and *Invasion of the Bodysnatchers* played on the fear of invading Communists, brainwashing highlighted the fear of Communism *itself*: a sinister mental state wholly incompatible with free thought. Brainwashing was a perfect metaphor for the Cold War: we were free and the Soviets were automatons. What other reason could there be for their inhuman behaviour?

In a war portrayed by politicians in terms of dominoes and missile gaps, brainwashing was something that everyone could grab hold of. If the Soviets could persuade American servicemen and Catholic cardinals that they were traitors, what hope had the average civilian? The technique was brutal, barbaric—a rape of the mind, or the soul. With the advent of brainwashing, the fear of Red subversion was carried into every American household. Everyone had to be on their guard: if the Russians had their way, we would not only be forced into slavery but brainwashed to *enjoy* it. It was scary stuff.

It was also complete fiction, and had been from the beginning.

CIA documents analysing the Korean confessions and the Show Trials make it clear that the Agency suspected, from the outset, that the Soviets did not have a secret technique capable of wiping minds. A memo of 24 February 1953 concludes that 'We have no indications that [the Russians] know any methods not known in this country for determining the truthfulness of information obtained from prisoners.' Four months later the CIA's chief of operations was told that 'The Communists did not employ sinister techniques such as drugs, serums, etc.' Two years later, 'Reports lead us to believe that the Communists do not use stimulating drugs or narcotics routinely to interrogate.' Again, two months later, the same office concluded that 'There is nothing mysterious about personality change resulting from the brainwashing process' since 'the techniques used to produce confessions . . . have been used, especially by police states, for centuries.' In fact, for every scary report the CIA promulgated about Soviet interrogation techniques, there are two that confirm they consisted of nothing other than brutality and repeated threats.

British Intelligence soon came to the same conclusion. Cyril Cunningham, the War Office's indoctrination and brainwashing expert, examined the Show Trials and the behaviour of Allied prisoners in Korea and found that confessions had been beaten out of them with violence, threats, starvation and intolerable living conditions. 'As far as the confessions were concerned,' he says today, 'it was being forced on them to make these remarks, otherwise nasty things would happen to them. I've *never* come across a single confession where the individual truly believed what they were saying. Absolute nonsense!'

In many cases, he realised, the confessions could only have been written by the Soviets: 'The language that was used in these confessions was enough to tell you that these guys hadn't written it themselves,' he says. 'As far as we were concerned in AI9, we were very sceptical.' On other occasions, prisoners had written their own confessions, deliberately couching them in preposterously pro-Communist terms in an attempt to warn their colleagues that they were being tortured. But while the sheer incredibility of the confessions persuaded AI9 that they were false, it had the opposite effect on other audiences. 'Unfortunately,' sighs Cunningham, 'the world press and the powers-that-be didn't see it that way.'

Cunningham, who had access to all the available intelligence on Soviet interrogations, learned that there was no psychological programme at work either in the USSR or in China. Interrogation techniques were the tried and tested ones, handed down over generations by interrogators and torturers. Brainwashing, he concluded, was a 'bogeyman'.*

Like many of the Korean prisoners, Cardinal Mindszenty had also tried to warn the West that his confessions were false. Declassified Hungarian Secret Service documents reveal that a number of his written statements were signed 'Mindszenty, CF'. To his interrogators, he explained that 'CF' stood for 'Cardinalis Foraneus', his rank in the Catholic Church. To students of history, however, 'CF' was ominous. It was a Latin term dating back to earlier Church persecutions: 'coactus feci'—made under torture.

To Western governments, however, the Korean confessions were embarrassing. If there was nothing new about the Communist interrogation techniques, why were so many Allied troops collaborating with their captors? In the case of the British, the problem was not so severe: without exception, all of the confessors were non-commissioned men. But many of the Americans were officers, who should have known better. It turned out that in captivity the American troops' morale had collapsed, leading their officers to comply with orders to ensure their own survival. A later study at George Washington University concluded that 70 per cent of US servicemen in captivity had caved under pressure and made at least one

---

* Cunningham's conclusion was borne out by later events. Of the forty 'converted' British Communists who returned home from captivity at the end of the war, none remained Communist for very long. One man, Royal Marine Andrew Condron—apparently fully brainwashed—remained in China. He eventually returned to the UK in 1960. Of the Americans that remained in Korea, all but three returned to the West.

contribution to enemy propaganda. This was uncomfortable for the Pentagon. The men were said to have been plagued by 'giveup-itis'. A facesaving operation was needed. Two months after Colonel Frank Schwable's famous confession, one was put into action.

In early April 1953, the US ambassador to the United Nations, Senator Henry Cabot Lodge, met with a pair of CIA officers. At the time Lodge was trying to counter Soviet bloc accusations that the Americans had used biological weapons in Korea but was facing stiff opposition: why, if this had not happened, were American officers queuing up to say that it had? Lodge recounted bitterly that 'he had a profound distaste for the matter . . . principally because of the difficulty explaining the film and the statement of the American flyers'. The CIA men offered him an escape route. They had heard, they said, that there was a Soviet method of inducing false confessions: 'the technique of "brainwashing"'. A month later, at an ARTICHOKE conference, the officers recounted that Lodge had seized upon their explanation:

> [Deleted] stated that . . . Senator Lodge had expressed a great interest in the potentiality of Chinese and Soviet use of "brain washing" as a propaganda weapon for use by the United States at the United Nations' sessions. Senator Lodge stated he was seeking a very dramatic word which would indicate horror and would condemn (by its sound) Soviet practices

The next step, reports another document, was a 'public offensive . . . to combat the fears and questions arising from public discussions . . . in relation to PoWs held in North Korea'.

What the CIA men do not appear to have told Senator Lodge was that the term they were suggesting he use to explain the Korean confessions was not a result of top secret intelligence hot out of the Soviet Union. Actually, it had been coined in 1950 by a popular journalist, Edward Hunter, in the *Miami Daily News*. And they certainly kept him in the dark about another key fact: that Edward Hunter was a salaried propagandist for the Central Intelligence Agency. In this way, 'brainwashing'—a term created at the behest of the CIA—was peddled to the United States Government, the United Nations, the press and the world public.

The tactic was effective for both parties. Senator Lodge's 'public offensive' spread the word all over the world, lodging Edward Hunter's term firmly in the public consciousness and making the Soviets look thoroughly evil. The fact that brainwashing was on everyone's lips, meanwhile, gave the Agency a perfect excuse to start a 'defensive' programme to investigate its capabilities. Enter projects BLUEBIRD, ARTICHOKE and MKULTRA.

Unfortunately, there were side-effects. Half a century after the fateful meeting between Lodge and the CIA men, the story is still running.

'Brainwashed' is a useful term because it can be used to describe anybody who performs actions out of character. If your kids become Moonies or Muslims, plant bombs or shoot civilians (or themselves)—well,—they must have been brainwashed. After all, normal people don't *do* things like that, do they? Although no one really seems to know exactly what 'brainwashing' entails, how it works or who uses it, the term is applied all over the place. It makes sense. Besides, we've read about it in the papers.

When people strap explosives to themselves and blow up buses and trains, there are only two possible explanations. If they're foreign, they're EVIL. If they're not, they're BRAINWASHED. Why would John Walker Lindh join the Taliban? Why would Richard Reid put a bomb in his shoes? Why would John Muhammad and Lee Malvo shoot ten people dead, and injure three more, from the back of their car? Why would anyone fly a jet into the World Trade Center? Because they were *brainwashed*, of course. The solution is as simple as it is elegant. Brainwashing eliminates the need for complicated explanations that involve research, analysis or thinking. It makes complicated situations simple. And because of that it makes us feel better.

Unfortunately, while brainwashing may be a great comforter, there are a number of reasons why applying the term is a bad idea. The first is that it distracts us from the true causes of destructive or uncharacteristic behaviour, leaving us unable to eliminate them, and susceptible to further similar behaviour. The second is that brainwashing itself, while reassuring us that we are normal and others abnormal, can become a scare story in its own right. At various points in the phenomenon's history, brainwashphobia has reached near-epidemic proportions: it makes our enemies seem even more cunning and sinister than they really are. If they're clever and evil enough to do *this*, well, what *aren't* they clever and evil enough to do? And so, like Chicken Licken, we run around panicking, warning our friends, 'The sky is falling down! The sky is falling down!' Brainwash paranoia is horribly contagious.

There is one final reason why use of the term is dangerous: the 'brainwash' label tends to lead us into all kinds of places that we don't really want to visit. Tragically, this is partly the result of the publication of John Marks's *The Search for the Manchurian Candidate*.

By the early 1980s, Marks's investigative triumph was feeding the arteries of a rich network of conspiracy theories. JFK's assassin, Robert Kennedy's assassin, Charles Manson's Family, the Jonestown suicide victims and Patty Hearst: all 'brainwashed'. To individuals with the right take on things, brainwashing offered a brilliant way of incorporating the CIA into any conspiracy theory. All that was needed to construct a plausible story was the following piece of beautifully warped logic:

(1) The CIA worked on brainwashing.
(2) Religious cults, assassins and terrorists either use brainwashing techniques or are themselves brainwashed.

Therefore:

(3) The CIA is behind religious cults, assassinations and terrorism.

Turn on your computer, type in an Internet search for 'mind control' and watch the conspiracy theories fall out. They multiply daily (112,000,000 websites, according to Google in February, 2006), each as implausible as the last, each citing Marks's book as evidence of their veracity. Want to know about alien abduction? Nazi mind control? Roman Catholic brainwashing? Or how *Scooby Doo* controls your mind? The truth is out there.

Such is the allure of the brainwash story that a recent UK survey declared 'mind control' to be the world's favourite conspiracy theory—ahead of the JFK assassination, the death of Marilyn Monroe and the faked moon landings. If there's no evidence, if first-hand testimonies disagree or if no one can remember anything, it's because the protagonists were brainwashed. In the world of mind control, the less evidence there is the more fiendish the conspiracy (after all, the victim of *true* mind manipulation does not know he is a victim). Marks's real-life exposé has become a web of desperate paranoia.

An example. Three years before Marks's book was published, another non-fiction book on brainwashing came out. Donald Bain's *The Control of Candy Jones* related the story of an American model unwittingly recruited by the CIA. Under hypnosis by her husband, radio presenter 'Long John' Nebel, Jones recalled a number of horrific experiences at the hands of the Agency, whose scientists had used hypnosis to split her personality and create an *alter ego* called 'Arlene Grant'. When the CIA wanted a piece of dirty work done, they would summon Candy Jones, hypnotise her and in-struct Arlene to come out. At the end of their agent's usefulness, the CIA doctors concerned apparently instructed Arlene to commit suicide, elimi-nating all evidence of their meddling.

The Control of Candy Jones was a great story—a number of feature films, including *Conspiracy Theory, The Long Kiss Goodnight* and *The Bourne Iden-tity*, have explored the same premise—and appeared to mesh with a lot of what Marks's documents were saying. In the 1950s the CIA had indeed meddled with hypnosis, and at one point it *had* toyed with the idea of splitting the human personality to create *alter egos* that could be used to convey secret messages with impunity.

Naturally, when Marks heard about the story he was excited. Had Candy Jones really been a guinea pig in the Agency's MKULTRA pro-gramme? Bearing in mind that the book had been published before his CIA documents had been declassified, how could the story be anything other than true? At the request of the book's author, Donald Bain, he spent months following up every lead in it, listening to the tape recordings of Jones's hypnotic sessions and trying to cross-reference them with his sixteen thousand pages of CIA documents.

Nothing matched. 'I couldn't get one cross reference that worked!' he recalls. 'Not *one!*' As he followed up the story, he realised that the whole thing was distinctly fishy. It turned out that Candy Jones's husband had pulled a number of similar stunts on his radio programme and was lectur-ing at a major American university on the use of hypnosis for the purpose of uncovering repressed memories. 'Nebel had been a hoaxster', says Marks. 'He made up the story, he put it into her and then he took it out of her . . . The whole thing was bullshit.'

Unfortunately, the fact that the story is almost certainly complete fic-tion has not stemmed the flow of copycat revelations from women who believe that they, like Candy Jones, were also hypnotically programmed by the CIA. The more recent the accounts are, the more lurid the stories.

Kathleen Sullivan of Tennessee is the author of *Unshackled*, which details her sale to the CIA, as a child, and subsequent programming. Brice Taylor's book *Thanks for the Memories: the Truth Has Set Me Free* alleges that she was used as a hypnotised sexual slave by Bob Hope and a senior U.S. cabinet official. Carol Rutz's *A Nation Betrayed* explains how she was sold to the CIA at the age of four. According to her, she was experimented on by Wilder Penfield, Ewen Cameron and Sidney Gottlieb, who instructed her to call him 'Daddy Sid' and trained her to assassinate foreign enemies by causing aneurysms.

But the prize for the single most offensive, fantasy-laden account must go to authors Cathy O'Brien and Mark Phillips, who have produced two books detailing Cathy's experiences at the hands of the CIA. According to them, Cathy was programmed by the Agency to become a 'presidential model' sex slave. Cathy was then apparently sexually abused at the hands of current and former presidents of a number of countries (and one of their hunting dogs), a U.S. Senator, Catholic priests, 'mobsters,' 'satanists,' police officers, and at least one internationally famous country music star.

It's hard to know whether to feel anger or sympathy towards people who write this kind of thing. What is immediately clear, however, is that we have unwittingly re-entered the world of repressed memory and satanic ritual abuse: a *Through-the-Looking-Glass* Wonderland where 'no evidence' means 'lots of evidence' and the rules of logic run backwards.

Stealing from John Marks's account where it suits them and discarding it where it doesn't, proponents of the theory argue that satanic ritual abuse emerged in Nazi Germany, where mind-control techniques were honed to a high level before being brought to the United States as part of Operation Paperclip, the Allied programme to round up useful scientists at the end of the war. Since then they have been applied by a monstrous clique of depraved brainwashers including police, doctors, politicians, judges, the FBI, the CIA and NASA. Abusers hope one day to take over the world and run it, funding their operations with profits generated by pornography, illicit drugs, prostitution and the arms trade. They communicate via hidden messages in pop songs, movies, books, newspapers and greeting cards. And they keep their sordid activities hidden by controlling the minds of their victims.

I might be making this up. But I'm not. Colin Ross, a psychiatrist from

Texas and one of the first proponents of the brainwash/abuse theory, has treated numerous patients whom he has diagnosed as suffering from 'iatrogenic' dissociative identity disorders (split personality created deliberately by a doctor), many of whom believe that they were sold to the military or the CIA when they were young and were programmed to be assassins or slaves. 'It's basically one or two pathways', he says. 'Either the father was in the military, had a lot of military friends, lived near a military base, or was a military contractor. And they ended up going to some sort of special classes or special trip to the base . . . There's some sort of financial transaction, or bribery or pressure or something like that between the father and the military.'

Since the heyday of the satanic abuse/CIA brainwashing theories in the late 1980s, Ross has toned down his approach—at one point he likened people who denied the existence of such cults to those who deny the Holocaust. But there is still, he says, something in it. 'If I had, like, a billion dollars,' he told me, 'and I created, like, a little detective intelligence agency of my own, I don't think it would be hard to find evidence of, obviously, organised sex trafficking, organised pornography, and some sort of connection with some sort of cult activity—and with government mind control.'

There are so many problems with this theory that it's hard to know where to start. The jaw-dropping implausibility of the plot might be a good place, or the lack of physical evidence. But it's worth noting one key fact. Colin Ross and other believers argue that the surviving MKULTRA documents point to the fact that the CIA's brainwashing programmes were a success. In fact, the evidence all points the other way: brainwashing *didn't work*. Outside the recovered memories of 'survivors', there is not a shred of evidence to indicate that the Agency ever succeeded in creating a Manchurian Candidate.

John Gittinger, one of the leading MKULTRA men, admitted as much in front of a Senate Select Committee in August 1977. 'By 1961, 1962,' he told Senator Richard Schweiker, 'it was at least proved to my satisfaction that brainwashing—so-called—as some kind of an esoteric device where drugs or mind-altering kinds of conditions and so forth were used, did not exist.' The movie of *The Manchurian Candidate*, he said, 'really set us back a long time because it made something impossible look plausible'.

Of course, Gittinger might have been lying but the fact that several CIA interrogators, including him, were unable to work out whether Yuri

Nosenko was telling the truth after three and a half *years* of interrogation in the early 1960s should persuade most that the techniques they were seeking either never existed or remained elusive. The MKULTRA boys had taken a wrong turn.

Hopelessly optimistic, in the 1950s and 1960s the CIA's experts saw the brain as something that could easily be tampered with, using chemicals or physical methods to achieve specific ends. But it was rather more complicated than that. Gottlieb and his team discovered that it was possible to make people freak out, forget things and scare them out of their wits—but that there was no magic bullet to induce subservience. 'Truth drugs' delivered as much fantasy as truth; LSD did something different every time; hypnosis was unreliable; subliminal techniques didn't work, full stop; and trying to induce amnesia with ECT was like shutting down your laptop with a mallet. As intelligence historian Thomas Powers later wrote: 'Powerful drugs can indeed wipe out the memory, but the sweep is clean. If the year in Berlin went, the wife and kids went with it.'

There are more pragmatic reasons for believing that the Agency's dabbling resulted in few useful techniques. 'There is no evidence at all that there were magic bullets in this field,' says John Marks today. 'Because the other thing about it—and something that you have to accept—is that if science had really discovered stuff that worked as well as they said it would, it wouldn't have stayed secret more than a year or two. That kind of stuff, *nobody* keeps secret.'

As a result of such reasonable conclusions, Marks has since been labelled a CIA stooge by the conspiracy theorists. According to these guys, the Agency did indeed perfect a way of creating a Manchurian Candidate. They just didn't want anyone to know about it. *The Search for the Manchurian Candidate* was a cover story, designed to conceal the real truth. 'Of course,' one interviewee told me confidentially, 'you know Marks was working for the CIA all the time, don't you?'

Like the CIA in the early 1960s, the satanic ritual abuse/brainwash theorists have constructed their own onion-like Monster Plot, where every skin removed reveals another, deeper skin. These days even Colin Ross, the godfather of the Manchurian Candidate movement, who first 'proved' that the CIA had been successful in its attempts to create a Manchurian Candidate, has fallen out of favour. A public register of 'MKULTRA and psychotronic-experimentee friendly professionals' specifically recommends *not* consulting Dr Ross any more. Apparently he advised a recent patient that her 'psycho-electronic and mind-control' issues were 'all in her mind'.

One can't help but wonder whether we haven't finally wandered into the true domain of brainwashing: the arena of the genuinely mentally un-well. A number of psychological problems produce paranoia, and it is not uncommon for schizophrenics to believe that people are maliciously inter-fering with their thoughts. A survivors' group at mindcontrolforums.com contains telling contributions from MKULTRA 'victims' who hear voices, experience headaches, can't sleep or feel strange. The accounts make heartrending reading.

According to David———, his symptoms are caused by 'an elaborate system of computer-controlled bio implants along many of the nerves of my brain'. He's not alone: a number of contributors complain of implants, either in their brains or teeth. Johan———receives messages from the US military: 'It's a voice I am feeling inside my head,' he writes, 'telling me to jump in front of a lorry or go and kill myself.' 'JD' also hears voices. When his family had him committed for treatment he pretended to accept his psychiatrist's diagnosis to get himself discharged. 'Now I have been la-beled schizophrenic,' he writes, but 'I know that I do not have schizo-phrenia that I have full body and mind implants . . . but no one believes me.'

Of course, the fact that 'brainwashing' was coined out of fiction from the Cold War does not mean there is nothing in it at all. As researchers such as Robert Jay Lifton, Edgar Schein and Margaret Singer have shown, there *are* techniques that can be used to assault the brain, to try forcibly to coerce people into reversing their beliefs. Many of these techniques were indeed used in Korea and are still applied, to some extent, by religious or-ganisations today. Removing someone from their social milieu, for exam-ple, is a good way to reduce access to potentially damaging criticism. Depriving them of sleep and proper food will break down their resistance. Inducing fear, subservience, imposing a 'closed' or private language, teaching them techniques to combat doubt and keeping them busy help, as does playing on their guilt feelings.

In the end, though, even when applied together, there is no sure-fire way of forcing people to reverse their beliefs. Admittedly, we would do well to beware of such techniques and keep our wits about us—but the same advice might be offered regarding advertising, television, political spin and everything you read, including this. There is no magical scientific 'brainwash'.

'People are rational,' says Richard Ofshe, who still testifies in court on religious indoctrination and mind-control techniques. 'They have the capabilities to make choices. But that doesn't mean you can't manipulate them and exploit the hell out of them . . . Brainwashing, the popular notion of it, I don't think it exists. There's no permanent change: an individual's capacity is not changed . . . They don't lose their will. They make bad decisions because they find themselves in situations that are built to get them to make those decisions.'

Brainwashing, a comforting bedtime story that made us all feel better, should have outlived its usefulness years ago. Such was the myth's potency, however, that it didn't. When we were scared or unsure, we called it up again to explain away the things that made us nervous. In the 1950s and 1960s it was Russians. In the 1970s it was new religious movements and advertising agencies. In the 1980s it was heavy-metal music. Like Batman, brainwashing came to save us. 'It's not your fault,' it told us. 'There's nothing you could have done. You're not responsible: you're just a victim.' Of course, this was exactly what we wanted to hear—which was why we called it up so often. 'It was a cultural manifestation of the time,' says Robert Jay Lifton, 'and we're not through with it—by any means.'

Today, once again, 'brainwashing' has been dusted down and given a new coat of paint. This time the threat is a heady combination of terrorism and religion. Why would anyone want to bomb the World Trade Center? How could these people do this to us? Is it the virgins and the rivers of wine? There must be a *reason*.

There is, of course. There are lots of reasons. But none of them is 'brainwashing'.

But, then, I would say that, wouldn't I? I'm working for the CIA. So is my publisher. We *all* are.

Epilogue:
'Truth. In the shortest possible time'.

As I was conducting the research for this book, the one thing everyone asked me about was interrogation: what was going on at Guantanamo Bay? At Abu Ghraib? How did this stuff work? Where did it come from? Who did it?

Here are the answers to some of those questions.

Here's a game you can play at home.

Imagine that you are an MI5 officer, fast asleep in your bed. Suddenly, the batphone rings. Three terrorists have been arrested. Evidence indicates that they have planted a bomb in the City of London. You don't know what kind of bomb it is, where it is or when it's going to detonate. You do know that the City is Europe's financial hub, that three hundred thousand people work there and that rush-hour is only seven hours away. You also know that none of the arrested men will say a word to the police.

How are you going to get these guys to tell you where the bomb is? Ask them nicely? Or storm in, like Jack Bauer, shoot one through the kneecaps and tread on him? These people have rights, remember. But, then, what about the guy with the bomb under his desk? Doesn't he have rights too?

The clock is ticking. What are you going to do?

Interrogators are a rare breed. Colonel Robin Stephens, head of MI5's spy interrogation unit, Camp 020, and probably the most experienced British interrogator of the Second World War, knew how hard it was to find good staff. 'An interrogator,' he wrote in his classified account of the unit's activities, 'is born and not made.'

According to Stephens, the effective interrogator needed a number of specific qualities. Personality was crucial, as was linguistic ability. He needed experience, common sense, a wide range of interests and an ability to identify with a broad array of people. But the main quality was simple: 'an implacable hatred of the enemy'. This hatred fed the interrogator's aggression, giving him the 'relentless determination' necessary to break down a spy, however long it might take. According to 'Tin Eye'— Stephens wore a monocle—such people did not crop up every day. So rare were they in MI5 that 'their total over the war can be counted on the fingers of one hand'.

Barristers—who might have been expected to make the best interrogators of all—proved useless. They were too analytical. 'On the one hand something is possible,' wrote Stephens, of the lawyers' intelligence take. 'On the other hand, however, the contrary is reasonable. And what manner of use is this in war?' None whatsoever: after all, the objective of the exercise was not an interesting legal debate, it was 'truth in the shortest possible time'. Logical analysis was all well and good but frequently an agile brain, with the ability to think laterally, was more important. 'The interrogator proceeds by paradox,' he wrote. 'He expects the unexpected.'

Stephens's account, parochial though it may seem today, rings true. Interrogators *are* a rare breed. It's hard to track them down, and harder to get them to talk openly about their methods. And yet, when you do, they are surprisingly normal. No fangs. And no respect for the old MI5 hawk's views on 'born, not made' supermen, schooled in the dark art of truth extraction.

'Rubbish!' says Chris Mackey, senior US Army Echo (interrogator) at Kandahar and Bagram airbases in Afghanistan. 'That's a public perception. I don't think it's a dark art at all. It never was. All the time that we trained, and all the preparation we had . . . we never felt that we were part of something weird.'

John Hughes-Wilson, a former Army Intelligence Corps interrogator, agrees: 'A tradition has grown up,' he says, 'a folklore about how interrogation is: black gloves, black rubber hoses, beating on the soles of the feet.' But this is inaccurate. 'Most interrogators, in my experience—which is limited to Northern Ireland and training with people, MI5, MI6, the SAS—will confirm that most people will talk to you if they find you congenial.'

Congeniality was certainly the key to the interrogation technique favoured by Roy Giles. According to Giles, trained as an interrogator by the British Army in 1963, the lead weapons in his armoury were not brutality, pliers or electrical clips but manners, a couple of glasses and a bottle of Scotch. 'To my mind,' he says, 'that was very good. And I've kept that as my way.'

Three different military interrogators, three different generations, same point. Most interrogations are conducted in public: in pubs, parks and restaurants, over cups of coffee, pints of lager and packets of chips. The ideal interrogation subject doesn't even realise he's being interrogated. He doesn't know who the interrogator is working for, or even that he's working at all. He's just having a chat. Interrogators engaged in this kind of operation are essentially reporters working for newspapers that never publish. The similarity between journalists researching stories and intelligence officers hunting information is the reason that the latter so often pose as the former. They're not supposed to, of course. But it works.

Unfortunately *your* three suspects are unlikely to respond to Scotch, packets of chips or assurances that you're from the *Daily Mail*. If they have just planted a bomb, they are unlikely to respond to much at all. Which presents you with a problem: how are you going to make them talk? 'In a perfect world,' says Hughes-Wilson, 'where we're all full of deep, liberal convictions, we sit down and say, "Will you tell us about the PRF [pulse repetition frequency] of the radar?" and he says, "Fuck off!" And you say, "Oh dear! *Do* tell us, please! We *really* want to know!" Sadly, the real world isn't like that. It never has been and never will be.'

In some ways, the situation is worse if you have caught someone red-handed. Incarcerated suspects are seldom well disposed towards their captors. They may demand a lawyer, become abusive or clam up altogether. Worst of all, on realising that they are in for a grilling, they will immediately start planning how they're going to resist. The lines are drawn. The subject will not want to lose this battle for a number of reasons, not the least being that no one likes losing a fight. The moment a subject is arrested, there is every chance that his incarceration will strengthen his resolve not to talk. And that's happening with your three guys at the moment.

Luckily for you, the odds remain in your favour for a short period. Most people involved in criminal acts don't expect to be caught. When they are, the result is a wave of panic, a psychological state that military interrogators refer to as 'the shock of capture'. Another Intelligence Corps veteran explains: 'When a person is captured, they go through a psychological process of shock—the same way you go through shock at school when somebody says to you, "The headmaster wants to see you at nine on Monday morning." You spend the entire weekend wondering what he wants to see you about. Your heart will race, your hands feel clammy.'

A prisoner-of-war is probably the most defensive person on the battlefield. He doesn't know what's going to happen to him, doesn't know when he's going to see his family again, doesn't know when he's going to get his next meal or his next drink. 'All he knows,' continues the Intelligence Corps veteran, 'is that he's in the hands of the enemy. That's all he knows. And it is, frankly, a very upsetting experience. It really is.'

While the prisoner is in this state he is extremely vulnerable to persuasion. This is the moment when the interrogator must pounce. He must use every technique he can to prolong the shock, to allow him to access the intelligence the prisoner possesses before he pulls himself together and musters his resistance. 'The whole idea,' says the Intelligence Corps veteran, is 'to maintain the shock of capture, and to decrease the chance of resistance in further interrogation.'

Capitalising on the shock of capture is universal in military and law-enforcement circles. It is the reason, for example, why police tend to swoop on suspects in the small hours of the morning, when they are likely to be most tired and surprised by their arrest. The greater the shock surrounding the pickup, the greater the confusion and fear, and the lower the chance of effective resistance.

In Afghanistan, Al Qaeda suspects were transported to Bagram and Kandahar airbases with hoods over their heads, not allowed to talk to each other and handled brusquely to stop them reassuring each other and to remind them of their impotence. Unloaded from their transport planes, they were frogmarched one by one into an in-processing area with a coloured square painted on the floor and ordered to stand still. Military Police then used scissors to cut off their clothes until they were naked.

There was a practical reason for this. Many of the Taliban men, who had been living rough in the desert, were crawling with parasites, so they ' had to be washed and dusted down with anti-louse powder before they could be moved to the cells. But the process served another important purpose: to be forcibly undressed in front of your captors is a humbling—and terrifying—experience. It reminded prisoners that they were in serious trouble, setting the stage for the interrogation. 'You try to do everything you can to advance and prolong the shock of capture,' explains Chris Mackey, who ran the process. 'As perfunctory handling as you can possibly muster. Like, two big, burly MPs for every prisoner, picking up each prisoner by the armpits and moving him over to the next station and standing him up. I encouraged that. I thought that had a positive effect.'

Shouting at captives and shoving them around is not the only way to maintain the shock of capture. Silence can be just as unnerving. 'One of the great things we strove to keep secret,' says Hughes-Wilson, 'is that interrogation is silent most of the time. If you're there in a high-security unit and you're being interrogated by professionals, it's *totally* silent.' To the captive, the silence may be interpreted as a sign that no one is paying attention. In fact, the opposite is true: everyone is paying attention. 'If, for example, you're a lifted nuclear submariner, with good stuff,' he continues, 'when you came in and you were being examined by the doctor, I'd be watching. The doctor probably would be a real doctor, doing a real job, but I'd be watching you, and when you were bagged up and hooded, I'd be the guard behind you.'

Shock of capture is further prolonged by removing anything that might remind the prisoner of his own identity or status. The quicker this takes place, according to Tin Eye Stephens, 'the more profound and depressing is the effect'. The removal of personal items such as watches and wedding rings is often extremely distressing for prisoners, who don't know if they will ever see them again—or even if they will be allowed to live. Clothes are likewise removed and searched (in Camp 020, one prisoner was found to be carrying coding materials in his teeth) and the prisoner reclothed in prison garb. The British Army tends to use shapeless outsize boiler suits; the CIA recommends providing prisoners with 'an outfit that is one or two sizes too large and to fail to provide a belt, so that he must hold his pants up'. It might be worth shaving the man's head, too. 'The point is,' explains the CIA's *KUBARK* interrogation manual (1963), 'that man's sense of identity depends upon a continuity in his surroundings, habits, appearance . . . etc. Detention permits the interrogator to cut through these links and throw the interrogatee back upon his own unaided internal resources.'

Interrogation subjects need to be given a good reason to talk. In criminal cases, a promise of freedom from prosecution might work, or it may be possible to appeal to the suspect's morality. In war or in the intelligence world, though, subjects who talk to the enemy are traitors. Apart from the penalties for treason, they are unlikely to want to betray their comrades. The same is probably true of your three bombing suspects. As far as they are concerned, they're going to go to prison for a very long time. Knowing this, their objective will be to do so without giving you the location of the bomb and nullifying the reason for their future discomfort. Frankly, they'd rather die than help you.

If this is so, you're going to have to apply some pressure, to *persuade* them that it's in their best interests to talk. The best way to do this is with stress.

There are all kinds of ways to induce stress in interrogation subjects. Almost anything that will annoy or disturb them will do. KGB officer Yuri Nosenko was given prolonged 'medical' examinations in which CIA staff probed sensitive parts of his body. But doctors aren't necessary. Kandahar interrogator Chris Mackey was taught various ways of annoying captives to increase their stress levels. 'When you in-process somebody', he says, 'all the person's possessions would be placed on a table and they'd be standing there without any clothes on. So they're standing there, ready to go into the cage, the cell. You say, "OK, you can have any three items on this table. Go get 'em." And he would pick whatever items he wanted. So you'd then take those away and say, "You can't have those. Pick your next three." We used to do this at all our exercises and, *man*, did it piss people off! Very useful.'

Other techniques can be added to enhance the captive's discomfort. Keeping his cell cold will stress him, as will overheating it. Or, better still, making it too hot one day and too cold the next. Likewise, ensuring that the cell is filthy should prove an effective stressor. The presence of rodents or insects is a strong incentive for many people to want to get out. While you're at it, to make sure that he has nothing to look forward to, it's worth feeding him bland, tasteless food that will sustain him but no more.

The best stressor of all, however, is fear. This is why interrogation subjects must never be allowed to talk with their comrades, to relax or to know what's going on. It's also a good reason for hooding them: being blind is terrifying when you might fall down a stairwell or walk into a wall—or a fist. At all times when you are interrogating suspects, keep them on edge. If you're not doing anything with them, you want them back in their cell, worrying about what you're going to do next. That way, they will fuel their own fear, saving you time and effort. Sometimes the best thing to do with a captive is to treat him roughly, give him no information about what's going to happen to him, then leave him— preferably somewhere uncomfortable—to ponder his situation.

To heighten the prisoner's stress levels, it's also worth keeping him tired. The easiest way to do this is to stop him sleeping, a process as simple as making a lot of noise throughout the night, or leaving a bright light on in his cell. At the first sign that he appears to be sleeping, pop into the cell, give him a shake and ask whether he's awake. If the cell has no natural light (it shouldn't), it won't be long before he loses all track of time and, with it, reality. He becomes jet-lagged. Has he been asleep for hours? Or minutes? How long has he been in the cell? He has no idea—and this lack of certainty is extremely distressing. The effect will be cumulative: the more tired he becomes, the harder it will be for him to concentrate and pull himself together, and the more he will exhaust himself trying to do so.

The prisoner should also be physically exhausted. Make him stand in a corner, or adopt a stress position, such as crouching on his haunches with his hands on his head. CIA research in the 1950s and 1960s showed that situations where individuals caused *themselves* physical pain (by prolonged standing, for example) were more effective at inducing confessions than those where the interrogator induced pain directly by beating. If the man is made to stand until he feels like talking, it's his own stubbornness that is causing the pain, and you can present this to him quite reasonably as the result of his own intransigence.

In all of these situations, it is crucial you make it clear to the subject that there is an alternative to this regime. 'They can stop all this by talking to you,' says the Intelligence Corps veteran. 'Simple! "All you have to do is put up your hand: 'I want to talk with an interrogator.' "Of course! Come along with us! Nice cup of tea! Once you're finished you'll be on your way to a nice prison camp, wherever. Not a problem."'

'You use the various techniques,' he continues, 'to break him down, to make him talk, to convince him that really resistance is a complete waste of time: "The more you resist, the more uncomfortable life is going to be. Therefore, talk to me. Make it easy now." ' By presenting the subject's submission as inevitable, you offer him a clear choice: the regime can continue for months, or he can end it here and now. If you treat him right, you won't need to explain the score to him. He'll catch on soon enough.

Chris Mackey agrees. Prisoners should be kept in a state of either extreme stress or despondency: 'High, high anxiety suits you to get tactical information quickly,' he says. 'Resignation and futility helps you to get the strategic info. We needed to set it up so that the anxiety gave way to futility as quickly as possible.'

'The aim,' says John Hughes-Wilson, 'is to develop the point where the individual *wants* to tell you because he sees no other way. What usually happens in my experience is that people don't break and burst into tears and say, "I'll tell you everything you want to know!" It's more like running into the wall on a marathon. They run out of steam. They're just so tired, they're so worn down by it all. They've got no more lies left to tell.'

If you've read a newspaper over the last couple of years, most of these techniques will probably ring a bell. They are all being used on the front line of the so-called War on Terror. But don't be deceived: they are not twenty-first century inventions. Most of the stressing methods currently in use at Guantanamo Bay and other US interrogation centres date back to the thirteenth century. Nicolas of Eymeric, Grand Inquisitor of Aragon, recorded many of them in his fourteenth-century handbook on torture, *Directorium Inquisitorum*. Sprenger and Kramer's *Malleus Malleficarum* (The Hammer of the Witches, 1486) took up the subject and became the standard textbook for two hundred years. Fear, prolonged standing, poor nutrition, uncertainty: all featured.

The sixteenth-century lawyer Hippolytus de Marsiliis is credited with the invention of sleep deprivation as an interrogation technique. According to him, prisoners should be marched up and down until they collapsed, and vigorously shaken or pricked with needles the moment they fell asleep. '*Tormentum insomniae*' was adopted in Britain in the sixteenth and seventeenth centuries where it was found to be not only highly effective but to leave no tell-tale scars. A later version was described by French lawyer Jean de Grèves: one of the subject's nostrils was pierced with a needle threaded with a length of fine, tar-coated yarn. This way the victim could be kept awake by a simple tug from outside the cell. According to de Grèves, fewer than two out of a hundred prisoners could withstand this treatment without confessing.

In addition to depriving their interrogation subjects of sleep, witch-hunters and inquisitors also understood the importance of tiring them physically. Like Allied interrogators, they used stress positions. One chronicler reports how a witch should be positioned in the middle of the floor, cross-legged 'so that all the weight of her body must rest on her seat'. The result was impaired blood circulation and extreme pain. Within twenty-four hours of this treatment, subjects became 'weary of their lives' and confessed.

Sleep deprivation, prolonged standing and isolation were cornerstones of Soviet interrogation techniques, too. Capitalising on Church inquisitors' discoveries, immediately after the Revolution the Russians developed a system called the Conveyor, which involved the grilling of captives by a permanently rotating shift of interrogators until they collapsed. 'Continued lack of sleep,' wrote Alexander Weissberg, a former victim, 'has a severe toxic effect. The need for sleep ultimately displaces every other sensation, even hunger and thirst, and overcomes all resistance and all power of mental concentration.' Eventually, sleeplessness led to hallucinations: '[The victim] sees flies buzzing about, he is surrounded by beetles or mice, smoke seems to rise before his eyes.'

In Russia the effects of sleep deprivation were combined with physical discomfort caused by stress positions. After forty-eight hours of prolonged standing or sitting on an uncomfortable stool, prisoners' limbs swelled. The muscles in the groin cramped so that the merest movement became agony.

'The Conveyor worked automatically and silently,' reported Weissberg. 'All the examiners had to do was wait patiently. Time was their ally. For the prisoner suffering the torture of the "Conveyor" there was no break.' After five days of this treatment—without sleep—he felt as if his groin was being pressed in a vice. He began to hallucinate and went partially blind. Instructed to sit on a low stool, he fell off it repeatedly. After 140 hours without sleep, he capitulated.

Many men interrogated by the Soviet secret police withstood physical torture but only one man is recorded as ever having beaten the Conveyor: a fifty-five-year-old Jewish tailor called Eisenberg survived thirty-one days of constant interrogation without uttering a word. Shocked Soviet interrogators called in a doctor to examine the man, and swiftly concluded that he had no capacity to feel pain. He was sent to an asylum.

There are two key differences between this kind of treatment and what Allied interrogators are up to today: the first is that such methods are—hopefully—applied briefly as a form of conditioning rather than over prolonged periods as a form of torture; the second is that we understand better how they work.

In a landmark study of interrogation techniques conducted at the behest of the CIA in 1961, psychiatrist Lawrence Hinkle studied the physiological states of interrogation victims. According to his account, stressing techniques such as wall-standing, hooding and malnutrition were not simply attacking the prisoners' willpower. They were actually working on the chemical balance in the subject's brain: physically lowering his will to resist. Hinkle noted that stressing techniques threw the brain's chemical balance out of kilter: dehydration, malnutrition, sweating, fatigue, hyperventilation and stress caused it to shut down, producing what he termed 'brain syndrome'. Taken too far, it led to 'loss of contact with reality and loss of consciousness' but in the early stages the techniques were an invaluable aid to the interrogator. 'Disordered brain function,' he concluded, 'is easily produced in any man.'

According to Hinkle, the deliberate induction of 'brain syndrome' produced a state similar to shell-shock in the victim. Isolation, in particular, brought about a condition 'much like that which occurs if he is beaten, starved or deprived of sleep'. The result, for the interrogator, was frequently positive. As brain function became progressively impaired, concern about loyalties and moral rectitude fell away. 'The "attitude" is likely to change,' wrote Hinkle, 'and the man becomes more "willing" to do whatever is necessary to secure his own comfort and survival.'

Professor Tim Shallice of the Institute of Cognitive Neuroscience at University College London, who campaigned on behalf of the first twelve Irish suspects to undergo 'interrogation in depth' at the hands of the British Army in 1971 agrees: while each of the stressing techniques is probably harmless on its own, he says, when they are combined the effects are pronounced. Stress positions induce fatigue, which manifests itself in faster breathing and hyperventilation, which in turn produces more stress and more fatigue, which is never allowed to dissipate through sleep. Hooding further cranks up stress levels, which in turn produce more fear, more sweating and a heightened need to rest. With the application of all the techniques, the interrogation victim enters a vicious circle in which everything he does heightens his own sense of terror. His mind begins to cannibalise itself. The only solution is the one the interrogator wants: complete submission.

Sounds unpleasant, doesn't it? It's supposed to. John Hughes-Wilson explains that an interrogator, submitting his subject to stressing techniques, is constantly on the alert, watching for symptoms that might indicate they are working: 'Is he weeping? Has he pissed himself? . . . You're trying to get to the nuclear personality as fast as possible . . . All the time you've got a psychological attack going on, which is just as damaging as beating the guy with rubber hoses.' Hughes-Wilson shrugs. 'Everyone ends up with psychological problems afterwards. Of course you would: everyone who has been through an interrogation—practice, training or for real.'

Bizarrely, the threat of psychological problems helps the interrogator. 'People fear interrogation,' says another Intelligence Corps veteran. 'They always have. And I'm not denying that we keep up the pretence: this is a *really* nasty thing to happen. The fact is that when you go through SAS combat selection, if you don't get through the interrogation, you don't get into the SAS. You just don't get in. It has a real fear factor.'

Bill Lowry, former head of the Royal Ulster Constabulary (RUC), recalls that after the 1971 interrogation-in-depth incident, IRA suspects arrived at the organisation's main interrogation centre in a state of abject terror. 'Castlereagh frightened the living daylights out of them,' he says. 'Some people were actually shaking as they were arrested. There was that fear, that menace. You always let that menace be there for the new people coming in. You made them think, 'It's just around the corner! This torture! This white noise!' . . . Cutting off of fingers and putting electrodes on to their testicles—it's just around the corner if you don't speak. You let that fear be in them.'

'I've never, cross my heart and hope to die, been involved in the really deep techniques for spies,' says one military doctor, 'but I have been involved in helping train the special forces. I find the psychology of the interrogators very interesting. They're *weeeird*! But,' he continues, 'I want them on my side. I want them to find out where the bomb has been placed. And where the next lot of bombs are.'

★　★　★

How do you feel about all this? Are you glad that these guys are on our side, too? Or do you find the idea of wall-standing and stressing techniques appalling, a step away from systematic torture? Would you be willing to use them? Under what circumstances? Remember: there's a bomb somewhere in the City and you don't have long to find it. How far would you be willing to go to get your three suspects to talk? If you don't have the mettle to exploit their shock of capture, you're going to have trouble getting information out of them. And you're going to *hate* what comes next.

Thanks to academic research following the Korean confessions, there is no doubt that treatment of terror suspects today involves more 'scientific' methods of stressing and confusing them.

The CIA's *KUBARK* interrogation manual explains that sensory deprivation is highly effective in heightening stress levels. The technique, says the manual, is a short-cut to hallucinations, delusions and 'other pathological effects'. 'The more completely the confinement eliminates sensory stimuli,' concludes *KUBARK*, 'the more rapidly and deeply will the interrogatee be affected.' Psychological disorientation that might take weeks or months to produce in an ordinary cell can be duplicated in hours or days in a properly soundproofed, lightproofed one. 'An environment still more subject to control, such as water-tank or iron lung,' the manual advises, 'is even more effective.'

It seems that a version of John Lilly's water tank is still part of the US Army's interrogation-training syllabus. Chris Mackey was shown a film of the technique in action during his training in the 1990s. 'It looked like somebody was in a Jacuzzi with a lid,' he recalls. 'There was a square-looking thing, much bigger than a bathtub, and there were people looking down, because they were up high, on walkways that were around it.'

In addition to sensory deprivation, it is worth adding sensory *overload* produced by bright flashing lights and loud noises. To heighten the sense of fear and unreality, these should be applied when the prisoner is least expecting them. This might be done by allowing him to fall asleep for a few minutes, then waking him up with a deafening discothèque effect in his cell. White noise can work for this purpose but there are other options. In the last twenty years, Britain's Intelligence Corps has experimented with the sound of babies crying, discordant car horns, bloodcurdling screams and Chinese opera tapes. In Guantanamo Bay, US experts from the

Behavioural Science Consultation Team, known as 'Biscuit', have recently used the sound of cats miaowing, lifted from a TV petfood advertisement, and thrash-metal music—Drowning Pool's 'Bodies' was a favourite at one point. Other white noise stressors used in Iraq have included ghostly laughter, Metallica's 'Enter Sandman' and Barney the Purple Dinosaur's 'I love you' from the children's TV series *Barney and Friends*.

The actual choice of noise doesn't appear to make much difference: what matters is that it's loud, repetitive and annoying. To an interrogation subject who hasn't been allowed proper sleep for a couple of days, an unexpected cacophony will cause him to jump out of his skin. This is how the big boys maintain the shock of capture.

KUBARK goes on to recommend the combination of such techniques with others, such as the manipulation of the subject's 'diet, sleep pattern, and other fundamentals'. Making these routines irregular disorients the subject, creating 'feelings of fear and helplessness'. Clocks, where visible, should be constantly shifted around to confuse and stress the subject. 'Day and night are jumbled,' says the manual. 'Interrogation sessions are similarly unpatterned.' If the preparations are done correctly, the victim's connection with reality will be severed, leaving him isolated and so confused that he is unable to muster any resistance.

It should be noted that since 1971 the British Army has not been allowed to use the so-called 'Five Techniques' that constituted 'interrogation in depth' (hooding, wall-standing, white noise, sleep deprivation, bread-and-water diet). Prisoners may be transported in hoods but not interrogated in them or left in them for inordinate periods of time. Apparently, the techniques are used only to train special-forces personnel to resist interrogation. Even when they were used in Ireland, the army appears not to have been terribly interested in the psychological rationale behind them. The goal was to make the suspects uncomfortable and isolated so that they would be willing to volunteer information to halt the treatment.

The Americans, perhaps predictably, had a more high-tech outlook. In the CIA's analysis, the goal of stressing interrogation subjects was not simply to make them uncomfortable but to forge a relationship between the interrogator and his subject. Ideally, this relationship was a form of 'transference': the phenomenon that takes place between a psychoanalyst and his patient. Eventually, loaded with enough stress, the victim would begin to see his captor as a father figure, the only person capable of stopping his suffering. When that happened, he would try desperately to please the interrogator. *KUBARK* terms this phenomenon 'regression'.

Stealing wantonly from academics' analysis of events in Korea, *KUBARK* states that the goal of the interrogation is to induce in the captive a state of 'debility, dependence and dread', which will eventually cause him or her to regress. 'All coercive techniques' states the manual, 'are designed to induce regression.' Once that point had been reached, it was not unusual for feelings of great affection to develop between interrogator and subject.

Professor Alexander Kennedy of Edinburgh University, a former officer at the Combined Services Detailed Interrogation Centre in Cairo, wrote later that the British had come up with a similar—but more sinister—technique during the Second World War. Advocating sleep deprivation, sometimes enhanced by the use of stimulants such as thyroxine and amphetamine, with partial sensory deprivation, the subject could be made to hallucinate by the application of 'ambiguous sounds and visual stimuli'. If these stimuli were presented when he was in a light sleep they would influence his dreams, which could now be predicted and, to some extent, controlled by his captors. Knowledge of the dreams permitted the interrogator to appear omniscient, and thus to reduce resistance during the next day's interrogation. 'The purpose of this device,' wrote Kennedy, 'is not only to destroy the distinction between uncontrolled dreaming and waking thought, but also that between the thoughts of the interrogator and of his prisoner in the mind of the latter. This accelerates the process of destruction of his personal identity.'

Kennedy also recommended the enforced association of unnaturally high stress levels with particular stimuli, such as sounds or light patterns created by a revolving coloured disc. Once the emotional response was firmly linked with the stimuli in the prisoner's mind, stress could be induced at will at a later date, simply by producing the disc or the noises.

Kennedy's revelations, delivered during a lecture 'The Scientific Lessons of Interrogation' in February 1960, created consternation, and led to perhaps the most disturbing revelation of all concerning British brainwashing research.

Two weeks after the lecture, the *Daily Mail* picked up the story and began looking into the Intelligence Corps' resistance-to-interrogation techniques, publishing an account on 9 March of how special forces personnel were made to stand naked for up to eight hours at a time, were put into stocks, locked into narrow lockers that were then rolled around the parade-ground, doused with water and made to sit for prolonged periods on a low, one-legged stool. The next day, the prime minister, Harold Macmillan, stepped in. 'What is this Psychological Warfare Unit?' he asked the Minister for War. 'Why is it at Maresfield? . . . I really think your colleagues would be interested to hear about this.'

Questions were duly asked in Parliament regarding British involvement in 'the process commonly known as brainwashing'. Macmillan responded that 'The techniques to which these questions refer have never been used by any organisation responsible to Her Majesty's Government.' But files in the Public Records Office indicate that the very next day, his briefing from the War Office was altered to read 'so far as the War Office know'.

But by now the *Daily Mail* was on the case. On 18 March, the paper sent a list of allegations to the War Office concerning torture at the Combined Services Detailed Interrogation Centre. According to two former guards, senior Nazi officers had been tortured with sleep deprivation for up to four days at a time, hooded, subjected to mock execution—Fritz Knoechlein was led to a gallows and told he was to be hanged—beaten and made to lie in cold baths for prolonged periods. As a result, four officers had committed suicide. 'There may be,' cabinet papers record, 'some substance in these allegations.' The editor of the *Daily Mail* was shortly summoned to a meeting with War Office representatives, and the story appears to have been killed.

Two years after Macmillan's denial to the House that the British had ever employed brainwashing tactics, the prime minister received a letter from Francis Noel-Baker, a former intelligence officer, in which he was informed that, contrary to his Parliamentary answer, the British services had indeed been testing brainwashing techniques during the war.

It is within my own personal knowledge—and that of people with whom I served in the war—that a technique of brainwashing certainly was used by Major Kennedy (as he then was) and other interrogators at the CSDIC outside Cairo and elsewhere, during the last war. Unfortunately, similar techniques were also employed during the Emergency in Cyprus.

I understand that Kennedy's methods included such devices as the suggestion of thirst in interrogations under drug-induced hypnosis and the deprivation of sleep . . .

The extent of Professor Kennedy's experiments on prisoners-of-war at CSDIC with hypnosis and drugs has never been revealed.

To these techniques we can add another important stressor: humiliation. If the subject is male, sex is an excellent place to start. John Hughes-Wilson recalls an old chestnut from special-forces resistance-to-interrogation training: 'Get a woman doctor to come in,' he says, 'and examine him when he's bollock-naked and get her pencil, lift his penis up, then drop it down again. Then look the subject in the eye—and smile—and say to the clerk behind the desk, "Small." ' A military doctor who assisted with this training in the 1980s recalls going through the procedure himself: 'At some critical moment,' he says, 'when you are completely knackered and naked, some woman comes in and looks at your parts, and she is seductive and feminine and has lots of lipstick on. She says, "Your tool! You must be suffering from that disease where it draws into the body—it's so small!" '

Sex as a means of humiliation can be especially productive when used against Arabs because they are more sexually inhibited than Westerners. Erik Saar, a translator at Guantanamo Bay, recalls the discovery of a micro miniskirt and lingerie in one of the civilian contractors' offices. The clothing belonged to a female interrogator, who entered the interrogation booths of Saudi suspects skimpily clad to provoke them. Another interpreter recalled that at one point she had conducted an entire interrogation clad only in a bra and thong.

Chris Mackey used a modified version of the technique at Kandahar and Bagram airbases in Afghanistan in 2002 when he deliberately tasked a junior female soldier to search the new detainees' pocket litter in front of them while they were standing naked and being deloused. 'I put her up against the wall, clearly dressed as a female,' he says. 'I made her put her hair in a ponytail, not in a bun. She looked female. She stood there and went through the pocket litter. It *freaked the prisoners out!*' Although the soldier concerned was specifically ordered to keep her back turned towards the prisoners at all times so that she could not see their bodies, the Arabs hated the experience.

These techniques raise questions concerning legality: isn't there something in the Geneva Convention about not humiliating captives? Mackey argues that his technique was acceptable because the female soldier concerned was not looking at the interrogation subjects. At one point she found something in the pocket litter and turned round to show him. '*That* I wouldn't allow,' he says. 'I said, "Whatever you find, don't turn round. Just call me."' In the end, to the US interrogator, there was a huge difference between using the presence of a woman to create anxiety, and using it to humiliate detainees. The former was acceptable; the latter was not.

Again, the technique is not new. In Britain during the Second World War, potential German hostiles were interrogated at the 'London Cages'. The Cages' commanding officer, Colonel A.P. Scotland, later reported that 'We never went in for any sadism. Still, there were things we did which were mentally just as cruel . . . One fellow we had up before us was really cheeky and obstinate. We told him to undress and eventually he stood before us completely naked. That deflated him. Then we told him to start doing exercises. That killed his resistance completely. He soon started to talk.'

Humiliation was likewise applied to bodily functions: 'Sometimes we would keep them standing on their feet round the clock,' wrote Scotland. 'If a prisoner wanted to pee he had to do it there and then, in his clothes. It was surprisingly effective.'

Is humiliation through sex worse than being forced to soil oneself publicly? Is either acceptable? An Intelligence Corps interrogator suggests another technique: 'You blame an officer for letting down his men,' he says. 'That's a great one for officers: "You've let down your men." Great one!'

Is this any better? How far would you be willing to push your luck with your three suspects? Would you bend the rules? If you do, you may be trampling on their rights.

Assuming that you have authorised the use of all available stressing techniques, your three bombers are now tired, isolated, cold and very scared. In a perfect state, in fact, for the next step: the interrogation. But have you thought about what you want to say to them? You may be able to rely on their confused state to make them come up with something useful, but if you can't sort out your strategy, you're unlikely to learn anything.

Before beginning any interrogation, there is a great deal of preparation to be done. If you skimp here, the process will probably be a waste of time. 'Only a novice,' wrote MI5's Tin Eye Stephens, 'will plunge into an interrogation unarmed.' If you have no intelligence on the suspects, you'll have no way of knowing whether what they're saying is true. They will pick up on this immediately—and then you're in for a runaround. 'PLAN,' wrote Stephens, in capital letters. 'There *must be one.*'

The MI5 interrogator's plan invariably depended on current intelligence about the prisoner concerned. If nothing was known about him, it became crucial to *learn* something. This could frequently be done through trickery. Some tricks were so simple that they probably wouldn't work on anyone unless they were seriously confused or scared. Others, however, were ingenious.

The first, and most important, of these techniques was so secret that it was not revealed until a quarter of a century after the Second World War. It was the use of hidden microphones. Even in MI5's own accounts, these are referred to only cryptically as 'M Cover'. Initially, microphones were used to record various stages of the interrogation, but during the Blitz it was suggested that the cells of the prisoners should be wired for sound so that investigators could hear what they were saying to each other when they thought no one was listening. A department was established to handle the monitoring process. Cyril Cunningham recalls how the system worked: 'CSDIC was a highly technical business. Mics all over the place, listeners—armies of men from the Royal Corps of Signals who had to be hidden from the prisoners—and the acoustics of the room had to be attended to. There were 101 things there. A proper interrogation centre needs special construction for all the recording.'

Of course, high-level German agents suspected that they were being recorded, which led to a problem: they wouldn't say anything, even to each other, in their cells for fear of being overheard. 'If you think about it,' says Cunningham, 'the use of microphones would be deadly passive if you didn't do something to get the people talking . . . You think of an interrogator as somebody who asks questions? Well, forget it. That's only a tiny little aspect of it. Particularly when you're using microphones.' As one MI19 man later wrote, once the microphones were installed, 'the chief aim . . . became the creation of a frame of mind suitable to the use of such devices'. But how was it possible to get German agents to forget the microphones and talk openly among themselves? One way was to put a stool-pigeon into the cell.

The use of stool-pigeons in interrogations goes back to the witch trials. In 1486 *Malleus Maleficarum* recommended the insertion of 'trustworthy men' into witches' cells to engage them in private conversations while 'spies stood outside in a convenient place' and listened in. In 1939, the technique was so well known in German military intelligence circles that every agent Stephens came across, he wrote, had been warned in their elementary training that it might happen to them if they were captured.

There was also a problem in locating suitable stool-pigeons. While it was possible to dress a British officer as a PoW and insert him into a cell with a suspected spy, agents who could pull off this act were even rarer than good interrogators—'found perhaps once in a generation'. The other alternative was to use a German spy now doubled and working for the British. But Stephens didn't like this, either. 'Essentially,' he wrote, the stool-pigeon 'is a despicable character, treacherous to a degree, mistrusted by both sides . . . To call a man [a stool-pigeon] is worse than the casting of doubt upon the parentage of a man down Silvertown way.'

While clued-up spies might expect stool-pigeons in their cells, smart permutations of the formula were soon devised. KUBARK suggests planting not one but *two* stool-pigeons in the cell with a spy. One man should win the subject's trust by specifically warning him that the other is a stool-pigeon, throwing suspicion from himself. He should then show the spy the location of a hidden microphone in the cell and warn him not to speak openly near that spot. Persuaded that his cellmate was friendly, the spy might then start talking in whispers in the area of the cell that he had been assured was furthest from the microphones. Of course, unknown to him, the area would be monitored especially closely.

Almost invariably the technique failed during the Second World War, making future interrogations more, rather than less, difficult. It also raised further problems. There was a question of how to handle a stool-pigeon in prison—'The man becomes bloody nuisance number one in an espionage prison for months, maybe for years.' Then there was the issue of how to get rid of him at the end of the war. According to Stephens, stool-pigeons tended not to want to go home, instead blackmailing the intelligence services they had formerly assisted and demanding increasing payoffs for their silence. 'It is not overstressing the case to suggest that creatures of this kidney should only be used as a last resort,' he wrote.

Sixty years on, there is no sign that intelligence organisations have heeded his warning. Stool-pigeons are being used in the 'War on Terror'.

One who has come to light is Canadian Abdurahman Khadr. In July 2002 Khadr, who had been captured in Afghanistan, signed a contract with the CIA for five thousand dollars in cash and a monthly payment of three thousand more. He was transported to Bagram airbase in shackles and put on to a container flight to Guantanamo Bay, where he was tasked to talk to recalcitrant inmates and see what they might reveal to a fellow prisoner.

The operation seems to have been a failure. Although he helped the Agency to recognise some inmates, Khadr was unable to persuade anyone to talk, either to him or to their interrogators. In October 2003 he was released at his own request, upon which he abandoned the CIA. Since then he has become the kind of 'bloody nuisance' Tin Eye Stephens so abhorred, giving widespread interviews about his time in Guantanamo—apparently because he wants more money. A Hollywood film about his experiences is planned. Rumour is that Johnny Depp will play Khadr. Tin Eye would turn in his grave.

Once you've generated some background intelligence and formulated a plan for your interrogation, it is crucial that you brief your team properly. Regardless of what you might have seen on TV, interrogation is a team effort. The interrogator himself is merely the focus of that effort, like the diamond at the head of a drill bit. All of the pressure must be applied through him, searching out inconsistencies in stories, looking for weaknesses and homing in on the cracks to weaken them further. 'It is attack at the maximum force at the critical moment that is decisive,' wrote Stephens. 'The fascination of gambling is present, and with it the strange urgency of war. And if ever a cliché could be justified it would be in relation to this subject. It is a war of nerves.'

Assuming you are suitably prepared, you should consider your approach. Like opening chess moves, there is no shortage of tried and tested methods for starting the game. Once again, many date back to the Inquisition and the witch trials. But for an example of a good opening technique, you could do worse than follow MI5's example.

Stephens prided himself on the vehemence of his initial confrontation. To him it was crucial that any spy be left in no doubt that the penalty for espionage was death and that this was the fate that awaited him. If he talked, there was a chance he might save his life—but it was only a chance. The prisoner was marched into the room containing the interrogators and ordered to stand to attention. He was not permitted to move, or speak unless spoken to and then only to answer the questions put to him. 'Figuratively,' wrote Stephens, 'a spy in war should be at the point of a bayonet.'

Questions were put forcefully and fast, giving the subject no chance to reflect on them. 'The requirement,' wrote Stephens, 'is a driving attack in the nature of a blast which will scare a man out of his wits.' If the subject was female it made no difference. 'As with a man, so with a woman—no quarter . . . Never promise, never bargain. The man's neck is in your grasp. Never forget it; never let him forget it.'

American police interrogation manuals advise less formality but recommend that the situation is manipulated to gain the psychological advantage. Suspects should be allowed to sit, but only in an upright chair bolted to the floor. In front of the chair should be a table, likewise secured to the floor—just too far away for the suspect to rest his elbows on it comfortably. The interrogator, meanwhile, sits in a swivel chair with wheels so that he can move around and rest his elbows where he likes.

Clever use is made of the prisoner's sense of personal body space. Ideally, the interrogator should begin his questioning at a comfortable distance, but as the confession nears, he should slide his swivel chair towards the suspect until he is violating his 'intimate zone'. When the time comes to press for a full confession, the interrogator will end up with one of his knees between the subject's legs, the two men's faces almost touching. This will make the subject very uncomfortable.

Interrogation can be a nerve-racking business but don't panic: if your background research is accurate and your interrogator astute, the cards are stacked in your favour. 'No spy,' wrote Stephens, 'however astute, is proof against relentless interrogation. Some unforeseen circumstance, some trivial lapse, is pounced upon, exploited by the interrogator, until a break is complete.' To engineer a trivial lapse, in addition to verbal and mental dexterity and thorough background research, he had a few tricks up his sleeve—all passed on to future generations, who still use them today.

The British Army teaches that there are four main approaches for the potential interrogator. He can be harsh—shouting and screaming—or he can be benign, offering consolation and solace. He can be boring and grind down his opponent, or he can play dumb in an attempt to trick him into indiscretion. These techniques can be mixed and matched to suit the mindset of the subject.

Predictably, the American military has a few more categories. Eight more, in fact. These range from challenging a suspect to prove his identity, to scaring the life out of him, to being as friendly as possible and reassuring him. Once again, however, there is very little that is new. Many of the CIA's *KUBARK* techniques date back to the witch trials; virtually all were honed by MI5 at Camp 020—no great surprise, since the faculty provided training for American interrogators during the Second World War.

If two men were arrested together, the situation offered a great opportunity for what MI5 called 'The X-Ruff'. The pair should be interrogated separately. Eventually, inconsistencies in their stories would emerge. Each man could then be played against the other to the interrogator's advantage. To start the ball rolling it was not necessary for either man to make a confession. All the interrogator had to do was hint to one subject that the other had implicated him, and cracks would show.

KUBARK takes the technique further. The manual suggests concocting a 'confession', at the bottom of which the weaker of the two men's signatures is affixed. In the confession it should be clear that the 'confessor' is trying to shift all of the blame on to his friend. Tapes of the 'confession' can likewise be faked to persuade the stronger man that he has been betrayed, or he can be positioned where he 'witnesses' his friend making a statement to the interrogators—the 'Outer and Inner Office Routine'. Convinced that all is lost, he can be asked whether, since he will be punished anyway, he would like to make a statement to set the record straight.

Playing one prisoner off against another is an old trick, as is the next MI5 ploy, 'blow hot, blow cold' or, as *KUBARK* terms it, 'Mutt and Jeff'. Fans of detective movies will immediately recognise this technique as the 'good cop/bad cop' routine. Essentially a cross between a 'fear up' and a 'fear down' approach (alternately scaring the subject, then reassuring him), the process involves one mean interrogator and another kindly one. The two are alternately released on the victim in the hope that he will appeal to the good cop to escape the bad cop's treatment. To enhance the situation, the bad cop can threaten to become violent and the kind one be seen to restrain him before warning the subject, alone, that his colleague is crazy and will do anything if he's not watched. The good cop then offers to intervene—but needs information to do this.

A variant on the good cop/bad cop routine is MI5's 'sympathy men' technique, in which other members of prison staff offer to assist the subject. The technique worked extremely well on Cardinal Mindszenty in 1949, when the Hungarian secret police planted an agent outside his cell dressed as a prison guard. When the interrogators had left, the guard whispered to the cardinal that, although he was a police officer, he was also a Roman Catholic and suggested that the pair flee the country together. He offered to deliver a letter to the US Embassy if Mindszenty promised to provide the four thousand dollars necessary to hire a pilot, and take him along too. Mindszenty duly wrote a letter to the American ambassador requesting assistance for himself and his friend in their daring jailbreak. The letter, in which the cardinal appeared to be abandoning his Catholic comrades, was the first piece of evidence produced at his trial.

The technique also seems to have been used in 1971 by the British Army in Northern Ireland. Joe Clarke, one of the twelve 'hooded men', recalls being made to do sit-ups by a British soldier prior to the application of the five techniques. Another soldier came up and ordered him to stop, restraining the first man and leading him away, then returned alone. 'Don't worry,' he told the IRA suspect. 'You'll be all right. I'll look after you. I like you.'

Other techniques to make men talk—even among themselves in their cells, for the benefit of the microphones—include the interrogator playing dumb and showing up apparently drunk, or putting questions to the wrong suspect. Once the victim of such a ploy is sent to bed for the night he finds it hard not to explain to his cellmate how stupid their captors are so that the two can have a good laugh. There is every chance that something useful will emerge from such an encounter. Equally, faked newspaper reports can be leaked into the cells to persuade the captives that fictitious events have taken place to see how they react.

Techniques to be used in interrogation vary according to the discretion of the interrogator and the personality of the subject. Will he respond best to encouragement or fear? What is he afraid of? Shouting or silence? The moment a cover story breaks down under this treatment, even an inch, the subject must be ordered to write a confession covering the point so that in the future he can't deny having made it. This technique also dates from the witch-hunter's manual, *Malleus Maleficarum*. Even apparently small concessions may prove crucial later on. 'Such admissions', wrote Tin Eye Stephens, 'one after another, are the milestones on the road to surrender. Pressure must be maintained.'

The opposite of the 'dumb-interrogator trick' is to fire relentless questions at the subject that he can't possibly be expected to answer. One US prisoner in Korea recalled how the technique had worked on him: after a verbal battering of questions he couldn't understand, let alone answer, he was offered a simple one: 'I know it seems strange now,' he said, 'but I was positively grateful to them when they switched to a topic I knew something about.' A modified version of this method recommended by the CIA's *KUBARK* manual is known as 'Alice in Wonderland'. In this case, the subject is brutally battered with an unending series of absurd and meaningless questions with the aim of confounding his expectations and disorienting him. 'The confusion technique,' states *KUBARK*, 'is designed not only to obliterate the familiar but to replace it with the weird.' Although he may laugh at first, eventually, after several days, the treatment becomes 'mentally intolerable' at which point the subject is liable to say something just to stop the flow of babble assaulting him. 'This technique', notes the manual, 'may be especially effective with the orderly, obstinate type.'

The key to loosening the tongues of people who won't say a word—military captives who have been instructed to remain silent in interrogations, for example—is to persuade them to reveal information about matters so insignificant that they cannot possibly be secret, then use these small lapses to open up a dialogue. One way of forcing an initial indiscretion is to lie. 'Doctors' conducting medical examinations might not really be doctors. 'Representatives of international human-rights organisations' are frequently not to be trusted. Offers to send postcards home to inform relatives of the subject's well-being are seldom sincere. The moment a subject agrees that he'd like his wife to know where he is, he is asked for his home address, telephone number and the names of all his relatives. All sorts of information emerges that can be used to exert leverage later on.

The 'this-interrogation-is-over' trick often works beautifully, too. Chris Mackey, the Kandahar interrogator, recalls using it when training with the British Army in Europe. Since none of his English subjects would speak under direct interrogation, he dressed up as a British officer, instructed them that the exercise was over and handed them back their personal possessions, having made sure to remove a few key items. Money inside wallets was missing, as were identity cards and watches. When the men complained, they were instructed to report to a Military Policeman. 'Right!' stated the MP, authoritatively. 'Fill out a report!' Mackey laughs at the story today. ' "What's your name?" "Colin Hewitt." "Unit?" "We're with the 34th Hampshires." "What were you doing in the field?" "We were placing mines." "What type of mines?" "Why do you need to know that?" "For the report!" We wrote the whole thing down!' he says. 'It only worked with about two guys out of thirteen—but it was good enough.'

Sometimes the trick in making a man talk lies in persuading him that there is no shame in breaking his silence: that he is not letting himself down by breaking under interrogation. One effective way to achieve this is to administer a 'truth drug'. Not a real truth drug, of course. No such thing exists. But you could administer a shot of something and convince the subject that he has been given a truth drug. As CIA analysts concluded in the early 1960s, sometimes the threat of a truth drug, and its administration, will serve to persuade a suspect to talk—because he feels that there is no way he can offer any resistance to such techniques. Defeat is inevitable.

Sodium amytal or pentothal would be good choices to start with, since both lead to loss of consciousness, offering fertile ground for further trickery should the drug not produce the goods. When the subject wakes up, he won't remember what has happened or what he has said. If you can convince him that he has talked extensively under the effect of the drug, he may be persuaded that the game is up and buckle completely.

Hypnosis can be used in the same way, to help a suspect justify to himself that he has talked. Both techniques, conclude *KUBARK*, 'provide an excellent rationalisation of helplessness for the interrogatee who wants to yield but has hitherto been unable to violate his own values or loyalties'. Faced with an intolerable situation, hypnosis and drugs offer the victim a way out of their predicament: ' "I was drugged," ' states the CIA manual, 'is one of the best excuses.'

In the same way, a polygraph test can be useful, not because the machine can detect when people are lying—although it can give a pretty good indication when this is the case with someone untrained in beating such a test—but because a gullible subject can be made to *believe* that the machine is infallible and can expose him scientifically. As with the use of 'truth drugs', a large part of this operation should consist of the theatre surrounding the test. 'A good operator', one CIA man told investigator John Marks, 'can make brilliant use of the polygraph without even plugging it in.'

On paper these tricks may sound silly, the kind of thing that *you* would never fall for, but when someone is cold, tired, wet, hungry, physically and mentally exhausted and terrified, all kinds of things can seem credible. Used singly, consecutively or in combination, such techniques have worked on interrogation subjects for hundreds of years. They still do. Through a series of assaults on the subject's will, contradictions in stories occur. These are prised open immediately to reveal more. Small breaks lead to larger ones and the confused prisoner finds himself revealing all kinds of things he thought he would never disclose. 'Blow hot, blow cold,' instructed Tin Eye Stephens. 'No respite, no time to recover, no time to plan.' The end result for the interrogation victim was 'mental hell. Worn out, dispirited, a time will come when there is absolute surrender. The man can stand the strain no longer.'

'It is an assault on personality,' says John Hughes-Wilson. 'All the time as an interrogator, you are trying to jemmy through the social personality to get to the nuclear personality and prise it out. All the time you're looking for weaknesses and because the subject is tired and hungry, and because he's dull and he doesn't know what time it is—and presumably you're relatively sharp—you have all the advantages. You can strike from all the angles.'

When it comes to intelligence officers, the process can be far more tortuous. Professional agents are trained to concoct 'legends', back-up stories to fool hostile interrogators. When the officer breaks, he produces the legend rather than the truth. 'You lift the MI5 guy and you know that he's got a legend and you say, "Why are you here in Folkestone?"' explains John Hughes-Wilson. 'And after he's waited twelve hours, he'll say, "All right, OK, I'll come clean." Get out the notepad, and he says, "Well, actually, I've got a girlfriend in Folkestone. Don't tell my wife!" to which the answer is, "Well, what's her name, where does she live?"'

The interrogator and his researchers now set about trying to verify the story, which can take some time. Eventually, when the girlfriend proves not to live where the subject said she lived, the interrogation starts again.

'You get back to him and he says, "Oh, well, she must have moved." ' Interrogations like this demand vast resources of patience on the part of the
interrogators. 'You're going through these stories, peeling the onion,' says
Hughes-Wilson, 'trying to get to the core. But eventually—and you can
speed up the process—people run out of stories through a combination of
all the techniques.'

Sometimes, however, they don't run out of stories. William 'Jim' Skardon, MI5's main cold-war interrogator, saw things differently. No Five
Techniques for him. His subjects were too smart. When it came to the really big fish 'You must be almost utterly sympathetic. You have to be, in
order to get right inside the man's mind, for only then do you discover
why he does things.' To do this, Skardon made his subjects as comfortable
as possible, giving them drinks and cigarettes if they asked for them. 'After
all,' he said, 'the whole purpose of my talking to him is to get on terms
with him.'

An MI5 contemporary agreed: 'You treat a professional almost with kid
gloves,' he told researcher Peter Deeley in 1971.' 'You sit him in comfort
in a good room without gimmicks. You deal with him on a perfectly
man-to-man basis.' According to this source, there was little chance of
getting such a character to break, no matter what you did, because he had
been so well briefed about what to expect from interrogation. Such men
also tended to be too bright to trick. 'They are by nature shrewd and intelligent,' he continued. 'They are the one type of person who will talk
quite a lot and say nothing. This can be very confusing. They will set you
off on false leads, but the critical stuff you really want—names, meeting
places—will never emerge.'

On occasion Skardon's approach certainly bore fruit. In 1949 he broke
the atomic spy Klaus Fuchs using his softly-softly technique. After his defection to the Soviet Union in 1963, Kim Philby later wrote that his MI6
interrogators, 'ineffective' and 'blustering', had never concerned him too
much. Skardon, however, 'was far more dangerous'. Faced by a barrage of
media questions from a tenacious *Daily Express* reporter, Philby later joked
that 'he should take a fortnight's course in interrogation with Skardon'.

Undoubtedly Hughes-Wilson is correct when he says that such people
should be worked on over time until the core of the onion is finally revealed,
and there are techniques that can be used to confuse even wily intelligence

officers—forcing them to relate their legends in reverse chronological order, for example, is sometimes enough to bring about a slip—but the problem is that this process takes time. When the man finally breaks, if he ever does break, any information he gives you may be long out of date. SAS recruits under training are instructed to hold out for twenty-four hours after capture, forty-eight if possible. By that time, the soldier's comrades will have realised he is in enemy hands, and any intelligence that he may be able to compromise will have been rendered obsolete.

Unfortunately for Allied interrogators, such methods of resistance to interrogation are not limited to intelligence and special-forces operatives. In February 2002, a document surfaced in the Al Farook Al Qaeda training camp in Afghanistan that demonstrated how far the techniques had spread.

Chris Mackey helped to translate it. 'It was a stack of paper, about sixty pages,' he recalls. The cover carried a handwritten note: 'Brothers—this is the book about prisoners.' Initially the Americans thought it was a book on how to handle Allied prisoners but it soon turned out that it detailed techniques that the Americans would use to interrogate Al Qaeda captives, and suggested various methods of defeating them. For a start, captured fighters should only reveal their *noms de guerre*—*cunyas*—and should remain silent for as long as possible. After a few days, they should tell false stories backwards, sideways and any way other than forwards, mixing truth with lies, to lead the interrogators 'in circles'.

Perhaps most damaging, the booklet stated in no uncertain terms that no matter what the Americans threatened, or appeared to threaten, Al Qaeda operatives should not be afraid because 'they will not harm you physically'. The Americans would never torture suspects, said the manual, because they were weak and lacked the courage. Mackey recalls the reaction inside the camp on the arrival of this document. 'The most infuriating thing about the Al Qaeda manual,' he says, 'was that its core diagnosis was dead-on.' The Americans don't have the stomach for torture.

There is a certain amount of truth in this assertion. But the reason that the Americans tend not to torture suspects is not because they don't have the stomach for it: it's that torturing people tends to produce unreliable information. MI5 came to this conclusion early on in the Second World War. 'Violence is taboo,' concluded Tin Eye Stephens, 'for not only does it produce answers to please, but it lowers the standard of information.' The CIA agreed. Under the influence of pain, reported Professor Hinkle in 1961, 'the source is, indeed, more prepared to talk, but he is also more likely to be inaccurate and to give false, misleading, inaccurate or inexact information, of a type like that which his interrogator happens to be seeking'.

Worse, torture is often counter-productive. According to *KUBARK*: 'Pain inflicted on a person from outside himself may actually focus or intensify his will to resist.' 'Pain doesn't work,' agrees a British Intelligence Corps veteran. 'There is a limit to the amount of pain you can take, no doubt about that, but it actually induces resistance. We used to equate it to playing a game of rugby or soccer. If you deliberately hurt the opponent, he's going to get fired up—and come back at you.'

Despite these conclusions, torture comes back again and again: it seems like it *ought* to work. In 2004 one SAS veteran, a qualified interrogator, told me that he would use it, even though he had been taught in the classroom that torture was counter-productive: 'If your life and the lives of your men hang on whether someone speaks or not, he's *going* to speak. There's no two ways about it. I would start at his feet and chop him slowly to bits. With a bloody knife or something. He *would speak.*' The veteran shrugged. 'You can say what you like about civilised carryings-on. If lives are at stake, for somebody who's a prisoner, I'm afraid it's not going to count. Their life wouldn't count a damn against one of my blokes.'

Perhaps he is right: everyone has a breaking point. But perhaps he's not. A 1969 CIA document advising officers on how to withstand interrogation advises that, should they face torture, they focus on their faith. 'Persons who have strong religious beliefs,' concludes CIA officer George Stanton, 'are able to resist much more effectively than those with a weak faith or none.' This is probably true. But if it's true for CIA men, it's just as true for Al Qaeda operatives, too. And they have a great deal of faith.

Chris Mackey doesn't advocate the torture of prisoners but isn't so sure that this is for practical reasons. 'Our experience in Afghanistan,' he says, 'showed that the harsher the methods we used . . . the better the information we got and the sooner we got it . . . But the reason the United States doesn't torture prisoners is not because it doesn't work. It is simply because it is wrong.'

It is also *politically* counterproductive. In 2004, reports of activities at Abu Ghraib in Iraq surfaced. Mackey was horrified to learn that one of his colleagues had been present. 'If I saw——today,' he says, 'I would take him out and kick the shit out of him till he could barely talk his native Russian or English. You know what they call those guys at the Pentagon now? "The six guys who lost us the war".'

In 2005, further reports emerged, detailing the handling of 'high-value' Al Qaeda suspects at the hands of the CIA. If anything, they were more appalling than the Abu Ghraib allegations. Suspects were kidnapped from various countries, drugged and flown secretly to undisclosed locations around the world. The process—'extraordinary rendition', in the CIA's bland bureaucratese—has resulted in a number of innocent people being flown to third-world countries and tortured viciously. Some have emerged, innocent, to tell their stories. Others languish in jails around the globe. One of the techniques that has been used on them—by Americans, not willing foreigners—is 'water-boarding', which involves strapping a suspect to a wooden board and immersing his head in water until he begins to drown. Presumably personnel responsible for such treatment hold that it does not constitute 'torture' because the victim will not be allowed to drown. It's unlikely, however, that any court of law would support this notion.

But the issue of torture is frequently more complicated than this. In 1973 the British Government was taken to the European Court in Strasbourg and found guilty of inhuman and degrading treatment for its handling of the twelve 'hooded men' in Northern Ireland. Such treatment, it promised, would not happen again. Perhaps the British are not using the Five Techniques. But the Americans clearly are. Do they constitute torture? Or are they justifiable ways of forcing dangerous terrorists to talk? At what point does 'a little bit of smacky-face', as one American interrogator recently referred to it, become torture? Is there such a thing as 'torture lite'?

Other techniques likewise straddle the border between acceptable and unacceptable behaviour. Under the Geneva Convention, it is illegal to humiliate prisoners. But isn't stripping and ridiculing them just that? Chris Mackey agrees that it's unacceptable. Army Intelligence Corps staff feel differently. John Hughes-Wilson says that enforced nudity and ridicule is pretty much par for the course: 'Is that a humiliation technique?' he asks.

'Of course it is! Is it a *reasonable* technique? By my judgement, yes. And by the standards of wartime, yes. It may not be by the standards of Matrix Chambers [leading London barristers, known for arguing human rights cases], though.' Hughes-Wilson sighs. 'We're not supposed to do that in the West now, because we mustn't make anyone unhappy . . .'

Under the Geneva Convention, it is illegal not only to kill or torture prisoners but also to *threaten* either to kill or torture them. But this clearly happens, too. Bill Lowry, former head of the RUC, recalls an incident in the 1970s in which an IRA suspect was brought in after a bombing. 'One of the detective sergeants went out and got Marigold gloves,' he says. 'And they were actually rewiring the place at the time with this big black armoured cable.' The detective put on the rubber gloves and grabbed a loose length of electrical flex. 'You fucking hang on there! I'll go out and get this one,' he announced to his colleagues, then approached the suspect with the supposedly live wires. 'The boy crapped himself,' says Lowry. 'He actually *crapped himself.* He thought he was going to be electrocuted.'

Does the fact that the wire was not connected to the mains make this technique acceptable? Or that the man confessed to the bombing in the end? Chris Mackey thinks not. 'That's no better,' he says, 'than what the people did in Abu Ghraib, when they had that guy stand on that box with the wires on his fingers.' To Mackey, it's acceptable to threaten actions that might happen, but not those that won't. One of his tricks was to show pictures of the electric chair in a US prison to an interrogation subject, telling him that terrorists received this kind of treatment in America and explaining that, since he had not been wearing a uniform when he was arrested, this could await him if he was deported there. 'My rule was that you can use that approach,' he says, 'because we *do* execute terrorists.'

This is a neat semantic trick. According to the rules of war, it's not acceptable to pull a gun on a prisoner and threaten to shoot him if he doesn't talk. It *is* acceptable, however, to sit in an interrogation with the victim and put the gun on the table in front of him, giving him the *impression* that you are about to shoot him, as long as you don't specifically state what you are about to do. His fear creates the illusion for him; you're not culpable.

Similar tricks have been used by the British military for half a century or more. A common technique used in the Malayan campaign when interrogating female suspects (who proved harder to break than the men, incidentally) was to arrest their boyfriends or husbands and march them into a neighbouring interrogation cell in full view of the suspect. A few minutes later, bloodcurdling recordings of screams would be played to persuade the women that their husbands were being castrated. 'It was all a put-up job,' reported one officer of a particular case, 'but it was enough to finish her.'

John Hughes-Wilson recalls a more theatrical performance in Aden. In this case a subject was marched past a recently whitewashed cell on the way to his interrogation. In the course of the questioning, tape-recordings of screams were played at great volume from the neighbouring cell. When the interrogation was over, the man was led past the white cell again—to discover that it had been liberally daubed with blood, as if someone had been disembowelled inside it. Hughes-Wilson mimics the interrogator: ' "Now then, Rashid, we can play this two ways. You've seen what's happened to the last chap . . ." and here's screams and there's blood! That's a technique that was often used in Aden. *Very* effective!' The prisoner wasn't to know it was goat's blood.

Such techniques are not only apparently legal but make use of the CIA's discovery that the *threat* of physical pain or death is more useful than their imposition. 'The threat to inflict pain,' states *KUBARK*, 'can trigger fears more damaging than the immediate sensation of pain . . . in fact, sustained for long enough, a strong fear of anything vague or unknown induces regression, whereas the materialisation of the fear, the infliction of some form of punishment, is likely to come as a relief.' The manual recommends indirect threats (if a direct threat is not carried out, the bluff loses its effectiveness and the interrogator loses credibility), 'delivered coldly' rather than in rage.

This lesson was learned during the Inquisition. According to Eymeric, the 'father of interrogation', when suspects failed to talk they should be submitted to 'The Question'—torture. But there were five levels of this process. The first involved threatening the use of the torture 'engine'. If this didn't work, the suspect was taken to the chamber and shown it. The next stage was theatrically to undress and prepare the subject, and the next, to place them slowly on the machine and tie them down. Only once these four stages had been carried out, by which time most suspects had confessed, should the torture be administered. The most effective torture of all, it seemed, was the threat of torture.

Tin Eye Stephens agreed that physical pain was a bad idea. Apart from anything else, if it failed, it left the interrogator with no further options: the game was over, and the interrogator had lost. But the threat should be ever-present. To suspects who proved entirely intransigent, he developed a threat designed to be worse than death. It revolved around the mysterious, and terrible, 'Cell 14'.

'You will now,' Stephens told victims, on whom no other interrogation techniques had worked, 'be sent to Cell Fourteen. In times of peace it was a padded cell, so protected that raving maniacs could not bash out their brains on the wall. Some recovered. Some committed suicide. Some died from natural causes . . . the mortuary is conveniently opposite.' After assuring the suspect that a number of spies had committed suicide in the cell, he bade them farewell. 'I shall not see you again. I do not know how long you will be there . . . You will be interested, perhaps, in the movements of the sentry who will cover you each quarter of the hour. Perhaps he comes to check. Perhaps he comes with food. Perhaps he comes . . . to take you away. For the last time.'

The entire process, Stephens later admitted, was 'unadulterated drama' and it depended on a suitably theatrical delivery. But results were often good. One Italian spy immediately 'gesticulated wildly for writing materials' and confessed. While the trick worked on occasion, it was only for use as a last resort. 'If it failed,' he concluded, 'then little hope remained of a break.'

Is there a difference between specifically threatening to kill someone if they don't talk, and merely hinting strongly that this will happen? Do you approve of this kind of trickery? How about 'torture lite'? Will you use it on your three suspects? If you won't, how do you propose to get them to talk? If it comes down to it will you, like the SAS man, be willing to use the third degree?

How far would *you* be willing to go?

'If you have a terrorist who has planted a plutonium bomb in London,' says Hughes-Wilson, 'do his human rights override the rights of the hundred thousand people [who might be harmed by it]? I have no doubt as a human being where *my* sympathies lie. And therefore I would say that pressure to make the subject give you the information that you require to save lives is perfectly reasonable.'

It's hard not to agree with this statement. But it is also hard to know what level of 'pressure' is acceptable. Wall-standing? White noise? Or 'water-boarding'? Today, as you read this, these techniques are being applied somewhere in the name of our security. Where would you draw the line?

Another Intelligence Corps veteran has little time for well-meaning liberals who bleat about the human rights of terrorists. This character served in Northern Ireland and watched a number of his comrades die. 'It's not the Irish Republican *Tea Party*, is it?' He raises an eyebrow. 'It's the Irish Republican *Army*. If you're gonna be in the *Army*, you have to play by the big boys' rules . . . I don't give a toss about them. If you're going to be a terrorist, I don't say, "Play by the rules," but I do say, "Expect the full weight of the security force reaction." '

Perhaps surprisingly, one former IRA member who was interrogated in depth in 1971—and who still suffers from nightmares of the event thirty-five years later—agrees. 'My attitude to this is, there was a war going on,' he says. 'These things happen. I was a soldier . . . They done what they done, and we done what we done . . . At the end of the day we knew: if you've been active and you're in—you're going to get a good hiding.'

He does not agree with the goings-on at Guantanamo and Abu Ghraib, however. 'It's horrific, so it is. Horrific. And by all accounts a lot of these people are totally innocent. They're doing basically what they did to us but a bigger version of it, and for a longer time. It's morally wrong. Simple as that. It's morally wrong to torture anyone. I can understand it in a war situation but I don't understand it in Cuba.'

John Hughes-Wilson sees things differently. 'As a professional interrogator,' he says, 'I thought the treatment of the Guantanamo suspects was par for the course. I thought they were being conditioned, handled as high-category prisoners. I do *not* hold with the ritual humiliation of prisoners at Abu Ghraib whatsoever. I hold to getting intelligence out of people without causing physical damage. Mental damage is what the law and society tells us we can do.'

Another Intelligence Corps veteran has a different take on the Cuban situation: 'I can understand why they do it,' he says, 'but I still thought it was barbaric. Conditions like that for two years: some of them will come out round the bend.' For how long should stressing techniques be applied? I asked. 'If they don't get anything in three months,' he said, 'forget it. It's not working.'

'We have to decouple our subjective sense of moral outrage from the practicalities of the situation and be very objective about it,' says Hughes-Wilson. 'You can say it's right/wrong/indifferent. My feeling about interrogation is, does it provide the intelligence the decision-makers require to enable them to make the appropriate decision?

'We should be very careful' he concludes. 'But not for deep moral reasons. For practical reasons. As an intelligence officer, I'm interested in: is the intelligence accurate? Is it timely? Is it true? That's all you're interested in. Lawyers can worry about the niceties. And if lawyers put restrictions on it, then so be it. We have to operate within the constraints of the law.'

Perhaps there is an alternative to these crude physical and psychological assaults.

Perhaps we should start researching new interrogation techniques, or ways of enhancing the old ones. Perhaps, in the light of the War on Terror, the CIA's escapades with BLUEBIRD, ARTICHOKE and MKULTRA seem more reasonable.

There is no doubt that drugs have been used in the apprehension and 'rendition' of Al Qaeda suspects. One wonders where, since all records of drug research by the CIA were apparently destroyed, information about which drugs to use came from. Author Mark Bowden, who usually has excellent sources, states in his article 'The Dark Art of Interrogation' that his intelligence contacts confirm that drugs are being used in 'critical' cases, usually amphetamines, barbiturates and cannabis: the same combinations explored by the CIA in the 1940s and 1950s.

Since there is apparently no CIA research data left on drug-based interrogations, it's hard to tell who is calling the shots. Brainwashing research—whisper it quietly—has made a comeback. One military psychiatrist I interviewed became hesitant to talk when the issue of drugs and interrogation came up. 'I can't speak for what the security services might do in their guidebooks,' he said, 'although I—I'm involved in something that I can't really talk about on telephones and stuff.'

In the summer of 2004 I met up for a drink with a psychologist who worked as a consultant to MI5. We chatted about brainwashing and, since I was researching the development of sensory deprivation in the 1950s, I asked whether he had heard anything about its use, its development by

Donald Hebb, or its application in Northern Ireland in 1971. 'I don't know anything about sensory deprivation' he told me, 'apart from the stuff that's going on at the moment.'

This was an interesting development. 'What stuff that's going on at the moment?' I asked.

'Oh, nothing,' he said. 'Another beer?'

Acknowledgements

Unfortunately there just isn't enough space to name everyone I interviewed in the course of researching this book. No doubt, bearing in mind the nature of the subject, some will not want to be identified anyway. Of those who might appreciate a mention, however, I would like to thank:

For their assistance in the world of brainwashing, intelligence and military interrogation: John Marks, Alan Scheflin, Cyril Cunningham, Chris Mackey, John Hughes-Wilson, Roy Giles, Nick van der Bijl, Adrian Weale, Nigel West, Chapman Pincher, MRD Foot, The Reverend SJ Davies, Major Patrick 'Stan' Weller, Ken Connor and the other SAS veterans who shared their time with me. Also Philip Knightley, Rob Evans, Anthony Glees, Phil Sabin, Phil Davies, Richard Aldrich, Alan Care, the Right Reverend Monsignor Denis Faul, Bill Lowry, Chris Ryder, Tim Shallice, Paddy Hillyard and Lord Hattersley of Sparkbrook.

Crucial with background research and information were Gisli Gudjonsson, Ben Shepherd, Robert Jay Lifton, Rhodri Haywood, Stanley Smith, Michael Neve, Joel Elkes, Hugh Jordan, Finn Abrahamovitz, Peter Naish, Werner Creutzfeldt, Wolfgang Eckart, Rick Ross, Steve Hassan, Gary and Barbara Scharff, Joe Szimhardt, Adrian Greek, Kent Burtner, Wellspring, Mary Alice Crapo, William Shaw, Sam Jordan, Ian Haworth, Steve Kent and Nigel Leigh.

For help in uncovering the work of William Sargant special thanks go to his widow, Peggy, Drs Anne and Peter Dally, Ronnie Sandison, Lord Owen of the City of Plymouth, Malcolm Lader, Henry Oakeley, James Birley, Henry Rollin and Desmond Kelly. I am particularly grateful to the 20 or so former nurses who took time to share their recollections of Deep Narcosis in Ward 5 of the Royal Waterloo Hospital—and to the Nightingale Fellowship for putting me in touch with them. Most wanted not to be named—but you know who you are!

For help in Canada I am eternally grateful to Ron Melzack, Karen Brown at the BBC, Alan Stein, Peter Roper, Maurice Dongier, James Turner, Jay Peterzell, Rich Sokolow, Seeta Ramdas and Paul Kofira.

In the chapter on false memory, thanks are due to Daniel Brailey, Jim Rabie, Neil McClanahan, Lawrence Wright and Saxon Rodgers. Colin Ross provided an

ACKNOWLEDGEMENTS

interview, as did Richard Ofshe. I should like especially to thank Madeline at the British False Memory Society for her help and advice.

Ken McKenna and Tim Post were very kind in providing memories of the Judas Priest case. Judge Jerry Whitehead shared his recollections; Bill Peterson and Suellen Fulstone gave me the side of the case as Sony/CBS saw it. Wilson Key provided a memorable afternoon outside Reno, while Tim Moore at Toronto's York University and Stuart Rogers assisted with the background to the subliminal story. Particular thanks go to the staff at Washoe County Second Judicial Court, who allowed me to access their files on the case itself.

Thanks are also due to the staff of the Imperial War Museum in London, who allowed me to view their filmed collections of war trauma, interrogation and counter-interrogation instructional films, and to the Public Records Office at Kew, the staff of the British Library, the Wellcome Library and the National Security Archive in Washington, DC.

I am particularly grateful to those who took the time to tell painful stories associated with this book: Robin Reid, Susan Wall—who lost her memory in Mallorca in the 1960s, only to recover it at the hands of William Sargant and his abreactive techniques—and Dr Anne White, whose memories were intact until Sargant treated her in the 1970s; Don Webb and Derek Channon, unwittingly fed LSD at the request of MI6 in the 1950s, and Janine Huard, who is still suffering forty years after her treatment at the hands of Dr Ewen Cameron in Montréal. Also Joe Clark and Paddy Joe Maclean, interrogated by the British in 1971, Louise, an English victim of the false-memory panic (but for whose story there was not, alas, enough room here); Catherine Ono and Ford Greene, the former kidnapped by the latter in the late 1970s. And Paul Ingram and his new wife, Catherine.

Thanks are also due to the handful of people desperate enough to assist me with my research at various points. Sam Miller for sterling work at Colindale and Kew, Andras Gerevich for locating and interpreting Hungarian texts, Philip Wahl and Dirk Majer for their work at Auschwitz, Dachau and Merck in Germany. Thanks, also, to Anna Louise Meinke who read, digested and noted three separate accounts of the Hardrup case in Danish before translating them all for me on the spot in a café in Covent Garden.

Special thanks go to everyone who helped to get this project off the ground and to bring it to fruition: Julian Alexander, and Rupert Lancaster and Hugo Wilkinson at Hodder. My parents were ridiculously supportive; Jonny and Matthew distracted me from Chapter 9; Thomas, Amelia, Elizabeth and Christopher stopped me going loopy by taking me waterskiing when I was stuck on Chapter 1. And, of course, to Rollo, without whom any book seems to be incomplete. And Diesel. Thank you.

Notes

Instead of an exhaustive breakdown, what follows is a select bibliography of the most important sources used in the research for this book. For reasons of space I have not included the source of every quotation or fact, or page references to the books concerned. Instead I have named the main texts at the top of each chapter.

There are two key works for aspiring researchers of brainwashing and mind control: *The Search for the Manchurian Candidate* (Norton, 1991) by John Marks, and *The Mind Manipulators* (Paddington Press, 1978) by Alan Scheflin and Edward Opton. The former is still deservedly in print; the latter, tragically, is not. Both are cited throughout.

Primary Sources

Most of the CIA quotes in this book come from the 16,000 pages that John Marks succeeded in declassifying in the late 1970s. These can be accessed at the National Security Archive in Washington, DC. Alternatively, it is possible to trace them on CD-Rom. Where cited, I have endeavoured to list the title of each document, its date and the filing (Mori) number listed on my CD-Rom copy. Where they were legible, I have also included the original CIA filing references.

William Sargant's personal papers can be viewed at the Wellcome Library in London. Court papers from the Judas Priest trial in Chapter 6 are held at the Washoe County Courthouse in Reno, Nevada. British Foreign Office and other military documents are held at the Public Records Office in Kew, London.

Quotations in the book not otherwise attributed are from personal interviews with participants.

Chapter 1: Brain Warfare

Books:

Andrews, George, *MKULTRA The CIA's Top Secret Program in Human Experimentation and Behaviour Modification*, Winstont-Salem, NC: Healthnet Press, 2001
Balogh, Margit, *Mindszenty, Josef, 1894–1975*, Budapest: MTA Torénettudomány: Intézete, 2002

Beck, Frederick, *The Russian Purge and the Extraction of Confession*, Cape Town: Hurst & Blackett, 1951

Burgess, Frank, *The Cardinal on Trial*, Daventry: Sword, 1949

Conquest, Robert, *The Great Terror*, London: Pimlico, 1992

Cunningham, Cyril, *No Mercy, No Leniency*, London: Leo Cooper Ltd, 2000

Gergely, Jeno, *A Mindszenty-per*, Budapest: Kossuth, 2001

Hunter, Edward, *Brainwashing: The Story of the Men Who Defied It*, London: Farrar, Straus and Cudahy, 1956

Hunter, Edward, *Brainwashing in Red China: the Calculated Destruction of Men's Minds*, New York: Pyramid Books, 1951

Huxley, Aldous, *Brave New World Revisited*, London: Chatto and Windus, 1958

Lifton, Robert Jay, *Thought Reform and the Psychology of Totalism*, New York: Norton, 1961

Meerloo, Joost, *Mental Seduction and Menticide*, London: Jonathan Cape, 1956

Josef, Cardinal Mindszenty, *Memoirs*, London: Weidenfeld and Nicholson, 1974

Rogge, O John, *Why Men Confess*, New York: Nelson, 1959

Ruff, Lajos, *The Brainwashing Machine/House of Torture*, London: Robert Hale, 1959

Sargant, William, *Battle for the Mind*, London: Heinemann, 1957

Seed, David, *The Fictions of Mind Control*, Kent, Ohio: Kent State University Press, 2004

Swift, Stephen, *The Cardinal's Story*, London: Macmillan, 1949

Weissberg, Alexander, *Conspiracy of Silence*, London: Hamish Hamilton, 1959

pp3–5   press reports on the Mindszenty trial come from the Newspaper Library at Colindale. See *Daily Mail* 31/12/48, 7/2/49, *BUP Vienna* 1/1/49, *Daily Telegraph* 2/2/49, *Reuters* 5/2/49, *Evening Standard* 8/2/49, *The Times* 21/1/49 and 8/2/49. The Mindszenty file in the Public Records Office is at FO371 1789. The final quote from Linebarger ('they took his soul apart') comes from *The Fictions of Mind Control*.

pp5–6   Schwable's full confession can be found at: www.umsl.edu/skthoma/schwab.htm.

pp6–9   British government reports on the returning Korean POWs (including Cunningham's assessments) are in the Public Records Office at AIR40/2762 and WO208/402. CAB158/5 contains the charter for JIC's Evasion, Escape and POW Intelligence Sub-committee.

p10   'I joined the Communist side' comes from George Blake's biography *No Other Choice* (Jonathan Cape, 1990).

p10   'There is adequate historical evidence': 'Report No1 on Trip to EUKOM', 22 June-7 August 1949, #144892.

p11   Hinkle and Wolff's assessment, 'A Report of Communist Brainwashing', 15 August 1955, #173492.

p17   'The Soviet Government requires': (untitled), dated 10 November 1955, filed under 'Survey on Lysergic Acid' 4 May 1953, 11 October 1955, #184428.

p20   The 'plastic' case appears in numerous CIA documents, first appearing 1 September 1951.

p20   'SHE' appears in 'Report Number 1' (as above).

p20   Details of Khokhlov's testimony and 'The Chamber' comes from Thomas Powers' introduction to *The Search for the Manchurian Candidate*, pxvi.

p21   'Characteristic of hypnosis': 'Defence against Soviet Medical Interrogation', 1 January 1943, #184374.

p21   'The cardinal was drugged': 'OSI Study, Strategic Medical Significance of LSD-25', 30 August 1955, #146133.

p21   'Strong evidence': 'Interrogation Techniques of Foreign Countries', 24 February 1949, #184367.

p22   Cigarettes 'of a peculiar odour': 'Proposal for a Project in the Field of Stimulants' 2 August 1951, #144826.

p22   'The individuals who had come ...': 'ARTICHOKE Conference, 18 June 1953' (filed 15 July), #144996.

p22   'Nikita Botanical Gardens': 'Defence against Soviet Medical Interrogation and Espionage Techniques', 4 February 1953, A/B, 4, 23/47, #147390.

p23   'Signs of a changed personality': Briefing, Psychological Strategy Board 13 May 1953, #146086.

p23   'Take selected human beings': Dulles Princeton speech, 10 April 1953, #146077

p24   Charles Mayo's quote at the UN comes from the *American Journal of Psychiatry*, May 1954, 'Pavlovian Strategy as a Weapon of Menticide' by Joost Meerloo.

p24   Analysis of the 'Psychopolitics' document comes from *The Fictions of Mind Control*. Intriguingly, it seems that the document was a forgery, probably written by L. Ron Hubbard, the founder of Scientology. Hubbard had been treated by LA psychiatrist Oscar Janiger, and hated the experience (to this day, Scientologists revile psychiatry and its practitioners). According to the FBI report, 'the author . . . is expressing primarily a dissatisfaction with methods of treatment of mental patients in this country'.

p25   'Shadow takes form and form becomes shadow': Edward Hunter's testimony before the Committee on Unamerican Activities, 13 March 1958, entitled 'Communist Psychological Warfare'.

p26   'Discovering means of conditioning personnel' (goals of project BLUEBIRD): 'Behavioural Drugs', 1 January 1975, #146193.

p26   'Black psychiatry': 'Overt and Covert Activities of [deleted]' 1 January 1950, #190882.

p27   'We are facing an implacable enemy': 2nd Hoover Commission, Secret Report, submitted May 1955.

Chapter 2: Truth Drugs

Books:

Biderman and Zimmer, (eds.), *The Manipulation of Human Behaviour*, London, Wiley & Sons, 1961

Boyce, Fredric and Everett, Douglas, *SOE: The Scientific Secrets*, Stroud: Sutton Publishing, 2004

Horsley, Stephen, *Narcoanalysis*, Oxford: Oxford University Press, 1943

Klee, Ernst, *Auschwitz: die NS-Medizin und ihre Opfer*, Frankfurt, Fischer, 2001

Lifton, Robert Jay, *The Nazi Doctors*, London: Macmillan, 1986

Lovell, Stanley, *Of Spies and Stratagems*, New Jersey: Prentice-Hall, 1963

Rolin, Jean, *Police Drugs*, London: Hollis & Carter, 1955

Sargant, William, *The Unquiet Mind*, London: Pan, 1967

Shephard, Ben, *A War of Nerves*, London: Pimlico, 2000

'SOE Syllabus: Lessons in Ungentlemanly Warfare', Richmond (PRO) 2001

p33   Sargant's personal papers. Correspondence with Brigadier Rees is located in Box 9.

p35   'MOST SECRET' (German truth drug experiments in the Ukraine): 'German Police 35/42, 24/7/42', in the Public Records office at HW14/44.

p35   'They're in the kitchen' comes from Rolin's *Police Drugs*.

pp37–   Details of Nazi medical experiments can be found in Wolfram Sievers'
38   duty diary for 1942, Sievers' trial papers (July-August 1942) and the Nuremberg Military Tribunal, vol. 2 p254 onwards (he was hanged for war crimes). Quotes from eyewitnesses to drug tests came from the Auschwitz archives; details of mescaline tests at Dachau are in the papers of Henry Beecher at Harvard University; copies are held at Dachau, along with a few other details, including an interview with Kurt Ploetner dated June 1967. It seems that drugs for use in the trials came from Merck, which produced 18,120 kgs of scopolamine in a compound called Skofetal—'Skopalamin-Eukodal-Ephetonin'—which would later be specifically mentioned in CIA documents as the drug used on Cardinal Mindszenty. Merck also produced mescaline at the time but records have been destroyed.

p38   'The best results': Technical Report 331–45, German Aviation Medical Research at the Dachau Concentration Camp.

p39   'The use of the so called truth drugs': PRO: HO454/25333, dated 3 July 1950, signed 'EJZ'; sparse details of MI5's tests with the drugs come from PRO releases in September 2005 and January 1999. The MI6 psychiatrist who declined to be named was interviewed in 2005.

p40   'The United States-Britain combined operation': 'Use of Special Interrogation Techniques by Foreign Countries', 22 June 1948, #184372.

p41   details of Lovell's recruitment and subsequent escapades are to be found in his memoir, *Of Spies and Stratagems*.

p42   'The experiment was negative': Development of 'Truth Drug', 21 June 1943, #184373.

p44   'Knock myself out': papers of G White. Diary: 24 May 1943.

pp43–44   other early reports on the development of the truth drug include: 'Truth Drug (TD), Memo for the File', 5 April 1945; 'Experimental Methods' (undated but probably 1943–5); 'Development of Truth Drug' (interoffice memo) 21 June 1943; and Report: 'Investigation of use of TD in Interrogation' (undated).

p44   'The needle should be thrust': 'Truth Drug (TD), Memo for the File', 5 April 1946, #144773.

p44   'Notorious' gangster: 'Memo on Truth Drug', 27 May 1943, #184373.

p46   'Do all the talking himself': 'Memo for the File TD Material', 31 April 1946, #148382.

p47   'SUGAR': 'BLUEBIRD Project', 4 November 1950, #144920.

p47   The diabetic drugging kit plan is labelled 'TD material': 5 April 1946, #184373.

p48   'Extraction of information from unwilling subjects': 'Organisation of SO Components Dealing with ARTICHOKE' (undated, filed 1 January 1951), #190716.

p48   'Crack teams': a number of documents refer to the assembly of such teams. See, for example, 'Special Interrogations', 12 February 1951, #149491.

p48   'Using aliens as subjects': 'Special Interrogations', 13 March 1951, #144927.

p48   Qualifications necessary for 'special' interrogators are addressed in 'BLUEBIRD Special Recommendations re: Personnel Requirements and Training', March 3 1951, #149453.

p49   'The subject is given an injection': 'Latest ARTICHOKE Project Method', 17 October 1952, #144748.

p50   References to operational use of the teams include BLUEBIRD files for 12 March 1951, 13 March 1951, 19 March 1951, and numerous others.

p50   ARTICHOKE operation June 1952. Details of the case can be found in 'ARTICHOKE Cases June 1952–deleted' (8 July 1952, #149427), 'ARTICHOKE Cases June 1952' (8 July 1952, #149441) and 'ARTICHOKE Cases' (9 July 1952, #148476).

pp51–52   The Wendt fiasco is reported in some detail in 'Test of New Interrogation Technique', 9 September 1952, #148286. A complete breakdown of the interrogation procedures used features in 'Rough Draft re: Chronological Description of an ARTICHOKE Team Interrogation Case', misfiled 1 January 1952, #148473. Morse Allen's comments come from 'Untitled Rough Draft Providing List of Questions Which Arose during the ARTICHOKE Process', likewise misfiled 1 January 1950, #148286.

p53   'Pure gravy': 'ARTICHOKE Techniques (deleted) and (deleted)", 21 June 1952, #184471.

p53   'It was tricky to persuade someone that they really needed to eat more syrup': 'Truth Drugs in Interrogation' by George Bimmerle in the CIA journal, *Studies in Intelligence*, Spring 1961

p55   Henry Beecher's 1957 study on truth drugs: 'Psychopharmacological Studies on Suppression', *Journal of Nervous Mental Disorders*, 1957, pp125, 316–21.

p57   'There is no truth serum': Gottschalk's comment comes from 'The Use of Drugs in Interrogation', in *The Manipulation of Human Behaviour*.

Chapter 3: Eating the Flesh of God

Books:

Allen, John, 'Mushroom Pioneers', Seattle: (privately distributed CD-Rom), 2002

Estrada, Alvaro, *Maria Sabina: Her Life and Chants*, Santa-Barbara: Ross-Erikson Inc., 1981

Hofmann, Albert, *LSD: My Problem Child*, London: McGraw-Hill, 1983

Huxley, Aldous, *The Doors of Perception*, London: Chatto and Windus, 1954

Lee, Martin and Shlain, Bruce, *Acid Dreams: the CIA, LSD and the Sixties Rebellion*, New York: Grove Press, 1985

O'Prey, Paul (ed.), *Between Moon and Moon. Selected Letters of Robert Graves 1946–72*, London: Hutchinson, 1984

Seymour, Miranda, *Robert Graves—Life on the Edge*, New York: Doubleday, 1995

Seymour-Smith, Martin, *Robert Graves—His Life and Work*, London: Hutchinson, 1995

Stevens, Jay, *Storming Heaven: LSD and the American Dream*, New York: Atlantic Monthly Press, 1987

Wasson, Gordon and Valentina, *Mushrooms, Russia and History*, New York: Pantheon Books, 1957

p65   LSD 'of great interest to national security': 'Development of Research in connection to Project ARTICHOKE', 21 November, 1951, A/B, 5, 25/7, #147406.

p65   LSD purchased through 'cutouts in Switzerland': 'Subject: Attached', A/B, VII, 9, 1, #148093, misfiled 1 January 1951.

p66   'If we picked up a *Newsweek*'. David Rhodes' quote comes from Anne Collins' *In the Sleep Room* (see Chapter 7, 'Sleep').

p67   I will write you a letter': 18 February 1963, cit Scheflin p151.

p67   'Our experiments on tolerance to LSD': 'NIH Addiction Research Center', 14 July 1954, #151524.

p67   Tusko's demise is described in *Science*, 1962, pp1100–1103.

p68   'It was awfully hard' testimony comes from the ABC News documentary, *Mission: Mind Control*, (1979).

p68   LSD tests where 'he gave all the details': 20 July 1954

p68   'Eliciting true and accurate statements': 'Potential New Agent for Unconventional Warfare', 5 August 1954, #148381.

p68   Henry Beecher's trip to Europe is reported in *Anesthesiology*, vol. 88(1), Jan 1988.

pp69– Elkes' experiments with LSD are detailed in his own book, *Selected Writings*
70   *of Joel Elkes*, (Animula, 2001)

pp70– Documents on the British testing of LSD and 'truth drugs' by MI6 and the
75   British military come from PRO: DEFE 10/36, 6 March 1956 and WO32/20163, 19 June 1964. The quote, 'subjects to whom the drug had been administered' comes from 'Note by JIB (DSI) DRP/P(56) 4', which is located at DEFE 10/35, as is 'Abreactive Drugs (note by JIB)'. Ronald Wilkerson's account of his truth drug trial is in his statement, (MG11(T)) given 17 December 2003. British testing with other drugs, including psilocybin, mescaline sulphate, LSD, harmine hydrochloride, 'East African Arrow Poison', 'Dart Poison' from Borneo and several 'curare-type' compounds are found in CDEE's six-monthly reports at WO188/710. Don Webb and Derek Channon recalled their time at Porton during interviews in 2004.

As this book went to press in 2006, three of MI6's LSD recipients (Webb was one) were awarded undisclosed compensation by the British government.

p76   'fifty million' doses of LSD: 'Survey on D-Lysergic Acid Diethylamide (LSD-25)' 4 May 1953, A/B, 1, 38/17, #184428.

p76   'This is a fantastically large amount': 'Discussion at (deleted) 4 September, 1953', filed 6 November, #145002.

p77   Decision to buy Sandoz's LSD: 'File: LSD', 23 October 1953, A/B, 4, 23/51 #147026.

p77   'Tonnage quantities': 'Memo for the Director, Central Intelligence': 26 October 1954, #144957.

p77   'Sort of truth serum': 'Piule', 14 November 1952, A/B—13/15, #147399.

p78   'Hidden treasures': 'Exploration of Plant Resources in the Caribbean Region', 7 February 1956, A/B, VII, 9, 5, #148092.

p78   'Swamped by deliveries': 'Reports, Requests from TSS' 10 August 1954, A/B, 1, 39/5, #184431.

p78   'We have approached the problem': 'Case (deleted) Crocodile Gall Bladder', 7 February 1962, #184583.

p79   'Very strong indications': 'ARTICHOKE Conference, 18 June 1953', #144996.

p79   'My man is very elated': Robert Graves, letter to Martin Seymour-Smith, 24 December 1956.

pp79–80   The Graves-Sargant MoD connection emerges in Box 3 of Sargant's private papers.

p80   'An amateur mycologist': 'INFO report: intoxicating mushrooms of unidentified species', filed 8 December 1955, A/B, 1, 34–6, #146215.

p81   Wasson 'unwitting' of CIA interest: 'Memo for the Record, MKULTRA subproject 58', 21 March 1956, #17457.

pp83–87   MKULTRA documents pertaining to George White's safe-house trials are in subprojects 3, 14, 16, 42 and 149. Details of the houses themselves, and receipts for purchases (including the portable toilet), are in the 823–page file on subproject 42, filed 15 December 1954 (#17440). White's diary is cited in Scheflin's *The Mind Manipulators* and Marks' *The Search for the Manchurian Candidate*. White wrote an autobiography, *Diet of Danger*, which has never surfaced.

pp84–87   Details of the Agency's work on sex as a means of extracting information come from Marks, along with interviews cited in ABC's *Mission: Mind Control* (1979).

p84   'borderline underworld': ABC's *Mission: Mind Control*.

p86   'P1, C1 and C9'. Drugs available for use come from an undated report: 'Influencing Human Behaviour', filed 1 January 1957, #146167.

p86   'I think every last one of us felt sorry': ABC's *Mission: Mind Control* (1979).

p87   'Professionally unethical and in some instances border on the illegal': 'Influencing Human Behaviour', 1957, #146167.

p87   The CIA inspector-general's report is dated 26 July 1963, #17748; further debate between the inspector-general and the Agency about the legality of safe-house testing, including the suggestion to continue, using 'foreign nationals' as guinea pigs, is dated 29 November 1963, #146165.

p88   James Thornwell's interrogation (use of LSD on 'Negroes') is dated September 21, 1961, 'Trip Report'. Full details of the incident, including an interview with Thornwell, are reported in *The Mind Manipulators*. Thornwell also appears in ABC's *Mission Mind Control*.

p89   'Not merely a red-letter day': Graves-Wasson, 7 February 1960, cit *Between Moon and Moon*.

p90   'Don't be deceived': Graves-Sargant, 8 January 1960, Box 3.

p90   Harris Isbell's report: 'Comparisons of the Reactions Induced by Psilocybin and LSD in Man', 5 May 1959, #151875.

p94   'There is information that some non-Agency groups': 'Memo for the Record', 1 November 1963, #146149 (195).

Chapter 4: In The Black Room

Books:

Biderman and Zimmer, (eds.), *The Manipulation of Human Behaviour*, New York, Wiley & Sons, 1961

Faul, Fr. Denis and Murray, Fr. Raymond, *The Hooded Men*: self-published, 1974

McGuffin, John, *The Guinea Pigs*, London: Penguin, 1974

McGuffin, John, *Internment*, Atlanta: Anvil, 1973

Solomon (ed.), *Sensory Deprivation: Symposium at Harvard Medical School*, Harvard: Harvard University Press, 1961

Vernon, Jack, *Inside the Black Room*, London: Souvenir Press, 1963

pp106–108 Details of the Tizard meeting come from the CIA's 'Report of Special Meeting, Montréal Meeting Report 1 June 1951', A/B, 1, 38/5, #184422; a Canadian document, 'Meeting at Ritz Carlton Hotel, June 1 1951'; and British documents at the PRO: DEFE 9/21, including Tizard's invitation and the letter regarding 'drugs, hypnosis etc in war', and a list of the names of the participants.

p108 'The American programs through Dr Webster': 'Minutes of Meeting' 6 June 1951, #144788, and 'For the Director's Log', 6 June 1951, A/B, 4, 19/18, #148317.

p109 'When the aircraft is flying straight and level': AM Hastin-Bennett, 'Sensory Deprivation in Aviation', in Solomon (ed.), *Sensory Deprivation*.

pp109–112 Canadian documents relating to Hebb's Project X-38, and his attempts to declassify it, include: DRBS 2–1–44–38 (CD(D)), 15 December 1952, and letters: DRBS 2–1–44–38 (CD(D)) 1 January 1953, 3(D) 2 November 1953, DRBS 2–1–44–38 (CD(D)) 16 November 1953, 11 January 1954, PA/CDRB 25 January 1954, TB 472907 6 July 1954.

p110 'The subject is paid to do nothing 24 hours a day': D. Hebb 'The Mammal and His Environment', *American Journal of Psychiatry*, May 1955.

p112 'It is one thing to hear that the Chinese are brainwashing': D. Hebb: 'The Motivating Effects of Exteroceptive Stimulation', *American Psychology*, 1958.

p115 'Deprived of information, the brain does not function "normally"': 'Physiological State of the Interrogation Subject as it Affects Brain Function', in *The Manipulation of Human Behaviour*.

p116 Information about John Lilly can be found in his books (there is no shortage of them) as well at his website, www.johnclilly.com, which includes pictures of the masks he designed for underwater sensory deprivation.

p117 'After an hour of crying loudly': Marks, *The Search for the Manchurian Candidate*, p147.

pp117–118 '[Baldwin] frankly admits that unless he can carry out 'terminal experiments': 'Total Isolation', 21 March 1955, 16 March 1955.

p118   '[Baldwin] stated that he would not want': 'Diary For Thursday 17 March 1955', #184610. This entry gives further details of the horrific plan's genesis: '[deleted] stated that the isolation, plus the specialized interrogation technique he had developed at [deleted] would, he believed, result in complete psychic breakdown, if enough time were permitted. The volunteer [deleted] personnel used to date could never be brought to this state . . .'. '[deleted] stated that he might want [deleted] to conduct a single experiment on an antagonistic subject which would result in complete psychic breakdown'.

pp118–119   Stanley Smith's experiments are written up in the *Lancet*, 2, 1959, p342.

pp119–120   Alexander Kennedy's lecture 'The Scientific Lessons of Interrogation' is published in the *Royal Institution of Great Britain, Proceedings*, vol. 38, 1960–1.

p120   'It is not the intention of this chapter to present': 'Sensory Deprivation in Aviation' in Solomon (ed.), *Sensory Deprivation*.

p122   The Army's instructional film *I Can't Answer That Question* is at the Imperial War Museum, DRF6993.

p125   MI5 Director-General Sir Dick White's visit to Northern Ireland is recorded in Chris Ryder's *The Fateful Split* (Methuen, 2005).

pp127–129   The Compton Committee was established 3 November 1971.

pp129–130   The Parker Committee report was adapted 31 January 1972.

pp130–131   Robert Daly's quotes come from the *Irish Times*, 9 July 1973.

p132   'As a reporter it would be irresponsible': BBC's *Letter from America*, Alistair Cooke, 5 February 1972.

Chapter 5: Building The Manchurian Candidate

Books:

Abrahamowitz, Finn, *Hypnosemordene*, Kóbenhaum: Host & Son, 2004
Condon, Richard, *The Manchurian Candidate*, London: Michael Joseph, 1959
Estabrooks, George, *Hypnotism*, New York: Museum Press, 1943
Hardrup, Palle, *Sandheden om hypnose mordene*, Copenhagen: Palle Hardrup, 1973
Janet, P., *Psychological Healing*, London: Allen & Unwin, 1925
Lovell, Stanley, *Of Spies and Stratagems*, London: Prentice-Hall, 1963
Nielsen, Schouw, *Slambert, altid Slambert*, Copenhagen: Stig Vendelkaers Forlag, 1958
Reiter, Paul, *Antisocial or Criminal Acts and Hypnosis: A Case Study*, Munksgaard, 1958

p143   'It is a reasonable certainty': 'Report No 1 of trip to EUKOM and USFA, 22 June-7 August 1949', filed 15 August 1949, #144892.

p143 'It can be said with certainty': 'Overall Report on Two-month [deleted] Trip', 26 September 1949, A,B, 2, 30/2, #149611.

p144 'In a minute you will slowly open your eyes': Watkins' experiments are reported in the *Journal of Abnormal and Social Psychology*, XLIII, 1947, cit Reiter.

p147 'I gave the money to you': cit Abrahamowitz.

p149 'I put him under deep hypnosis': 'Hypnosis Comes of Age', Estabrooks, *Science Digest*, April 1971.

p149 Estabrooks' letters to various law enforcement and intelligence organisations are to be found in his personal papers at Colgate College. Colin Ross, author of BLUEBIRD, has copies.

p150 'In the September, 1947, issue of *Reader's Digest*': 'To Director, Central Intelligence', 30 April 1948.

p151 '[Hypnotist] stated that he had constantly used hypnosis': 'Untitled' 9 July 1951, A/B, 5, 28/1, #147378.

p151 The Gulf of Mexico experiment is included in 'SI and H Experimentation' 10 July 1951, A/B, 3, 2/135, #190570.

p152 'During a demonstration with an excellent subject': 'Hypnosis and Covert Operations', 5 May 1955, A/B, III, 6, 13, #190713.

p153 'It demonstrated that a person having no ability': 'SI and H Experimentation', 7 August 1951, A/B, 3, 2/129, #190564.

p154 'If hypnotic control can be established': 'Hypnosis and Covert Operations', as above.

p159 'Experiment 1, N-18, Hypnotically induced anxieties': 'Visit to Project [deleted]', 11 May 1953.

p159 '[subject] was told that she would go to the small room': 'SI and H Experimentation', 18 September 1951, A/B, 3, 2/116, #190556.

p160 *The Black Art*: the script for the CIA's hypnosis film is located in 'I&SO Training Film: Hypnosis', 1 March, 1953, A/B, 1, 3, #149585.

p160 '[Subject was told to open her eyes': 'SI and H Experimentation', 25 September 1951, A/B, 3, 2/112, #190527.

p161 'Can we induce a hypnotic condition in an unwilling subject?': 'Special Research, BLUEBIRD [deleted]', filed 1 January 1951, A/B, V, 110, 1, #148197. Other interesting questions include: '8) Can we 'alter' a person's personality? How long will it hold?; 16) Is it possible to find a gas that can be used to gain SI and H control from a gas pencil; odorless, colorless, one shot etc?'; and '20) Can we, using SI and H, extract complicated formula [sic] from scientists, engineers etc, if unwilling? Can we extract details of gun emplacements, landing fields, factories, mines?'

p161 'Individuals could be taught to do anything': '[deleted], Interview with', 25 February 1952, A/B, III, 6, 7 #190597.

p162 Lloyd Rowland's snake experiment is reported in the *Journal of Abnormal and Social Psychology*, 1939 (34).

p162 'Suppose that while under hypnosis a subject': 'Hypnosis and Covert Operations', 5 May 1955, as above.

p162 Allen's pistol experiment appears in 'Hypnotic Experimentation and Research', 10 February 1954, A/B, 3, 2/18, #190691.

p163 Hardrup a 'rank amateur': 'Hypnosis and Covert Operations', May 5, 1955, as above.

p164 'As a trigger mechanism for a bigger project': 'ARTICHOKE 8–15 January 1954', B/3, #149438, misfiled January 1 1954.

p165 West's 'unique laboratory' is referred to in documentation for Subproject 43, filed 21 March 1955, titled 'Psychophysiological Studies of Hypnosis and Suggestibility', #17441. In his proposal he specifically suggests the deliberate induction of stress with hypnosis and sensory isolation, and the latter's role in the process of hypnotising unwilling subjects. A good account of the interrogation possibilities hypnosis and the 'Magic Room' is featured in 'Hypnosis in Interrogation', Edward DeShere, *Studies in Intelligence* (Winter, 1960).

p166 'The operator then presses the right thumb': 'Report Concerning Certain Techniques of Hypnosis', 17 January 1958, #146144.

p167 'A great deal of work and effort': 'Operational [deleted] Activity in [deleted], June–July 1963', filed 8 July 1963. #184627. Details of the operation can be found in *The Search for the Manchurian Candidate*.

p168 'A well trained person', 'It cannot be done by everyone' and 'Creating a Manchurian candidate' quotes come from *The Search for the Manchurian Candidate*.

Chapter 6: 'Do it'

Books:

Haberstroh, Jack, *Ice Cube Sex*, Chicago: Notre Dame, 1994
Key, Dr Wilson Bryan, *Subliminal Seduction*, New York: New American Library, 1994
Key, Dr Wilson Bryan, *The Age of Manipulation*, Lauham, Maryland: Madison, 1993
Key, Dr Wilson Bryan, *The Clam-Plate Orgy*, Signet: New York, 1981
Packard, Vance, *The Hidden Persuaders*, New York: McKay, 1957
Pratkanis, Anthony and Aronson, Eliot, *The Age of Propaganda: The Everyday Use and Abuse of Persuasion*, New York: Freeman 1992

Good papers on the subliminal phenomenon include 'Subliminal Perception: Facts and Fallacies' (*Skeptical Inquirer*, vol. 16, Spring 1992), 'Subliminal Delusion' (*Psychology Today*, July 1985), 'Subliminal Advertising: What You See is What You Get' (*Journal of Marketing*, Spring 1982), 'Subliminal Psychodynamic Activation' (*American Psychologist*, Nov 1989), 'Subliminal Self Help Auditory Tapes, an Empirical Test of Perceptual Consequences' (*Canadian Journal of Behavioural Sciences*, 27:1, 1995), and 'Subliminal Influences in Marketing' (*Psychology and Marketing*, vol. 5, #4, Winter 1988). All of these papers were written, or co-written, by Tim Moore. See also Vokey and Read's 'Subliminal Messages', *American Psychologist*, 40, 1988, and Stuart Rodgers' 'Subliminal Advertising' (*Encyclopaedia of Advertising*) and 'How A Publicity Blitz Created the Myth of Subliminal Advertising' (*Public Relations Quarterly*, vol. 37, 1992). Professor Rodgers was also kind enough to allow me a copy of his unpublished paper, 'Subliminal Advertising: Grand Scam of the 20th Century'. The best overview of the case, and of the way that bad science is frequently presented in courts cases as fact, is to be found in 'Scientific Consensus and Expert Testimony: Lessons from the Judas Priest Case' (Tim Moore, *Skeptical Inquirer*, Dec 1996)

Records of the Judas Priest case come from the following documents at Washoe County Court in Reno, Nevada, case #86–12915:

p171   'You knew I'd listen to it . . . : court deposition, James Vance, Sept 26, 1988 (reel #3, 174–86).

pp171–   Details of the morning of December 23rd come from the statements of
176   Aunetta Margaret Roberson and Rita Skulson (reel #2). Also 'Hypnotism of James Vance by Dr Danton' (19 November 1987, reel #4) and 'Statement of Phyllis Vance', 16 November 1987 (reel #2). See also 'Depositions, James Vance' dated 2 December 1987 and 6 January 1988 (reel #2).

p175   Details of the 911 calls and the crime scene come from Policeman Dan Kelly's 'Continuation Report' of 23 December 1988 and the statement of Detective Sergeant Dave Zarubi 11/6/87, which gives details of James' condition in hospital and their conversation ('life sucks') there.

p181   'Hypnotist: 'he said "I sure fucked my life up"' : 'Hypnosis of James Vance by Dr Danton', 19 November, 1987, (reel #4).

p182   'Motion for summary judgement', case 86–3939, 'Points and Authentication in Opposition in Motion to Dismiss' (reel #1).

p183   'Below threshold': Nickloff's two letters to Ken McKenna are dated 30 Sept 1988 ('I detect sounds') and 6 October 1988 ('DO IT') (reel #3, 174–86).

p183   'INVISIBLE ADS TESTED': *Printer's Ink*, 20 September 1957.

p185   'Within a few years': Huxley-Humphrey Osmond April 8, 1957, Huxley, *Collected Letters XX*.

pp185–   'There are no references to subliminal projection': *Brave New World*
186   *Revisited*, Aldous Huxley, Chatto and Windus, 1959.

p186   Huxley's relationship with Dr Louis 'Jolly' West emerges in a letter to Humphrey Osmond dated 1 June 1957. Huxley was impressed by the young doctor, who was at the time feeding human subjects mescaline, then trying to hypnotise them. Huxley suggested that he should reverse the procedure, hypnotising them first, then feeding them LSD, and afterwards trying to bring back the hallucinogenic experience through the reintroduction of a hypnotic state. History does not relate whether this technique worked

p186   'It might be that in order to lessen the resistance': [CIA] 'Report Concerning Certain Techniques', 17 January 1958 (389), #146144.

p186   William R Corson recorded the Agency's experiments with subliminal techniques in his book, *The Armies of Ignorance* (1977).

pp187–188   'CBS couldn't find it'. There is a string of documents describing the hunt for the multi-track master tapes. A formal request for the tapes was lodged in November 1987. A year later, the search was still going on. In February 1988, CBS admitted that 'their location is presently unknown' and asked for an extension. Jamie Young testified that CBS 'never did and does not have custody [of them]'. A two-track tape was sent instead. In April, CBS was ordered to turn over the tape within 45 days. That September, CBS suggested that the tapes had been borrowed by The Who and subsequently lost. The plaintiffs asked the judge to impose sanctions. Later that month, CBS finally admitted that the tapes really were gone, and forwarded the only master they could find: 'Better by You, Better Than Me'. This one track—coincidentally at the heart of the case—had apparently been recorded separately from the rest of the album, hence its survival.

p190   Judge Whitehead's denial of CBS's motion for summary judgement is dated 23 August 1989, 86–5844/86–3939.

p191   Ray's past run-ins with the law come from the statement of Aunetta Roberson; the pair's plan to 'commit mass murder' is from Dave Zarubi's statement, 11 June 1988.

p191   'He was seriously weird': 'Deposition of Lisa Davis', 20 January 1988 (reel #3, 124–86).

p191   James' history of drug abuse is indicated by the statement of his mother, Phyllis, 16 November 1987 (reel #2).

p195   'Worse than the timing': 'Today it's Just a Historic Flashback for Researcher Vicary', *Advertising Age*, 17 September 1962 p203.

p195   'There are several mighty leaps': [CIA] Studies in Intelligence: 'Operational Potential of Subliminal Perception' by Richard Gafford, Spring 1958.

p202   'I very specifically remember': 'Deposition, Susan Rusk', 23 May 1990 (reel #5 176–86).

p204   'You have seen subliminal messages': Cross-examination by Peterson, 29 March 1990 (reel #8).

p207   'They simply do not work': 'Subliminal Messages', *British Psychological Society*, 1992.

p208   Wilson Bryan Key's CV: reel #3 174–86.

Chapter 7: Sleep

Books:

Bromberger, Brian and Fife-Yeomans, Janet, *Deep Sleep: Harry Bailey and the Scandal of Chelmsford*, New York: Simon and Schuster, 1991
Collins, Anne, *In the Sleep Room*, Toronto: Key Porter, 1988
Gillmor, Don, *I swear by Apollo*, Fountain Valley: Eden Press, 1981
Sargant, William, *The Unquiet Mind: The Autobiography of a Physician in Psychological Medicine*, London: Heinemann, 1967
Sourkes and Pinard (eds.), *Building on a Proud Past*, Montreal: McGill University Press, 1995.
Weinstein, Harvey, *A Father, a Son and the CIA*, Toronto: James Lorimer & Co, 1988

p216   'Dormiphonics: A New language of learning': Max Sherover: *Modern Language Journal*, 6 Oct 1956.

p223   'Disposal of Maximum Custody Type Defectors': 7 March 1951, #184586.

p223   'Any operation requires . . . war is a grim business': 'Evaluation of the Medical Staff's Contribution to BLUEBIRD', 3 March 1952, A/B, 4, 23/32, #147392.

p223   'Alcoholic' CIA man: 'ARTICHOKE conference, 30 July 1953', #144999.

p223   'Some individuals in the Agency': 'ARTICHOKE conference', as above.

p224   Blast range and concussion-producing equipment: 'Subproject 54', filed 6 December 1955, #17453. The project proposal suggests that 'if a technique was devised to induce brain concussion without giving either advance warning or causing external trauma, the person upon recovery would be unable to recall what had happened to him'. A handwritten memo concurs: 'This looks like what we want.'

p224   'The other Technique was': Testimony by Charles Geschickter in 'Human Drug Testing by the CIA', 1977, p90.

p224   'Short of cutting a subject's throat': 'AMNESIA', filed under 'Drug Card Index', 1 January 1956, A/BI, 75–13, #189903.

p225   'Whole head was on fire': 'ARTICHOKE, 3 December 1951', A/B, 5, 134/3, #146342. The agent concerned was particularly interested in the idea of attempting to hypnotise a subject in the 'groggy' state immediately after ECT.

p226   'Repetition of Verbal Signals': 'Application for Grant', 21 January 1957, 68/37, in MKULTRA Subproject 68 files, #17468.

p227   Mary C's experience is related in 'Observation in Alaclitic Therapy' by Hassan Azima, in *Sensory Deprivation: Symposium at Harvard Medical School*.

See also 'Prolonged Sleep Treatment': Azima. *Journal of Mental Science 101*, 1955.

p227   'Cameron was irresponsible': Hebb's interview with film-maker, Ronald Blumer. This interview, together with more information on Ewen Cameron and the court cases that have followed his treatment, is available at www.turnerhome.com. Affidavits concerning psychic driving can be read at the site, including those from Donald Hebb, Ormondt Solandt and Robert Jay Lifton.

p233   'The work of the Devil': *The Sunday Times*, 22 February 1976.

p236   'A long full course of . . . ECT/We had accidentally found': Sargant's papers, Box 1.

p246   'Cameron was a victim of his own kind of brainwashing': interview with Donald Hebb, at www.turnerhome.com.

Chapter 8: Jesus Loves You

Books:

Conway, Flo and Siegelman, Jim, *Snapping*, New York: Lippincott Williams & Wilkins, 1978

The Cult Awareness Network: *Anatomy of A Hate Group* Los Angeles: (Freedom Magazine, 1995)

Freed, Josh, *Moonwebs*, Toronto: Virgo, 1980

Hassan, Steve, *Combatting Cult Mind Control*, Maine: Park Street Press, 1990

Lifton, Robert Jay, *Thought Reform and the Psychology of Totalism*, New York: Norton, 1961

Patrick, Ted, *Let Our Children Go!*, New York: Ballantine, 1976

Shaw, William, *Spying in Guru-land*, London: Fourth Estate, 1994

Singer, Margaret, *Cults in our Midst*, Hoboken: Jossey-Bass, 2003

Underwood, Barbara, *Hostage to Heaven*, New York: Clarkson N. Potter, 1979

p275   'An absolutely correct account of a devastating technique': *Guardian*, 4 October 1976.

p277   Details of CAN's demise come from 'Did Scientology Strike Back?', Susan Hansen, *American Lawyer*, June 1997.

Chapter 9: Believing the Impossible

Books:

Medway, Gareth J, *The Lure of the Sinister—The Unnatural History of Satanism:*, New York: New York University Books, 2001

Nathan and Snedeker, *Satan's Silence*, New York: Basic Books, 1995

Ofshe, Richard and Watters, Ethan, *Making Monsters*, New York: Scribners, 1994
Pendergrast, Mark, *Victims of Memory*, Hinesburg: Upper Access Books, 1995
Wright, Lawrence, *Remembering Satan*, New York: Knopf, 1994

p281   'merely the ketchup on the corndog': Black Lake website: www.black-lakebiblecamp.com

pp283–   Julie's notes to Kristi Webster are often undated; 'I wonder what will
284   happen' comes from a letter of 27 October 1988.

p284   'Cut her up': 'Statement of Marianne Manoogian', 3 November 1988, Case 88–27067–11.

p285   'abuse had started . . . in the fifth grade;: 'Interview with Julie Ingram' (Joe Vukich) 3 December 1988, conducted 21 November 1988.

p285   'Wet and yuckey': 'Officer's Report (Paul Johnson)', 5 December 1988.

p286   'I know that if this did happen': Ingram's arrest and initial interrogation are described in 'Supplemental Report', 28 November 1988, by Neil McClanahan. Also 'statement of Paul R Ingram, 28 November 1988', an 81–page interview transcript from which most of the original charges were derived. In this interview he recovers his first memories, names Jim Rabie as a perpetrator and 'sees' the tombstones. During the course of the interview, Dr Peterson tells Ingram to relax and he begins to relive the past.

p286   and elsewhere. 'Statement of Paul R Ingram', 1 December 1988, contains other memories, along with some of the quotes cited in this chapter in which Paul prays, and is encouraged to relive the past through his religious beliefs ('You don't wanna go to Hell . . .'). This interview is also the source of the quotes from Paul's attorney, Gary Preble, telling him to be quiet and the allegation that Jim Rabie pointed a gun at him. Rabie tells Ingram to shut off the Christian music ('didn't believe in God'). Paul concludes 'I see evil'. Interestingly, Ingram specifically states a date on which some of this abuse took place. Rabie's bank details showed that he was in Canada on the day concerned; Paul soon remembered that the date he mentioned was wrong, and had another go. Rabie was unable to find an alibi a second time.

p292   'Totally truthful'. Records of Rabie's behaviour prior to his arrest are in 'Supplemental Report', 5 December 1988, along with a summary of his first interview.

p293   'Is this about Paul?' Ray Risch's arrest is recounted in 'Supplemental Report', 1 December 1988.

p293   'I honestly do not have any recollection': 'Rights Statement: Jim Rabie', 1 December 1988 is a transcript of the first recorded interview.

p298   Green River Killings. Ingram's confession comes from 'Supplemental Report' by Brian Schoening, 14 December 1988.

p299   'I signed a contract with them': 'Statement of Paul R Ingram', 17 December 1988.

p299   'The baby would be put on a table': Handwritten statement, Exhibit No
        117, dated 6 February 1989.

p300   'Sometimes he would go for 5–10 minutes': 'Interview with Chad Ingram,
        Statement of Schoening and Peterson', 8 December, 1988.

p302   'I don't know who performed the abortion': Defendant's Exhibit No 117,
        6 February 1989.

p303   'Mild acne on back': 'Statement of Judith Ann Jacobson', 20 April 1989.

p304   'I've dug people out of pits.': Interview with Mark Papworth, dated 3
        January 1996. This interview can be found at http://members.aol.com/
        ingramorg/papworth.htm.

p305   'Bondage items and a knife': 'Supplemental Report', Joe Vukich, 23
        March 1989.

p305   'Baby's arm/spiders': handwritten note from Julie, dated 26 April 1989.

p307   'Daytime. Probably Saturday or Sunday afternoon': Defendant's Exhibit
        No 40, dated 22 January 1990.

p309   'How's my very special little girl?': Details of the letter, and the revelation
        that it was written by Julie herself, are in 'Supplemental Report', 9 March
        1990. The letter itself is undated.

p310   'Paul, I think your daughter is lying': Conversation with Ofshe, Exhibit
        42, admitted 29 January 1990.

p311   'Please see that I will not have to live in fear': Ericka and Julie's letters to
        the judge are dated 9 August and 31 July 1989, respectively.

p313   Julie's accusation against Isidro Archibeque is dated 29 August 1985.

p314   'Satan's Underground': Interestingly, Ericka admitted to reading this book
        before making her first satanic accusations. See 'Supplemental Report', Joe
        Vukich, 7 January 1988.

p316   'Hunting snarks and exploring mare's nests': *An Introduction to Physical
        Methods of Treatment in Psychiatry*, William Sargant and Eliot Slater, Liv-
        ingston, 1944.

p317   I'll tell you something': Interview with Chad Ingram, 'Statement of
        Schoening and Peterson', 8 December, 1988.

Chapter 10: The Monster Plot

Books:

Epstein, Edward Jay, *Legend: The Secret World of Lee Harvey Oswald*, New York:
    Hutchinson, 1978

Mangold, Tom, *Cold Warrior: James Jesus Angleton, the CIA's Master Spy Hunter*, New
    York: Simon and Schuster, 1991

Westfield, H Bradford (ed.), *Inside the CIA's Private World—Declassified Articles from
    the Agency's Intelligence Journal, 1955–92*, New Haven: Yale University Press,
    1995

pp323– quotes from the Nosenko story come from *Cold Warrior, Legend*, and Edward
330   Jay Epstein's autobiographical website, www.edwardjayepstein.com, as well
            as 'Paths to Judgement' (Richard J Heuer), in *Inside the CIA's Private World*.

p326–   quotes from Murphy and Nosenko come from 'HSCA Security Classified
330   Testimony (TOP SECRET)', dated 9 August 1978 (Murphy) and 20 June
            1978 (Nosenko).

p331   'Acoustic Kitty'. Efforts appear to have been under way to procure suitable
            kittens in late 1966. 'Summary Information on [deleted]', filed 27 Septem-
            ber (#21815), announces that the 'going price for show stock is $150 and
            up', and advises that 'we will need to get a copy of *Cat* magazine and *All
            Pets* magazine' to facilitate the hunt for suitable suppliers. Details of the
            trial itself are missing but 'Proposed Agenda [deleted] Show and Tell', filed
            14 February 1967 (#173986), is the source of the 'secure gear' quote.

p333   Documents relating to the death of Frank Olson are scattered throughout
            CIA records for 1953 and 1954.

p338   'We have no indications': 'Communist Mental Conditioning for Confes-
            sions', 98, 24 February 1953, #145896.

p338   'The Communists did not': 'Report on POW Situation', 15 June 1953,
            #146093.

p338   'Reports lead us to . . .': 'Soviet Mental Conditioning', A/B I, 2, 1, 21
            July 1955, #184363.

p338   'There is nothing mysterious . . .': 'A Report of Communist Brainwash-
            ing', 15 August 1955, #173492.

p340   'He had a profound distaste': 'Follow Up on BW Resolution, (United Na-
            tions)', 11 April 1953, #146078.

p340   '[deleted] stated that . . . Senator Lodge': 'ARTICHOKE Conference, 16
            April 1953' (filed 11 May 1953), 224, #146085.

p346   'Powerful drugs can indeed wipe out the memory': Thomas Powers' in-
            troduction to Marks' *The Search for the Manchurian Candidate*.

Epilogue: 'Truth. In the shortest possible time'.

Books:

Bowden, Mark, *Road Work*, New York: Atlantic Press, 2004

Deeley, Peter, *Beyond Breaking Point*, London: ArthurBarker, 1971

Gordon, N. and Fleischer, W., *Effective Interviewing and Interrogation Techniques*, London: Academic Press, 2002

Hoare, Oliver (ed.), *Camp 020: MI5 and the Nazi Spies*, London: PRO, 2001

Inbau/Reid, *Criminal Interrogation and Confessions*, Baltimore: Williams & Watkins,
   1986

Innes, Brian, *The History of Torture*, London: Blitz, 1998

KUBARK 1963 [CIA]

Mackey, Chris and Miller, Greg, *The Interrogator's War*, London: John Murray, 2004
Philby, Kim, *My Silent War*, New York: Random House, 1968
Rolin, Jean, *Police Drugs*, London: Hollis and Carter, 1955
Saar, Erik and Novak, Viveca, *Inside the Wire*, London: Penguin, 2005
Scotland, AP, *The London Cage*, London: Evans Books, 1957
Summers, M. (tr.), *Malleus Maleficarum*, London: J. Rodker, 1928

p357   'The Conveyor worked automatically': Weissberg, *Conspiracy of Silence*, 1959.

p358   'Brain syndrome': 'The Physiological State of the Interrogation Subject as it Affects Brain Function', Lawrence Hinkle in *The Manipulation of Human Behaviour*.

p363   'What is this Psychological Warfare Unit?': Papers relating to Professor Kennedy's lecture are in the Public Records Office at PREM 11/2900 ('Brainwashing'), CAB21/3184 ('Psychological Procedures in the Services: Brainwashing') and WO208/5572 ('Interrogation Policy and Training'). The latter contains the letter from Francis Noel-Baker.

p368   Abduraman Khadr was interviewed on the BBC Radio 4's *Today* programme, 17 March 2004; further details are available from CBC News Online, 23 December 2005.

pp372–373   The use of truth drugs and hypnosis to trick interrogation subjects is detailed both in *KUBARK* and in 'The Use of Truth Drugs in Interrogation', in *The Manipulation of Human Behaviour*.

Index